LIFE LESSONS
from the
HIDING PLACE

In My Father's House

Tramp
for the
Lord

LIFE LESSONS
from the
HIDING PLACE

Other Books by Pam Rosewell Moore:

The Five Silent Years of Corrie ten Boom
Safer than a Known Way
When Spring Comes Late: Finding Your Way
  through Depression

With her husband, Carey Moore:
If Two Shall Agree, later published as *What Happens When Husbands and Wives Pray Together?*

LIFE LESSONS
from the
HIDING PLACE

Discovering the Heart of
CORRIE TEN BOOM

PAM ROSEWELL MOORE

Chosen
Grand Rapids, Michigan

ISBN:0-7394-4342-9

Original Scriptures quoted by Corrie ten Boom are quoted from an original Dutch
translation from the Hebrew and Greek and are not, therefore, identical to any of our
English versions, although they are probably closest to the King James Version. In some
cases, however, the author has changed Miss ten Boom's wording to the New International
Version (NIV) in order to make it more easily understood by modern readers. Unless
otherwise indicated, all other Scripture quotations are taken from the HOLY BIBLE,
NEW INTERNATIONAL VERSION®, NIV® copyright © 1973, 1978, 1984, by
International Bible Society. Used by permission of Zondervan. All rights reserved.

Scripture marked KJV is taken from the King James Version of the Bible.

Scripture marked PHILLIPS is taken from The New Testament in Modern English, revised
edition—J. B. Phillips, translator. © J. B. Phillips 1958, 1960, 1972. Used by permission
of MacMillan Publishing Co., Inc.

Scripture marked TLB is taken from *The Living Bible* © 1971. Used by permission of
Tyndale House Publishers, Inc., Wheaton, IL 60189. All rights reserved.

Scripture marked RSV is taken from the Revised Standard Version of the Bible, copyright
© 1946, 1952, 1971 by the Division of Christian Education of the National Council of
the Churches of Christ in the USA. Used by permisson.

For those interested, the centuries-old house containing the hiding place is now a
museum.

For Carey, with all my love

Contents

Acknowledgments

I would first like to express my grateful appreciation to the Corrie ten Boom House Foundation in Haarlem, the Netherlands, and to the Billy Graham Center Archives in Wheaton, Illinois, U.S.A., for their permission to quote from the Ten Boom family letters and other documents. Some of the references have been printed earlier in various of Corrie ten Boom's more than twenty books of past decades, but the above two organizations hold the original material. In addition, a few of the letters are from my personal archives.

The excellent Dutch book *De Eeuw van mijn Vader* (My Father's Century) by Geert Mak was very helpful to me in describing the history, culture and people of the Netherlands in chapters 2 and 3.

I deeply appreciate the contributions made to this book by many family members, friends and professional contacts. These include my sister, Sylvia Baker, who helped me develop the concept; Terry Bensmiller, my research assistant; and Jane Campbell, Grace Sarber and Stephanie Vink, my editors.

Invaluable help was also given to me by Dr. Michael E. Williams, dean of the College of Humanities and Social Sciences and professor of history, Dallas Baptist University and by Dr. Ronald D. Rietveld, professor of history, California State University, Fullerton.

Introduction

The Power
of a Good Story

One evening in 2001, a handful of children from a Christian school in Stalybridge, a small town in the north of England, performed a short play based on Corrie ten Boom's life. The setting was a simple school hall. As the boys and girls acted their parts, a hush descended on the parents and friends in the audience. The riveted attention in the room went beyond what would normally be expected of proud parents watching their children act. When the play ended, several parents commented on the story.

A mother exclaimed, "What a powerful story! I was so moved by it."

One father said, "I want to see it again; it was so good."

What makes this story powerful?

Robert Pickle came to visit me one day from east Texas. He was one of the biggest men I have ever seen. I am fairly tall, but the broad-shouldered biker loomed above me. He was middle-aged and wore a ponytail and a thick black jacket studded with silver. Robert wanted to tell me how the story of Corrie ten Boom changed his life completely. While in prison, he was given a copy of *The Hiding Place*. Although he was not normally given to reading, Robert picked up the book and became engrossed in the story. Skeptical at first, he went on to read Corrie's *Tramp for the Lord*.

"There is nothing you can think of that I have not been guilty of," Robert told me, "but after I read those books I asked the Lord Jesus Christ to be my Savior. I gave Him all my life. He has changed me and given me a ministry to prisoners." Robert Pickle told his story with passion and joy, expressing his love for and gratitude to Corrie ten Boom.

How did a woman he had never met have such a strong influence on the hardened heart of Robert Pickle?

≈

Diagnosed with bipolar disorder and later with clinical depression, Cindy suffered mental anguish for decades. She read *The Hiding Place* and said, "God has given me a second chance. He collects our tears. There are always tears in the heart when one is sad. Our wonderful Lord is deeper than the deepest pit in this fallen world. He is my Hiding Place."

≈

Mindy told me how one story from Corrie's life helped her regain peace. It was the story of Corrie's meeting with one of her former tormentors at a speaking engagement in Germany shortly after World War II. The former guard from Ravensbrück concentration camp asked Corrie to forgive him for the way he had treated her and her dying sister, Betsie.

"And she forgave him," said Mindy. "This had a huge impact on me because at the time I read *The Hiding Place* I was personally dealing with serious issues of unforgiveness. Corrie taught me how to forgive, and I did forgive."

Gail was a young mother with three preschoolers when she first heard Tante Corrie's story. Her husband supported her fully and helped her during all the hours he was not at his job, but it still seemed to Gail that life was filled with diapers, baby bottles, cleaning and seldom a good night's sleep. "My life was the Lord's," she said, "but deep inside I yearned for fresh inspiration for my walk with Christ. I found the model I was seeking in *The Hiding Place*. Strangely, in my twenties, I found this much older, never-married woman's story to be one that lifted my heart and brought richness and purpose to my ordinary, daily steps. She gave me a completely new perspective on life."

Melody told me, "As a single woman I have always been challenged by how Corrie ten Boom lived so fully for Christ and did not settle into bitterness or hopelessness or self-pity. As I get older, I find myself often looking to those who have gone before me, and through them God says to me, 'Keep walking in faith, in the direction of hope. I am faithful. You can trust Me.'"

Thousands more have their own stories. And most of them have never met Corrie ten Boom, let alone have the insights into her life and death that I, as her companion for the last seven years of her life, was allowed to receive.

Many concentration camp survivors have written autobiographies. What makes the story of *The Hiding Place* so powerful? Why does Tante Corrie's life have such unusual and lasting influence? The question intrigues me as much now as it did on that night in East Africa in the mid-1960s when, unknowingly, I was about to take part in her story.

one

Meeting Tante Corrie

It was during an evening meeting in tropical East Africa that I first heard her name. The year was 1966. In my early twenties, I was working as a volunteer assistant for the Anglican Church of the Province of East Africa and had been invited to attend a nondenominational prayer meeting in a suburb of Nairobi, Kenya. Crickets chirped loudly outside. This was still a novel sound to me. I had never heard it in my home country of England. Nor had I ever before caught the sweet, heavy scent of the white and waxy frangipani flower that drifted through the wide open yet iron-barred window of the single-story suburban home where the prayer meeting was taking place.

Dozens of missionaries, men and women, filled that warm living room. Many of them described their work and asked for prayer. Seated at the back of the room, I kept quiet. I had never been one to speak up in public. But in my inner self I joined in the enthusiasm and prayers of the group.

15

Near the front of the room a middle-aged lady in a floral-printed frock raised her hand and stood up. "I would like to ask for prayer for Corrie ten Boom," she said. "She is in her mid-seventies now and has recently spent many months in Uganda. Her doctor had prescribed a sabbatical rest for her. But now she has resumed her world journeys."

I had never heard of Corrie ten Boom, but it seemed to me that the words of the woman in the floral dress were received with a kind of reverence, as if this elderly Corrie ten Boom were a legend in her own lifetime. I was intrigued. Not wanting to ask who she was, I listened interestedly as several missionaries volunteered experiences they had shared with her. From these reports, I was able to assemble my first impressions of the life and work of this Dutch missionary evangelist who had hidden Jewish people in her home in Holland during the Second World War and had been imprisoned by the Nazis for doing so. I also ascertained that after her release she had traveled the world for twenty years telling how she had proven God's love to be stronger than the deep darkness of Ravensbrück concentration camp and had learned to forgive those who had caused the deaths through imprisonment of her father, sister, brother and nephew. Inexplicably I was drawn to this old lady and her story. As the group prayed for her, I felt grateful I had been invited to the prayer meeting.

A chorus from the cricket choir greeted me as I left the house in that Nairobi suburb. *I would like to know more about Corrie ten Boom*, I said to myself. *I wonder if she has written any books about her work.*

First Impressions of Tante Corrie

In August 1968, the summer after my return to England from that short-term assignment in Africa, a friend invited me to go with her to a mission conference comprised of Dutch and English young people. It was to be held in the town of Matlock, Derbyshire, a beautiful, hilly part of north central England.

"Corrie ten Boom is one of the Dutch speakers," said my friend. I knew the name sounded familiar. Then it was as if I heard again the cricket chorus outside the suburban East African house a couple of years earlier, and I remembered the elderly lady who had saved Jewish lives in the Second World War. Recalling my intrigue about her story and curious to learn more about her, I traveled with my friend to Matlock and found myself part of the most unusual conference I had yet attended.

For one thing, there did not seem to be many halfhearted Christians among the fifty English and fifty Dutch young people. And for another thing, these Dutch were so different from the average English young person with whom I had grown up. They looked different; many of them were above the average English height, and they were mainly fair-haired and long-limbed. They also acted differently in that they spoke more loudly than I had been taught to speak. And they laughed a lot and heartily. I found this contrast with the more circumspect and cautious approach of the British a bit daunting.

One morning during the five-day conference, for example, it was discovered that about half the participants had contracted food poisoning from the meal the night before. I was fortunate to escape the affliction but not the frank questioning of a young Dutchman with whom several others and I sat at the half-empty breakfast table.

"Have you diarrhea?" he inquired with apparent interest as we began breakfast.

From the beginning of my acquaintance with them, I could see that there was no beating about the bush with the Dutch. On the whole they seemed to be honest, friendly, noisy, unpretentious, straightforward and opinionated. And I really liked them.

A Dutchman known as Brother Andrew was the main speaker. Also called "God's smuggler," he had a powerful message about what he called "the Suffering Church" under communism in Eastern Europe and the Soviet Union. He challenged us Western Christians to personal involvement, whether that meant taking Bibles and other help behind the Iron Curtain, giving or praying.

But his main emphasis was on going, whatever the personal cost or danger involved. I learned that he had carried out a Bible-smuggling mission from the Netherlands since 1955.

Soon it was Corrie ten Boom's turn to speak. She was 77 years old and physically strong-looking with a chin that can be well described as determined. Her height was about the same as mine—five foot seven. As I contemplated her size, I thought of the description on the army uniform my father was issued in England in the Second World War. "Slightly Portly" was the diplomatic British army description of Jim Rosewell's size. Not "Portly" or "Large," just "Slightly Portly." This phrase certainly described Tante (Aunt) Corrie, as the Dutch contingent referred to her. Just back from working in Asia, she was tired and always surrounded by people. I do not remember being introduced to her at that conference and had no idea that her life and mine would one day be closely bound together.

As I had learned was characteristic of the Dutch, Corrie ten Boom's messages during the five days of that conference were delivered with no sentiment or emotionalism. She just gave us the facts as she had experienced them.

"There is no pit so deep, the love of God is not deeper still," she said, speaking of her imprisonment in a concentration camp.

"We do not know when the Lord Jesus will return, but we do not know of one moment when He may not return. Are you ready? Have you forgiven your enemies? There was a time when I could not forgive those who had been so cruel to me and to my dying sister, Betsie. But God has taught me how to forgive.

"The Lord Jesus is coming again soon," she told us young people. "Are you obeying the Lord? Are you His ambassador?

"The Lord Jesus has promised to return. And He will. It may be very soon. In the meantime, are you taking hold of all the riches God has given us in Jesus Christ? We so often live like paupers when we are really children of the King of kings."

During that first week of August 1968 I heard Corrie ten Boom speak for the first time on the truths that formed the basis of her work and life. Later I was to hear the same consistent messages hundreds of times.

As the conference in the beautiful Peak District progressed, I noticed something in Corrie that went beyond the straightforward, frank and honest approach I had already noted in the Dutch participants—something harder to define. Her words seemed to carry an impressive authority and were delivered with unusual energy and dynamo. I felt rather intimidated by her powerful personality. But at the same time, observing her interaction with the young people through our five days together, I saw her love for them and their loving and interested response to her. She extended the same love with the same results to the conference leaders, the cooks, cleaners and gardeners as well. And I could not help noticing that every time Corrie ten Boom entered a room or took part in conversations, she was immediately the center of attention. It did not seem that she sought this. It simply happened.

A Surprise Invitation

As the conference drew to its close, I received a surprise invitation. Brother Andrew, whose book *God's Smuggler* had been released the previous year, told the group that he needed help. In response to that book, a large amount of correspondence in English arrived weekly at his ministry headquarters in Holland—mainly from American readers. He had even brought some items needing attention to the conference, and I volunteered to help him take care of them. Soon he asked if I would come to the town of Ermelo in central Holland, where his mission was based, to assist him. All the other team members were Dutch, and he wanted somebody whose first language was English to deal with the hundreds of inquiries being generated by the new book. I was free to go, having recently resigned from a temporary secretarial position, so I agreed to join him and his team in Holland for what

I thought would be a short time—perhaps three weeks. Little did I know my stay was to be much longer than that.

To Holland

After the conference ended, I said good-bye to my new friends, some of whom I would meet again in Holland. Returning to my family home in Hastings in East Sussex on the south coast of England, I packed my suitcase and took the cross-channel ferryboat to a port in Belgium, then a train to Holland. Before it stopped at Utrecht, a main railway junction, the train had introduced me to a land whose history, culture and people I was soon to love deeply. The landscape was orderly, green and flat with plenty of well-planned, open country areas between the cities. And forever remarkable to me, it was diffused with a clear and beautiful light.

I knew that Holland, although small, was one of the most densely populated countries in the world. From my seat in the train I saw that most of the cars the Dutch drove were small. Nearly all of the houses seemed small, too. They were mainly very clean and inviting. Most front room curtains were drawn back, and I was offered clear views into family living rooms, sometimes with many occupants, through high and wide polished windows.

I changed trains at that large junction and took a slower one that traveled in a north-easterly direction toward the small town of Ermelo, where Brother Andrew had said he would be waiting for me. To my relief, he was. We shook hands and observed each other briefly. Andrew (not his real name) was dressed in slacks and a casual shirt. His build was slight, his hair brown, his voice quiet. I contrasted his bearing with the loud and boisterous Dutch people I had met at the conference. *Perhaps it is easier for Andrew to keep anonymous in the Eastern European countries he visits,* I thought. He would be less conspicuous in those places than if he were tall and fair. As he shook my hand he studied me, a 23-year-old woman with dark brown hair, brown eyes and fair skin. I was wearing a

1960s minidress and Dr. Scholl's wooden sandals, which clacked noisily.

"Welkom in Holland, Pam," he said in his warm and charming way. As we hoisted my luggage into an oversized gray car—*Why such a large car for a missionary in a country of mainly small cars?* I asked myself—Brother Andrew explained he would drive me first to his home. He and his wife, Corry, had four children with a fifth on the way. We drove through quiet, tree-lined streets, and after reaching a busier street Brother Andrew stopped outside a house with a pointed red roof. Here Corry welcomed me, and then God's Smuggler led me up two flights of steps, the second of which was a steep, short, ladder-like staircase to the third floor—the attic under the pointed roof. It had been converted into an office and was large enough to contain four desks with chairs, typewriters and a few bookshelves and filing cabinets. The setup became even more fascinating when through the back window I saw a couple of station wagons parked on the property. Three large cars in one family? I also saw a medium-sized shed.

"We keep Bibles in the various languages of Eastern Europe in that shed," he told me. "And these cars belong to our mission. You may have noticed that they are larger than the average car in Holland, but they need to be. On our journeys to Eastern Europe we take as many Bibles as we can pack into them."

The intrigue was mounting. Was a dangerous international smuggling ministry really being carried out from this ordinary house in this fairly small town? I wanted to know more.

We descended the steep staircase, and I said farewell to Corry and the children. I supposed I would be back the next day to start my duties.

Brother Andrew then drove me to a small town nearby named Harderwijk, where he had arranged for the rental of two rooms in the little home of an elderly Dutch midwife, Miss Jo de Graaf. She spoke no English and I as yet no Dutch, but from the beginning we liked and understood each other. As he took leave, Brother Andrew told me that one of his team members would pick me up and take me to the office in the morning. And then he said, "Here you are. You will want to read this book to find out what our work is all about." And he handed me *God's Smuggler*.

My new landlady showed me to my bedroom. It was quiet, with a large picture window overlooking the backyard. The walls were white and so were the ceiling, sheets, pillowcases and candlestick bedspread. My room was comfortingly clean and inviting. I made myself ready for bed, propped myself up on pillows and started one of the most fascinating journeys of my life up to that time.

I do not remember how long I read that night, but *God's Smuggler* transported me to another world. I learned of the 1955 beginning of Brother Andrew's mission to Communist countries, of God's provision for his family, of his learning to listen to and obey the Holy Spirit. As the story progressed I was caught up into the fast-moving adventure of Bible smuggling. It sounded rather risky. I wanted to help by carrying out administrative work in the Dutch headquarters. I also wondered with a certain apprehension if in the future I would be invited to make journeys to any of those mysterious lands behind the iron curtain.

Beginning Work

As I began work the next day there were lesser mysteries to uncover. "Why is this country known by two names?" was one of my first questions to my co-workers. They told me that the country's official name, the Netherlands, refers to the low-lying nature of the country (*nether* meaning "low"). The name Holland is frequently used instead of the Netherlands, but it actually refers to the two western coastal provinces, North and South Holland, which have played an important role in the country's history.

And why were the language and the people of the country called Dutch? I learned that the noun derives from the word *Deutsch*, meaning "German." Europe was widely inhabited by Germanic and other tribes for countless centuries, and the German influence is still evident in the name of its language.

Another question I put to my new colleagues had to do with Dutch surnames. Brother Andrew's surname, which he did not publish for the sake of the Christians in Eastern Europe, had two words in its prefix. And then there was *Ten Boom*. I knew that *Boom* meant *tree,* but what did the prefix *Ten* mean, and why did I sometimes see the first letter T written in upper case and sometimes in lower?

Ten, it turned out, means "to the" in old Dutch. In Dutch grammar, when the word *Ten* stands alone, as it does when one refers, for instance, to the *Ten Boom* family, the first letter of the surname is capitalized. When the surname is combined with a Christian name, or family title such as Betsie *ten Boom* or Father *ten Boom,* lowercase is used for the first letter of the surname. Being a perfectionist in nature, I wanted to learn Dutch quickly and correctly and colloquially, but my unpretentious and down-to-earth new friends soon put me in my place, often laughing at my mistakes. They were kind and helpful, however, and eventually I learned their language—and to take myself less seriously.

Acclimating to Dutch Life

A couple of months after arriving in Holland I purchased a bike and pedaled my way to work and back each day, but for my first six weeks in the country in that autumn of 1968 I rode the bus because it rained incessantly. There was not one day when the sun appeared.

"Pam, you must make sure that you have plenty of sunshine inside when you live in Holland," said my new boss, "because there is not much outside."

My stay in Holland was to last more than seven years, during which time I came to love Holland and its people deeply. I made new friends and was often invited to team members' homes for meals, where I entered into a delightful Dutch state called *gezelligheid.* There is no translation for that word. *Coziness* is perhaps the nearest English word, but that does not capture *gezelligheid* at all. The dictionary says it means "companionable, convivial, sociable, clubbable and pleasant," but it is much more. It is togetherness in a deep, trusting, open, safe and enjoyable way. Coffee and cookies, low lights, flowers and laughter often accompany it. There are so many Dutch people that it is impossible for them to get away from each other. A person cannot be *gezellig* alone.

But being single, I was often alone. There were bike rides on Sunday afternoons on the trails in the woods just outside Harderwijk. It was exhilarating. I rode there in all seasons, autumn being my favorite. There were also many times when I left my lodgings and Miss de Graaf on Sunday afternoons and rode my bike a short distance to the dike and the low-lying polder lands beyond. Rows of tall and slender trees acted as windbreaks along the road to the polder and on the polder itself—trees that, along with grass plantings, stabilized the land so recently reclaimed from the sea. It was often very windy there, and when the wind was against me I leaned closer to the handlebars and kept going as quickly as I could pedal.

I persevered in my work, too. It was fulfilling, very busy, youth-oriented and adventurous. Eventually it did include several visits to Eastern Europe, where I had encounters with the persecuted Church that changed the way I looked at life. I was to learn many things from the Dutch and East European Christians, including how to pray so as to get what you ask. And I spent much time thinking on such things as the ethics of smuggling. Of course, the years contained disappointments and loneliness and some sadness. Life always does. But although there were many rainy days, it seemed to me there were a lot more days when that beautiful light appeared.

My First Encounter with Tante Corrie

But I must return to the time when my Dutch adventure was just beginning.

"One of the first things I want you to do," Brother Andrew told me upon my arrival in the Netherlands, "is to help my friend Corrie ten Boom."

He told me that the American authors John and Elizabeth Sherrill, co-writers of *God's Smuggler*, were now writing a book with Tante Corrie. It was not yet named, but work had begun. Hours of interviews with the writers and their subject had been audiotaped, and a typist was needed to transcribe them.

"I have volunteered you," said Brother Andrew.

And so my first personal encounter with Corrie ten Boom came to pass. She was usually absent from her home country on world journeys—her favorite title of the several ascribed to her by her friends was "Tramp for the Lord." But she spent several months in Holland during that autumn of 1968, mainly for the purpose of working on the new book. Her temporary residence was a borrowed apartment in the town of Soestdijk, about 45 minutes' drive from Brother Andrew's mission base.

As I traveled from my lodgings in Harderwijk to Tante Corrie's residence on that first misty, mellow autumn day, I looked forward to what promised to be an interesting undertaking. But I also felt rather apprehensive. This was the lady whose powerful presence I had found rather overwhelming at the mission conference in England two months before. Self-confidence had never been a strong point with me. And this lady seemed so very confident. I knew I had much to learn about the culture of the Dutch, and I certainly had never worked closely with Americans—or writers of any nationality for that matter—so the prospect of working with John and Elizabeth Sherrill was daunting as well. Would I be able to complete this assignment in a satisfactory way? I thought, *There must be many others more capable than I of helping with the production of a book.*

I arrived at Tante Corrie's lodgings, which were in a beautifully appointed apartment owned by a member of the Dutch nobility who was working in Israel and had made her home available to Corrie. My fears were put to rest quickly as I was welcomed so warmly. Blue, discerning eyes looked into my brown ones. I noted the healthy, olive-toned skin and the silver and gray hair arranged around a doughnut-shaped roll on the crown of her head.

"Come in, child," she said, "and let's have a talk. The Sherrills will be arriving soon. We will all travel together to Vught. That was the first concentration camp where Betsie and I were imprisoned. My co-authors want to be sure about the site of the camp and its surroundings and how it looked in 1944."

During the few minutes we had together before the arrival of her American friends, I was immediately drawn into Tante Corrie's world. We drank a cup of coffee, ate cookies made with butter and took each other in. It was *gezellig*.

"I am so glad you are going to help us with this book," she said, somehow conveying the assurance that I was a vital part of its birth.

A little later, as Tante Corrie, Elizabeth, John and I were driven to Holland's most southerly province and the site of the concentration camp, I watched the swiftly passing trees all dressed in gold, red, brown and yellow and reflected on the coffee time of half an hour before. Corrie ten Boom may have done courageous things during the war, traveled the world for decades, addressed hundreds of thousands of people and possessed a very powerful presence, but she certainly knew how to make an individual feel important and valuable. She had talked as if I were indispensable to her current project. And I believed her!

Beginning Work with Tante Corrie

We soon arrived at the site of the concentration camp, and I began to witness the care and determination with which the Sherrills recorded the facts of Corrie ten Boom's incarceration and, indeed, whole life story. At one point they asked Tante Corrie to describe how the tree-lined avenue on which we were walking had looked on the night in 1944 when she and her sister were brought to the camp.

"Corrie," said John Sherrill, "you told us that when you and Betsie were brought here soldiers stood near the trees on each side of this avenue. Where were the soldiers exactly—in the trees, or beside the trees? And those floodlights you told us were shining on you—were they in the trees or between the trees?"

"I don't remember," Corrie responded with no hesitation and with emphasis, unwilling to unlock memories of her wartime experiences. They were clearly hard for her to recall, but she stated that fact very honestly. This forceful personality was not afraid to show her fears and vulnerability.

During the coming months of the writing of the book, however, she made herself remember. I transcribed many tapes, and when *The Hiding Place* was published in 1971 it was fascinating to see how the skillful blending of such details as soldiers and trees with the element of danger for the Ten Boom family and the rescue of the Jewish people made this a book about which many still say, "I could not put it down."

Brother Andrew's work expanded, and so did the number of co-workers. We moved from the attic office under the pointed roof to a much larger headquarters, which housed more vehicles, Bibles and Christian book supplies in the various East European languages. An increasing number of people for whom English was their first language joined the team. I was no longer the only person who dealt with the continuing correspondence.

Asked to Be Tante Corrie's Companion

After I had worked with Brother Andrew for seven years, Corrie invited me to become her companion. Her Dutch companion of nearly nine years, Ellen, was soon to marry an American minister. I wondered how I, by now a rather independent Englishwoman in my early thirties, could possibly blend my lifestyle with that of a determined Dutch lady more than fifty years my senior. Was I cut out to be a companion? I did not think I was the type.

Deciding to accept Tante Corrie's invitation to an interview, however, I left Brother Andrew's headquarters on a March day in 1976 and drove to Overveen, a suburb of her hometown of Haarlem. She had a house there that had been her base since the previous year. A bunch of yellow tulips, a gift for Tante Corrie, lay in the passenger seat of the small, French, yellow-green car I was driving. As I entered the ancient city of Haarlem above which rose the roofs of the St. Bavo Dutch Reformed Church, also called the Great Church, I could not help but reflect on what had happened there. I thought of the small house lying almost in the shadow of that church on a street named Barteljoris where, more than thirty years before, Corrie ten Boom and her family were arrested for their part in saving Jewish lives.

Light rain was falling as I entered Juliana Avenue, where I would find Tante Corrie's home and headquarters. The wind blows across the Netherlands on most days, and this day was no exception. The cyclists on the bicycle paths on each side of the avenue had their heads down, those on the right side battling into the wind and rain from the nearby North Sea.

Pulling up to the curb as near as possible to house number 32, I parked the car. A short walk took me through part of the tree-lined street with its large and well-kept houses. The street was clean and neat in spite of its fairly heavy traffic. As I turned in at 32 Juliana Avenue, I noticed that the front yard had no gate. Dutch houses normally did. I later learned that since her imprisonment, Tante Corrie did not like to be shut in.

I rang the front doorbell and a few seconds later, Ellen de Kroon, Tante Corrie's companion, let me in.

I stepped into an atmosphere of peace and acceptance. I had experienced this several times before on visits to Tante Corrie over the years in whatever house she might have temporary residence. And from reports I heard, nearly everybody felt the same at her house—peaceful and welcome. Needed even.

Ellen welcomed me and said, "Let me take your coat."

She was tall and blond and, having seen her in action many times previously, I knew Ellen was a very able woman. Depending on the travel circumstances, her job responsibilities included, among many other tasks, those of chauffeuse, cook, cleaner, speaking schedule organizer, nurse, public speaker and counselor to many. She dealt with thousands of people and always tried her best to see that Tante Corrie got enough rest.

As she led me to the bottom of the stairs, Ellen explained that on the advice of her doctor Tante Corrie, then nearly 84, had recently begun to take one rest day each week. On this day of my visit, she was resting in her room on the second floor of the house.

"Tante Corrie is waiting for you. You know the way to her room, don't you?" asked Ellen. "Go on up, and I will bring tea in a little while."

I had visited this house before and did know the way. Clutching the yellow tulips, I climbed the steep staircase with slight trepidation but also with a sense of mounting adventure.

That Is Settled!

How on earth does Ellen do all those tasks and at the same time provide almost constant companionship to Tante Corrie? I asked myself. I did not know how the coming interview would turn out, but I was certain that I could not fulfill all of Ellen's roles as companion to Tante Corrie, should this elderly lady ask me to take her place. I was not a nurse, and Corrie's doctor had told me that her heart was not strong. I did not like cooking or driving, and I had a reserved personality, which might make dealing with thousands of people rather difficult. And although I had deep respect for Tante Corrie, I could hardly imagine being in this strong personality's presence 24 hours a day for an open-ended time.

Reaching the landing I knocked on her bedroom door, and Corrie ten Boom's firm and clear alto voice invited me to come inside. Entering her bright, fresh, colorful bedroom, I found her sitting up in bed wearing pale yellow nylon pajamas. The bedspread was covered with books, notebooks and writing implements, and her Bible was at her side. *This elderly lady may be resting her body,* I thought, *but she is not resting her mind.* We greeted each other with smiles, and I handed her the yellow tulips.

She thanked me, deposited the flowers on a bedside table and invited me to sit down. Drawing a comfortable chair closer to her bed, I looked into her blue eyes and thought how good she looked. Her silver-gray hair was not arranged in the usual roll around her head on this, her rest day. Fine and straight, it was neatly combed and rested on her shoulders, somehow making her look rather vulnerable. These observations did not last longer than a few seconds, however, because, characteristically, Tante Corrie came straight to the point.

"Well, child, what has the Lord told you?"

"I am willing to help you, Tante Corrie ..." I ventured, by way of a start.

"Praise the Lord! That is settled then!"

But for me it was not settled at all. I had not even finished the sentence. I had been going to say, "I am willing to help you until you have found a more suitable companion."

Tante Corrie began to tell me about her plans for the coming months, which included returning to the United States, where most of her work in latter years had taken place. "I have so many opportunities in America," she said. "*The Hiding Place* has been read by thousands of people. And now there is a new movie giving the story of the book. I have many more invitations to speak than I can accept."

She went on to tell me that among many other appointments, she was soon to speak at a sunrise service in Florida, work for several days with a pastor in Brooklyn, be interviewed for a television program in Toronto and receive an honorary degree from Gordon College in Massachusetts. After all this, she was to speak to prisoners in Chicago and Hawaii. At the same time she told me she would work on several writing projects, including a new book.

"The whole journey will take seven months," she stated matter-of-factly. "Do come with me to help me."

Seven months for a person in her mid-eighties. How ever would she get through it? How would I get through it? But I was beginning to catch her enthusiasm, and besides, it sounded like a good adventure.

"I'll go with you for the next seven months, Tante Corrie," I promised. My boss, Brother Andrew, knowing of her need for a new companion, had told me he would give me a leave of absence for several months to help his old friend Corrie, should she ask me.

Getting to Know Tante Corrie

Ellen joined us, bringing the tea, and we three spent a couple of hours talking about the travel itinerary and what my duties would be. While Ellen went to the kitchen to prepare supper and Tante Corrie took care of some items on her desk, I looked at the many items on the walls of her room. I had seen them briefly on a previous visit to this room, but now I could inspect them more closely. Tante Corrie obviously loved these objects and had hung many of them as closely as space permitted. Some were original oil or watercolor paintings, somehow kept safe in the War. Others were reproductions of works by old Dutch masters, including Rembrandt with his enchanting use of light. Other items on the wall included plaques on which were written Scripture texts of special meaning to her. Some were framed, and most were small. I read them all and was struck by one in particular. It was not particularly pretty, but it did stand out. It was a rectangular plaque without a frame. Its background was reddish pink with the words *Mijn tijden zijn in Uw hand*— "My times are in your hands"—written boldly in black. Underneath was the Scripture reference—Psalm 31:15.

Ellen produced a good meal in a short time, and after some more planning I took leave of them, turning the small, light-green car toward Harderwijk and home. As daylight dissolved to dusk I reached the last half of my journey where the lighter traffic allowed me to think about the events of the day. It looked as though I would be returning soon to Haarlem to accompany Corrie ten Boom on her journeys for seven months. Yet I did not feel as though I had been pushed into accepting her invitation to go with her. Although she had been quite sure that it was right for me to be her new companion and I was not so sure, I knew

31

her well enough to know that she would not act presumptuously or force a decision on me.

What remarkable faith and trust in God Corrie has, I thought. *She is so sure about the work God has given her and how to carry it out. She lives close to Him, and her decisions have been proven right on countless occasions. She believes it is right for me to join her.* Although I did not share her certainty, I did feel a kind of peace about it. There was comfort in the fact that God always seemed to honor Tante Corrie's decisions.

I decided to leave things as they were for now and see what happened in seven months' time. In the meantime, perhaps I would gain insights into what made her the woman she was. What kinds of things had influenced the peaceful and purposeful life she was living? How could I learn to live like that?

A few weeks later, with Brother Andrew's blessing, I arrived again at Tante Corrie's front door, with two suitcases. We began our work together on April 1, 1976. Several days before our departure on April 6, Tante Corrie began packing for the long journey. Here I caught a glimpse of her very pragmatic side. We were in her bedroom and placed the suitcases on her low bed. For the first time I saw some of the things that the long years of traveling had taught her. It was of real importance to her that we be ready in plenty of time to prevent a last-minute rush. Between us we had seven pieces of luggage, including small and large cases. She asked me to count the luggage carefully as it was loaded at the airport and again upon arrival. We began by packing her items, and I noticed that she worked methodically, never pausing to ponder or worry that she might forget something important. Last of all, she packed a copy of the New Testament translation by J. B. Phillips right at the top of a small bag for easy access. Judging by its rather worn black cover, it looked as if it had accompanied her on many journeys.

At one point Tante Corrie packed a folded piece of shiny blue material with yellow threads hanging from it. I asked if it was some embroidery she was working on.

"No, child," she replied, her blue eyes alive with some secret, "this is what I call 'the crown.' You will see how I use it later." Saying no more, she slipped it into a cloth bag.

And so I left the Netherlands, the land I had grown to love so deeply, with its straightforward people, its language, poetry, history, the flat green lowlands on which the wind always blew and the mysterious light from the huge dome of a sky. And that short assignment, which I originally thought would last seven months, turned into seven years—time spent mainly in the United States.

From Travel to Rest

Tante Corrie traveled, wrote books, spoke at gatherings large and small and in February 1977 moved into a rented house in Placentia in Orange County, California. Her heart needed rest, but Tante Corrie disliked rest. It seemed to me she worked as hard as ever, although she did not travel as much as in previous years. She wrote several books, conducted telephone and letter correspondence, gave interviews and received many guests.

Eighteen months later, on August 23, 1978, I took tea to her room as I always did early in the morning. I knew I would find Tante Corrie propped up on her pillows, her J. B. Phillips translation of the New Testament open on her chest. The thick curtain on the big picture window facing east, which had shut out light during the night and early morning, would have been determinedly drawn back and Tante Corrie would be planning her day.

Teatime together was a time of quiet fellowship and prayer before each busy day began. We talked about the day before and the day lying ahead. The talks were always about people—ones she had worked with decades before, others she had met on her world journeys who were passing through Los Angeles, our neighbors and the children down the road, and the many unknown people who did not yet know the Lord Jesus. And we read the Scriptures together and prayed for those we discussed. It was perhaps the one part of the day when I could expect things to be the same as they had been the morning before.

But this day was different. For one thing, as I carried the tea tray along the corridor leading to her bedroom, I saw that all was dark inside. This was unusual, but I was glad she was sleeping in. She had complained of bad headaches in previous days.

I felt my way into the darkened room, put the tray down and extended my right hand to draw the heavy curtain. It pulled slowly back. Then I pulled on the rope that drew back the light green, filmy sheer.

I turned around and faced a completely different Tante Corrie from the one I had bid good night the evening before. She was conscious but looked very confused. I was so shocked that it seemed I froze in place for a few seconds. I greeted her, but there was no response. I ran to her and took her right hand. "Let's pray, Tante Corrie," I said. She immediately closed her eyes, and I asked the Lord to help her. Then I summoned an ambulance, and she was taken to the local hospital, where a stroke was diagnosed.

After a few weeks, Tante Corrie came home, but her brain was permanently damaged. She could not do the normal things we do with language—she was unable to speak, write or comprehend as she had before. Sometimes, but rarely, she managed a few words appropriate to the occasion. She never learned to write again. Those of us who helped her during the next five years became sure that there were times when she could comprehend, but we were unsure as to what degree and when.

It was a different Tante Corrie with whom I lived for the next five years, yet in spite of some pain and much discouragement, not a less resolute or consistent one. During what I call the five silent years that followed, in what seemed to be a very slow movement of time, I watched closely and I saw that Christianity really works. On April 15, 1983, her 91st birthday, Corrie ten Boom passed away at her rented home in Placentia, California.

Discovering the Heart of Tante Corrie

Corrie ten Boom's speaking and writing ministry reached hundreds of thousands of people, and in the years since her death the impact of her story has remained strong. She frequently told her audiences, "We are living in one of the darkest times of the history of the whole world." I wonder what she would think now. More than two decades after her death, the times appointed to you and me seem even darker. What can we discover about the heart of Corrie ten Boom that will help us to persevere with a better understanding of our own times—and with less fear and real victory?

I invite you to come with me on a journey into her story in which we will see afresh the kinds of things that influenced the peaceful and purposeful life Corrie lived.

We can learn from her how to put into practice the how-tos of faith that are essential to real Christian living in our times. We will discover things like:

- Learning to tell our own story
- How to maintain strong family relationships
- How to develop strong community relationships
- How to live a single life
- How to forgive our enemies
- How to get along with less
- The secret of simplicity

Corrie ten Boom told her story many times. And it was in the telling of that story that lives were changed. Deep within each human being is an ancient, profound desire for a good story. You and I have a story, too, without which every other Christian is the poorer. Perhaps in learning how Corrie told her story, we will learn how to tell our own stories as well—and in so doing we will affect our world in ways that only eternity will tell.

It was 1892 when Corrie's story began.

two

Corrie's Early Life and Influences

1892–1910

Corrie ten Boom was thoroughly Dutch, in large part a product of her time and her nation. As with each of us, the history, environment, spiritual, physical and social conditions of the country of her birth had indelible effects on her and on the story she told us.

The Holland into which she was born in Amsterdam on April 15, 1892, had enjoyed peace for decades—longer than most people could remember. This followed centuries of conquests, control, invasions, wars and raids by, for example, the Romans, Germanic tribes, Vikings, Hapsburgs, Spaniards, English and French. As a result of Napoleon's march across Europe, little Holland (14,103 square miles in area—the size of Massachusetts, Connecticut and Rhode Island combined) was incorporated into the French empire in 1810 and was ruled by Napoleon's followers.

Corrie's great-grandfather Gerrit ten Boom, a staunch Calvinist, lived in Napoleonic times. A master gardener on an estate, he lived and worked in the outskirts of Haarlem. Gerrit stood up to the Napoleonic government several times. On at least one occasion, after he had rallied the members of his Dutch Reformed Church to remember their true freedom as Dutch citizens and Christians, he was brought before the authorities. Had his influential employer not intervened he would probably have been sentenced to prison. Corrie's father, Casper, was proud of his grandfather Gerrit and told Corrie, "I am glad he was a real man."

Gerrit's influence on his grandson was evident more than one hundred years later. When people warned Casper, "Stop having Jews in your house—you will be sent to prison," he answered, "I am too old for prison life, but if that should happen, I would be honored to give my life for God's ancient people, the Jews."

And great-grandfather Gerrit's son Willem (Corrie's grandfather) also made a large contribution to the coming generations of Ten Booms. In 1844, while in his late twenties, he began a weekly prayer meeting for Israel, to "pray for the peace of Jerusalem." He had become part of a revival movement in the middle of the nineteenth century started by Willem Bilderdijk and Isaac Da Costa, a Jew of Portuguese descent who converted to Christianity. The influence of both these men on the Ten Boom family was profound. Father Casper ten Boom told Corrie that a picture of Da Costa always hung in the family home while he was growing up. (appendix 1 to this book further explains the influence of Isaac Da Costa on Corrie's grandfather Willem in regard to the Jewish people, for whose sake several of the Ten Booms would later lose their lives.)

Jewish people had found a refuge in Holland ever since the first Prince of Orange (of the Dutch royal family's House of Orange) delivered the country from Spanish rule in the seventeenth century. Holland became a land of freedom and security for oppressed people from many countries. The Jews settled mainly in Amsterdam and even called that city "the New Jerusalem."

Years later Corrie told her audiences: "We never know how God will answer our prayers, but we can expect that He will get us involved in His plan for the answers. If we are true intercessors, we must be ready to take part in God's work on behalf of the people for whom we pray."

"A Very Little, Weak Baby"

Corrie's mother, Cor ten Boom, kept a diary of sorts. Her entries were made once or twice a year, from 1887 until 1909. Her purpose was to keep notes about her children: "It seems to me it might be so nice for them, when they are grown up (the Lord sparing them) to read some things about themselves when they were small."

This is part of her entry on December 31, 1892:

> What an eventful year we have had. At times it was so dark and difficult, but the Lord spared us for one another and we also received a very small baby, which we had been expecting in May, but which arrived a month early, on Good Friday. We will never forget the happenings of that day, the awful fear in those dark hours, our crying out to the Lord to spare me. The Lord heard and gave us a very little, weak baby, Corrie. Oh, what a poor little thing it was. It was nearly dead and looked bluish-white at birth. I never saw anything so pitiful. Nobody thought it would live.

Child of a Godly, Loving Marriage

Corrie was the fifth and youngest child of Casper and Cornelia ten Boom, known to each other and to their friends as Cas and Cor. Born in 1858, Cor was the seventh of the eight children of Arent Luitingh and his wife, Cornelia Frings. Shortly after the birth of the couple's eighth child, Anna, at the end of 1860, father Arent died at about fifty years of age, leaving his 42-year-old wife with a small store to manage in Amsterdam. As soon as they were old enough all the children worked to support the family.

When Cor was in her late teens, she and her youngest sister, Anna, taught in a kindergarten started by Jans, their resolute older sister. Jans then added a Sunday school, and it was here that Cor Luitingh met Casper ten Boom. The two of them found they had much in common, including the same birthday, May 18.

Their friendship grew, and one day when Cor decided to visit her grandmother in Harderwijk, Casper missed her so much that he followed her there the next day. In view of the limited means of transport, Cor must have realized there was more to Casper's being there than just a visit. Indeed, the next day he made a proposal of marriage to Cor. Their wedding took place on October 16, 1884.

About fifty years later, Corrie and her father visited Harderwijk, a fishing village on the Zuider Zee, Holland's inland sea, now reclaimed polder land. I can still hear Corrie tell the story:

> As we walked along the Bruggestraat, Father said: "This is where I proposed to your mother. There were cobblestones instead of pavement at that time, but many of the old houses and the sea gate are still the same." I asked him if Mother had said yes immediately. "No, not until the next day," he answered, "and I spent a very restless night waiting for that decision!"[1]

> When Corrie asked him if he had ever regretted his decision to marry Mother his voice was firm. "Never! Until the last day of her life, I was just as much in love with your mother as I was on that day in Harderwijk. We did not have an easy life—we had many sorrows—but God led us by His extraordinary providence."[2]

The Watchmaker Ten Booms

Casper ten Boom was the eldest child of the second marriage of Willem ten Boom, whose first wife Geertruida died

Ten Boom Family, 1900   PHOTO COURTESY OF THE CORRIE TEN BOOM HOUSE FOUNDATION

of tuberculosis in 1856 after giving birth to thirteen children, most of whom also died of the same disease. Corrie's grandfather Willem was a watchmaker by trade, and in 1837 he set up shop in the city of Haarlem.

Casper followed his father's profession and established a business in Amsterdam, where each of his five children was born. In 1892, after the death of his father, Casper and his family moved to Haarlem where he took over his father's business at 19 Barteljorisstraat (Barteljoris Street). Since the full name of that street is a bit of a mouthful, the Ten Booms contracted their particular address to Beje, the Dutch spelling for the letters B and J—B for Bartel and J for Joris. This is pronounced *bay-yay* in Dutch. Actually, over the centuries there probably had been a corruption in the street's name. It is said that Bartel may really stand for Martel or *martyr*. Martyr Joris was put to death in the Dutch city of Dordrecht in 1558. Barteljorisstraat commemorates him and, to those who know the story, four other martyrs from number 19 nearly five hundred years later during World War II.

I am looking at a photograph taken in 1897 of Casper and Cor ten Boom's children—Betsie, Willem, Nollie and Corrie.

Betsie, Willem, Nollie, Corrie, 1897   PHOTO COURTESY OF THE CORRIE TEN BOOM HOUSE FOUNDATION

The children are facing the camera and are depicted in decreasing height. The oldest child, Betsie, is on the left. Twelve years old, she is wearing a white dress with big frilly sleeves and a high neckline. Her long brown hair is pulled back and a thick ringlet hangs over her left shoulder.

Next to her is brother Willem, wearing a white shirt and black jacket that seems too big for him. His black hair is cropped short. Like that of Betsie, his expression is enigmatic. The two were born within fifteen months of each other, and Willem is half a head shorter than Betsie.

The next step down is a longer one. Beside Willem is sister Nollie, wearing a white dress with a splendid, large ruffled collar and a wistful expression. A gap of three and a half years separated Willem and Nollie. Had he lived, their brother Hendrik would have filled the middle space in this line-up of the Ten Boom children. But he died at six months from "a terrible brain fever."

Then, at the far right we see the youngest child, five-year-old Corrie. She, too, is wearing something white, but time has faded the details of her clothing. She is looking into the camera with a most serious expression.

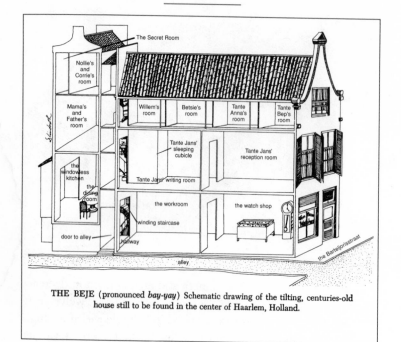

THE BEJE (pronounced *bay-yay*) Schematic drawing of the tilting, centuries-old house still to be found in the center of Haarlem, Holland.

The Beje

Five-year-old Corrie's home was near the marketplace that bordered the pre-Reformation St. Bavo Cathedral, the family's Dutch Reformed Church. It was then known as the Grote Kerk, the Great Church. The Beje itself, as the Ten Booms called their home, was actually two houses joined together. The first house was built in the 1400s. Like many of the ancient houses in Haarlem it was very small, with three stories, two rooms deep and one room wide. This was the house Father ten Boom inherited, and he soon found that it was too small for himself and Cor, their four children and Cor's three sisters—Bep, Jans and Anna—who one by one had joined the household. The three did not have the means to support themselves, although Tante Jans did have a small source of income, a pension as the widow of a minister.

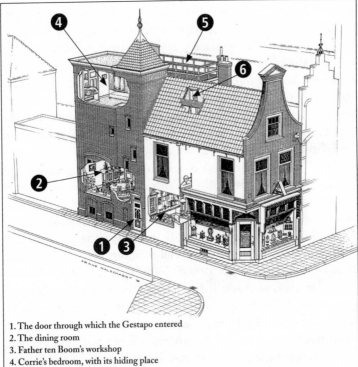

1. The door through which the Gestapo entered
2. The dining room
3. Father ten Boom's workshop
4. Corrie's bedroom, with its hiding place
5. The balcony on which those in hiding took fresh air
6. This location was once considered as a hiding place but was never used.

COURTESY OF THE CORRIE TEN BOOM HOUSE FOUNDATION

There was no question in Father ten Boom's mind that his wife's sisters should live with his family, but he knew he had to supply more space. He was able to purchase the very narrow house behind the existing home. A narrow alley separated the two houses, so Casper arranged for the houses to be joined by breaking through walls, building extra outside walls and adding a steep, winding staircase to join the two. Since the houses are on different levels, doorways issue out of the staircase at unusual intervals, and the family stepped up or down into a room, depending upon which part of the house they were entering or exiting.

To this day I find the house confusing. Perhaps the Nazis did, too, when they failed to find the secret room built to hide Jewish people. Behind a false wall in Corrie's small bedroom at the top of the house was an area about two feet wide and eight feet long. Entrance to the hiding place was gained by crawling through a wooden sliding panel at the back of the linen cupboard that was built into the false wall. It was professionally built with real bricks by a co-worker in the underground work. There was no hollow sound when the Nazis hammered on it or any other wall in the house, and even when the Ten Booms were led away to prison on February 28, 1944, it did not give up its secret.

Tante Bep, the children's oldest aunt, had never married and had a rather dour disposition. Tante Corrie always said that it was because she had worked as a governess all her life and had never had a home or family of her own. Tante Anna, also never married, was the youngest aunt. Being close in age, she and her sister Cor had always had a special relationship, and Anna had been with the family since Betsie's birth. The third aunt, widowed Tante Jans, was an evangelist, a strong-minded woman who took over most of the second floor of the house. The four children, Tante Anna and Tante Bep had their bedrooms upstairs on the third floor. Nollie and Corrie shared a room not quite ten feet by seven feet in size. Mother and Father slept in a small room on the second floor.

The Oval Table

The Beje's dining room was at the back of the house overlooking an alley. Lit by gas lamps, it was five steps higher than the watch shop but lower than Tante Jans' rooms. Its oval table was a place of much *gezelligheid*, that untranslatable Dutch word meaning fellow-feeling, comradeship, laughter and trust. Meals would consist of two *broodmaaltijden* (bread meals) each day and one other meal. The bread meals were simply that—bread with butter, thinly sliced cheese, sometimes thinly sliced meat, jam, milk and plain yogurt. The main, hot meal consisted primarily of vegetables—cabbage, for example, or peas, green beans, kale or beets—normally with a small amount of meat. And, without exception, potatoes.

At the oval table, which was usually covered by a black and red cloth, the Ten Booms read the Bible from various translations. Casper ten Boom wanted to broaden his children's thinking, and he held Bible studies in several languages simultaneously. While they studied the same passage, different family members read from Dutch, French, German, English, Hebrew and Greek Bibles.

During mealtimes they made plans, some of which must have been about their frequent travels and stays away from Haarlem and the Beje. They must have confided their hopes and dreams to each other, too, but on the simplest of levels they wanted to know what each family member had done that day. "Tell me every detail," Tante Corrie used to ask me when we lived together in California and I came home from a day away. "You stepped into the car. What happened next?"

Two recurring problems must have surfaced at times at the oval table—Father's financial difficulties and Mother's chronically delicate health. Father was a good watchmaker, but he had a hard time making ends meet in his household of nine, especially when he sometimes failed to send bills to customers whom he knew would find it hard to pay for his repairs.

In keeping with Victorian modesty Mother's health problems are not described in the family letters, but they necessitated frequent times of recuperation away from the city through most of the years of their marriage. Betsie, who suffered from a blood disease, was also often away convalescing, and Willem, Nollie and Corrie made many more journeys away from home than would have been normal for a family of their means. Because the family members wrote to each other almost every day during their times away, a rather remarkable record of their daily lives is preserved.

All accounts given in the many preserved letters between the Ten Boom children and their parents, aunts and friends are so full of love and admiration for each other that the family seems perfect! Since they were a normal family, this surely could not always have been the case, but there is little trace of disharmony in any letters or diaries, or in the stories Tante Corrie told me. Therefore, when John and Elizabeth Sherrill, writers of *The Hiding Place*, were looking for a way to describe life in the Beje that would reflect some of the tensions inevitably found in families (thus making them real), they were glad when they were finally able to say with relief, "We were delighted to find a few abrasive aunts!"

There was one serious disharmony, however. Mother's diary entry on New Year's Eve 1895 reads:

> Some very dark clouds have come up…it concerns my husband and his mother. That battle has been going on for such a long time. What a terrible thought—that a mother is not living in peace with her own children. . . . So many prayers have been offered for this very sad state of affairs. I only trust that the battle will not grow too heavy for my dear husband. He looks so unwell.

We do not know the end of that part of the story, but it seems that Casper's mother was permanently estranged from the family. Corrie never wrote about or spoke of her grandmother, Elisabeth Bel ten Boom (after whom Betsie was presumably named) in any of the papers I have studied, even though she lived and died in Haarlem.

Corrie's World in the 1890s

Looking outside their house, five-year-old Corrie would have seen a densely populated city with many houses the same shape and size as that of her family. Streets were narrow and houses tall, some of them leaning and many with distinctive gables. Most houses adjoined each other except at intersections of streets, alleys and canals.

One of the first paved roads in Holland ran the short distance between Haarlem and Amsterdam. It was less than four-and-one-half yards wide. A few times each day an automobile would be seen traveling down it.

From the Dutch census of 1899 we know that Holland had a population of about five million at the time of Corrie's birth. Three-quarters of the population lived and worked on the land. Many houses and farms built in the seventeenth or eighteenth centuries were still in daily use.

There is a well-known Dutch poem that describes Holland beautifully:

> When I think of Holland I see broad rivers moving very
>   slowly through endless lowlands
> And rows of very tall poplars that look like long feathers
>   standing on end. . . .[3]

Rivers, canals and other watercourses with their locks and sluice gates crisscrossed the flat Dutch landscape. Much of the land is below sea level, and the sea had always been the fiercest enemy of the lowlands. Disastrous floods mainly from the North Sea had caused untold numbers of deaths throughout the centuries. From the air the lowlands can be clearly seen for what they are—a very large delta.

Young Corrie's Holland continued a hurtling journey begun decades earlier. With the rest of Europe her little country moved frantically through and toward far-reaching and inexorable change. Between 1880 and 1914 nearly all the big towns underwent fast alteration—boulevards were built in the cities, along with squares, new housing districts, warehouses, museums, theaters and train stations. People slowly gained more free time, more convenience, better food and better education in hygiene.

The French elite gave a name to the years 1890–1914—*La Belle Époque* ("The Beautiful Time"). Freedom reigned throughout Europe, and new innovations such as electricity and cars were changing the continent rapidly. So were advances in medicine and welfare. But the increasingly comfortable changes of "The Beautiful Time" were mainly for the upper class. In Holland, more than a quarter of the population lived in housing consisting of just one room, even though there were often four, six or even eight people in a family. A high percentage of the people did not reach their fiftieth birthday. Every 45 minutes someone died of tuberculosis. Mother Cor's diary entries were full of prayers and pleadings that she and Casper might be able to "keep their children." She wrote about times when the children were so ill with diseases such as diphtheria, flu and scarlet fever that she could not see how they could live. She never referred to their future without saying "the Lord willing."

Corrie also used the expression "the Lord willing" quite often, and so did many Dutch Christians in the Calvinist tradition. They took very seriously the New Testament's admonition through James, "Listen, you who say, 'Today or tomorrow we will go to this or that city, spend a year there, carry on business and make money.' Why, you do not even know what will happen tomorrow. . . . Instead, you ought to say, 'If it is the Lord's will, we will live and do this or that'"(James 4:13–15).

Religious Changes

Corrie's family belonged to the Dutch Reformed Church, the state church in which Corrie was christened in July 1892. The Ten Booms were uncomplicated people who believed that Christians could know God personally and discover and follow His will. For them and many others in their day faith was not a theological construct but a daily, self-evident reality. Father ten Boom knew his Bible from cover to cover. He was widely read and always ready to discuss theological issues.

Father ten Boom was a Calvinist, but he did not live in a rigid theological system. Corrie was influenced greatly by him and by her church's theology. She, like him I believe, talked less about "the sovereignty of God" than about "my times are in His hands." Corrie wrote in 1976, "Father was not quarrelsome about his biblical beliefs, but he stood fast in theological debates. . . . I heard him speak frequently about predestination. I never quite understood what he meant, and one time I asked him, 'What is predestination?' He answered, 'The ground on which I build my faith is not in me, but in the faithfulness of God.'" She was to repeat that statement many times in the years that followed.

The census of 1899 tells us that only two percent of the population admitted to having no church affiliation. The Renaissance (1400s) and the Enlightenment (1700s), with the resulting new thinking and scientific discoveries, had caused differences in theological thought and had divided Protestant churches in Holland and across Europe.

Dr. Abraham Kuyper, journalist, pastor, statesman and strongly Orthodox theologian, was used by God to turn the Dutch people's dissatisfaction with modernity and liberalism into a strong mass movement. Although theologically conservative, Kuyper was a radical reformer socially and politically. He was the leader of the mainly rural conservative Dutch Christians whom he called the *kleine luiden* (the "little people"). In 1880 he founded the Free University of Amsterdam on theologically reformed principles. Kuyper's influence on the religious and national life of Holland from about 1870 until his death in 1920 and later was immense. He declared "the absolute sovereignty of God" and believed that the only true Holland was a Calvinistic Holland.

Kuyper and his followers wanted to take over the Dutch Reformed Church, but an attempt to seize power in 1886 was unsuccessful. A break with that church then occurred, and Kuyper became the leader of the *Gereformeerde* (Re-reformed) Churches. The theology of Kuyper's churches was that the promises of God were no longer made to the Jews, since they had rejected the Messiah. The Church, not the Jews, was now the recipient of the promises of God. The theology of Father ten Boom's church, on the other hand, emphasized the importance of the Jewish people and the restoration of the Jewish nation.

In 1901, when Corrie was nine years old, Abraham Kuyper became prime minister of the Netherlands. Although they remained in the Dutch Reformed Church, the Ten Booms were certainly influenced by him. "Father voted for him," noted Corrie decades later.

Kuyper began Christian schools throughout the nation. Corrie and her sister Nollie attended Haarlem's Christian school, of which their father was one of the founders.

Come as a Little Child

Corrie often told the story of the most important decision of her life, made in 1897. She has recorded this in books, films, videotapes and letters. These are her own words:

When I was five years old, I learned to read: I loved stories, particularly those about Jesus. He was a member of the Ten Boom family—it was just as easy to talk to Him as it was to carry on a conversation with my mother and father, my aunts or my brother and sisters. He was there.

One day my mother was watching me play house. In my little girl world of fantasy, she saw that I was pretending to call on a neighbor. I knocked on the make-believe door and waited . . . no one answered. "Corrie," said my mother, "I know Someone who is standing at your door and knocking right now."

Was she playing a game with me? I know now that there was a preparation within my childish heart for that moment; the Holy Spirit makes us ready for acceptance of Jesus Christ, of turning our life over to Him.

"Jesus said that He is standing at the door, and if you invite Him in He will come into your heart," my mother continued. "Would you like to invite Jesus in?" At that moment my mother was the most beautiful person in the whole world to me. "Yes, Mama, I want Jesus in my heart."

So she took my little hand in hers and we prayed together. It was so simple, and yet Jesus Christ says that we must all come as children, no matter what our age, social standing or intellectual background. When Mother told me later about this experience, I recalled it clearly.[4]

Early Signs of Corrie's Gifts

Mother's diary entries in the last years of the nineteenth century describe Betsie, Nollie and Willem as beautiful children who developed quickly. Corrie is depicted as a very sweet but ugly child, except for her large and beautiful blue eyes. Compared to her brother and sisters she was slow developing.

A few months before Corrie's tenth birthday in 1902, Mother ten Boom's diary gives us the first glimpse of a gift her daughter would later develop to such an extent that she would become one of the most influential women communicators God has given to the Church in our time. Her mother wrote, "Our 'baby,' Corrie, is the family's darling, particularly because of her lovely way of putting things into words. She is a surprise to everyone because of the way she talks, and she is so cute sometimes that it astonishes us."

Corrie was part of a family who loved life and lived it with passion, and this was evident in each of them—but especially in Corrie. Their hope and prayers for their queen and her baby serve as evidence of that.

The Ten Booms, like most other Christians, were strongly patriotic, but not at all nationalistic. They loved their queen and country. They offered many prayers for Wilhelmina, Queen of the Netherlands, because after years of her marriage to German Prince Hendrik the couple remained childless. Royal families still played a central role in international politics, and the people knew the lack of an heir to the throne of the Netherlands could have big political consequences, especially if the crown came to rest on the head of some distantly related German. In 1902, Queen Wilhelmina became critically ill with typhus, and some feared that before too long Holland might become part of Germany.

But at last, in 1908, the queen was expecting. The prayers of the Ten Booms and their friends became even more urgent. Betsie, away from home for recuperation from an illness, wrote on April 17 to the Beje, "Everyone is waiting for the prince here, too!" The Netherlands had already had two long-reigning queens, so the hope of a prince was strong.

Betsie, Nollie, Corrie, 1905   PHOTO COURTESY OF THE CORRIE TEN BOOM HOUSE FOUNDATION

Tante Jans, writing from the Beje on April 28, said, "At 10 a.m. this morning we received the news from The Hague that things had 'begun.' Toward sunset the great event is expected."

Willem wrote to the Beje the same evening: "Dear Father, Mother, Sisters, Aunts . . . it gradually looks as if my joyful expectation, together with that of the whole nation, will be fulfilled."

At 7:30 a.m. on Friday, April 30, seventeen-year-old Corrie learned the news of the safe arrival of Princess Juliana through a telephone call. She wrote to Betsie:

I shall never forget how I felt when I heard it was a princess. I shouted, 'A Princess!!!' I quite forgot to be quiet and walk softly, which is always best before 8:00 a.m. I even wanted Tante Jans to get out of bed, but she had not slept yet, although she did not sleep much afterward because nobody kept quiet.

In just a few minutes, flags were flying everywhere, except on the church tower, because of which Tante Anna did not dare to believe it. We all went and stood in front of the mayor's house, where we sang the "Wilhelmus" [the Dutch national anthem] as loudly as we could.

Corrie's response shows her never-ending enthusiasm for life, so evident in her obvious joy at the arrival of a baby girl, even though they had hoped for a prince. It is an example of her rather mischievous sense of humor, revealed by the teasing reference to her rather daunting Tante Jans.

Her wonderful sense of humor, as well as her merciful heart, is evident in other letters. Earlier in that month of April, for example, in a letter to Betsie, Corrie makes reference to the family cat. But first she teases Betsie, whose household duties she has temporarily taken over:

Dearest Betsie,

I have washed fifteen pairs . . . let me say it again . . . *fifteen* pairs of gloves today. I had to gather every bit of my small amount of perseverance, and I did it this evening. As a result it feels as if my hands are glowing. Not all of them are thoroughly clean (the gloves that is) but they are washed. You enjoy that thought, don't you?

Poor Blackie is meowing. There is talk of getting rid of him because of some little accidents, and Mother does not want all the work that causes. In one word, I would find it *terrible.* I think that I am much too attached to him because I just don't want to think about his actually being sent away.

Monday morning: The question about Blackie has been solved! We have decided to keep him. Oh good!

It is encouraging to see how normal Corrie ten Boom was. She wanted to keep the cat, yet even at seventeen years old she was aware that she might be holding onto a personal desire too tightly. In later years she often said, "I must learn to hold earthly things lightly because if I do not the Lord might have to pry away my fingers, and that hurts."

Corrie with two cats, 1909   PHOTO COURTESY OF THE CORRIE TEN BOOM HOUSE FOUNDATION

"A New World Opened Up to Us"

Willem was the first child to leave home. In 1906 he went to study theology at the University of Leiden. Nollie took teachers' training and gained her diploma in 1909. Corrie studied at domestic science school, and she and Betsie were involved, with the aunts, in the household. The women of the Beje, like many Dutch, were scrupulous housekeepers.

In the old family letters to which I have access, there are no references to any other European countries during the time of the many comfortable and enriching advances mainly available to the European upper class of *La Belle Époque*. But in the rest of Europe "The Beautiful Time" also contained a strong military element. Nations were arming themselves, military parades were common and there was talk of unrest among Prussian princes.

The four young Ten Booms were often found at missionary conferences, where they would spend days learning from missionaries or overseas Christians. They studied other religions. When Corrie was in her late teens she, Willem, Betsie and Nollie got involved in a missions movement. Many years later, she recalled their first attendance at a missions conference:

> That first day I was so moved when the hundreds of people sang under the perfect guidance of an elderly missionary. Nollie was given the job of being a soloist for the first time in her life. The lectures were beautiful and deep, and in our spare time we talked things over in smaller groups. A new world opened up to us. . . .
>
> We had always been interested in missions, but now our horizons widened as real missionaries told their experiences.

The Ten Boom family members' bond was so strong that Mother once wrote, "We can hardly do without each other." They did not know the term "family values" or even talk about such a concept, but love, loyalty and commitment were clearly a normal reality for them.

The record shows, however, that community was as important to them as family. The Beje always welcomed anyone in Haarlem who was in need of advice, supper, prayer or fellowship with the Ten Booms. The whole family was deeply involved in the community, and as they grew up the children's involvement began to include the people of other countries.

And Afterward Receive Me

Eighteen-year-old Corrie wrote: "Today I had a quiet Sunday, not as pleasant as at home, but still Sunday. I went to church this morning and heard a fine sermon on an Old Testament text—that beautiful one from Psalm 73: 'Thou shalt guide me with thy counsel and afterward receive me to glory (KJV).'" In that letter she again refers to the good sermon and says that the singing was so beautiful that shivers ran down her spine.

Afterward You will receive me to glory. Even Corrie ten Boom, who had the most vivid imagination of anybody I have ever met, could not have envisaged her experiences in the 73 years that lay between that summer of 1910 and *Afterward.*

Although her country was able to remain neutral, it would not be long before World War I began. By the time it ended, 13 million lives would have been lost on both sides of the conflict. And that war would pave the way only 22 years later to another World War—for Corrie, "the deepest hell that man can create."

three

World War I

1912–1921

*T*he Belle Époque, "The Beautiful Time," as the elite called it, was drawing to its close. From our vantage point in history, the sinking of the *Titanic* was the beginning of the end of the peace and prosperity that Europe had known for many decades.

Tuesday, April 15, 1912—Corrie's twentieth birthday—was also the date of the loss of the world's biggest ship, heralded as unsinkable, on its maiden voyage from England to America. The *Titanic* was fitted with the latest furnishings and contained electric elevators, several kitchens, libraries and even mechanical exercise machines shaped like camels and horses in the vast ship's gymnasium. Reports from survivors tell of passengers continuing to receive training on the mechanical animals even as the ship went down.

"When news of the disaster reached the Ten Boom household," described Corrie more than sixty years later, "Father went into the living room with Mother and called everybody who was at home to come together. We all had heard about the big ship—it was so safe, so luxurious. He was shocked by the news and could not take it in at first. I remember how he talked about it with us—and even with the customers.

"'Just imagine,' Father said, 'The passengers on the *Titanic* were not thinking much about danger. Those who belonged to the Lord Jesus were ready. Perhaps God called some at the last minute. The band played "Nearer My God to Thee" until the ship sank.'" Father ten Boom was implying perhaps that the music and words might have led many passengers to trust the Lord Jesus in the last moments of their lives.

The loss of 1,513 lives and the huge *Titanic* was a kind of precursor of the enormous destruction of people and property that Europe was about to face in the twentieth century.

A Time for War

After the establishment of the German empire in 1871, Germany quickly became an industrialized nation whose power challenged that of England, Russia and France. As Germany's wealth and power increased in the decades leading up to 1914, so did its people's glorification and military fortification of their fatherland. In response to this, other European lands began to arm themselves, spurred on by the ever-growing weapons industry. From 1910 onward, armies were mobilized and weapons arsenals were stockpiled in a way that Europe had never seen in peacetime.

Slowly two blocs came into being: Germany and Austria on one side and France and Russia, later joined by England, on the other. As 1914 approached, more than 25 million trained soldiers were at the ready on the European continent. Although there was no clear reason to declare war, it was as if the European powers wanted it. The Ten Boom family must have been deeply concerned about the rumors of war, but I have not found any trace of it in their frequent pre-war writings to each other.

Early in November 1913, nine months before World War I started, Willem moved out of the Beje. His studies had taken him away from home for years already, but this was a permanent move prompting his 21-year-old youngest sister, normally not a sentimental person, to write a letter in which we are given a glimpse of the love and admiration she had for him. Corrie wrote:

The morning you left was wretched. It never occurred to me that we would all find it so difficult. Saying goodbye must have something to do with the "Fall." Perhaps this is very stupid of me because it is obvious, but please don't mind if I sound rather silly in this letter because ever since you left I have been wanting to write you a sentimental letter in which I tell you how much I love you, what a large place you fill in my life and perhaps thank you for I don't know what and that, of course, between a brother and sister would be too silly for words. I would be the first one to point out to somebody else how silly it would be to act in that way.

Therefore, I think it would be better just to write and tell you that all the photographs came out well. Mother knows only about the two taken in the church. She will receive the others at [Christmas]. The large photograph of you is particularly good and full of life, perhaps a bit "great-manlike" but you are a "great man" in my eyes. I think my feelings are going in the wrong direction again and I had better close. Bye, Willem. Your Corrie.

Matters of health always featured strongly in the family's letters to each other, and this is evident in another letter from Corrie to Willem later that November, written while Father ten Boom was away for a few days:

It was so nice that your letter came this particular day. I read it to Mother while she was still in bed. She could not sleep after Father left, but this afternoon she slept for a whole hour. Later in the afternoon I took her to Dr. van Veen, and his nurse took Mother's blood pressure. It was much too high. It should have been 140, but hers was 210. The doctor took it very seriously and told her that if Mother did not do anything about it, she would have increasing problems with it, especially in about ten years' time.

Mother ten Boom was to die of a stroke eight years later.

Meanwhile, outside Holland's borders, the arms buildup continued. On June 28, 1914, the Austrian heir to the throne, Franz Ferdinand, was murdered in the Serbian capital of Sarajevo with his wife, Sophia. Germany rushed to the aid of Austria, which probably would have been capable of handling its own crisis, and World War I began in the first week of August.

Holland tried hard to stay neutral and succeeded. It was a small, militarily weak country living off the wealth of its large and rich colony of Indonesia. The Dutch could not possibly have defended the sea routes between Holland and Indonesia, and they certainly could not have defeated any state that might try to attack Indonesia. Germany was reluctant to occupy Holland because England would then have the excuse to take over the rich Dutch colony.

In a letter to Willem two months after the outbreak of war, Corrie refers to a military funeral:

Last week there was a funeral procession for the English officer who died here. The music played by the marine band was very beautiful and sadly impressive. Then the main band stopped playing and only a recorder sustained the tune, accompanied by some drummers on covered drums. That recorder was so beautiful and spooky. It was as if the sound came from another world, as in a fairy tale. Behind the carriage, on which lay the coffin covered with the English flag, was a large procession of soldiers and sailors, all walking very slowly. It was so strange to see these soldiers filing by step—step—step. The procession took half an hour to pass by. Perhaps it was because of all the artificial saddening things, or perhaps also because we knew that this was one of the thousand thousands, but we all felt unhappy inside.

This is the first reference to war. She was presumably referring to the many deaths taking place in the countries just outside Holland's borders. After initial advances, the war amounted to slow battling in the trenches, with resulting high loss of life on both sides.

Holland was an island of peace in the hell that most of Europe had become. In the first years of the war, industry, farming and shipping even made big profits. The British government oversaw the supply of food and other goods to Holland, with the proviso that these were not to be smuggled through to Germany for sale on the black market. But that happened to some extent. Between 1914 and 1917 the national income rose by almost fifty percent.

Less favorable conditions were to affect Holland soon, however, and the watch and clock business at the Beje would feel those effects. Writing to one of the girls' clubs that she and Corrie ran, Betsie gives us a picture of the family's circumstances in January 1916:

Dear children,

Please excuse me if my writing becomes incoherent. Nollie and Corrie are singing and playing the organ in the background, and I am finding it hard to concentrate. You have all been to our house, so you can probably picture me here in the living room. It is Sunday evening and the lamp is burning. Nollie is playing the organ near the window and all the family is upstairs reading. Everything looks Sunday-like in the house. I don't know why, but things look different from the way they do on weekdays.

As for my work, it is a strange time in business. I have never experienced anything like this in the fifteen years I have worked in the shop. At the moment we have enough clocks, but nobody, not even the cleverest economists, knows what the future will bring. However, if the war continues we will see some strange things. For example, for months not one clock came across the borders. Then a large wholesale Dutch dealer exported wagons full of chocolate. In exchange he received clocks. Watches are still coming through. Corrie needed a coat but could not find one. There were hardly any in a clothes shop where we have always had a lot of choice. In the end she bought a velvet one. You should see her—she looks so *chique*! She is worth a shilling more!

[Here Corrie adds a note:] I don't feel flattered at all. The shop assistant said, "You do need something chique," and Father said, "You really must take an elegant coat; you do need that."

A Time for Love

The Ten Boom family wholeheartedly supported Willem's decision to become a minister. As the only son and the sole university-trained member of the family, his career was followed with intense interest. He was ordained in the Dutch Reformed Church in April 1916. For the next month the Ten Booms lived at high-level mutual alert for Willem to be called to the pastorate of a church. They knew that it might come from the small village of Made in the beautiful southern province of Brabant, where a church had shown some interest in Willem. But the family knew that another candidate was also being considered.

When the decision to call Willem finally was made on May 16, the family's joy and cohesiveness was expressed in a letter written the next day from Corrie at the Beje to Betsie:

There is inexpressible happiness and gratitude in our hearts. Yesterday was a strange day. None of us wanted the other family members to know what we were thinking, but when the 1:15 p.m. post was expected we caught ourselves acting unusually. Nollie was sewing near the window from which she would be able to see the approach of the postman. Mother said goodbye to everybody on her way to her bed for an afternoon nap. Then I decided to shake out the mats in the passageway near the front door and found Mother sitting on the staircase. Both [of us] would have been near the letterbox through which the mailman might drop the good news. But the news did not come at 1:15 p.m. or at 4:00 p.m. . . .

When a telegram from Willem finally arrived, Corrie wrote, "Mother was jubilant! Tante Anna clapped her hands, and I threw my hat, coat and gloves in the air."

Now that Willem's call had come, plans could be made for his wedding. He was engaged to Christina (Tine, pronounced "Tina") van Veen, younger sister of the family doctor. The length of their engagement is unknown, but Dutch couples often had long engagements, probably due to the scarcity of suitable housing and work. Willem's wedding took place in the St. Bavo church on the market square near the Beje on August 23, 1916, when he was 29 and Tine was 32.

In a photograph of Tine and Willem seated in the Great Church at the end of the wedding ceremony, they are sur-rounded by about forty family members and friends—mainly unsmiling in the custom of the day. Corrie is in the top row of the photograph, standing near a handsome young man called Karel (not his real name). Karel and Willem became friends when they were theological students together. Corrie had first met him when she was fourteen and Karel had accompanied Willem to one of the Beje's many celebrations—perhaps a birthday party.

Corrie recalled later that from the moment she looked up into Karel's deep brown eyes, she fell irretrievably in love. Two years later, in 1908, while visiting Willem in his room at the University of Leiden, she met him again. He remembered her, and Corrie's hopes rose that a lasting friendship would develop that would lead to marriage. Now and then, through the years, Corrie and Karel came across each other at various family events.

In *The Hiding Place*, Corrie allowed her co-writers John and Elizabeth Sherrill to tell the story of Karel. They deal sensitively and respectfully with a subject to which Tante Corrie made no reference during the time I was with her, except once near the end of her life.

Another Route for Love to Travel

Shortly after Willem and Tine's wedding, Corrie and her family and many friends went to the village of Made to hear Willem's first sermon as pastor. A first sermon was always a momentous occasion in the Dutch Reformed Church. Corrie had looked forward to the occasion with extra excitement because she knew Karel would be there.

Indeed he was, and during the days they spent in Made, he showed much interest in Corrie. They took many walks together and even talked about the future. Although the word "marriage" was not mentioned, Corrie was led to believe that Karel had a serious intent toward her—until Willem explained that his parents, who had sacrificed much for his theological education, were determined that Karel should marry into a wealthy family. Corrie protested that his parents' wishes did not necessarily represent what Karel wanted. Her brother's response must have dealt the biggest blow Corrie had yet received in her 24 years. She describes it in *The Hiding Place:*

Willem fixed his sober, deep-set eyes on mine. "He will do it, Corrie. I don't say he wants it. To him it is just a fact of life like any other. When we would talk about girls we liked—at the university—he would always say at the end, 'Of course I could never marry her. It would kill my mother.'"[1]

Willem's prediction soon proved true. Karel announced his engagement to the daughter of wealthy members of the church where he was assistant pastor. It was Father ten Boom who comforted a grieving Corrie that fall of 1916.

"Corrie," he told her when they were alone, "do you know what hurts so very much? It's love. Love is the strongest force in the world, and when it is blocked that means pain. There are two things we can do when this happens. We can kill the love so that it stops hurting. But then, of course, part of us dies, too. Or, Corrie, we can ask God to open up another route for that love to travel."[2]

That hour Corrie gave up her feelings for Karel: "Lord, I give to You the way I feel about Karel, my thoughts about our future—oh, You know! Everything! Give me your way of seeing Karel instead. Help me to love him that way. That much."[3]

Although without doubt Corrie had the same deep emotional longings of most women, it was not long before she realized that there never would be another Karel and that her life would be spent as a single woman.

Perhaps the contents have nothing to do with Karel or her future, but in an undated letter to her mother written at approximately the time of her prayer of relinquishment of marriage, the normally effervescent and humorous Corrie displays a vulnerable side. She had just attended a mission conference:

> I must tell you about a wonderfully treasured moment at the conference. We women were lying in bed in the dormitory. We shared difficulties and comforted each other. And then all became quiet . . . even in the noisy rooms around us. We were dozing, and all of a sudden we heard very softly from far away, yet quite distinctly, the "Ave Maria" being played on a flute, and oh, you don't know what a lonely sound that is, a flute in an open field. It gripped me so much that I sat on the windowsill crying softly.

She never spoke to me about Karel except with joy in 1978 when, during the reading of a newly published Dutch book about the Second World War, she told me that Karel had been among the Dutch Reformed ministers who had not gone along with the edicts of the Nazis. "I have often wondered about that," she told me. When, in her eighties, Corrie learned of Karel's death in the Netherlands, she wrote a note of sympathy to his widow. This was the last I know of Tante Corrie's thoughts about the man she once had loved.

Life During the War

In 1917, the third year of the war, rations were cut and the Dutch, especially the laborers, suffered hunger and cold from then until the end of the war. In June of that year Mother wrote to Willem and Tine in Made that she had been able to buy a basketful of purslane (an edible weed) for a couple of guilders and that Corrie made eight bottles of preserves from it. She asked Tine if she had any potatoes. At the Beje they were able to purchase a few kilos quite frequently.

Corrie's zest for living is indicated in a letter dated May 1917 from Betsie to the family, although we do not know what caused Betsie's merriment: "My handkerchief was wet through with tears of laughter when I read Corrie's postcard. I could not even read it aloud to Tante Jans."

At about the same time, in another letter, Corrie expressed her love for travel: "I will be going to Leiden tomorrow on an errand for Tante Jans. Lovely! Whenever there is an opportunity to celebrate or to travel, I am happy!"

On July 8, 1917, while Betsie was in Made awaiting with Willem and Tine the birth of their first child, Corrie wrote to tell her, "This week I gave a private demonstration of the cooking bag and the newspaper case for a family. We made the cooking case from a suitcase and it held three large pans. It was a success."

Sixty years later, when I was living with her in Placentia, California, Tante Corrie explained this strange activity to me. She volunteered to cook supper for guests one evening and told me she wanted to use a cooking method she had learned during World War I. It involved partially cooking the food, wrapping each item very thoroughly in newspaper and then placing the items in a cooking case all packed together with the lid closed. The idea was that the food in its tightly enclosed wrappings would continue to cook slowly. Less fuel was used, of course—a good and economical wartime method! That night a truly excited Tante Corrie presented her meal which, after having sat in newspaper wrapping for several hours, could not be described as tasty. Although he thanked her profusely, one of the guests said to me privately, "That was terrible."

We can tell from that same letter to Betsie in early July 1917 that Corrie was not particularly fond of housework. She addresses it while referring to her course at Bible school in Haarlem:

> Earlier this week I had some exams. As you know, I had excellent opportunity to get ready. The day before the exam I got up at 5:00 a.m. There were two boxes of trash that I dragged from the cellar to the street with great difficulty. Then I made Nollie's sandwich for her lunch and cleaned the living room. When the trash man came he did not want to take the rubbish with him. I pulled it into the house again and had to sweep the passage, the staircase and the street. By 8:00 p.m. I had not studied one letter.

Corrie goes on to tell Betsie that she thought the exam went well and wrote, "I am glad about that, for there is nothing more discouraging than bad papers and looking after the housekeeping with no help."

Although the terrible war continued to cost the lives of hundreds of thousands of Europeans outside the Dutch island of neutral safety, life went on for the Ten Booms. Named after his grandfather, Tine and Willem's expected baby, "Little Cas," arrived on July 13, 1917. The next week, on July 22, Father Casper wrote to Willem, Tine and Betsie, telling of his longing to come to them and explaining why at the moment it was not possible.

I am fairly well and do have some income, but I have such an excessive amount to pay in bills that I am in straightened circumstances. Bills seem to be coming from all sides. Yet I have nothing to complain about and no doubt I will be helped through. . . .

We greatly long to see that child, our little grandchild, and hold him in our arms. But it seems the time for this has not yet come, otherwise the Lord would have given me some more money. . . . May the Lord bless you and the little one and may He enable us to send something, though it is not possible yet.

He must have received a quick answer to prayer because four days later Mother Cor sent twenty guilders to Betsie: "Ten guilders are for you so that you can give a guilder to the nurse and pay your travel costs with the rest. The other ten guilders are for the cradle and other expenses for little Cas."

From correspondence in early August we learn that the Dutch government had to restrict the use of gas. Betsie and Corrie were away from home at a conference, and a letter from their mother offered the mysterious advice: "Corrie, you must not stay away too long for, oh child, I fear it will all be too much for you. Don't use too much *zieleleven* (soul-life, spiritual life) for that is as bad as using too much gas. Betsie, please look after her. Keep each other calm."

A P.S. from Tante Anna indicates that the Beje household missed Corrie's power of organization: "Corrie, cubic meters of gas are being burned! I tremble to see your face when you come home! I keep reminding Father to watch his meter usage continually. You must come home soon again in order to keep us close to being economical."

Two days later Mother wrote about the arrival of electricity at the Beje, paid for by Tante Jans: "We do like the electric light, but oh dear, Mr. Koen said that gas light was really cheaper, and now Tante Jans is very crestfallen."

In mid-August Nollie, a trained schoolteacher, left the Beje to take a teaching position in Amsterdam. Sufficient housing has been a problem in Holland to this day, so there was no question of her finding even so much as an apartment. She was able to rent rooms in a large house. She and the family were impressed with this very independent move.

In November 1917, Corrie wrote to Betsie, again referring to the fuel situation:

> Now that we have to use fuel so economically we often eat upstairs, which makes the living room a terrible mess. The table becomes a dresser and the side window a steam funnel to take away the smells of cooking meat and cabbage.
>
> This week I wanted to put everything aside in order to prepare for the big examination in dogmatics, which awaits me tomorrow. It is filling my thoughts day and night. In every free moment I am trying to learn a sentence, and my dreams are filled with talks on original sin, the unity of the human race, evolution theory and Pelagianism.

Corrie's Bible Education

During this time Corrie was growing strongly in her knowledge of her faith. In 1910, when she first took courses at the Bible school, Corrie had written to Willem: "There are so many problems assailing me at this time that I cannot handle them. The interpretation of the liberal pastors sometimes gets me very confused. If I did not have Father, I would never manage."

Several years later, during the war, she sent another letter to Willem that is evidence of her level of spiritual growth:

> I feel there are plenty of dangers around us. They cause us to look for reality, for a living faith, some solid point in this ocean of influences. We keep hearing about Christian moral consciousness, denial of man's corrupt nature and glorifying

of man's intellect. In this atmosphere, many ministers are losing ground.

Maybe I am exaggerating a little, but I feel a little out of balance myself. I do not belong in our Reformed Church, nor in the Christian Reformed Church. . . . Also, the other smaller fundamentalist circles do not satisfy me. I have studied too much church history for that. But then, where do I belong?

In a letter to Nollie in December 1917, Corrie describes the beauty of her previous day's outing at yet another conference while expressing her early love for theology and teaching:

What Christmas-like scenes we saw! At 4:00 p.m. the moon was already shining brightly, and its reflection on the white snow made it as clear as midday. We went to the Wilhelmina dune, and the view from there over the snowy dunes and the white roofs in the clear moonlight and the lights of Haarlem . . . it was so unreal and so like a fairy story that I would not have been surprised if I had met dwarves or nymphs.

Pastor Creutzberg gave a beautiful sermon. It was so stalwart and Calvinistic, and he had such beautiful diction! The whole church, full to overflowing, hung on his every word. He set our thoughts in motion in such a way that when I went to bed I quickly wrote part of my sermon. The consequence of this was that I got to sleep very late and preached the rest of the night. Don't be afraid that I shall ever deliver that sermon, at least not in the near future. But it is a very good exercise to write down one's thoughts. You then become aware that your subconscious is a store of thoughts, and that while you are writing, the sentences and ideas come all on their own.

On January 20, 1918, Betsie wrote a letter to Corrie, who was shortly to receive her Bible school diploma. Apart from discussing household affairs, ration coupons and the availability of bread, Betsie tells about a visit from Nollie, who had now been living in her own rooms in Amsterdam for about six months:

Tonight again we had a long discussion about feminism, especially Father and Nollie. That funny child has only just started thinking of these matters now that she has left home. Funny, isn't it? She is greatly enjoying Father's counsel and conversations. I am also in the middle of feminism affairs because I am reading Naber's book about our aunts and great-aunts. It deals especially with the forerunners of feminism.

Child, how easy things are for us. Without realizing it, we are reaping the fruits of their troubles. Fifty years ago you would not have dared to think of studying, as you are doing now. Girls had to wash the dishes and embroider and marry. And it never entered their minds to live like Nollie, having rooms of her own and earning her living. You really should read the book.

The Ten Boom sisters could never have foreseen the work that Corrie would later undertake as a single woman, especially that of speaking. In her early twenties, she enjoyed singing at gospel meetings but was not yet convinced that it was proper for a woman to preach. This was an important issue in the Church at the time, and she wrote Willem about her feelings on the matter:

Pastor B. sent me a request to preach on December 12. I discussed it with Father and, following his advice, I declined the invitation.

In the evangelism course I took we did not agree on the question of whether the women of our present day may preach or not. Father says it will cause me to lose my femininity; I am 75 percent in agreement with him but would like to have your opinion on this.

This urge to evangelize—to tell people the glorious message of the Gospel—gives me a deep longing to speak out loud, as loudly as I can. But as far as that is concerned, I am afraid there is some vanity connected with it.

There is no record of Willem's response, but Corrie obviously eventually changed her mind about the propriety of a woman teaching the Gospel! See appendix 2 for her views on the subject in 1960.

The End of the Great War

In 1917 the United States came to the aid of the French and the British. The Germans had lost ground and on November 10, 1918, the German kaiser fled to the Dutch border for refuge from the revolution in his own country. The official end of the First World War took place at 11:00 a.m. on November 11, 1918. The Allies had lost five million men in the previous four years and three months, and on the German-Austrian side three million had died.

On November 11, President Woodrow Wilson announced to the American people: "The armistice was signed this morning. Everything for which America fought has been accomplished. It will now be our fortunate duty to assist by example, by sober, friendly counsel and by material aid in the establishment of just democracy throughout the world." On that same day, however, a news release told of the German foreign secretary's "earnest" appeal to President Wilson "to mitigate the fearful conditions" of the Versailles agreement, which "the German government had to accept."

Mother Cor's Strokes and Death

At the end of 1918, Mother Cor, who a few years earlier had experienced a mild stroke, suffered a major one. Corrie, busy with housework in another part of the Beje, decided to check on her mother. Running into the kitchen, she found Cor at the sink with the water running out of the basin and onto the floor. Her mother was "staring strangely," Corrie said later, and could say just one word: "Corrie." Assisting her mother to bed, Corrie called for the other members of the household and dispatched the shop apprentice to fetch Dr. van Veen. At first it seemed that Mother would not live, but after two months of serious illness and semi-consciousness, she opened her eyes and looked around her. Though she suffered initial paralysis, she regained the use of her arms and legs and was even able to be present at Nollie's wedding on July 23, 1919. But she never spoke again. Communication was possible through a little game, something like Twenty Questions:

"What is it, Mama? You're thinking of someone!"

"Yes."

"Someone in the family?"

"No."

"A woman?"

"Yes."

Mother passed away in 1921. Nearly six decades later, Tante Corrie and I were standing at the sink in her bathroom. The previous year she had suffered a stroke that had taken her powers of speech, but she had made a fairly good recovery from initial paralysis. On this morning of her second and major stroke, I was assisting her in getting ready for the day. As I helped her find the sleeves of the jacket to her dress, Tante Corrie looked at me strangely and began to lean to the right. I took hold of her and led her to her bed. She lost all the strength regained on her right side and was in a partially conscious state. It seemed she could not live. But one day after several weeks of serious illness, as suddenly as she had lost consciousness, she woke up and looked around. Although she regained strength and lived for four more years, her speech never returned. We worked out a system of communication very similar to the one she had used with her mother decades before.

"Tante Corrie, are you thinking about a person?" (The Ten Booms were usually thinking of people other than themselves.)

"Yes."

"A man?"

"No."

"Does she live in the United States?"

We were to play the Twenty Questions guessing game for nearly five years.

four ❧

The Years between the World Wars

1921–1939

In her later years Corrie was fond of saying, "Every experience God gives us, every person He puts in our lives is the perfect preparation for the future that only He can see." During the two world wars God brought many experiences and many people into the lives of the Ten Booms. Between the wars Corrie and Betsie worked with young women and became foster parents of many children. And the letters during this time help us to know Betsie better.

Father Casper

"This is the saddest day of my life," said Father when his wife passed away in October 1921. "Thank you, Lord, for giving her to me."

For me, these words sum up the attitude and living faith of the Ten Boom family. In the deepest grief he had yet known, Casper simply stated that fact, and then turned to the Lord with a thankful heart that his deeply loved Cor had been given to him for 37 years. Years later, telling about that day and the months that followed, Corrie said that her father displayed no self-pity. He knew where his wife was, and he knew that life and the Lord's work had to go on.

In Corrie's writing and speaking of Casper, we see a resolute, not-in-a-hurry kind of Christian leader. His matter-of-fact Dutchness was part of that, but this watchmaker's stability was based on an active and daily living faith that "all our times are in God's hands, even the difficult ones." Theologians call this the sovereignty of God, which, simply said, means that He who is all-loving and always good determines the paths His children take, allowing pain and suffering to come to them for an eventually good purpose. Casper ten Boom lived his life from that perspective. So did his daughter Corrie. It was the basis for all her witness and work and is the main life lesson of this book.

Tante Corrie's Greatest Lesson

I am often asked to tell the greatest lesson I learned during my seven years with Tante Corrie. The answer is "a high view of the sovereignty of God." But I do not usually say those words because through overuse they have lost their real meaning for some, and for new Christians in our generation they can sound a bit pompous and not very practical. But the truth is that I can describe just about any lesson I learned from her and it will come back every time to: "All my times are in His hands."

From Corrie I learned, for example, how to deal with my tendency toward self-pity. During the months we traveled together my tasks as her companion included things like travel arrangements, stage arrangements, diet needs and crowd control—all in fast-moving repetition as we journeyed from city to city. I was busier than I had ever been, and my tendency to feel sorry for myself was encouraged by the way I was treated sometimes by those who invited Corrie to speak. One such difficult occasion took place in a flat, northern city in the United States when her host, a minister, seeing that I was Corrie's servant, began to treat me in a cold and distant manner—as though I were his servant, too. I found this most unfair. I had enough to do already. Why was this unpleasant man making life more complicated?

Tante Corrie was aware that I was feeling off-balance about this, but she did not really understand the effect the minister's behavior was having on me. This does not mean that she was uncaring. She was just resolutely doing her job as speaker and counselor. In her mid-eighties she could have been forgiven if she had complained about fatigue and inconvenience, but I never saw in her any hint of self-pity in all the time we were together.

On this and another occasion, she took me to task quite firmly about self-pity, calling it a particularly destructive sin. She helped me see that even the most difficult things in our lives cannot occur unless the Lord allows them. "It is not so much what happens, but how we take it that is important," she taught me. "All our times are in God's hands, even the difficult ones." I can see now that while the minister's treatment of me was wrong, so was my reaction. A "poor-me" attitude blinds us to God's larger purposes. After her imprisonment Corrie prayed that God would help her see her sufferings "a little bit" from His point of view. He answered that prayer. He showed her that her sufferings could be used in a far-reaching, redemptive way in the lives of others.

Children Join the Household

As soon as the war ended, the Ten Booms looked for ways to help German children. Many of them were suffering from severe malnutrition as a result of their country's defeat. Always happy when making plans, the sisters discussed the possibility of bringing some of the children to Holland, providing them with good food and loving care and sending them back to their country healthy. Father had many contacts among the watchmakers of Holland, and he wrote letters to them asking if they could provide temporary homes for German children. Many responded, and arrangements were made for the children to arrive by train on a certain day to be met by their prospective host families. Father, Betsie and Corrie went to Haarlem's railway station to see that each child went with the proper family.

One shy, thin girl of about ten had not been assigned to a family. "We'll take her home with us," said Father. And the host family of eight-year-old Willy, who lived on the streets of Berlin, was not at the station to meet him. Father discovered that because of illness at their house, the family was unable to take Willy. He, too, was taken home to the Beje. These were the first of many children who went to live there during the post–World War I years.

A Change at the Beje

In the early 1920s, after the German children returned home, a change occurred in the division of labor in the Beje. Of the three aunts, only Tante Anna was still living. All the years the children were growing up and during the final illnesses of her sisters, she had worked hard at housekeeping. Now her own health was failing.

Betsie had long been her father's helper in the watch shop, although she and Corrie did change tasks now and then. Corrie's main job had always been in the household assisting Tante Anna. Although as a younger woman she had not shown a particular liking for housekeeping, Corrie grew to find the work "challenging and creative."

When Betsie became ill during a flu epidemic, Corrie had to take her place in the watch shop, where she had previously spent little time. "I felt as if I had two left hands," she said, recalling those early days. "It was a different world—meeting people, remembering their particular likes and dislikes, seeing in facts and figures the precarious balance of the family business."

After Betsie recovered, Corrie made a suggestion: "Why don't we exchange jobs for a few months, so I can learn more about shopkeeping? I am so terribly ignorant of what goes on in the business." Her sister agreed. As the months passed, both sisters were happy with the arrangement. Betsie had a particular flair for beauty and order, and this was reflected in rearranged cupboards, flowers on the table and new variety at mealtimes. The new working arrangement became permanent.

Holland's First Woman Watchmaker

Corrie settled into her new work with characteristic enthusiasm. She saw ways to improve the business, such as asking Father why he closed the windows of the watch shop in the evenings when far more people walked through the Barteljorisstraat at that time than during the day. Realizing that the stock of watches and clocks was insufficient, she purchased more and soon had a larger inventory than the watch shop had ever known. That side of the business was soon left in her hands.

After a while, Corrie realized how useful it would be if she were able to help not only by running the shop but also in actual watch repairing. She asked her father if he would teach her the trade. Immediately Father agreed, telling her that he would like to send her to Switzerland for training and that she could well become a better watchmaker than he was.

"He had a great trust in my abilities," she said. Corrie inherited this trait from him—trust in the abilities of others. She was able to make a person feel he were the only person in the world who could fulfill a particular task.

Through the sale of an expensive watch, Father was able to send Corrie to Switzerland to learn watchmaking by serving apprenticeships in two factories. She gained her certificate in 1924 at the age of 32 and became, as she liked to tell, "Holland's first licensed woman watchmaker."

The Foster Children

After Tante Anna's death in 1925, only Father, Betsie and Corrie were left in the Beje. The same year, a new way of life came to the old house with the arrival of foster children. Many Dutch missionaries worked in Holland's large colony of Indonesia, and their children completed elementary and some high school grades in that country. But when the time came for further education they were sent to the Netherlands. Many of the children did not have relatives or friends with whom they could stay. Having visited the large institution-like housing where many of them stayed, Corrie and Betsie felt sorry for the children who were paying such a high price of separation and loneliness. When Willem, therefore, came to the Beje one day with a special request, they quickly responded, and after saying, "Let's pray about it first," Father did, too.

Willem, a member of the boards of several mission societies for Indonesia, had just heard about three missionary children who urgently needed somewhere to stay in Holland. Before long, Betsie (40), Corrie (33) and Father (65) became the foster parents of two girls and a boy: Puck (14), Hans (12) and their brother Hardy (15).

Betsie and Corrie shared their new responsibilities. Betsie took care of food and clothing, and Corrie, who reckoned her tasks were more fun, was responsible for sports and music.

The Generosity of the Ten Booms

There was never much money at the Beje. Most Dutch families had to economize as much as possible. Many were out of work in the years between the wars, and there was much poverty. This meant there were fewer clients in the watch shop. Most people did not have the means to buy items such as clocks and watches.

In spite of this, the Ten Booms' generosity to needy children increased. More children joined the household, including two girls named Lessie and Miep. At one point the Beje was home for seven children. "I never had so much fun as in those years when the foster children were with us in the Beje," said Corrie, recalling memories later in life. But it must be noted that Corrie frequently used that expression. She lived firmly in the present with an eye to the future. I heard her say "I have never had such fun" countless times, and I am sure she was right in each case!

More than fifty years after she came to live at the Beje, Hans, one of the first foster girls, described life there in a letter:

> Life with the Ten Booms was simple but a lot of fun. They understood the art of enjoying every small thing. I remember especially that Tante Corrie and Tante Betsie both enjoyed life intensely because they believed that everything that was given to them was a gift from God. But they did not over-spiritualize.
>
> Tante Corrie was a very gifted person. She would say about her gifts: "Those are things a person cannot make for herself. You must, therefore, thank God for the gifts you have been given."

Hans went on to tell about Father's attitude in a house that was always busy not just with the foster children but with the friends whom they often brought home:

> Opa (Grandfather), as we young ones called him, was never bothered by all the noise going on around him. He just kept working quietly. He always saw good in us. "They are wonderful children," he used to say. "They never quarrel."
>
> In those years at the Beje I grew from a girl to a young woman. I thank God even now that he gave me these substitute parents while my own father and mother were missionaries in

Indonesia. It was a privilege to spend those important years with the Ten Boom family.

Of course it was actually not always the case that the children never quarreled. As in all normal households they needed discipline now and then, and Corrie applied it. Father, however, was never aware of disharmony.

It might seem that Corrie was busy enough in the watch shop business and in caring for the foster children. But she also gave Bible lessons in schools and held classes and a special church service on Sunday afternoons for mentally disabled children, for whom she had particular respect and love.

The Clubs

And there was to be much more work. In keeping with her family's enthusiasm for learning of the needs of others, she found herself one day at a meeting of the Association of Women Friends of the Young Girl. She heard a speaker talk passionately about the help and guidance needed by girls aged thirteen to eighteen. Sunday school classes ended when a child reached the age of twelve or thirteen, and the YWCA (Young Women's Christian Association) provided group meetings only for girls of eighteen and above.

Betsie and Corrie talked about the need for structured Christian activities for the young girls who in their early teens would be faced with decisions that would affect their whole lives. They began making plans.

Betsie, who had taught Sunday school at the St. Bavo, the Great Church, for many years, obtained lists of her former pupils. Invitations to be part of a new club were issued, and teenage girls responded. The name of the first club was the Church Walk Club. Corrie and Betsie met the girls on one of Haarlem's bridges each Sunday at 8:30 a.m. They took a long walk together to the dunes, where they played games and talked before walking back to the 10:00 a.m. service at church. The club grew in number and soon began to meet on Wednesdays, too, for an evening of games and a short Bible story with a practical application.

From this small beginning many other clubs were formed. It was soon necessary for Betsie and Corrie to find and train more leaders. Both were strong motivators—"even Betsie in her quiet way," said Corrie—and it was not long before an enthusiastic group of able young women began to get together every week to discuss activities for the next club meetings. They learned games from each other to play with the girls, and Corrie taught them how to give a Bible message with a short story so that each leader knew how to do it in her own club. Soon, more and more girls showed the desire to be part of these clubs, officially known as Haarlem's Girls' Clubs. Their purpose was to teach the girls the Gospel and keep them off the streets. During weekly meetings of the club leaders, everybody took a turn telling a story from the Bible while the rest critiqued. The types of questions asked were:

Was the Gospel clear?

How was her first sentence? Did it attract attention?

Was there humor?

What help was offered for the girls this week?

What importance did the story have for eternity?

Did she describe colors, movements?

Did she draw clear pictures with good illustrations?

Was it an inspiration for action, for faith, for endurance?

This training was invaluable not just for the girls but for Corrie herself. In thousands of talks across the world in 64 countries she applied the speaking principles she taught her club leaders in the 1920s and 1930s. When I was with her in the mid-1970s, she still took each speaking appointment very seriously, preparing arduously for each talk. Sometimes we went over her talks together. My respect rose when she, who had given basically the same message countless times, asked me to be sure to tell her if there was anything she had left out.

In the 1920s so many enthusiastic members joined the clubs that the garden and park areas where they had been meeting were no longer suitable. Premises were rented.

There was a club for every activity in which the girls showed interest: music, singing, folk dancing, English, sewing, embroidery, gymnastics, and so on. Eventually Corrie was to start a mixed club, almost unheard of at the time, where boys and girls could get to know each other in a natural setting. Halfway through the evening, the club leader gathered the girls together and read a short piece from the Bible, after which they had long discussions.

Once each year the clubs came together for a performance in Haarlem's concert hall, where nearly every club had the opportunity to demonstrate its abilities. The performance started with all 250 to 300 girls marching onto the platform. They then sang a song, and Corrie gave a five-minute talk to the approximately one thousand people in attendance. One year her subject was "God's Telephone Number Is Never Busy," and another year, "Have You Tuned Your Radio to the Right Station?"

The young men of the mixed Friends' Club provided musical accompaniment for the whole evening. Describing the first performance, Corrie later wrote:

> They were nervous about playing, and I wanted to boost their confidence. I took a violin in my left hand and the bow in my right hand. Then I turned the bow over so that it could not touch the violin's strings and acted as if I were a real musician. I don't know how many people in the concert hall saw my antics. There was no music coming from my violin, but we had lots of fun. And I needed to help the boys only that one time.[1]

Under Corrie's leadership, a Christian Girl Scout movement, the Triangle Girls, grew out of the Haarlem's Girls' Clubs. Many girls became part of the movement, including some with physical handicaps. As the club work grew, Corrie began to hold summer camps for the girls. At first they used tents, then later a building that had room for about sixty girls.

Decades later, Kitty, one of the club girls, wrote about her experiences:

> I came to know Tante Corrie when I was fourteen. I first met her in the Haarlem Girls' Club where I took the catechism class. After that, I was confirmed in the St. Bavo. In those days nearly all the club girls belonged to the working class. Our families had little money. There was a lot of unemployment. But because of the Girls' Clubs I was able to attend several camps and even went on a journey along the Rhine River.
>
> At the camps we had a campfire each evening and we always paid good attention to what Tante Corrie said in her talks. Her simple way of telling things made a deep impression on me and many others. And she always gave us something to think about after the talk ended. I always listened closely, looking at her beautiful, friendly eyes, which spoke so much love to us. Tante Corrie was a wonderful pedagogue. And she had such a great sense of humor that I can hardly describe it. She laid in my heart the basis of faith.

The Rise of Anti-Semitism

Willem ten Boom, after working in village pastorates—first in Made and then in Zuijlen—began to be increasingly concerned at the rise of anti-Semitism in Europe. He spent much of his spare time studying the subject at the University of Utrecht.

He said to Tine, "I was captivated by the subject of anti-Semitism from the start, but now that I am really getting into it, it is taking possession of me. I can no longer get away from it. The Jewish question is haunting me. It is so dangerous. Anti-Semitism has repercussions that will affect the whole world." Leaving the pastorate in 1926, he began working for the Society for Israel, and this led to doctoral studies at the University of Leipzig in Germany. The title of his thesis was "The Birth of Modern Racial Anti-Semitism in France and Germany."

From Leipzig he wrote to Tine, who was home with their four children: "I expect that in a few years' time there will be worse pogroms than ever before. Countless Jews from the east will come across the border to seek refuge in our country. We must prepare for that situation."

Betsie

It would not be long before the gathering clouds of war would darken and Betsie would lose her life. She and Corrie shared a deep sisterly love, respect and closeness. They enjoyed being co-workers, co-conspirators and co-planners for the good of thousands in their home city—those in their Bible classes, Girl Scout and club members, their foster children, neighbors and friends, many of whom visited the Beje. Photographs, writings and stories from this time show us what Corrie was like—a strong, extroverted leader and an unconditional lover of people with a huge sense of humor and an infectious faith.

But what was Betsie like? In the few photographs we have of her she allows no smile and even looks a bit formidable. I think Corrie wanted us to know Betsie better because in her mideighties, when we were living in California, she sent letters to friends, relatives and previous club girls and foster children asking them to send her their written remembrances of Betsie. She wanted to write a book about her sister. Her stroke in 1978 prevented that desire from materializing, but I often thought about the slim, cream-colored file hanging in its green casing in the left-hand drawer of her desk with the tag "Book, Betsie" in her handwriting. And I felt regret that Corrie's version of Betsie's life would never be told.

She had written notes, however, that were intended for her proposed book, and she had kept several letters about Betsie.

These give us insight into some of the lessons Corrie wanted us to learn from Betsie's life. She starts with a reference to foster child Lessie:

Several years of Betsie's and my life were occupied with our foster children. When the girls were all in their crowded bedrooms at night, Betsie, Father and I came together and talked over what had happened during the day. Then we prayed and committed all of them to the care of the heavenly Father whom we knew loved them and from whom we expected the wisdom and love we needed to guide these teenagers. . . .

I do not remember ever to have laughed so much as in that time. Once Betsie said, "I told Lessie today to give a spring cleaning to the kitchen cupboard. She did it with much joy, singing the whole time, but boy, how impractical she is! Girls who grow up in Indonesia do not learn housekeeping because their parents have servants who do that work. But as for my girls here, I will teach them housekeeping."

"How will you find time for it?" I asked her. "They all are studying to be teachers."

"Yes, and the day they finish they will find a job and leave the care of their Aunt Betsie. But I have found a solution. I have written to their parents about my plan. I told them: 'There is a great chance that your daughter will marry in the future. I can congratulate the young man who will bring Puck to the altar and is willing to stay with her for better and for worse. I know that as soon as she has her teaching diploma she will get a job. How can I teach her the noble art of cooking and housekeeping when she is so busy at the moment with her studies and later with her job? What about giving me permission to keep her at home for a year before she goes to the last class at college?'

"I also have written about my plans to the mission board and wonder what they will think of my revolutionary thoughts."

I remember how in the following days Betsie received enthusiastic letters one after the other from the parents and mission boards. So Betsie took the girls away from school one at a time, and she taught all of them how to cook, clean and organize the big household. We also found we could finally enjoy the music, sport and other hobbies for which we had not had enough time when they were studying. And most of the girls helped me at the Clubs, first as Club girls and later as assistants.

How did it work out? Later when I went to the house of one of the married girls, I remember that the kitchen, closets and rooms all were arranged in the same way as in our house. Hans' daughters told me that when there was an argument about a household decision their mother said, "Tante Betsie said . . ." and that convinced them. Certainly the menus were like Betsie's—Betsie's soup, Betsie's puddings. Betsie's spirit was alive in that home. She had the art of making everyday life important and joyful."

What did Betsie look like, and how did her voice sound? In a letter written six decades later, a woman named Jo who as a child visited the Beje one afternoon in 1911 gave her perception of the difference between Corrie and Betsie: "Betsie had a soft speaking voice, which suited her angelic and fragile being. She kept working at the housekeeping very quietly—a very caring woman. It seemed to me that Tante Corrie was the strong one, someone everybody could depend upon whenever that was necessary."

Previous club girl Henk van Langelaar described, "Once I was at the Beje for a meal. Tante Betsie reminded me of fine china." And a family friend said, "She always reminded me of a cameo brooch." Another foster child recalled: "I remember Betsie as a 'Martha' figure, an always-serving Christian."

A relative wrote:

You asked me to tell you my memories of Tante Betsie. The thing I remember most is the connection she maintained with the family ancestors through old letters, daguerrotypes and old pictures, which she lovingly colored and framed. The past lived for Betsie (in contrast with her brother and sisters who much more—sometimes exclusively it seemed—looked toward the future). How Betsie enjoyed books like David Copperfield and those by Louisa May Alcott! She loved, understood and knew about antiques, and especially art. She transferred her love for paintings to me during the various visits I made with her to the Frans Hals Museum. At first I went with her reluctantly to do her a favor, but her enthusiastic descriptions of the pictures won me over and I developed a permanent interest in art. I also remember her scrapbooks in which she glued colorful advertisements for recipes and foreign newspaper clippings.

Sometimes she received letters from Indonesia from the parents of the Beje foster children in which they requested that she buy and send them certain items that could not be found in Indonesia. Those were not always easy errands. She once told me she had to go to many shops before she found the desired article. Nothing was ever too much for her. I remember that she was always cheerful and very neatly dressed

Hans Kapner, whose home I just described and whom I mentioned earlier as one of the first foster children to come to the Beje, wrote:

The first thing I want to say about Tante Betsie is that she was *there*. She was always *there*. She was a balanced, quiet woman who was involved in every part of the life of the Beje. You could really say that she had a central place in the Beje. She never sought the limelight, but if for some reason she had to give the lead, she stepped forward with controlled grace.

Betsie was the only member of the family who could not sing and who did not play an instrument. Even so, she was very musical and enjoyed good music intensely. She was able to determine musical nuances and to direct our attention to them.

She was definitely before her time in the way she used language. I always noticed this trait, for instance, when Grandfather and Tante Corrie were not there and Betsie prayed at the table. The first time I heard her address God without using "Thou" or "Thine" I felt a bit shocked, as she just called Him "You" in the modern way. But later I thought, "Yes, that is how it should be. That is how we speak to each other, that is how you talk to your friend; so why not talk to your great Friend in such a way?" That helped me a lot later when I was a teacher. It meant much more to the children if I did not use old-fashioned terms in prayer.

I think Betsie was a very intelligent woman. When we arrived at the Beje as foster children, she was auditing a class in Hebrew in the top [last] class of high school. She used the Hebrew often at home, following Grandfather's Bible reading in her Hebrew Bible. Sometimes she would say, "I thought that this is the way it should be translated." And when Grandfather or Tante Corrie had to give a talk somewhere, it was often Betsie who suggested a subject or came up with the idea on which the speech would be based.

She was always happy when I came to the kitchen to study while she cooked. She liked me to study aloud and often commented, "Oh, how interesting." She was particularly interested in history.

She had a great need of *gezelligheid*, both for herself and for others. She showed this in all kinds of small ways in ordinary daily life. On Sunday afternoons, for example, we always drank tea upstairs in the parlor. She laid a large tray with a matching mat and took the best cups from the cupboard and the silver candy dish. Then we all drank tea together with a cookie. Oh, it was so *gezellig*!

As Christmas approached each year we polished all the silver in the house—tableware and everything that had to do with Christmas—until it shone. The Christmas table was always tastefully decorated and cheerful.

Tante Betsie had the idea, which became a tradition, of taking tea in bed to every member of the family on Christmas morning. She took me into her confidence about it and gave me a large tray, telling me how she would like it to be set with a cup of tea for everybody and a slice of Christmas bread. And she wanted there to be a lighted candle on the tray. I served everybody, after which I ran back to bed and under the covers because soon the Salvation Army would play Christmas carols behind the towers of the St. Bavo in the early Christmas morning. Everybody in the house always enjoyed hearing these carols while still in bed. We always had wonderful celebrations, especially Christmas, New Year's Eve, *Sinterklaas*, Grandfather's birthday, etc.

There was a very small roof to the Beje, rather like a balcony, next to Grandfather's room. Betsie grew plants there. She tended to them every day. One would have thought they had little chance to grow there, as they received so little sun, but with Betsie's care they thrived. She also took good care of her plants in the parlor. She did this kind of task with a lot of warmth.

Betsie had a strong sense of humor. She laughed a lot when we came from school with silly stories. Sometimes Grandfather told us slang Amsterdam words or popular expressions and Betsie would say, in a pretending official voice, "Now, Father. . . ." But you could see the fun dancing in her eyes.

On New Year's Eve 1891, when Betsie was six years old, Mother ten Boom recorded the following in her diary:

Our Betsie is a lovely girl, sensible in everything. She looks pretty with her long fair curls, and though she is very pale she is in good health. She is hypersensitive and must be treated very carefully because she notices everything and ponders it all. We have to take care that she does not see and hear too much. It is astonishing that she has such a strong memory. Things we have forgotten altogether she remembers exactly with all the details. She is very anxious to learn and carries pencil and paper or slate and slate-pencil with her. She likes this far better than needlework. It is lovely to see how much she enjoys all good things that come her way and how every time she has something special she thanks the Lord for it without you having to tell her to do so. I cannot but say good things of her. She certainly has her faults, but so few that I really should not know what to say about them.

Betsie must indeed have had her faults, but, of course, her family and friends do not describe them. We will, therefore, never know any weaknesses in her character. These descriptions make it hard for me to relate to her because it puts her in a saintlike position. But how could she have been so loved if she were not a real person, just like you and me, with lots of failings?

In 1917, 26 years after her mother described her six-year-old daughter, Betsie showed her true faith in a profound statement that Corrie in her notes described as a simple but serious message for us all. As Europe headed into the final year of the First World War, Betsie said, "It is going to be a harder winter than we have ever had before. We must show through our joy the worth of being a Christian. We should already be doing this, because seeing the dark clouds approaching is often harder than being covered by them."

five

"The Deepest Hell That Man Can Create"

1939–1944

In the late 1930s many in Holland did not recognize the signs of approaching war. Their country had remained neutral in the First World War, and they reckoned that would surely be the case with this war. The Dutch government tried to ignore the signs, assuring the people they did not need to worry because Holland's desire for neutrality would be respected. At the end of 1939 the prime minister assured the people in a radio broadcast that there was absolutely no cause for alarm. He quoted an old Dutch poem, whose author I do not know:

People often suffer the most
By anticipating suffering that never happens.
They, therefore, have more to bear than God gives them to
bear.

But many did take note of the warning signs. Queen Wilhelmina was one of them. In her autobiography she wrote, "By the spring of 1938, when Hitler invaded Austria, the answer [to the question of what national-socialism would mean for the rest of Europe] was plain to me. German policy would result in a European catastrophe."[1]

As daily life went on, news reports told of one country after another being overtaken by the Germans. In April 1940, Hitler invaded Denmark and Norway.

War!

At three o'clock in the morning of Friday, May 10, 1940, the first German shock troops invaded Holland's most southerly province and took some of the bridges over the river Maas. At the same time a large number of aircraft flew into Dutch airspace. And at about 3:15 a.m. the first ground fighting took place when German soldiers removed the Dutch border patrol in the north of the country to clear the way for an armored German train.

Corrie was jarred awake at about four o'clock by the sound of loud explosions coming from the direction of the airport. In *The Hiding Place* she describes the invasion:

> I sat bolt upright in my bed. What was that? There! There it was again! A brilliant flash followed a second later by an explosion that shook the bed. I scrambled over the covers to the window and leaned out. The patch of sky above the chimney tops glowed orange-red. I felt for my bathrobe and thrust my arms through the sleeves as I whirled down the stairs. At Father's room I pressed my ear against the door. Between bomb bursts I heard the regular rhythm of his breathing.[2]

When she reached her sister's room, Betsie was sitting up in bed. "I groped toward her in the darkness, and we threw our arms around each other. Together we said it aloud: 'War.'"[3]

Holland held out for five days, during which the large port city of Rotterdam was heavily bombed. Soon came a proclamation from the queen that she had decided to take the difficult but urgent step of moving the seat of government away from Holland for as long as necessary. When Corrie heard the queen had left she wept: "I had not cried the night of the invasion but I cried now, for our country was lost."[4] The Netherlands surrendered on May 15, 1940.

During the first year of German occupation, life was fairly normal, but slowly the enemy began to apply restrictions. Nobody was allowed outside after 10:00 p.m. This curfew later was changed to 8:00 p.m., and then 6:00 p.m. Total blackout was ordered. Food was rationed. As time went on radio sets, gold, tin, copper and even bronze church bells had to be handed over to the Germans. The number of people who were allowed to comprise a group was limited. In 1940 the Nazis shut down the Girls' Clubs.

Although attacks on the Jewish population were minor at the beginning of the war, it was not long before the Germans began discriminating against them, starting with the requirement that they all wear a yellow star bearing the word "Jew." Then came attacks on Jewish businesses and synagogues, and they were denied access to shops, restaurants and theaters. Next, the transportations began. Rumors circulated about what might be happening to those who were deported.

Hitler's vision for postwar Europe was that Holland would become a province of Germany. Aryan Dutch men and women who were favorably disposed to Germany would be allowed to stay in Holland. Everybody else would be transported elsewhere. All Jews would be exterminated.

The Underground

By the beginning of 1942 the family at the Beje was involved in underground work. They began finding hiding places for Jewish refugees.

Every Dutch citizen was required to have an identity card on his or her person at all times, and it had to be produced in order to claim ration coupons. As Jewish people began to seek underground addresses it became necessary to obtain coupons and false identity cards for them. These were also needed for the young Dutchmen who otherwise would have been transported to Germany to help with the "labor force."

A very effective motivator, Corrie soon was surrounded by able young Dutchmen whom she called her "boys." They carried out underground errands for her. Willem and Tine's second son, Christiaan, nicknamed Kik, was one of them.

The first to become a refugee in the Ten Boom household was Hans Poley, a young man who came under suspicion of being involved in illegal activities. Having heard of the underground work carried out at the Beje but never having been there, Hans' first meeting with the family was in May 1943:

Carefully following instructions, I turned right into a narrow alley. It was empty, so I pressed the button on the post of the green door. Quick steps sounded and the door opened. "Welcome! Come in, quickly," Corrie's cheerful voice greeted me.

"I am Tante Corrie," she said, "and I do hope you will be very happy here." She led the way, turning left up a short staircase onto another landing where she opened a door into a small room. The curtains were drawn to prevent light from being seen from outside. In the middle was an oval table where a stately lady was busy with her sewing. To the right, next to the stove, sat an older man who could have passed for a patriarch. He had snow-white hair with a beautiful full beard, and he looked at me over his gold-rimmed glasses.

"Father," Tante Corrie said, "this is Hans. He will stay with us for some time." I did not know who to address first—the lady or the obvious master of the house—but he solved the problem. "Well, my boy, we are glad that you trust us to offer you shelter, but we have to expect our ultimate protection from our Father in heaven. We do hope that our Lord will bless your stay. Sit down here."[5]

Barteljorisstraat 19 became a well-known address for illegal activities. It housed refugees, and many underground workers met there to discuss plans and act as couriers. But in spite of the danger and tension of which they were constantly aware, Corrie, Betsie and Father made the best of the situation. They invited their Jewish guests to lead classes in any subjects they might be qualified to teach. They held classes in Hebrew and astronomy, and everyone in the house attended the Italian lessons—including Father, who, always ready to learn a new language, arrived each time with a notebook in his hand. In the evenings the members of the household came together in the living room, sometimes with a wood fire burning, and sang.

A few years later Corrie wrote some notes that describe life in the Beje during the year of 1943:

> As was always the case, there was a happy mood that day. The house where "the three old people lived" was full of the kind of fun caused by the coming together of fourteen people. The overtone was provided by Eusie, who once again was asking whether he really did look very Jewish [or not]. Since there was nothing about him that did not look Jewish, the rest of the company never tired of naming every visible characteristic of his race. Especially Mary and Martha, the two Portuguese Jews, appeared to be very knowledgeable on the subject. There were three young men from Friesland having a meal with us. They had come to Haarlem in connection with their illegal work, and one of them asked how it was possible to keep our work secret from the neighbors when there were such noisy conversations going on.
>
> "First, tell me [if] I would be recognized as a Jew on the street, sir, and then I will tell you how we keep our presence here a secret," replied Eusie.

He had just received the comforting news from his house-mates that he would perhaps be able to walk fifty meters without being recognized as Meyer Mossel, a cantor in the synagogue in Amsterdam, and was about to make up a detailed speech about how the underground activities were kept secret when a ladder was placed against the window and the window cleaner started his work. The curtains were only partly closed, and the man had a good view of the whole company. We were not very pleased with that because we did not know him. It could not be guaranteed that he would keep quiet about what he had seen. Very quickly I, the three Frisian boys, four more boys of their age, our Jewish guests and the others who happened to be in the house at the time conferred with each other about how we could best distract his attention.

It was Eusie who came up with the solution: "Let's act as if it is Tante Betsie's birthday!" Without hesitating for a moment he started to sing that favorite birthday song:

Oh how happy we are today.
It's Tante's birthday, it's Tante's birthday.

The noise level increased, and the window washer could never before have heard a birthday song that could not be finished because of the laughter of the singers. The situation was saved, the size of the group explained. He probably did not notice that Father did not know what to do with himself for laughing and that Betsie could hardly stop her familiar noiseless laugh.

After supper, while those who had to stay inside (those who because of their appearance could not be seen outside) did the washing up, a serious talk took place with the Frisian young men about the technicalities of hiding refugees. They only knew about the hiding places in the farms in the countryside and could not imagine hiding such a large number of people in a city, near the police station and only a short distance from the notorious Nassau Square. What would we do if the Gestapo came?

We were able to calm down the boys. We told them of our system of locks, the opening of which would cause a delay of at least two minutes to anybody wanting to enter the Beje. The house had two doors, one on the main street leading into the shop and one from the alley to the corridor. Both doors had four locks, and if undesirable visitors arrived it was Betsie's job to go to whichever door had been knocked on and fumble with the locks for a while. She was then to maintain that she could not get that door open, but would make her way to the other door, which she surely would be able to open.

In the time that all this took, there was plenty of opportunity to press one of the many buttons that had been placed all over the house. They would cause bells to ring on all three stories. Everybody in the house would hear the alarm signal.

When they heard the alarm bell anybody whose presence in the house could cause difficulties was to go straight to the hiding place in my room. Every refugee was trained to disappear in ninety seconds. If the alarm went at night they first had to fold up their sheets and blankets and turn their mattresses over.

Corrie went on to explain that she and Betsie and Father had given a lot of thought to the situating of the hiding place:

It was quite a long time before we decided upon the false wall in my bedroom. Originally we thought the best place for it would be in a space behind one of the cupboards in the dining room. We worked out that it would hold four people, three sitting down with their backs to the wall with their legs stretched out and the fourth lying across the legs of the other three. But the space was closed off by only a thin partition. Also, as the number of refugees in the house increased, we started to think about a place that might hide them better.

For a short while we experimented with a small space in the attic above the front bedroom. This could be reached only through a hatch high in the wall of another bedroom. In order to help anybody to safety we would have to use the household stepladder. There were too many problems. The older people and the ladies did not want to climb. It would take far too long to hide eight people. Also, the people in hiding would have to make their way through a very narrow passageway past a big beam. We had tried to remove some of the beam with an ax and a saw, but the passageway was still too narrow. Another problem was that there would always have to be somebody in the bedroom to close the hatch after the last refugee was inside, and then that person would have to hang an improbably large etching of the Great Church in The Hague in front of the hatch. So that hiding place was rejected, too.

And then we found the right place. My own bedroom had a blank wall. A second wall was built a short distance from the first wall, and in the left-hand corner of that second wall a cupboard with shelves was built of which the lowest portion of the wooden back of the cupboard could be pushed up. It was ideal. There was room for six to eight people between those two walls.

Ready for use on June 2, 1943, the hiding place was about eight feet long, two feet wide and nearly ten feet high.

The inhabitants of the Beje began to drill with enthusiasm. At the most unexpected and confusing moments Corrie pressed one of the alarm bells. And then a lot of action took place. Nobody wanted to be the last person to disappear into the hiding place. Corrie wrote:

One cold evening when the whole family had just gone to bed, I pushed the bell for the first night alarm and the droll procession began. Piet was the first to get to the hiding place. He was wearing his pajamas and carrying his clothes. He knelt down somewhat frantically in front of the cupboard, poked his head inside and disappeared. It was as if he had been swallowed by an enormous monster. The last I saw of him was an arm, which reached quickly through the opening to grab his clothes. By this time the others had arrived. One by one they slipped behind the wall from a kneeling position. Eusie came in last, wearing monstrous pajamas with a blue stripe.

Once he was inside I quickly replaced a few boxes and linens on the bottom shelf and closed the sliding panel.

When the practice was completed and the refugees had been given the all clear, they talked about it. There were a few objections. Carrying clothes inside the hiding place cost unnecessary time. It was decided that from then on the refugees would hang their clothes in the hiding place before bedtime. There was also the difficulty about coming out at the end of an alarm. This time I just came into my room and called out "Everything is all right. Come out." But we had heard from acquaintances that sometimes the Gestapo would follow a person suspected of hiding refugees through his house and make him say a sentence like that. We therefore appointed Betsie to knock three times on the panel after every alarm and say: "Come out, children." If they heard any other words the hidden guests were not to raise the panel and were to keep perfectly still.

The "Blow" Comes

September 9, 1943, less than six months before the Beje was raided, Italy capitulated. That evening proved to be one of the busiest the Beje had yet known. The Ten Booms still had a radio because when the Germans demanded all radios be handed over, they had parted with only a very small, spare radio. The main radio was hidden upstairs in the hiding place. The rumor spread quickly through Haarlem that the Italians had given up the fight. People were even beginning to say that the Germans soon would surrender. Since many friends, co-workers and acquaintances knew there was still a radio in the Beje, they came from all sides to hear the great news of the capitulation for themselves. So many people came that it became impossible to listen through the headphones in the hiding place on the third floor and relay the news to the first floor downstairs.

In the end, they brought the radio downstairs and attached the loudspeaker normally used with their record player. Father sat cheerfully in the middle of a group of some thirty people, listening to the news reports that kept streaming in. Happily, there was no raid that evening. "It would have been a big catch for the Gestapo," said Corrie.

Some resistance workers visiting the house for the first time, after hearing about all the happenings at the Beje, would become fearful and act as if they wanted to leave as soon as possible. And Corrie would simply explain, as she did to a nervous courier:

> We do not do these things out of personal bravery. . . . We just live in the belief that God has given us this work, that we understand the danger, but that we know we are hidden under the wings of Him whose care and protection we experience daily.

Toward the end of 1943 the Beje became even more deeply involved with the underground, and a couple of close calls necessitated having to find temporary safer accommodation for the Jews on at least one occasion. In her papers, Corrie tells how all in the Ten Boom household understood the danger of what they were undertaking:

> Father was also completely aware of the possible consequences of our undertakings. We said to him more than once, "You do know, Father, it could happen that we are discovered. Then we will all go to prison and with your poor health you would not survive." Father was 84! He would then go quiet and say that he would obey if God asked him to give his life to protect the old people of the covenant.

The blow came on Monday, February 28, 1944, between five and six o'clock in the evening. Tipped off by a Dutchman who worked as their agent, the Gestapo raided the Beje, which was busy that afternoon. Four Jews were staying as guests, and they were upstairs. Willem had held a Bible study in the dining room, and some of the members had not yet left the house. Nollie also had come to the Beje with her son, Peter, to visit Father. Peter was playing the piano with his back toward two resistance workers who were discussing some plans when the alarm bell sounded. The Jews made straight for the hiding place, and the two resistance workers, whose presence would have aroused suspicion, were pushed up the stairs and through Corrie's bedroom into the hiding place. So the place held Martha, a Portuguese Christian Jew of about 60; Eusie the cantor, about 55; Mary, about 45, a Portuguese Jew; Ronnie, a Jewish young man of about 25; and the two young Dutch resistance workers, Hans and Reynout. Although the family was arrested and the house thoroughly searched, the hiding place was not discovered. After 47 hours those in hiding were released through the cooperation of Dutch police who were sympathetic to the underground and had been informed of the refugees' plight by other resistance workers.

In her papers Corrie describes her thoughts as she, Betsie and Casper were loaded into a police van that would take them away to the Scheveningen prison near The Hague: "In my heart was a great sense of peace. I had long expected this catastrophe. Now the blow had fallen, [and] I accepted it as the close of an exciting chapter of my life. In my mind I kept telling myself, 'Don't ever feel sorry for yourself.'"

Scheveningen

After a journey of about an hour, the doors of the prison closed behind them and Betsie and Corrie were ordered to stand with their faces toward a red brick wall. Father was allowed to sit on a chair. When the sisters' names were called they passed by Casper, who looked up and said his last words to them softly: "The Lord be with you, my daughters." He was to die in prison ten days later.

Corrie was suffering from pleurisy, which was later thought to be tuberculosis, and she was placed in solitary confinement for the three months of their imprisonment at Scheveningen. Betsie was confined in a cell with other women. Although officially they were allowed to write and receive very few letters, some were smuggled in and out, and it is these letters to family and friends that give us insights into prison life. Corrie sometimes wrote brief descriptions of her feelings about life in cell number 384:

> A cell consists of four stone walls and a closed door . . . how greatly a prison deprives people of the most elementary conditions of life. If God still grants me the opportunities, I hope to work in the area of rehabilitation. I will now also dare to visit a prison cell, although I did not dare before now.

Corrie's first letter to "Nollie and all friends" was written on April 11, 1944. She thanks them for the parcel they had sent: "It was perfect! All those colors! I am using the threads from the bath towel to embroider everything." She writes that her main difficulty has been her worry about Betsie and Father, of whom she had heard nothing. She also says, "I am grateful that I am alone, I who love company and people so much! I see my sins more clearly, my own SELF in upper case letters, and I see much more superficiality in myself than I had previously realized. I am continuously looking at Him and trying not to be impatient. I will not be here one minute longer than God deems necessary."

Every two weeks the Red Cross brought packages to the prison for delivery to each prisoner. On one occasion her cell door opened and the prison guard insisted Corrie come and take the package from her even though she was weak with her illness. Remarks Corrie:

> Unkindness is so depressing! I unpack the box. The items are nice and tasty. They were chosen by understanding people who knew what would be good for us. Will this be the last parcel? In another two weeks will we be . . . ?
>
> Look out, thoughts! It is better to concentrate on and contemplate the Savior. With Him there is certainty. With the

other there is only uncertainty and delayed hope, which hurts the heart.

Betsie was the first to learn of Father's death, but she did not receive that news until a month afterward in a letter from Nollie's daughter Cocky. She wrote back to her niece:

April 11, 1944

Dear Cocky,

So our dear father has been promoted to Glory. The Lord Himself crown his head with the martyr's crown. Many years ago I had a premonition of this, but I steadfastly put it out of my mind. I often thought that a person in whom Christ was shown to such advantage, who lived so close to the Savior, to whom eternal things were so real and who had the gift of prayer in such a wonderful way—such a person had all the conditions for becoming a martyr. And then I would think, *He is not going to die in his bed.* God did not let His sovereignty slip through His fingers. No, this all had to be this way, even my being here in prison. . . .

Cocky, tell everybody who is praying for me that they should especially thank God because miracles are happening here every day. The rush of great waters came to me, but I did not despair for one moment. The Lord is closer to me than ever before in my life. Even in those first terrible days I felt His nearness. I knew that this was not punishment because He suffered completely for me at Golgotha. This horror had come to us from His loving hand to purify me.

Corrie's 52ⁿᵈ Birthday—April 15, 1944

Corrie's birthday came while she was in Scheveningen. Later she recalled:

I was alone, given cold food (nothing hot) and had no opportunity to get fresh air. No books. Everybody was snarling, and I felt so sick and miserable. A doctor gave me a shot, and I told him that it was my birthday and then he gave me a firm handshake. He himself was a prisoner. Never did I appreciate a handshake so much as this one!

Betsie and Corrie were allowed no contact in Scheveningen, and Corrie did not learn of Father's death until three weeks after the news reached Betsie. She wrote to Nollie and family:

His going will leave a great emptiness in my life. The Lord will surely provide many others to whom I can give the love and help I gave him, but that which he gave me can never be replaced. But what a privilege it was that we could enjoy him so intensely for so long. For a few days I was upset. Now that has passed. During the last few days there was such tension inside me. I did not dare to think things through, and when you are so alone it is difficult to get away from your thoughts. Now that is gone and I am thinking much about the future. I am making plans and am experiencing much peace. How good the Savior is to me! He not only bears my burdens, but He carries me, too!

In a letter smuggled out of Scheveningen prison Corrie describes one of the few times she was allowed out of her cell into the fresh air. It is not clear whether while walking in the garden she actually came to the terrible yard she describes or whether she was mentally reliving a description somebody had made of it.

When I had gone through the door it was bolted behind me, and I was alone again. Even in the garden there was only loneliness for those of us sentenced to solitary confinement.
    After nine weeks, this was my first time outside. Red flowering shrubs, colorful little primroses, grass, yellow dunes and a wide blue sky. My legs were stinging from their unfamiliar movement, but I walked and walked, on and on, on the rect-

angular path around the center lawn. I drank in the colors and the air.

Tremendous emotion made my heart beat faster, and then an unspeakable melancholy descended within me. I saw the colors through my tears. In me and around me was more loneliness than in the cell, and all of a sudden I did not see any beauty, just a bare yard, and felt an atmosphere of death and cruelty. At the end, they had dug a long, narrow pit. It looked like a freshly dug grave. Half the shrubs were without leaves and were dead. Around the yard was a high, hard wall with pieces of broken glass in sharp points liberally cemented in its top. And in the north was the tall prison, bare and cold with rows of barred widows. Near the south wall was the gruesome stench of burned bones, and I could hear Kik telling me, "There are already three crematoria in Scheveningen." Behind the south wall the rattle of a machine gun broke the silence. And then, once again, everything was terrifyingly quiet. It was two o'clock and was as if everything around me was a ghost city and I the only one alive. I walked on and an uncontrollable homesickness surged up in my heart.

Then suddenly I remembered Enoch. He was not filled with homesickness when he walked with God, and so I was no longer alone either. God was with me. Hand in hand we walked on and saw the blue sky and the flowers and the flowering shrubs, and I could see the yard as part of a beautiful free world where I would be allowed to walk once again. In the same way, earth is a lonely garden and heaven the liberty where great joy awaits us as children of the light.

Vught

On June 5, the day before D-Day, Betsie and Corrie were reunited when they were suddenly transported from Scheveningen prison to Vught, a German concentration camp in the south of Holland. They were delighted to discover each other while waiting at the railway station for the train that would take them on a slow, twelve-hour journey to their new destination. With many other women prisoners they were placed in a large room, where for the next twelve hours they sat on wooden benches without back rests. They were given neither supervision nor food.

Betsie's diary:

Tuesday, June 6: Unexpectedly brought to Vught in the night to Barrack 4. Corrie and I were together in the train compartment. We enjoyed it immensely. Everything terribly strict here, but still so grateful not to be in a cell any longer.

Thursday, June 15: Transferred into the camp here. We sleep, eat and sew side-by-side and are now so happy! Both had physicals and are fine. Corrie's lungs fully recovered. Must get up at five each morning. Wear overalls and wooden shoes. Have fun walking on wooden shoes. Each day and by night we are experiencing thousands of miracles.

The sisters were assigned tasks at Vught. Betsie's first job was the braiding of heavy ropes, a job so hard on the hands that she eventually was released to lighter duties in the sewing room. Corrie worked in the nearby Phillips factory.

Through every preserved letter shine Betsie's trust, light-heartedness and love. Although often suffering from hunger, she was grateful for the smallest thing and her famous flair for living allowed her to be ever grateful instead of complaining. I cannot find the faintest trace of self-pity in any of her writing.

Sunday, June 25: We had to report to the sewing room. The morning flew by. In the afternoon, fifty of us gathered outside. Wonderful! Then slept and did laundry. In evening, a discussion circle. Nice. Had a wonderful Sunday. Beautiful weather.

Later she expressed thanks for a thimble and a piece of cake given to her by a Belgian woman prisoner:

Yesterday, many blessings. Had a good talk with Smid. Received butter and cheese. Washed a blanket. Cabbage soup. Corrie doing well at Phillips. We enjoy the beauties of nature, the skies, very much. The weather is cold, just right. Every day some sunshine. We receive amazing strength for this harsh life. I am often very hungry. Corrie brings me a warm meal from the factory, and I eat it while we stand at roll call.

On July 6, through a letter from the outside, Betsie and Corrie learned that the Beje and the watch business had been released by the Germans. "We understand that the condition of the house is not bad," wrote Betsie in her diary. "Just what I expected from the Lord."

While Betsie continually displayed such solid faith, joy and even cheerfulness, Corrie's strong imagination and descriptive powers cause us to sense deep emotion in these writings. On August 13, 1944, Corrie wrote to the family:

We are able to witness here and there, but not nearly as much as we had expected. There is much bitterness and communism, cynicism and deep sorrow. The worst for us is not that which we suffer ourselves, but the suffering we see around us. We are learning to put the worst in the hands of the Savior. We are very peaceful, in rather good spirits, but not cheerful. Our health is fine. My hair has turned gray. Life is hard. It is as if I have been drafted into the army but in the harsh German way. But don't worry too much about that. In many aspects it is not too much.

Betsie's letters seem to display a more childlike and pure faith than those of Corrie, as if she was somehow protected from the cruelty, murder and deprivation going on around her. She celebrated—no doubt, for her that is the right word—her 59th birthday on August 19.

Ravensbrück

On September 4 Corrie and Betsie, along with many other women prisoners from Vught, were transported to Ravensbrück concentration camp in Germany on a very slow-moving train. The boxcar should have held about forty women, but eighty were shoved into it. The conditions were terrible; there was no space to sit comfortably, very little water and hardly any fresh air. Tante Corrie told me once that those three long days and nights in the boxcar were the worst time of her ten-month imprisonment.

Ravensbrück was the only major Nazi concentration camp for women, and about twenty European nations were represented there. At the time of Corrie and Betsie's incarceration, the population of the camp was about 80,000. She and Betsie were officially registered as prisoners on September 8, 1944. By the end of the war more than 132,000 women and children had been imprisoned in Ravensbrück, and it is estimated that 92,000 of them died there by starvation, execution or weakness. One of them was Betsie.

The camp authorities forbade any receiving or sending of mail, so we have no written record between the end of August and the end of December, when Corrie was released. (Two dates, December 28 and December 30, appear on her discharge certificates.) But she described the happenings at Ravensbrück in her books *The Hiding Place* and *A Prisoner and Yet . . .*, the latter written early in the year after her release.

In Ravensbrück Betsie and Corrie encountered a world that they had never imagined. Lying, pushing, shoving, filthy words, lice, vermin, starvation, dirt, manipulation and hard labor were their daily lot. Tante Corrie called it "the deepest hell that man can create," where the guards had had "lessons in cruelty."

But God did not allow their spirits to be broken, their love of planning to cease or their prayers to stop. Corrie wrote in *The Hiding Place*:

As we prayed, God spoke to us about the world after the war. It was extraordinary: In this place where whistles and loudspeakers took the place of decisions, God asked us what we were going to do in the years ahead.

Betsie was always very clear about the answer for her and me. We were to have a house, a large one—much larger than the Beje—to which people who had been damaged by concentration-camp life would come until they felt ready to live again in the normal world. She would say, "It is such a beautiful house, Corrie! The floors are all inlaid wood, with statues set in the walls and a broad staircase sweeping down. And gardens! Gardens all around it where they can plant flowers. It will do them such good, Corrie, to care for flowers!"[6]

In the days before her death, Betsie described another phase of the work they would both carry out when they were released. Was she seeing visions or having dreams?

A camp, Corrie—a concentration camp. But we are in charge. The camp was in Germany. It was no longer a prison, but a home where German people who had been warped by his philosophy of hate and force would come to learn another way. There were no walls, no barbed wire and the barracks had window boxes. It will be so good for them . . . watching things grow. People can learn to love from flowers. . . .[7]

Corrie asked Betsie if this camp in Germany was to take the place of the house in Holland. No, Betsie told her, the house in Holland would come first. It was ready and waiting.

As she weakened, Betsie gave new details about that house, and of the barracks in Germany. "The barracks are gray, Corrie, but we will paint them green! Bright, light green, like springtime."[8]

Betsie's final instruction about the future was that she and Corrie would travel the world together. "We must tell people what we have learned here. We must tell them that there is no pit so deep that He is not deeper still. They will listen to us, Corrie, because we have been here."[9] Betsie always spoke in the plural when describing the future to Corrie, who desperately hoped that her sister would indeed live to see the fulfillment of her three dreams. Corrie asked her if they would be together when the work Betsie had described came to pass. "Always together, Corrie! You and I . . . always together."

And in a way they always were together because Betsie's story, forever combined with that of Corrie, would circulate the world. While they were in the camp, Betsie predicted that both she and Corrie would be free by the new year. She passed away on December 16. After her own release two weeks later, Corrie described her anguish at the loss of her sister but then used very comforting words to show us through her eyes her last glimpse of Betsie's face: ". . . full of peace, and happy as a child. She looked incredibly young. The care lines, the grief lines, the deep hollows of hunger and disease were simply gone. In front of me was the Betsie of Haarlem. It was a bit of heaven in the midst of the surrounding hell."[10]

In chapter 4 I quoted an excerpt from one of the letters Tante Corrie received in the last years of her life when she asked for remembrances of Betsie. The letter was from a woman named Jo who had visited the Beje when she was a child. I quoted her perception of the difference between Corrie and Betsie: "It seemed to me that Tante Corrie was the strong one, someone everybody could depend upon wherever that was necessary." But it was the next sentence, which I have saved until now, that really describes much about Betsie: "But it seems that during the war years Betsie was the stronger spiritually." Tante Corrie marked that part of the letter; it surely would have been part of her unwritten book about her sister.

In the coming chapters we will see how Betsie's words were fulfilled through the beautiful house in Holland, the former concentration camp in Germany and the more than three decades of Corrie's world travels.

six

Corrie Begins to Tell Her Story

1945–1947

*C*orrie was discharged from Ravensbrück concentration camp in the last days of 1944 and made her slow, cold and hungry way by train back to the Netherlands. Germany was in ruins. As the train passed through Berlin she realized that it was New Year's Day 1945. Betsie had been right. They were both free.

Upon her arrival in Holland, Corrie spent ten days in a nursing home in the northern city of Groningen and then stayed two weeks with her brother and family at their home in Hilversum. She was shocked to see that Willem looked very ill and to learn that Kik, the younger of Willem and Tine's two sons who had been active in the underground, had been arrested and sent to Germany. No news of him had been received. But she did learn that the Jews who had been in the hiding place were safe except for Mary, who for some inexplicable reason had gone out into the street shortly after finding another temporary hiding place, where she was arrested and transported to Poland.

Holland was not yet free, and permission to travel was limited. This was also the infamous "Hunger Winter" of 1945, during which, to save themselves from starvation, the Dutch ate even tulip bulbs.

After some difficulty obtaining transportation to her old hometown of Haarlem, Corrie arrived there during the last week of January, delighted to be reunited with Nollie and her family. Then she returned to live in the silent family home.

Home to the Beje

Much had been stolen from the Beje. After the Germans had "unsealed" it during the summer of the previous year it had been used to house homeless families. Four Oriental rugs were gone, as were her typewriter and the clocks and watches left for repair at the time of her arrest. But many priceless things were left, including her piano, the family's Frisian clock and an oil painting of her father given to him as a gift from the people of Haarlem on his eightieth birthday.

Corrie inquired about the many friends and co-workers from the underground work and learned that the group was still operating but on a smaller scale. When she asked about the mentally retarded children and adults she had formerly taught, she learned that their families had hidden them in the back rooms of their houses from the regime that did not think they were "fit to live." Their special schools and institutions had been closed down. Corrie took several of them into the Beje.

All this might be thought enough for a person to undertake in those first few months of recovery from imprisonment, but Corrie was busy with another time-consuming task. She was used to being awakened early in the morning at Ravensbrück for roll call and found that she still automatically awoke long before dawn, unable to return to sleep. Not wanting to waste those hours, she got up and began writing her first book, *Gevangene en Toch* . . . *(A Prisoner, and Yet . . .)*. Remarkably, this book was ready for the printer by the summer of 1945.

Corrie Begins Telling Her Story

Corrie often described the early days and months after her release as she began to tell others about her experiences. Remembering Betsie's words, "We must tell them, Corrie, what we have learned in this terrible place," she invited all her neighbors to come to the Beje. They all had been very sorry when the Ten Booms were arrested and wanted to know what had happened to Father and Betsie.

As Corrie recounted their experiences, one of the neighbors said, "I am sure it was your faith that carried you through."

"My faith? I don't know about that," replied Corrie. "My faith was so weak, so unstable. It was hard to have faith. When a person is in a safe environment, having faith is easier. But in that camp when I saw my own sister and thousands of others starve to death, where I was surrounded by men and women who had training in cruelty, then I do not think it was my faith that helped me through. No, it was Jesus! He who said, 'I am with you until the end of the world.' It was His eternal arms that carried me through. He was my certainty.

"If I tell you that it was my faith, you might say if you have to go through suffering, 'I don't have Corrie ten Boom's faith.' But if I tell you it was Jesus, then you can trust that He who helped me through will do the same for you. I have always believed it, but now I know from my own experience that His light is stronger than the deepest darkness."

From this beginning, Corrie began to tell her story to anybody in Haarlem who would listen. She rode her bike through the city streets and suburbs to bring the message that when the worst happens in the life of a child of God, then the best remains and the very best is yet to be. Whether she spoke to people individually or in groups, the message was the same, beginning in that Dutch Hunger Winter until the end of her speaking life decades later.

During one of the early meetings in Haarlem, after she had talked about Betsie's vision of a large home for rehabilitation, Tante Corrie was approached by a woman whose face she recognized. She was Mrs. Bierens-de Haan, the owner of a very large house in the wealthy suburb of Bloemendaal. The lady told Corrie that she had five sons, all of whom had fought in the war. Four had returned safely. She believed God had told her during the meeting that if the fifth son came back, she should make her house available for Betsie ten Boom's vision. The fifth son did return and Corrie was invited to visit the house, where she found inlaid wood floors, a sweeping staircase and bas-relief statues set along the walls just as Betsie had described.

On May 5, 1945, the Allies liberated Holland. And at the beginning of June, less than six months after Betsie's death, the beautiful house—named *Schapenduinen,* meaning "Sheep Dunes"—received its first guests. Through the coming years hundreds of people who had suffered mental and physical anguish during the war would receive rehabilitation there and in the larger house that eventually took its place.

For the rest of that year Corrie continued to receive and fulfill many speaking appointments, including one in the city of Nijmegen, where she gave her first talk in English to a group of Canadian servicemen. They told her they hoped she would one day come to speak in their country.

And during that year Corrie told her story to one very significant person. The Dutch collaborator who had betrayed the Beje by tipping off the Germans had been arrested, brought to trial and sentenced to death. His name was Jan Vogel, and Corrie wrote him a letter.

Haarlem, 19 June, 1945

Dear Sir,

I heard today that you are very probably the person who betrayed me. I went through ten months in concentration camp. My father died in prison after ten days and my sister after ten months.

That which you meant for harm, God meant for good for me. I have come closer to Him. A severe punishment is awaiting you. I have prayed that the Lord will accept you if you turn to Him. Remember that the Lord Jesus bore your sins, too, on the cross. If you accept that and want to be His child, you will be saved for eternity.

I have forgiven you everything. God will forgive you, too, if you ask Him. He loves you and sent His Son to earth to pay the price for your sins—to bear the punishment for you and me. You need to give an answer to that. When He says, "Come to Me, give Me your heart," then your answer must be, "Yes, Lord, I want to. Make me Your child."

If you find it difficult to pray, ask if God will give you His Spirit. He will give faith in your heart.

Never doubt the love of the Lord Jesus. He is waiting to receive you with outstretched arms.

I hope that the deep path you now must take will work toward your eternal salvation.

Sincerely,
Corrie ten Boom

To America on Fifty Dollars

It is not clear who suggested to Corrie that she visit the United States to tell her story, but she quickly made plans to go there. She saw it as God's guidance in fulfillment of Betsie's dream that they would go around the world with their story. In her diary on January 26, 1946, she recorded:

> Planning a foreign trip is wonderfully exciting, and for me it is doubly wonderful because it is such a contrast with my last foreign journey. Then I was being taken against my will to the land of the enemy, but now by my own free will I am going on an evangelization journey through a friendly country. What an adventure! I know so little about what is awaiting me. I will have $50 with me and some notes of introduction, but I do not know anybody there. What a privilege to have been called to evangelize in another part of the world—I, a weak, sinful, little person. But I know that God's power is made perfect in weakness. I experienced that in the camps.

Leaving the rehabilitation center in the hands of a Dutch board and a caring staff, Corrie moved on to the next challenge. After considerable difficulty in obtaining her visa, Corrie left Holland for America on a cargo ship. Fifty dollars was all she was allowed to take out of the country. An American businessman whom she had met in Holland, however, had given her two checks, one small and one somewhat larger, for her to use if necessary. "You can pay me back later," he said.

Arriving in New York City, Corrie went to the YWCA and found a room. One of the addresses she had been given in Holland was that of a group of Christian Jews who had immigrated to America and held meetings in New York City. She called them and learned that they were from Germany. They invited her to speak to them, but the English speaking notes she had made on the trip across the Atlantic Ocean could not be used. Her first talk in the United States was in German.

After staying at the YWCA for a week, she received a letter from somebody who had heard her speak at the Jewish meeting. Knowing how difficult it was to find rooms in New York, this lady whom she had never met offered Corrie the use of a room in her house. She accepted quickly and became the woman's guest for the next five weeks.

Corrie spent her days looking up the addresses she had been given in Holland. The Americans were polite and some seemed interested, but nobody asked her to speak. She even began knocking on the doors of churches, offering to tell her story. But few people were interested. After a couple of weeks she began to run out of money. Her daily food for some time was what she described to me as "a Nedick's breakfast." It cost ten cents and consisted of a cup of coffee, a doughnut and some orange juice.

"One day on that first visit to New York," she recalled to me late in her life, "I met some American girls. They invited me to have lunch with them as their guest. I had chicken and gravy and potatoes and vegetables. Oh, it tasted so good. That day I started to love the Americans!"

As the weeks progressed, Corrie felt increasing resistance to her message. Nobody was interested in an older Dutch woman who wanted to give talks. Nor did they seem to understand that there was such a thing as God's guidance.

"But God's guidance is much more important than common sense. I know He has told me to give this message in America. I can tell from my own experience that the light of Jesus is stronger than the deepest darkness."

"We have ministers to tell us that," was the response.

"Of course you have. But from my own experience I can tell people that what the ministers say is true."

"It would have been better if you had stayed in Holland. We don't need any more preachers. Too many Europeans are coming to America. Something should be done about it."[1]

After five weeks of no work Corrie was beginning to wonder if she should indeed return to Holland, when the first of a chain of events took place that were to lead to open doors all over the United States. First, she met a Dutch minister who had heard about her story. She stayed with his family in the pastoral manse for five days: "What a joy to eat good Dutch food again." A week later after a service in a different church she met Irving Harris, editor of the magazine *The Evangel*. He was interested in her story and asked if she had any written material he could publish in his magazine. She gave him a copy of one of her lectures and before they parted, Mr. Harris gave her the name and phone number of a Mr. Abraham Vereide in Washington, D.C. Reluctant at first, Corrie finally called Mr. Vereide and received a warm invitation to come to Washington.

More Than Sufficient Work

Twenty-five years later Corrie wrote about Mr. Vereide in her news magazine *It's Harvest Time*.

In the U.S.A. I started to bring the Gospel, but no doors were open to me until I met Abraham Vereide. He introduced me to many people. It was my joy to work with him in the International Christian Leadership Breakfast Groups. Abraham was a man full of the joy of the Lord, always prepared to tell everyone about Jesus, whom he loved. His introductions were always unusual. Once I was with a group of highly educated people. Abraham did not forget the title of any of the people in the group. I wondered how he would introduce Corrie ten Boom, just a licensed watchmaker. Without hesitation he said with a smile, "Corrie ten Boom was graduated from the University of Ravensbrück." It certainly had been training in that prison camp! I was still more moved when he put his arm around my shoulders and said, "Corrie ten Boom, God's own girl."

From that time on, Corrie had more than sufficient work. Soon she was able to pay back the businessman who had given her the two checks "to use if necessary." Something of the scope of her new work is shown through some notes she made in Toronto on June 2, 1946: "It is no small thing to be put to work in Canada. I see so many possibilities that I could stay for the rest of my life in Toronto and have enough work. In the last fourteen days I have held 24 talks, four newspaper interviews and a radio interview."

During her time in Canada she met a Mrs. Bobbie Halliday from whom she received much kindness through the coming years, not the least of which was the supply of clothes. When I started traveling with Tante Corrie in 1976 she told me that according to Mrs. Halliday she had only one dress on her first visit to America. "But," said Corrie to me thirty years later, "I cannot have had just one dress. I must have been wearing one and had another in my suitcase."

She began to write letters in English from time to time, which were mimeographed and sent to the new friends she had made, and she kept in touch with her Dutch friends through a column in a Dutch evangelical magazine. Because Mrs. Halliday kept copies of these letters we are able to follow Corrie's early travels with some accuracy.

The first of these letters, which I have been able to track down, was written from Prairie View, Kansas, on July 15, 1946, about four months after she met Abraham Vereide. Among other places where she had already spoken were New York City, Philadelphia, Washington, D.C., Staten Island, Vermont, Ottawa, Toronto, Detroit and Grand Rapids. She must have already shared with some of those new friends her difficulty in understanding Americans and her lack of fluency in English, for she said:

> The language difficulty is no more a real brake upon the work, or [my] not understanding the American people. I accept them now as they are. When they are different from the Dutch I don't judge but try to understand their elementary needs. To many thousands I brought the message during the last months . . . thirty lady lawyers at a dinner of the Women's Bar Association at Chicago accepted me extraordinarily. A Jewish Women's Congress did not accept me at all, and one asked me: "Why did you speak of Jesus? Did you not know that you were speaking to Jews?" I certainly did.

Underneath the mimeographed letter, Corrie added a note in her own handwriting: "Your dress, Bobbie, is a real blessing. I am sure that I am quite ladylike with it . . . when I spoke for the lady lawyers I was so glad I had that dress."

Two months later, in October 1946, after having spoken in California and Utah and 22 times in Iowa, Corrie wrote:

My health is splendid, and in my heart is an ever-growing joy. To bring the light makes you so happy. It shines into your own heart . . . to everyone I may tell about the victory of Christ! How good it is to know that all work in God's Kingdom is for His sake. Jesus works in our hearts the love of God by His Holy Spirit (Romans 5:5). What rich children of the King we are! Why do we so often live like beggars?

How do people respond? Sometimes they tell me I come over too strongly. I think they say that because I see more and more that we may not be content with living as if we are only partly a child of God. Sometimes God's Spirit shows the people their sins and brings them to the happy deed of giving their life to Him. Some have been strengthened by my telling of the small and large miracles God did and does in my life and dare now bring their own difficulties to Him. Yes, God does miracles even now in my life. Is it not a miracle that I might give more than 160 lectures and I am not tired?

On December 14 I hope to leave on the *Queen Elizabeth* for England and then be home at Christmas.

Corrie had much to do, however, in the intervening two months. On November 19 she wrote to Abraham Vereide requesting his prayers and the use of his influence to free Hans Rahms, a German judge at Scheveningen who tried to secure Corrie and Betsie's freedom after their arrest. He was then interred in Germany.

Will you try to get free Hans Rahms, at Hammelburg bei Bad Kissingen 9793 Internment Camp in Germany?

In April 1944 he questioned our family, set free 32 people who were in prison with us. He knew that most of them were underground workers. He changed my Protocol and tried in several ways to set free my sister and me but did not succeed because another judge got our trial. Hans Rahms listened with real interest when we spoke of the Gospel and allowed my sister to pray with him. When it is useful, I will take him in our house in Holland for a time with his family. Will you get permission for that? Pray that they may be saved for eternity.

In the same letter to Mr. Vereide she wrote: "People say that Molotov [the Soviet foreign minister] will be on the *Queen Elizabeth* on December 14. Pray that I may bring him my message. God is a God of miracles."

Because there is no further mention of Molotov, it seems that she was not able to bring him her message. But as for Hans Rahms, he must have been released because several years later she renewed her acquaintance with him on a visit to Germany and explained the Gospel and his need of the Lord Jesus as his Savior. Rahms accepted Him and later she wrote, "I know his sins were forgiven and that his name was written in the Book of Life."

Home Again

From that first of countless travels abroad, Corrie arrived back in the Netherlands shortly after the death of her brother, Willem, who passed away in December 1946 of tuberculosis of the spine, contracted in prison. Just before he died, Willem opened his eyes to tell Tine, "It is good, it is very good, with Kik." Although they had long surmised that Kik was no longer alive, not until 1953 did the family receive confirmation that he had died in 1945 in Bergen-Belsen concentration camp.

Father, Betsie, Willem and Kik—four Ten Booms—had given their lives for shielding and saving Jewish refugees.

seven

"We Are Able to Live as King's Children"

1947–1953

Corrie's home in Holland was now the beautiful rehabilitation center in Bloemendaal near Haarlem. It was to her room there that she returned from her ten-month adventure in the United States.

One of her first tasks was to tell the Dutch Christians what she had learned in America. Just as the Ten Boom family, under Father's example, had looked for and received fellowship and instruction from Christians outside their own denomination, Corrie showed the same spirit to her new friends across the Atlantic in a circular letter dated June 27, 1947:

> It is half a year since I left America. How much that time in your country has meant to me! All you many people I know are my friends who pray for me.

Amongst other things my work in Holland has been to tell people here what I learned in America. For example, I tell them about Youth for Christ, about Breakfast Groups, about the Christian Businessmen's Committee, about the Gideons, to show them how America understands the mission call. It inspires the Dutch. I hope that people here will get the same spirit of action. Many people in Holland have a wrong idea about America, just as I had before I visited you. During my trip through your country I learned to love the American people.

The house in Bloemendaal had been open for a year. Corrie wrote:

Most of the war victims are back into society. Now all sorts of tired people needing a period of rest spiritually and physically can come to the beautiful house with its large park. We also held eight conferences during a two-month period for young people who want to use their spare time for the spreading of the Gospel.

We need a far bigger house where we can have longer conferences, a Bible-school, a retreat and rehabilitation home at the same time. We know that God will give us the house and the money we need for it at His time.

In July 1947 she wrote to Bobbie Halliday, her clothes supplier from Canada:

My dear Bobbie,

Today I wear the green dress you gave me last year! So often I think of you, also during the winter when in the cold I had your nice warm cardigan.

Like most effective Christian leaders, Corrie read a lot. Until a stroke took her ability to read when she was in her mideighties, she read avidly with an attitude that always wanted to learn. Her letter to Bobbie continued:

Did I send you the book *In His Presence* by Kenyon? This book gave me much blessing. Write if you did not get it, and I will send it. I cannot believe everything that is in it, but it gave me much light and made Jesus' victory more real for me. We *are* God's children. We may go to God's throne every moment of the day or night. We have legal rights to take all the promises of the Bible. Demons reign over us by bluff; they have no real power. Perhaps they have a little bit, but the power of Jesus is far and far greater.

Then she made a request to Bobbie:

My house "Schapenduinen" is blessed. It is not large enough, and there is a chance I can get an unfurnished house where people can sleep in their own rooms. Can you perhaps help me by sending curtains or tablecloths? In America I saw those cotton bags for chicken food. Could you get them? Don't worry if you can't. God will take care of everything.

A Face from the Past in Germany

In the latter part of 1947, nearly three years after her release from imprisonment, Corrie went back to Germany. It was then that she had an encounter with one of her former guards. Those who know Corrie's story probably have heard the following many times, but I would not be true to her memory if I did not include this vital part of her message—forgiving our enemies:

It was at a church service in Munich that I saw him, the former SS man who had stood guard at the shower room door in the processing center at Ravensbrück. He was the first of our actual jailers that I had seen since that time. And suddenly it was all there—the roomful of mocking men, the heaps of clothing, Betsie's pain-blanched face.

He came up to me as the church was emptying, beaming and bowing. "How grateful I am for your message, Fraulein," he said. "To think that, as you say, He has washed my sins away."

His hand was thrust out to shake mine. And I, who had preached so often to the people in Bloemendaal the need to forgive, kept my hand at my side. Even as the angry, vengeful thoughts boiled through me, I saw the sin of them. Jesus Christ had died for this man; was I going to ask for more? *Lord Jesus,* I prayed, *forgive me and help me to forgive him.*

I tried to smile, and I struggled to raise my hand. I could not. I felt nothing, not the slightest spark of warmth or charity. And so again I breathed a silent prayer. *Jesus, I cannot forgive him. Give me your forgiveness.*

As I took his hand, the most incredible thing happened. From my shoulder and along my arm and through my hand a current seemed to pass from me to him while into my heart sprang a love for this stranger that almost overwhelmed me.

And so I discovered that it is not on our forgiveness any more than on our goodness that the world's healing hinges, but on His. When He tells us to love our enemies, He gives, along with the command, the love itself.[1]

I heard Corrie tell this story at every meeting to which I accompanied her. She gave this example of the importance of forgiveness for 33 years throughout the world.

1948-49

It was estimated that nine million people were without homes in postwar Germany. They were living on bombed sites, in half-standing houses and in heaps of rubble. Corrie was invited by a church group to speak to and work among one hundred families living in an abandoned factory building. Sheets and blankets divided each family's living space from the next in an attempt to provide some kind of privacy, but it was not possible to escape the sounds of babies crying, radios set at high volume or family squabbles. Corrie decided that in order to bring her message of the victory of the Lord Jesus she needed to thoroughly identify with the homeless people and live as they lived, not returning to the hostel room outside the city that the church had provided for her. After she had been living in the abandoned factory for several months, the director of a relief organization came to see her. He had heard about her rehabilitation work in Holland and wanted her to start something similar in Germany.

"We've located a place for the work," he told her. "It is a former concentration camp that has just been released by the government."

She drove with him to Darmstadt to see the camp. Rolls of rusting barbed wire still surrounded it, and a cinder path led to gray barrack buildings. But in her mind's eye Corrie saw something else. Betsie's dream was about to be turned into reality. I have before me a photograph of those buildings after they had been prepared to receive German people in need. They are clean and neat and painted spring-green. And there are window boxes.

These activities were interspersed with much travel. Although not many records of her comings and goings in 1948 exist, we know that she spent April 15, her 56th birthday, in Los Angeles, where she was speaking to students at the University of California. The student who acted as her chauffeur on that day later wrote:

She taught me what the true love of Jesus Christ can do in the life of a chosen vessel. Her spiritual depth and insight into Biblical truths, coupled with the compassionate understanding that had come from her time in a Nazi concentration camp, left me with the desire to do more with my life than just earn a good living.

Before the end of 1949, five years after her death, Betsie's dreams had already been established for several years, and a larger rehabilitation house in Holland had been acquired. This is confirmed in another letter Corrie wrote just before Christmas that year to her friends in America and Canada.

> After seven months in Germany and the rather rough crossing in the freighter, I had lost weight but gained it very soon in this land of plenty.
>
> From Holland, Bloemendaal, good news. The house, Zonneduin (meaning "Sun Dune"), bought in faith, had to be altered. We have now 28 beds. It is a home for people who need a time of rest—house mothers, patients who had to leave the hospitals but are not yet able to do their work, and many different kinds of people who find there a home with good nursing and—what is the most important—come in contact with the Gospel of Jesus Christ. The builders were not yet paid and telephoned that if we did not pay that week they should go to a lawyer. The lady director said, "Then I go to my heavenly lawyer." She went on her knees and told the Lord that there was no money to pay. The next day our Queen Juliana sent 4,000 guilders, about $1,300. So the King of kings moved a queen to help us out.
>
> In Germany, the former concentration camp where we have now 85 refugees, the barracks had to be painted and the walls here and there strengthened. We hope that the barracks will be less drafty now in the coming winter. One hundred forty refugees left to live now in their own built houses.

"Let Us Expect Much—Then God Gives Much"

In October 1950 Corrie wrote to her friends that she had arrived back in Holland in August. Tante Corrie always had a great sense of urgency:

> It seems as if the world is going down. We know it is. Romans 8:19: "The creation waits in eager expectation for the sons of God to be revealed." Knowing this, let us use our time

not in straightening pictures in a house on fire but jumping into the work of saving souls, losing our lives for Jesus' sake and thus finding them. Not with sad faces, but filled with the Holy Spirit and joy, knowing that Jesus not only cures but also renews. We have a Savior who not only died for our sins, but the moment He went to sit at the right hand of the Father He began to live for us. The devil accuses us night and day but our advocate, Jesus, says that we are God's righteousness in Him.

So we are able to live not like beggars, but as King's children—yes, God's children. Tell that to the devil; that is the best way to resist him. Act on the Word of God; you will experience that it is true. A believer is a possessor. Let us expect much—then God gives much. Let us not try to live a resurrection-life with Christ without following Him in His death. Then He can fill us with His love, which is victorious over all circumstances.

In December 1951 Corrie wrote again to Bobbie Halliday, who continued to keep her supplied with dresses:

O, that your prayers for me may be answered and that God may use me to "ignite the spark into flame," like you wrote. I am thankful but not satisfied. I have so many opportunities. Pray that I may be used one hundred percent everywhere. "Streams of living water" is what I pray for.

The Weaver

In February 1952 Corrie received a letter from the superintendent of the American Board of Missions to the Jews. It contained a poem called *The Weaver* by Grant Colfax Tullar, which from then on Corrie frequently quoted.

She used the poem in a very special way. Corrie liked to use visual aids in her work, and one principal aid was her crown

Corrie begins her travels, U.S.A., 1946   PHOTO COURTESY OF THE CORRIE TEN BOOM HOUSE FOUNDATION

embroidery. She often used it to help her audiences see their circumstances "a little bit from God's point of view."

She would begin, "When the worst happens in the life of a child of God—and for me it did—the best remains and the very best is yet to be." Then she would slip out of her bag a piece of shiny blue cloth which, you may recall from chapter 1, when she and I were packing for our first journey together I had mistaken for embroidery. She would hold it up backward so that the audience found themselves staring at the tangled, knotted, untidy,

130

yellow threads on the underside of the cloth, and she would quote *The Weaver:*

> My life is like a weaving
> Between my God and me.
> I do not choose the colors;
> He worketh steadily.
>
> Ofttimes He chooseth sorrow,
> And I in foolish pride
> Forget He sees the upper
> And I the underside.

As she spoke the last two lines, Corrie would turn the cloth around so everybody would see a golden crown instead of tangled threads, and she would continue:

> Not till the loom is silent
> And the shuttles cease to fly
> Will God unroll the canvas
> And explain the reason why.
>
> The dark threads are as needful
> In the skillful Weaver's hand
> As the threads of gold and silver
> In the pattern He has planned.[2]

A Blessed Life

In 1952 Corrie made her first visit to Japan. On her sixtieth birthday, April 15, 1952, Corrie wrote to Bobbie Halliday from the YWCA in Tokyo:

The weeks and days before leaving the States were full and fuller up 'til the last evening. Then I spent four days in Honolulu, where I spoke *sixteen* times. A time of great blessing, and I

Corrie at 60 years of age in Japan, 1952, with missionary Mrs. Mitchell

was not tired at all. . . . Japan is different from anything else. I preached Sunday and had to leave my shoes outside.

And in November 1952:

I traveled over the northern island of Japan. Here I learned to know the real Japanese life. Sleeping, eating and living in Japanese style was very interesting but not always easy for an old girl like I am. But the Lord gave me much strength. When my weakness leans on His might, all seems light. Thank you for your prayers and help! Yes, Ravensbrück was a good training. Sometimes when I sleep on a dirty bed on the floor in a small hotel far away in the country, I say to myself, "Ravensbrück was worse."

Corrie worked in Japan for nine months. Although she believed God had called her to proceed to Taiwan, New Zealand and South Africa, lack of funds for the journey prevented her leaving Japan when she had hoped.

But Corrie knew the joy of trusting in the Lord with a faithful heart, and this became very evident when she referred to her financial needs in her letters during this time. By now Corrie had a mailing list of thousands of people. In one letter she wrote:

Friends often ask questions and want to know more about the various projects that are supported by the funds I receive, so I will tell you about them and their prayer needs.

First, there is the International Home, Zonneduin in Holland. The small charge of two dollars a day, which includes meals, does not cover the cost of running such a home; yet it has been a haven of rest to many who could not pay even that much.

Second, there is the former concentration camp in Darmstadt, Germany, where 85 refugees are living while they work and build their own homes. When they move out, others take their place. This camp often needs repairs, in addition to helping these people become established.

Third, there is the sending of these newsletters to about 18,000 in fifteen different countries. Pray that the Lord will bless this letter and for the other people on my mailing list. Many have spiritual needs, and about a thousand are prisoners.

Fourth, there are my expenses to carry the message that Jesus is Victor around the world. Thanks to all the dear people who, as Phillips translates Romans 12:13, "never grudged me a bed or a meal." I seldom have to use God's money for personal expenses. Traveling from place to place is always the big item.

Although Corrie told her audiences about the financial needs for her rehabilitation house in Holland and for the work in Germany, she never asked for money for herself.

She did eventually continue with her planned trip into other parts of Asia. From Taiwan in January 1953, after describing her work there, she wrote:

I told you here a little snapshot of my life. What a blessed life I have! In churches, streets, prisons, Bible schools and missionary meetings, God uses me. Late in the evenings I am tired, but God gives me always a healthy sleep each night, and then I am peppy again. The joy of the Lord is my strength [see Nehemiah 8:10].

Is it always easy? No. Of course, I have moments that the spirit of self-pity asks entrance into my heart. One day recently cockroaches ate holes in my dress, the dirty scoundrels. I try to travel light and have not too many dresses with me, and just that day I had no money to pay my room, though it was no high amount at all. I also needed money for my air ticket, for the letters to my mailing lists in America and Japan. I did not really worry but asked God, "May I tell my friends about my shortage of money?"

The Lord answered only, "Trust Me!" I was so very happy about that answer and went to bed wondering how the Lord should help me out this time.

The next day was very busy, and I came home very late. For the first time mail reached me in Taiwan. There were 36 letters. The first I opened had a check of $150, and then there was a letter from [my representative in the U.S.] to tell me about many Christmas gifts for me in money. I had money for every need of that moment, even for the air tickets. It is no risk to trust the Lord. Faith is a problem for those who do not know the Lord and the Word.

Does that mean always answered prayers? Surely not, although no problem is too great or too small for the Lord, and He is far more ready to answer our prayers than we are ready to pray. Sometimes He allows deep ways.

eight

In the Power
of the Holy Spirit

1954–1959

On October 22, 1953, Corrie's beloved sister Nollie died at the age of 63. Away from Holland at the time, Corrie received the news by telegram. In a letter to her friends she wrote:

That afternoon Nollie had had a Bible study group at her home. In the evening she passed away, only one step from earth to heaven. What a joy for her to be with the Lord. For me earth is much emptier, heaven still fuller. Nollie went a train earlier. Not lost, but gone before.

Nollie wrote to me every week. We were very much united in the Lord. Three letters reached me still after her death. She helped me often with good illustrations. In one of her letters she wrote:

A king gave a little golden staff to his jester and said, "Keep this staff till you find a greater fool than you are, and then give it to him." When the king was dying, the jester came to him. "I am going on a long journey to a country far away," said the king. The jester answered, "But I do not see any suitcases. Did you not make any preparations?" "No," said the king, "I made neither reservations nor preparations." Then the jester gave him the little staff and said, "Now I have found a greater fool than I am."

Is not that a good one? By the way, how about you? Read 1 John 5:11–13.

A Turning Point

Shortly after Nollie's death came a turning point in Corrie's ministry—such an extraordinary one that her countenance changed. When I look at photographs of her from before and after that year, 1954, I see that she was given an unusual empowerment to continue her work. Her face had a new radiance and love, and it remained there until the end of her life. It began with a puzzling time. It is best that she tell the story in her own words:

As I stood in the railroad station in Basel, Switzerland, waiting for my luggage, I suddenly realized that I did not know where I was supposed to go. For the eight years after my release from prison, I had been traveling all over the world at the direction of God. Many times I did not know why I was to go to a certain place until I arrived. It had become almost second nature not to make my plans and then to ask for God's signature. Rather, I had learned to wait for God's plan and then write my name on the schedule.

But this time was different. Suddenly I was in Basel and had no idea why or who I was to contact. Besides, I was tired. Sleeping each night in a different bed and always living out of a suitcase had worn me down. I felt a sensation of panic in my heart and sat down, trying to remember to whom I was going. At 61 years of age, could it be that I was so overworked that I was losing my memory? Or even worse, had God withdrawn His conscious Presence from me and was letting me walk alone for a season?

In my suitcase I found an address. It had no meaning to me, but it was all I had to go on. I took a taxi to the place, but the people at that address were complete strangers and had never heard of me. By now I was desperate—and a little bit frightened. The people told me of another man I might contact. Perhaps he would know who I was and why I had come to Basel. I took another taxi, but this gentleman, too, was unfamiliar with my work.

For eight years the Lord had guided me step by step. At no time had I been confused or afraid. Now I was both—unable to recognize the Presence of God. Surely He was still guiding me, but like the pilot who flies into the clouds I now was having to rely on instruments rather than sight. I decided to turn around and go back home to Holland, there to await further orders.

Because of a severe storm, the planes were not flying. I had to travel by train. Arriving in Haarlem, I started toward the phone near the station to call our rehabilitation house in Bloemendaal where I was to stay. But on the way to the phone booth I slipped on the wet pavement, and before I knew it I was sprawled in the street. A sharp pain shot through my hip, and I was unable to stand.

"Oh, Lord," I prayed, "lay Your hand on my hip and take away this horrible pain." Instantly the pain disappeared, but I was still unable to get up. Kind people assisted me to a taxi, where a policeman asked if he could help.

"What is your name?" he asked.

"Corrie ten Boom."

He looked surprised and questioned me further. "Are you a member of the family of that name whom we arrested during the war?"

"That is right."

During the war, many Dutch policemen had stayed in the service of the Gestapo, not as traitors but for the express purpose of helping political prisoners. This man had been on duty that day my family was arrested.

"I am so sorry about your accident," he said sympathetically, "but I am glad to see you again. I will never forget that night in the police station. You all were sitting or lying on the floor of the station. Your old father was there with all his children and many of your friends. I have often told my colleagues that there was an atmosphere of peace and joy in our station that night, as if you were going to a feast instead of prison and death."

He paused and looked at me kindly as if trying to remember my face. "Your father said before he tried to sleep, 'Let us pray together.' And then he read Psalm 91."

"You remember!" I exclaimed. After eight years that policeman had remembered which psalm my father had read. For a fleeting moment, sitting in that old taxi on a Haarlem street while the rain pelted the roof, I allowed myself the pain of looking backward. It was in this same city that we had been arrested. In fact, the prison was only a short distance from where I was sitting. That was the last time our family had been together. Within ten days Father was dead. Then later Betsie. All gone. And this policeman still remembered.

"He who dwells in the shelter of the Most High will rest in the shadow of the Almighty" (Psalm 91:1). Now the message was clear. Although there was no light to guide me, I was still in God's will. Actually, when one is resting (abiding) under the shadow of the Almighty there will be no light, but that is only because God's Presence is so near.

I leaned back in the seat. "Dear God, when this shadow came over me I thought you had departed. Now I understand it was because you were drawing closer. I eagerly await whatever you have planned for me."

Eager I was, but not so patient. An x-ray showed my hip was not broken, only badly bruised. The doctor said I would have to remain in bed for several weeks for it to heal. . . . I was put to bed in Zonneduin, our rehabilitation house, unable to move or turn over without the help of a nurse.

I was a very impatient patient. I had only five days to get to a student conference in Germany, and as the days slipped by and I realized my hip was not healing fast enough to make the conference, I grew irritable.

"Is there not a Christian in all Haarlem who can pray for me to be healed?" I asked. My friends sent for a particular minister in the city who was known to have laid hands on the sick for healing. That same afternoon he came to my room. Standing beside my bed he asked, "Is there any unconfessed sin in your life?"

What an odd question, I thought. I understood he had agreed to come pray for my healing, but was it his job to get so personal about my sins and attitudes? However, I did not have far to look. My impatience and the demanding attitude I had displayed toward my nurse had been wrong—very wrong. I asked her to come to the room and I repented of my sin, asking both her and God to forgive me.

Satisfied, this gentle man then reached over and laid his hands on my head. Only a few months earlier, my sister Nollie had died. Ever since my heart had been broken with mourning. I had the feeling of being left all alone and knew that the insecurity I had experienced had contributed to my being here in this bed, rather than in Germany with the students. Yet as this tall, handsome man laid his hands on me and prayed, I felt a great stream of power flowing through me. Such great joy. The mourning left, and I wanted to sing with David, "Thou hast turned for me my mourning into dancing: thou hast put off my sackcloth, and girded me with gladness" (Psalm 30:11, KJV).

I felt the Presence of the Lord Jesus all around me, and I felt His love flowing through me and over me as if I were being immersed in an ocean of grace. My joy became so intense that I finally prayed, *No more, Lord, no more.* My heart felt it was about to burst, so great was the joy. I knew it was that wonderful experience promised by Jesus—the Baptism in the Holy Spirit.[1]

The Holy Spirit

Corrie did not use the term "baptism in the Holy Spirit" exclusively. She talked about the "fullness of the Holy Spirit." She taught the people, "The question is not whether you have the Holy Spirit [or not], but whether the Holy Spirit has you." A strongly grounded member of the Dutch Reformed Church, she knew that it is only through the Holy Spirit that a person can receive the Lord Jesus Christ. He comes to each person at his or her conversion. But she strongly believed that it was possible for a person to be only partly full of the Holy Spirit. She prayed for the fullness of the Holy Spirit every day and often said that Ephesians 5:18 contained the most joyful commandment of the Bible: "Be filled with the Spirit." And each time she used that text in her talks she explained that the Greek tense of the verb means "be being filled"—a continuous state.

After her hip healed, Corrie made her way to Germany for her speaking appointments, and she said she was "still filled with joy overflowing." It was only after she arrived that she realized why God had chosen that particular time to fill her with His Holy Spirit:

> For in Germany, for the first time, I came face-to-face with many people who were demonized. Had I gone in my own power I would have been consumed. Now, going in the power of the Holy Spirit, God was able to work much deliverance through me as we commanded demons to be cast out in the name of the Lord Jesus Christ.[2]

Hidden Behind the Cross

All through the 1950s, Corrie traveled and spoke constantly. Her journeys usually were made alone. When she and I first began to travel together in 1976 she told me she was glad she had a companion. "In the first years of my work I went around the world twice—six years each time. It was often lonely. Sometimes I bought a *Reader's Digest* for company as I left my new friends and journeyed to the next country," she said.

Corrie was completely undenominational. She worked with every leader who loved the Lord Jesus. At the beginning of 1955 she wrote to her friends that she was working in Canada "with much joy." She went on:

> God blesses the work very much. My schedule is very full, but the Lord is my strength. I speak not only in many different churches, but also in jails, universities, men's and ladies' clubs, high schools, etc. I am really ecumenical. Today I spoke in an Anglican church and wore a robe of a Baptist minister, and with me Dutch Reformed, I thought that was pretty good.

Corrie was also able to relinquish a work she had started but could not complete. She described an instance in Darmstadt, Germany, where she already had the camp for German refugees:

> There was a Deaconess House there that needed help to rebuild a ruined refugee home for girls. I had then just enough money to have the ruins removed and the foundation and basement built. Now I have a photo of the house, built and ready to use. So sometimes God uses me to start a work that I cannot finish but gives vision and courage to the people to go on.

Corrie also seemed almost indefatigable. In May 1955, having arrived to speak at Dr. Tozer's church in Chicago a few hours early, she took the opportunity to write to her friends:

> In Canada I had to have a little operation and was a week in the hospital. I took it easy afterward, during ten days, by speaking not more than once a day and doing little traveling. But now the Lord has renewed my strength and healed me one hundred percent. My schedule is now, God willing, June and July, Mexico, August–October, west coast of America from Vancouver to San

Diego. Pray much for me, will you? Pray that people who hear me may forget the channel, seeing only Him. Pray that Corrie ten Boom may be hidden behind the cross of Jesus.

Corrie received the voluntary help of secretaries during her stays in various cities and sometimes for a portion of her travels:

> For the last quarter of 1955 God gave me a very good secretary who has now returned to her home in Canada. I am praying that the Lord will give me a permanent teammate-companion-secretary who is willing to dedicate her life one hundred percent to the Lord's work. My, she must have so many qualities to be fitted for this work that I sometimes think I am praying for what is called in Holland "a sheep with five legs" [the impossible]. But the Lord knows the right person and the right time: I wait upon Him.

To Australasia with Revival Fellowship

Early in 1956 Corrie was invited by Dr. J. Edwin Orr to take part in revival meetings in Australasia as part of his Revival Fellowship Team. He was an authority in the study of revival, and Tante Corrie called his books on this subject "a great contribution to the story of the evangelical Church." She had the utmost respect for him and frequently referred to him and his work.

In June 1957 she wrote:

> Australia is not an easy country to work in, but God blesses the efforts of the Revival Team with whom I work. Sometimes we work together as a team in one place but often spread out over several suburbs and hold campaigns of one or two weeks' duration in each. We do not yet see revival but know that the Holy Spirit works in the hearts of many Christians, and prayer groups are formed to pray for revival. Our schedule is full. Three

meetings a day is the regular program, and often there is no free day between the campaigns.

But we work for a General who has never lost a battle, so it is worthwhile to give our one hundred percent. Will you please pray for us for wisdom to arrange skillfully and for strength from on high for our spirits, minds and bodies?

Not long after this Tante Corrie headed to New Zealand. From there she wrote:

Mrs. McKenzie, a dear saint in Otorohanga, had heard me in Auckland and organized a campaign in her own town. She wrote me: "Corrie, I love you already for the happy message you bring. I will take good care of you and not give you too many meetings. But there is a crippled girl in a hospital I will visit with you. She is very near to the valley of the shadow of death but hopes to meet you before she dies."

That same day Mrs. McKenzie herself died suddenly. I did not know the name of the crippled girl she had wanted me to visit. I prayed that the Lord would guide me to her, and I found her. Poor little Grace. She was a dwarf with hands out of place. I never saw such a poor body. But her soul was radiant because she was filled with the Holy Spirit. I could not understand everything she said—her voice was very weak—but I understood that she said, "Go to my mother, please, and bring her to the Lord." We prayed together for her, and that same day I had the joy of bringing the mother to the great decision for Jesus Christ. When Grace heard it she said, "Now I can die." Two days later she died.

Also during her time with Revival Fellowship Corrie met a special young man:

While in Melbourne I met a Dutchman from my own hometown of Haarlem, who asked me, "Do you remember that thirteen years ago you sent me a Jewish baby of two weeks old?"

"No," I answered, "I only remember that there were a hundred babies from a Jewish Orphanage and that we distributed them to a hundred families, but I really do not remember to whom I sent them."

"Well, here is one of them," he answered, and before me stood Martin, a lovely boy. He looked with interest at the Dutch lady who had saved his life thirteen years before. A bit later I had the great joy of bringing him to a decision for the Lord Jesus.

Next day in school he gave his first testimony, "Boys," he said, "yesterday I met the lady who saved my life when I was two weeks old, and boys, listen. I think I will be a good boy now, for she has told me how to ask Jesus to come into my heart, and He will make me good."

And also from Australia Corrie wrote about her love for prison ministry:

In a women's prison I gave an invitation to accept the Lord Jesus. One woman came to the Lord, and she told me, "I have been sentenced to two weeks in jail. I know why I had to be here, for I found here my Savior Jesus Christ." *Work in prisons is still the work that has my heart more than any other.*

In November 1957, Corrie's work with Revival Fellowship came to a close. "After two years in Australasia, I am now called to India, Borneo, Korea, Japan and wherever the Lord leads me."

Water Baptism

On March 20, 1958, Corrie was baptized by immersion in the William Carey Baptist Church in Calcutta by Walter G. Corbett. Later she was to tell about it:

I was re-baptized in a small Baptist church in India. In the morning I spoke to Baptists about baptism in the morning service. In the afternoon I was baptized again by immersion. I think baptism by immersion is Biblical—fuller than by sprinkling. This baptism is a better symbol of being "buried with Christ" by going under the water and then rising up with Him out of the water purified.

A Discovery of God's Provision

Finally in 1959, at the end of this decade, fifteen years after her release from concentration camp, Corrie was part of a group that revisited Ravensbrück to honor Betsie and the thousands of other women who had died there. Checking the records, she discovered that her own release had been the result of a clerical error. A week after she was released all women her age died in the gas chamber.

nine

Lessons from Argentina and Africa

1960–1963

In 1960 Corrie received the answer to her prayer for a permanent traveling companion. The solitary life had never become easy for the pronounced extrovert. I remember her saying to me when I joined her in 1976, "At the beginning of my travels around the world I went on a journey that lasted six years. Soon after that came another world journey that took six years. Then the Lord gave me Conny, who was with me for seven years, then Ellen, who was with me for nearly nine years, and now I have you."

Conny

Here is how Corrie described the gifted first companion God gave her: "The Lord saw and supplied my need in the person of Conny van Hoogstraten, a beautiful, young Dutch woman. . . . I met her on one of my visits to England, where she was attending a Bible school. We laughed much together, for the

Lord had given her an infectious sense of humor and a happy laughter."

Corrie and Conny were to undertake extensive work journeys together between 1960 and 1967. Corrie said of her companion, "We really do three times as much work than I did when I was alone."

In May and June 1961 Corrie wrote about one of her early travels with Conny:

> I am now sitting in the midst of a palm wood in Kerala State. The wind makes a beautiful music with the waving palm leaves. The weather is hot. Often I pray, "Lord, be my coolness!" And He is.
>
> Three months in India—what an experience! This country of millions of people gives such an opportunity to reach Christians and to show them the victorious life, and to tell sinners the way of salvation through Jesus. Conny reaches often the children. She arranges meetings for them in the time that I reach the grownups. Sometimes it happens that first the children come to the Lord and after that the parents come. A man told me that he was so happy that his little son had accepted the Lord Jesus. He wanted to do the same but was not able. I found out that he had fallen into witchcraft-sin. I read Deuteronomy 18:10–13 with him, and he confessed. But only after we had cast out the demons was he free to receive the Lord Jesus as his personal Savior. How we need wisdom and strength from on high. Without Jesus we can do nothing, nothing—with Him much, very much" [see John 15:5].

Lessons from Africa

Leaving India and going on to Africa, Corrie wrote to her friends about some of the most important lessons that helped her lead a victorious life:

147

Living for the Moment

Dear Friends,

The Lord gives me always the grace to live in the present, not in the future or past. In India I thought, "In this country is the most important work I ever had to do. How I love the Indians!" Now I am in Africa, and I can say the same. Africa is the most inspiring surrounding. Such openness and hunger for the messages I did not see elsewhere, and I surely can add—How I love the Africans!

The Answer for Problems of the Heart

The eight months Conny and Corrie spent in Africa from April to December of 1961 were particularly significant:

This year from April until December we traveled in active service from Ethiopia to Cape Town, working in eight countries. All the time I was conscious of the fact that I was in the midst of political tensions. It has made me still more thankful that God has called us here, for the root of all the controversies is sin, and Jesus is the answer.

To me the climax was again when I could speak in prisons. I wish that more Christian men and women felt the call to work in prisons and reformatories. We know the answer for the problems in the heart of every decent or indecent sinner. Jesus says to all, "Come to me, and I will give you rest." And how very precious is every soul in His loving eyes.

Walking in the Light

When Corrie and Conny arrived in East Africa for the first time in 1961, the famous East Africa Revival had already been taking place for many years. Its distinguishing mark was that Christians took very seriously the importance of "walking in the light with each other," following the New Testament's instruction: "If we walk in the light, as He is in the light, we have fellowship with one another, and the blood of Jesus His Son purifies us from every sin" (see 1 John 1:7). As soon as East African Christians found themselves out of fellowship with another, they became strongly convicted to confess their sin and ask forgiveness of each other and the Lord. Having been cleansed from sin with fellowship restored, they could experience victorious life. If Christians failed to reconcile with each other, it could be that the Lord would not answer their prayers for growth and continued revival.

I was to see "walking in the light" in action myself when I lived and worked in East Africa in the mid-1960s. Its practice is undoubtedly a big reason for the ongoing revival. Tante Corrie found it such an important lesson that she taught it for the rest of her life. And she definitely lived it—in the first place with Conny!

Every day I am more thankful that God gave me my "Timothy," my co-pilot and co-everything. We live "in the light" as soon as the enemy tries to attack the personal relationship between us, that strategic point for many missionaries. We repent together and to each other. I am an old veteran, hardened in the battle, and especially during those terrible months in the concentration camp I learned not to mind little hardships. As a "tramp for the Lord" I have lived in more than a thousand homes during the last fifteen years. [Conny] has still to get used to this life, and to learn that her sufficiency is of the Lord in all circumstances of life. I believe that it is one of the secrets of a happy Christian's life: to draw on the Unfailing Source—Jesus Christ—for every situation and every new adjustment we have to make. But the Lord gives us much grace, and we praise Him for giving us this work to do together. We both enjoy life.

The Sin of Worry

In her thousands of messages, Corrie often taught about the sin of worry. Nancy, one of her hostesses during that long journey through Africa in 1961, later wrote about this lesson that Corrie taught her:

> She was sitting in the front seat beside me in my old car, and I asked her, "Corrie, what is your secret? How do you live in the light?" As I spoke, the windshield wiper squeaked slightly as it cleared away the heavy raindrops of a sudden shower.
>
> "That is the secret," Corrie said, pointing to the moving windshield wiper. "It is the little decent sins—things like worry and unforgiveness—that cloud our spiritual vision. Don't wait until nightfall, Nancy. You started the wiper as soon as you could not see clearly."
>
> "But, Corrie, worry isn't a sin."
>
> "Oh, yes, it is, Nancy. Worry is a sin. If you are worrying you are not trusting God. Not to trust God is a sin."
>
> But still I pressed her, "You cannot tell me that things like impatience and irritability are really sins. These are character defects."
>
> "They *are* sins," she interrupted, "and there is no verse in the Bible that says God forgives excuses. You will never grow if you bring God only excuses."

Removing Rags in Argentina

Early in 1962, shortly after their eight months' stay in Africa, Corrie and Conny spent a month in Argentina. Her letter to her friends gives us another clear lesson from her life—how she quickly turned to the Lord, instead of complaining when plans seemed to have gone wrong.

> This was the first time God called us to go to this country. After forty hours of traveling by jet plane from Entebbe, Uganda, we arrived in Buenos Aires. It is always a thrill to be called to a new country, and we were looking forward to the blessings the Lord had in store for us.

The minister who met us at the airport asked us [if] we had not received his letter. He had written us that it was perhaps better not to come at this time to Argentina since it was holiday time. The key people were out of town, and no meetings could be arranged. After our talk I asked myself why the Lord had sent us here, but I trusted Him, for He never makes a mistake.

The first meeting I had was some hours' traveling away, and then I could speak for twenty ladies. The enemy told me that it was all wrong to go to this little church, since I am so used to speaking for large congregations. But then I repented of my pride. How often we forget that we are "nobodies," just gloves who cannot do anything by themselves. It is the Hand in the glove who is able. "Without Me you can do nothing," Jesus says [see John 15:5].

And now, after having been in Argentina for a month, I can tell about unusual blessings. Dr. Gwen Shepherd, a children's doctor and specialist for polio cases, gave me her furnished flat to live in, and I enjoyed it very much to be for a whole month in the same rooms. And God opened doors and hearts. Students, doctors, prisoners and Jews were reached.

Dr. Shepherd reported on Corrie's visit some years later:

For four weeks I translated Corrie's message into Spanish. One morning I came to the flat and found Corrie sitting on the blue divan tearing up a piece of cloth and stuffing the strips into her flashlight.

"Corrie, what on earth are you doing?"

"Preparing my props," she answered with a twinkle in her eye.

"Props?"

"Yes, props for my talks. Sometimes university students object to visual aids, but I find that even intellectuals sometimes need practical illustrations in order to understand my

151

message. Everyone can see that a flashlight cannot shine if it is full of rags." I was soon to see the effect of her "props."

"Gwen, have you ever been in a prison?"

"No, Corrie, I have not."

"Would you like to visit one?"

"Can't say I am especially keen."

But, keen or not, Corrie and I were flown in a small army plane halfway across the country as VIP visitors to the model prison at Santa Rosa de la Pampas, where she was invited to speak to the men.

"Men," she said, "I know what it is like to be behind bars and to be shut up in solitary confinement."

How they listened—a hall full of tidily dressed prisoners, with the Governor, his wife and little daughter and the rest of the prison authorities in the front row. They heard Corrie tell about God's love for each one of them and how life could be wonderful even behind bars, if they walked in His light. Out came her flashlight. A school-boyish sniggering swept over the hall as she vainly tried to click it—a reaction that quickly turned to a hushed silence as one by one the rags of sin were pulled out of it.

A few months later, shortly after her seventieth birthday, April 15, 1962, Corrie wrote to her prayer partners:

This morning I prayed again that I may decrease and that Jesus may increase. Then I received a letter from the mayor of my hometown, Haarlem, Holland, in which he wrote that it has pleased Her Majesty the Queen to give me the decoration of Knight in the Order of Orange Nassau. When I read that letter I fear that a little rag came into my flashlight. It was the sin of pride, but I brought it to the Lord. He forgave and cleansed me with His blood, and now I just accept this honor from the hand of the Lord and my Queen with great thankfulness.

Will you pray that more and more people in the meetings may see Jesus and that I may be hidden behind the cross?

Ever the Learner

After her Argentinean adventures, Corrie and Conny traveled to the United States of America. During Billy Graham's crusade in Chicago in 1962 they signed on as two of the many counselors who at the end of each evening would counsel those who responded to Graham's invitation to accept the Lord Jesus Christ. Although she had brought the Gospel to others since her childhood, she was ever the learner:

> Our days are so full and blessed, and I had a great experience to be in Chicago and join the campaign of Billy Graham. Conny and I both studied the training course for counselors, and like the other 4,000 counselors we worked as much as possible after the meetings in the inquiry rooms. We learned much, also for the future. To counsel standing in the midst of hundreds of people embarrassed me sometimes. I am sure I made many mistakes. But what joy it was to see people coming to a first decision for Jesus Christ, or to a new surrender.

Years later Corrie herself would be invited to give her testimony from crusade platforms.

And during that same time in 1962, Corrie wrote something that showed how she continually let her Lord teach her as well:

> On one occasion I was very cross with the important gentleman who had arranged my program. Everything was very badly organized, not because of incapability but through sheer carelessness. After the meeting I told him what I thought of him in no uncertain terms. He looked rather astounded but did not say a word.
>
> However, that night God had a word with me. I rang the gentleman up the next morning and apologized.
>
> "Oh, that's okay," he answered, "I told my wife about the dressing-down I had received last night and how I felt

like a guilty schoolboy being reprimanded by the teacher. But I also told her that I really deserved it, so please don't apologize."

"But," I said to him, "I do owe you an apology. What I said to you was right, but not the way I said it!"

A Movie?

Several times during the decade of the sixties, Corrie asked her friends and prayer partners to pray that her book *A Prisoner and Yet* . . . would become a motion picture. At the time of the Cuban missile crisis of 1962 she wrote:

Some weeks ago two American Christians met to discuss the possibilities of what they could do for their country. They both knew that in the USA much is being done to fight communism by organizations such as the Christian Anti-Communist League, which by means of literature and the spoken word informs the public about the nature and aim of communism. These men asked each other: "Is it necessary that we, too, use our time to fight communism? Is it not very necessary to show people that when the worst happens in the life of a Christian the best remains? Jesus is not limited in giving His strength and comfort in times of hardship."

The next day these two men heard about the possibility of making a film of my book, *A Prisoner and Yet.* . . . They saw this as an answer to their questions. In that book God gave me grace to show that in my life Jesus' light was stronger than the deepest darkness of the concentration camp. Now these men will do their best to have this book filmed.

Will you pray for that enterprise? Pray that good actors may be found and that the words of the Gospel may be spoken by people who stand behind the message with their faith and life. It is possible that this film will be used to bring the Gospel in places where it never has been heard before.

Corrie's faith and prayers would be rewarded in the coming decade when John and Elizabeth Sherrill developed and enlarged on the story in *A Prisoner and Yet* . . . The book *The Hiding Place* would be published in 1971. And in 1975, the movie of the same name would be released by World Wide Pictures, the filmmaking arm of the Billy Graham Evangelistic Association.

ten

When Bad Things Happen

1963–1968

The year 1963 would take Corrie and Conny to several places around the world. Each one offered unique ways for Corrie to share her message before she headed home to Holland for a forced rest.

A Retreat Center in Uganda

It was God's plan that Corrie spend more time in Africa as the 1960s unfolded. She wrote to her friends early in 1963:

Since a long time, some of my friends and I have prayed for people, a house and money to open an interracial, international and interdenominational center where races can find each other at the foot of the cross of Jesus Christ. We did not know where the Lord was intending to give us this center—Holland, Switzerland, Israel, Australia? A place where we can have conferences to train young people and where people can come for retreats and for rest.

In Uganda God brought me in contact with Christians who had the same vision. God gave there a house with a beautiful garden around it. In Uganda, East Africa, between Entebbe and Kampala lies Lweza. Men who have been mightily used in the continuous revival in Africa and over a big part of the world have joined hands, and so we are now in the process of rebuilding the house. An open-air church, guest rooms and cottages for workers and many more plans will come into being there, the Lord willing.

She then listed the men whom God so greatly used—members with her on the planning committee: Dr. J. E. Church, Mr. Festo Kivengere, Mr. William Nagenda, Bishop Eric Sabiti of the Anglican Church in Uganda, and Mr. Harry Campbell.

Argentina, Brazil and Holland

On July 8, 1963, Corrie wrote to Bobbie Halliday: "We are now in the jungle in northeast Argentina. A revival started in a church. Christians started to live in the light. Sinners were saved. Hallelujah. . . . We are now leaving for Brazil."

And two months later, from Holland to her friends:

This letter I have written partly in South America, partly in Holland. "Knocked down, but not knocked out." I had to leave South America because my health gave in. I had an infection of the liver. Now I am in Holland, and when the Lord has healed me, I hope to take a time of rest and finish a book that I began to write. The Lord has made it

157

clear to me that I had not taken sufficient rest between the campaigns, so I think it is His discipline to bring me alone with Him for a while. Will you pray for perfect healing? It was a very sad thing to have to cancel all the appointments for the rest of the year.

After five weeks of illness, of which I spent two in the hospital, I am completely healthy again. The Lord is guiding me to stay in Holland until the end of the year to spend much time alone with Him.

To Germany

In July 1964 Corrie was back in Germany. She wrote:

Oh, it is such a joy that the Lord uses me this time in Germany for many prisoners! But also for ministers. More than before, I am involved in their congresses and meetings.

The ministers and I got along well, working, praying and striving together. Although we differed in background and training, our common aim united us: the winning of souls for eternity and helping the children of God to learn that "Jesus is Victor."

Speaking at a ministers' meeting is another story. Frequently it was among them that I found my severest critics, and sometimes even my greatest opposition. Yet it seemed vital to be used by God among them, for these men who worked in over-large congregations and were weighed down with problems also needed to be reminded of Jesus' victory and His plan for the world.

A large group waited for me to speak. Should I try to convince them not to listen to me but to God and His message for us?

"Gentlemen, I am a lay person, a lay woman, a Dutch lay woman. Are there some present who would rather not remain?

"I intend to speak about conversion. Perhaps you have a label for me—a pietist? I shall talk about the Lord's return—that should label me a sectarian. I may even speak about the rapture of the Church—that makes me a fanatic. Or the fullness of the Holy Spirit—a Pentecostal. Keep your labels handy, gentlemen. Should my words touch your consciences, you have only to label me, set me in a corner and have nothing to fear."

A strange thing happened. The critical faces relaxed. There was laughter, after which we truly listened together to God's message: Germany's great need, and Christ the answer to this need. The world's history is a great embroidery by God, enough of which is made clear to us through His Word so that we can face the future calmly and securely since all is in His hand. Indeed, the best is yet to be—a world full of the knowledge of the Lord, as the waters cover the sea.

When I finished, with one accord the group turned to prayer.[1]

The following she wrote to her friends concerning Germany in that same letter of 1964:

When I spoke about our wonderful commission, given to us by the Lord in Mark 16:15–18, one minister said to me, "I know that there are people in my parish who are possessed. But is it my task to cast out the demons?" Then I answered, "Who else should do it? We who have the name of Jesus are the only ones who have this authority." Another minister said, "But how does one know whether it is a case of demons or of mental illness?" I answered, "Here we may take the promise given in James 1:5. All wisdom we need is given to us in this verse. We need only to cash the check."

The Gifts of the Holy Spirit

I am so happy that lately many people's eyes are being opened for the gifts of the Holy Spirit, in Germany as well as in

South America and many other countries of the world. I am convinced that the Lord will fulfill the promises of Joel 2:28, even in the main denominations. The whole atmosphere is changing. I believe that the Lord will do great things. When a person is open for the Lord Jesus Christ and all that He wants to give, and is closed to the world and all that the world wants to give, he is levelheaded. Here in Germany many people are still afraid of fanatics and excesses, but when we take the promises of 1 Corinthians 14:12 seriously and covet the best gifts earnestly (see 1 Corinthians 12:31), we have nothing to fear and God will do miracles. How unbiblical is the assertion that we need only to love and that the gifts of the Spirit are superfluous. On the contrary! Paul begins 1 Corinthians 14 with the twofold sentence: "Follow the way of love, *and* earnestly (eagerly) desire spiritual gifts."

Still writing from Germany in the summer of 1964, Corrie says:

During a meeting in East Berlin I received flowers from a group of young people from the town of Ravensbrück with the request that I come and speak in the church. We could arrange it with our program, and so it happened that we had a meeting in the old church at the border of the lovely little lake that I had seen when, tortured by thirst, I entered the concentration camp about twenty years ago. Betsie and I suffered so much there, but now I could tell here how I had come through alive and victorious, not through my faith, which was weak and wavering, but carried by Jesus Himself. Jesus, who is willing to sustain everyone who is in need and willing to surrender his or her life into His strong and never failing hands.

How wonderful is God's plan with my life! First a struggle with death in a terrible prison, and now I can bring in the same place the Word of Life to free people.

A Sabbatical

Near the end of this same year, Corrie was diagnosed with hepatitis. She was now 72 years old and had been traveling for seventeen years without any long break.

> The doctor has advised me to rest for some time, and the Lord has shown me that I must take a sabbatical year. No wheels of cars, trains and airplanes beneath me. Alone with the Lord and with Conny, I hope to receive new inspiration and strength and to be able to write.

Corrie was to spend most of her sabbatical year at Lweza, Uganda, East Africa, in housing provided for her and Conny at the beautiful conference center that had come into being partly through her own prayers and work. Before she left, however, she spent almost two months at the house of a German doctor:

> Never before have I had a medical treatment like during that time. There was so much prayer and care. God blessed that treatment, and now I am healthy again and can enjoy the sabbatical year. There are no meetings, no traveling, but I am walking, resting, studying and listening to the Lord. What a privilege!

But Corrie, who disliked rest in terms of it being the opposite of work, also found the prospect of a sabbatical daunting:

> Sometimes I regret that I cannot and may not travel and have meetings during this sabbatical year. I know God can use only obedient servants, and He has made it so clear that I must take this time of rest. I experience that just in the moments when I regret this time of different activity, the Lord always arranges it so I receive an encouraging letter to show me that the work is going on and the seed is sprouting out.

One of the secrets of Corrie's victorious life was that she carried out her work from a position of rest in the Lord. She absolutely loved work. To her it had nothing to do with personal attainment. It was obedience. In March 1965 she wrote:

> We have arrived in the little paradise of Lweza. From a cold winter in Europe to a heat wave in a country very near the equator. For six months there had been no rain at all, but yesterday it rained, and it is as if the flowers and trees are smiling with joy. We enjoy the singing of the birds and the stillness of the tropical nights, but most of all we rejoice because of the fellowship with the Christians here.
>
> I am still recharging my spiritual and physical batteries by reading the Bible, listening to the Lord and resting on an easy chair in this beautiful garden. Two nice dogs are lying at my feet. When I look to the right I see Lake Victoria in the distance. Crickets are chirping. A kind African brings me an extra pillow. The whole atmosphere is full of beauty and peace. It is a miracle how much one can do even during such a time of rest—correspondence, writing articles, revising a manuscript for a book, intercession and being quiet to listen to the Lord so that He will recharge our spiritual batteries.

Corrie's sabbatical year also included work with Conny in prisons, hospitals, schools and churches.

When Corrie started her sabbatical year at the end of 1964 she told her friends: "I asked the Lord that after this year of rest, if He has not returned, to give me another ten years of work with new strength and inspiration." The Lord gave her more than that.

And when her rest year came to a close in the autumn of 1965 she wrote: "There is great joy in my heart to begin again. The Lord willing, first in Africa, then in Aden and Israel, then perhaps for a short time in the U.S.A. and Canada and then in

Eastern Europe, where we hope that the Lord will open doors in countries we did not reach until now."

Following the Sabbatical

Before she left the African continent, Corrie was to work in several countries there, including Kenya, Tanzania, Ethiopia and the Congo. She also revisited two small countries south of Uganda—Rwanda and Burundi. On an earlier visit she had been deeply affected by the tribal warfare in Rwanda and Burundi in which hundreds of thousands of people, many of them Christians, lost their lives very brutally. Her own experiences of suffering gave her unusual authority to comfort.

> Once I spoke for about one thousand people in Rwanda. Many of them had burnt the houses of their enemies, and there were also the people whose houses were burnt. To speak to such people about the miracle that when Jesus tells us to love our enemies He will Himself give us the love He demands from us is a timely message. I could tell them about my problem. I had had hatred for the murderers of my family, but I brought that hatred to the Lord, and He forgave and cleansed me and sometimes even used me to bring my former enemies to Him. Those people there in Rwanda understood that what I told was not theory or theology but real experience.

The Greatest Joy for a Christian

Corrie had heard many Christians speak of the annual Keswick conferences for Christian growth in England. In the autumn of 1965 another appointment at the end of her sabbatical year was in Nairobi, Kenya, where she was a speaker at the East Africa Keswick Convention.

The Lord gave me to speak about the joy of total surrender. I mentioned the "if onlys" and told about my "if only I was married," which I had when I was young. The boy whom I loved chose another girl, and I surrendered that "if only" to the Lord Jesus to whom I belonged. It was a short battle, and then victory and peace came. The miracle happened that this "creative" part of a woman's life that she needs for marriage life and having children, the Lord used in His Kingdom. I never had the joy to bring a child to birth, but often God used me to bring someone to rebirth—and that is the greatest joy for a Christian. The Lord undertook and gave me a very happy life so that I never became a "frustrated old spinster."

It was the year after this that I arrived to work in Nairobi, Kenya, and heard Corrie's name for the first time at that momentous prayer meeting I described in chapter 1: "I would like to ask prayer for Corrie ten Boom," the lady in the floral dress at the front of the room had said. "She is in her midseventies now and has recently spent many months in Uganda. Her doctor had prescribed a sabbatical rest for her. But now she has resumed her world journeys." I had already made my own surrender to the Lord, the biggest of which was the laying down of the right to marriage. It would be ten years before I joined Tante Corrie in her work. I can confirm that she certainly was not a frustrated old spinster, and her example of the joyful acceptance of her singleness as part of God's plan was greatly encouraging to me.

A New Home in Holland

In the summer of 1966 the work she had started in Bloemendaal twenty years earlier became exclusively a rehabilitation home for Dutch people who needed rest and medical care. Corrie's work there ended rather abruptly and sadly. She seldom referred to her parting of the ways with those who helped her make reality of

Betsie's first vision, but years later, when she lived in California, she explained to me what happened.

At the time though, she wrote to her friends simply this: "Soon I hope to be able to give you my new address where Conny and I will have a home and an office, where we will live during the few days that we are from time to time in Holland."

Indeed a good home was provided. A Dutch baroness who spent most of her time working in Israel gave Corrie the use of her beautiful apartment in Soestdijk near the royal palace. It was to be her base for some years.

A New Teammate

Corrie's 75th birthday, April 15, 1967, was spent working with her old friend Brother Andrew in Vietnam. And in September of that year, Conny married Lykle Hoogerzeil, a Dutch missionary doctor to India.

During the weeks before Conny's marriage a day came when she was sure they had found the right person to take her place as Corrie's companion. It was the day that tall, blonde Ellen de Kroon came to meet with them about the unusual vacancy needing to be filled. Among other things, Conny noticed the loving way in which Ellen, thinking that Tante Corrie might be a little cold, found a blanket and tucked her into it as she sat in her chair. Again, God provided for Corrie. She wrote:

> The Lord gave me another helper, Ellen de Kroon. She has been a nurse but has surrendered herself to this quite new work of being my teammate. We appreciate your prayers for her. We are having lots of fun already, and it is a real challenge for her to start such an adventurous life of dependence on the Lord.
>
> Conny and Lykle are now in Utrecht preparing for the mission field. What joy it has been to have Conny during seven years as my fellow tramp for the Lord. Not only what she did, but also what she was has been such a blessing for

the work and for me. She herself is so thankful to the Lord for the time of preparation for the mission field these seven years gave her, with all the work in God's Kingdom all over the world together with me, as a team, side by side.

During the months that Conny and Lykle were preparing to leave for India, Corrie was happy that they lived nearby. They visited her often, and Conny and Ellen also had the opportunity to discuss what living and working with Tante Corrie involved. When time allowed, Conny was able to help Corrie now and then.

An Accident

Late in 1967 Corrie was involved in a serious car accident while on her way to record some messages in Dutch for her friends at Trans World Radio. She wrote to her friends:

For Trans World Radio I often give short messages in the Dutch language that reach many people who understand our language over all the world. This time I was asked to give a talk about our victory over demons. The Lord gave me three strong messages. The title of the first was *Are We Powerless Against Demons? No!* And I told about the authority of the name of Jesus and the power of His blood. We overcome by the blood of the Lamb and by the power the Holy Spirit gives us.

On the day that I [was to] give these messages over the radio, I got involved in a rather serious car accident. Conny, who was driving, was not injured. By a miracle both our lives were spared. The little combs in my hair were broken in pieces. So my head could have been severely wounded, but only my right arm was broken in four places. During the accident I could only cry, "Jesus, Jesus."

When I was lying in the hospital with my broken arm, I thought about what had happened and I understood that it was very well possible that the enemy did not like those messages about the Christian's victory over the devil. So he tried to get me knocked out. He really has got me knocked down, but the Lord has spared my life. But I had to stay in hospital for two months and suffered very much pain.

I also saw that this experience was a little bit of cross-bearing. When Jesus died on the cross, He destroyed Satan's head. In the Old Testament the promise was given: "The LORD God said to the serpent . . . I will put enmity between you and the woman, and between your offspring and hers; he will crush your head" (Genesis 3:14–15).

In the New Testament, Paul says, "By His death He (Jesus) might destroy him who holds the power of death, that is, the devil" (Hebrews 2:14). My radio messages were meant to show the Christians this victory over demons through Jesus. That is why I saw it as cross-bearing, too. Then I said to the Lord: "You have suffered terrible pain at the cross in your great love. Your pains and love were mixed together. Will you now make me to experience Romans 5:5? You have poured out your love into my heart by the Holy Spirit. Please mix your love with my pain." When I had prayed this prayer, I could bear the suffering.

I learned much in this time. It was one of the difficult classes of my life. But again Jesus stood in front of the class. I can praise His name.

The Foolishness of God

"Her life hung by a silken thread," said Hans van der Steen, the director of Trans World Radio in Holland, speaking of the time after the accident. He and Corrie were good friends, having first met in the late 1940s when Corrie returned from her first journey to the United States, full of zeal and new knowledge about how to spread the Gospel. She was very interested in Trans World Radio, and during her short times in Holland between her travels Hans recorded her messages for broadcast. One day they were having an animated conversation about how the radio work in Holland began and the wonderful things God did as a result of it.

"Stop for a minute," said Corrie. She walked out of the room, stood at the bottom of the stairs and called loudly, "Conny, come down quickly. Come and listen to the foolishness of God."

Corrie liked using that expression, and she liked teaching on the subject.

How we need to have good vision in this time when all is so dark. The Holy Spirit gives us good eyes that we may see God's plan in the midst of all the chaos of this time. In 1 Corinthians 1 and 2 we read about the "foolishness" of God and the "wisdom of the wise." Two realms they are: The wisdom of the wise is all we can grasp with our logical thinking, with our brains; the foolishness of God, the greatest wisdom, we can touch only with our faith knowledge. The Holy Spirit teaches us to lift up the wisdom of the wise to the height of the foolishness of God, and then we get the vision. When people do not know the Lord and are not born into the family of God, they cannot see and they cannot understand the Kingdom of God, because they have only their logical thinking, the use of their brains. And when you try to bring the foolishness of God under the criticism of the wisdom of the wise, then you may end up with a theology that says, "God is dead."

We live in a period [in which] one of the signs of the end time [that] Daniel gave becomes very clear: "Knowledge shall be increased" (Daniel 12:4, KJV). Some people expect that in the coming ten years the sum total of human knowledge will be doubled. [She wrote this in 1968.]

It is such a great danger when only our logical thinking gives us guidance. It may become a real weapon in the hands of the antichrist. I experienced that personally at a congress of communists in Ravensbrück. I heard that a reunion of ex-prisoners was to be held, and I hoped to find friends with whom I had suffered. Instead, forty thousand communists were present. I listened to their talks, and such darkness fell upon me that when I returned to West Germany I had the feeling that I had no message at all. Then people prayed with me, and the Lord liberated me totally, and I received a strong message from Him. But there I saw how dangerous it is to be permanently in the atmosphere of the wisdom of the wise without any knowledge of the foolishness of God, which is the highest wisdom.

The wisdom of the wise is not something that is wrong in itself. We belong to the Lord one hundred percent with heart and mind. And when we have surrendered both to Him, He will show us how to use that wisdom. I remember that when I was a watchmaker with my old father, he once said, "My name is on the shop, but really God's name should be on the shop, because I am a watchmaker by the grace of God." Sometimes we could not find what was wrong with a watch and then we prayed that the Lord would show it to us. And Father and I, we both had the joyful experience that in our dreams in the night the Lord showed us the fault in the watch. When it happened with me, I went down to the workshop and looked [to see] if my dream was true. Always I found the answer to the problem. Yes, there is nothing too great for God's power; there is nothing too small for His love.

The Right Side of the Embroidery

Corrie was very intelligent, but she was not an intellectual. On matters of suffering she was distressed but did not question God. She learned to ask God to show her a little bit of His side of the embroidery of her life.

I mentioned earlier that after her imprisonment she asked God to let her see her suffering "just a little bit from your point of view." God answered and Corrie obeyed. The lives of countless people were changed as she taught them that the Lord Jesus was able to turn loss into glory. When I worked with Corrie she frequently asked Him to show her things "more and more from Your point of view."

And she surely made that same prayer when Conny was diagnosed with a malignancy. Conny was never able to accompany her husband to the mission field because she became very seriously ill.

Conny was to pass away in 1970. It was then that Corrie wrote about the end of Conny's life:

Her illness became worse and she was in the hospital, finding it hard to breathe because of fluid on her lungs. When I got to her room she said, "Take an easy chair." She showed concern for the needs of others, was kind to the people around her and had no trace of self-pity. It was as if she did not know how to play the role of a critically ill person. She talked a lot about what she had read in her Bible.

Once she said, "Tante Corrie, I often thought I would have to bury you, and now you have to do that for me."

God does not make mistakes. We cannot understand His ways, but Conny already knows the answer. God has shown her His side of the embroidery of her life—the upper side—while we still see the wrong side—the underside.

At Conny's funeral I prayed: "Thank You, Father, in Jesus' name that Conny is now with You. Would You make us all ready to come into Your presence? Her work on earth is finished. Use us, make us faithful, to keep burning the lights which have been lit by her in Your strength. Fill us, therefore, with Your Holy Spirit. Make us also faithful unto death, so that we will receive the crown of life. Amen."

eleven

Extraordinary Years, Extraordinary Results

1968–1976

Ellen de Kroon and Corrie became close and effective co-workers for nearly nine years. Ellen's nursing ability must have been of great comfort to Corrie after the serious car accident and at many other times as she approached and entered her eighties. Ellen had a good sense of humor and love for people. In their first years together they traveled to Germany, Israel, England, Russia, Switzerland, France, Cuba, Mexico, Kazakhstan, Tajikistan, Uzbekistan, Cyprus and the United States, among other countries.

Ellen was to accompany Corrie through some of the most extraordinary years of her life—years in which a book and movie would make her message available to millions. But there were other significant events in which Ellen had the privilege to share.

Yad Vashem

One of the first foreign journeys Ellen and Corrie made together was to Israel. On February 28, 1968, the 24th anniversary of their arrest at the Beje, Corrie and her deceased relatives were honored by the state of Israel.

Corrie described this as a very moving experience in which she and a Dutch couple were honored. The ceremony took place in Jerusalem at Yad Vashem, a memorial and museum built in memory of the martyrs and heroes of World War II. Corrie wrote:

> Heroes are considered those who gave themselves to save Jewish people during the war. The staff of Yad Vashem invited me to come to them to give them the opportunity to honor my family and me. When I arrived, a large crowd was already present. Together with the Dutch couple I stood in the center of the big hall where they would honor us. First a rabbi chanted a litany in memory of the dead. The voices of Jews are so beautiful; they can express sadness and suffering in such a moving way. This rabbi sang in memory of those members of my family who died for the Jews. It was so intensely sad and moving. While he sang, however, birds came all the time, singing their happy song as a joyful background, an accompaniment to the chant for the dead.
>
> There was a litany in memory of the dead, a child read a psalm and speeches were made. This was followed by a visit outside to the "Avenue of the Righteous" where I planted a tree (with my healed arm, praise the Lord). Here every tree has a small plaque at its base bearing the name of the "Righteous Gentile" who planted it.

But to Corrie the most important thing was the opportunity to thank those who had given such a high honor to her and her family for their part in saving Jewish people. "What an opportunity the Lord gave me to bring the Gospel to many Jews in an official position who were present, just by simply telling about my family."

The Death of a Friend

In 1969 Corrie received news of the death of the Christian leader Abraham Vereide, one of her earliest friends in America. You will recall that when no doors opened for Corrie on her first visit to the States in 1946, it was he who wrote letters and made telephone calls on her behalf. Soon she had more invitations than she could accept.

Corrie wrote:

> Abraham Vereide went from his work to be with the Lord. He had traveled that week to speak at several breakfast groups. He read at the dinner table a word from the Bible and prayed. Then he said, "I am so very, very happy today. It is as if I have got a new baptism of the Holy Spirit." Some hours later he was with the Lord. No sickness, no suffering. He really died in the harness at 82 years old.

Tante Corrie longed that she might die "in the harness," too. She often told me that she wanted to go straight "from service good, to service best." I believe the Lord gave her that desire, but not in the way she would have chosen.

On Dutch Television

In 1971 Corrie received an unusual invitation that brought her much joy: the opportunity to appear as a guest on a very popular secular Dutch television program. Many people in the Netherlands had never shown interest in her story—a prophetess is without honor in her own country—but now she was asked by TV personality Willem Duys to tell about her trips around the world and to give a short Easter message:

> Because it was not a Christian television program, I reached many people who were not expecting to hear such a mes-

sage—perhaps six million people, I was told [nearly half of
the population of Holland at the time]. The results were tremendous. Letters, phone calls and visits made the next weeks
full of important work for Ellen and me. Many people who
needed spiritual help came for counseling. Doors and hearts
opened in churches and groups. Many found the Lord Jesus.
People who had seen me on the TV invited me to come to
various cities. And many people with whom I had had contact
during various periods of my 79 years now got in touch with
me again, including people for whose salvation I had prayed
decades before.

Some had become Christians earlier. Some Corrie led to the
Lord as a result of the program. She encouraged her friends:

God works sometimes slowly, but His work is perfect. Have
you already prayed a long time for your son, husband, wife
or neighbor? The devil will tell you, "You see, God does not
hear you. How long have you already prayed now?" He is a
liar. Do not listen to him. Not one prayer is lost. The devil
often laughs when we are up to our eyes in work. He giggles
when we make plans, but he trembles when we pray.

The Hiding Place

At the start of their work together neither Corrie nor Ellen
could have imagined the extraordinary results of the publication
of the book *The Hiding Place* in 1971 and the release of the movie
of the same name four years later. It all began with prayer.

As we have seen, Corrie had prayed for many years that *A
Prisoner and Yet . . .* would be made into a movie. But God had a
different plan, and before there could be a movie a new book had
to be prayed into being. While co-writers John and Elizabeth
Sherrill were working with Brother Andrew on his book *God's
Smuggler,* Andrew told them fascinating stories about his friend

Corrie's travels behind the iron curtain. At first they wondered if some of those stories could be part of Andrew's book, but finally they said, "We could never fit her into the book. She sounds like a book in herself." Shortly afterward the Sherrills met Tante Corrie when she gave her testimony at a church in Germany, and so it happened that plans were made for a new book about her.

In April 1969 Corrie wrote to her prayer partner friends:

Friends of mine in the U.S.A., John and Elizabeth Sherrill, are writing a book with me about my life. In January Mrs. Sherrill came to Holland as she wanted to see my hometown, Haarlem, and meet people here who could give information for the book. Together we visited many places, among them the prison in Scheveningen, where I was three months in solitary confinement.

The prison chaplain helped us get permission to see the prison inside. He also invited me to speak to the prisoners. What a joyful opportunity! In that building, where once I had suffered so much I spoke to the men and stood, as it were, beside them.

Although the reason for my imprisonment was different from theirs—as I had done something good (saving Jewish people during the last war)—I did not feel myself better than the criminals. It is by the grace of God that I am not a criminal myself. My sins are what you may call "decent sins." And although I am not guilty in the eyes of a human judge, still in the eyes of God I have been just as guilty as one who has committed a murder. For hatred was once in my heart, and in the eyes of God that is the same as murder. I brought a message to the men about our riches in Jesus Christ, which we can enjoy in the most difficult circumstances.

In Haarlem we saw the police station where my whole family and about 35 of our friends were kept before we were brought into the prison. It was there that for the last time we were together as a family.

During Mrs. Sherrill's visit we met several people who played a part in my life in that time of war. One of them was Eusie, the Jewish man full of humor who hid in our house. This time,

25 years later, he told me, "I appreciated it so much that I was treated in your house as a real friend of the family, and not just a Jew who needed to have a hiding place." And that is exactly what we all thought of him—a real friend of the family, as we all liked him so much. He is now a cantor-rabbi.

At the end of her visit to Holland, Mrs. Sherrill said that both she and her husband are praying much for guidance in all that writing a book involves. Will you pray with us that this book may become one hundred percent a blessing in the Kingdom of God? Thank you.

Then in April 1971 she wrote:

Sometimes I could not understand why the book has not been finished. The Lord used Catherine Marshall to tell me what the difficulty was. The last chapters tell about the sufferings of Betsie and about her death in the concentration camp. It was very hard for Tibby Sherrill to write these last chapters because she is living what she describes. That is why this last part of the book is such a great strain for John and Tibby Sherrill. Thank you for your prayers for them. I believe that this book will be a great blessing for many people, and I am sure that the Lord will use it to reach many more than my other books have done. The name of the Lord will be glorified. Hallelujah! Keep praying!

Four months later Corrie announced the publication of her book, at last with a name, *The Hiding Place*. It was released in the autumn of 1971 and quickly became a bestseller.

Movie Production Begins

Corrie had met Billy and Ruth Graham for the first time in the 1960s. Ruth was one of the first people to see the potential for a film in *The Hiding Place* book.

World Wide Pictures, the filmmaking arm of the Billy Graham Evangelistic Association, was headquartered in the Los Angeles area at that time. In 1972 Corrie wrote to a friend:

Next week we go to Glendale to meet the people of World Wide Pictures. Billy Graham is very happy with the book and that it can be worked out in a movie. It surely will reach many more people than we have ever been able to reach. I am so thankful. John and Elizabeth Sherrill's book is a good seller and has opened many doors and hearts for me. In April I will be 80 years old, and it seems that the Lord gives me more and more joyful work to do. I feel so privileged.

God uses Ellen much. Her testimonies are so powerful and always bring a blessing. We both feel happy to be in the USA.

Corrie was involved in the making of the movie from the start, enlisting the help of her prayer partners in the early days of planning.

With *The Hiding Place* there is better material for a movie than with *A Prisoner and Yet*.... Billy Graham's World Wide Pictures will make it. But ... a movie is not a book. God needs to do miracles in many ways: a scriptwriter, then finances, the right cast and many other things. I ask your special prayer for this.

Corrie's Eightieth Birthday

On April 15, 1972, Corrie celebrated her eightieth birthday, first with friends at Cape Cod. She described the event:

I wore the long dress my friends in Scottsdale gave me. It was very *gezellig:* There were many bouquets and even real Dutch tulips and more than sixty smiling faces. Then there was a three-tiered cake with eighty candles on it! I am afraid it took me three puffs to blow them all out. Finally we stood and sang *Stand up, Stand up for Jesus,* and the thing I want most for this

Corrie, U.S.A., 1974   PHOTO COURTESY OF THE CORRIE TEN BOOM HOUSE FOUNDATION

coming year is to "stand" for Jesus. He has stood with me for 80 years, so I think I can trust Him for the rest.

Some weeks later, Corrie again celebrated her eightieth birthday when she returned to Holland. Among her guests was Loren Cunningham, leader of Youth With A Mission, whose work she prayed for and encouraged. She called him at his mission base in Switzerland and asked if he would come to pray for her that the Lord would give her a new ministry. So Loren drove from Switzerland to Corrie's party and prayed just as she asked—for a new ministry—but he also prayed something for which Corrie had not asked—that God would extend her life and work by another ten years.

At the end of her sabbatical year in Uganda with Conny, Tante Corrie had asked the Lord to give her another ten years of fruitful work. At the time of her eightieth birthday in 1972, the Lord had already given her seven of those years, and their fruitfulness and effectiveness were increasing by the day.

Could there really be another ten years—not just of life but of real work? Tante Corrie was not happy when she was not working. Would she still be working when she was ninety? It is probable she did not ponder Loren's prayer for long. Her times were in God's hands. I am sure she thought that if she were to live until she was ninety, they would be good and blessed years, for God never makes a mistake.

A Surprising World Premiere

The world premiere of *The Hiding Place* movie was scheduled for the evening of September 29, 1975, in Beverly Hills. The stars of the movie, other prominent actors and actresses and friends—even some from Europe—were present. The audience had mainly filled the theater when a sound like a rifle shot rang out, after which everybody was requested to leave the theater, which was filling with tear gas. It was later learned that this was the work of a member of the American Nazi party, apparently as a gesture of hatred against love for the Jews shown in the movie.

Corrie wrote:

The Lord allowed it—otherwise, it would never have happened. How easy it is to become unforgiving at such a very important moment. But it seemed the Lord was teaching us in a very practical way the very lesson the film will bring to people. "Love your enemies, and forgive."

Corrie and Pam, Shalom House, Placentia, California, 1977   PHOTO CREDIT: RUSS BUSBY

A most wonderful thing happened that night. Across the street from the theater World Wide Pictures had arranged for bleachers so that people could sit and watch the many movie stars and others who came to the premiere. The street was roped off and when everyone had to leave the theater, the street was available for them.

Pat Boone, who was the M.C., was ready to go on, thinking that after the firemen had aired out the whole place everyone could return, but after ten minutes the manager of the theater told us that the stench was too much and the premiere could not continue. But we had a marvelous time out in the street, a place where we never could have had a street meeting. Billy Graham spoke, and Bev Shea sang *How Great Thou Art.* Cliff Barrows and Pat Boone led the singing. Many Hebrew songs were sung. It was all so different from what had been planned. But one thing is sure—Jesus got all the glory.

And, of course, the publicity generated by the tear gas incident resulted in many more people viewing the film. It was to become World Wide Pictures' most successful film.

Ellen Marries

In October 1975, a month after the release of the movie, Corrie and Ellen traveled to Oral Roberts University in Tulsa, Oklahoma, to fulfill speaking appointments. It was to mark the beginning of a big change in both their lives, for Ellen was to meet Bob Stamps, who had been chaplain at ORU for eight years.

Some months later, Ellen wrote to prayer partners:

"Delight yourself in the LORD and He will give you the desires of your heart. Commit your way to the LORD; trust in Him, and He will do this" (Psalm 37:4, 5).

In October 1975 two worlds met, and two prayers began to be answered. Two people had been praying that the Lord would lead them to the person whom God had prepared. Then Tante Corrie prayed for us: "Lord, thank You for not taking my daughter away, but for giving me a son."

Ours has been an international romance. Since the evening that Tante Corrie prayed for us, Bob and I have met in many different places.

Ellen announced that her wedding would be on August 1, 1976, in Holland, with a reception in Bob's hometown of Jasper, Texas, and then a dedication service at Oral Roberts University as soon as the students returned from summer vacation. And she said, "I have to thank many people, most of all Tante Corrie for all her love and care all of these years."

"How faithfully Ellen helped me in the nearly nine years we spent together, working in many different countries," wrote Corrie to her friends. "How the Lord is going to use her together with Bob."

And so it came about that I became part of the plan God had for the end of Corrie's life. When Ellen passed the care of Corrie over to me in April 1976, we did not know that another kind of imprisonment would be waiting for the one who had become a legend in her own already long lifetime.

twelve

I Am Yours!

1976–1983

I became Tante Corrie's companion only six months after the release of *The Hiding Place* movie. At the end of the movie the real Corrie ten Boom speaks to the audience. It should have been no surprise to me, then, when our international travels together began in April 1976, that she was widely recognized by American Christians who had seen the movie. "Recognized" is too mild a word. Mobbed is perhaps more descriptive. For the extroverted Tante Corrie this was no ordeal. The more people the merrier, as far as she was concerned. She found one thing, though, a bit of a trial.

She had cautioned me before we left Holland, "Americans like to hug necks." Part of my job was to try to shield her from neck huggers, many of whom we encountered at airports. Her dislike of that particular display of affection, however, had nothing to do with her love for and acceptance of people. When countless people asked her to pray for them she would say, "Let's go to the Lord right now." It did not matter how public the place. First things were always first with Tante Corrie. There was so much to do and so little time in which to do it, she often told me.

She met and prayed with people everywhere, and during those first few months of our work together we encountered people from Toronto, Honolulu, New York, Massachusetts, Charlotte, Williamsburg, Knoxville, Tulsa, Dallas, Des Moines, Chicago, Miami, Los Angeles, San Diego and San Jose. Tante Corrie did not like small talk, being put on a pedestal or any kind of silliness. She was not pious, staid, old-fashioned or prudish. She simply could not waste time.

I like people, too, but my personality is introverted. I like space and room to think. Whereas constant contact with people energized Tante Corrie, it had the opposite effect on me. To receive energy I needed to be alone and quiet for at least part of the day. That was hard to acquire in 1976 and 1977, but the next year there would be quietness such as I could never have imagined.

Corrie's books and the movie spread widely, and she received countless invitations to speak. To conserve her strength it became necessary to hold meetings in large venues where the maximum amount of people could listen to her messages. They were always the same: "God's light is stronger than the deepest darkness. Forgive your enemies. Live as rich as you are in Jesus Christ. Are you a child of God? If not, come to Jesus. Jesus is victor. There is only one person who cannot come to Him, and that is the one who thinks he is too good to come."

At the beginning of 1977, because it was becoming harder for foreigners to renew U.S. visitors' visas for more than a short time and because by now most of her work was carried on in the United States, Tante Corrie and I applied for and received resident alien status from the American consul in The Hague. This meant that we both could return to America for an indefinite time. Corrie, however, never became a U.S. citizen. The reason was quite simple. "As a Girl Scout I pledged total loyalty to the Queen of the Netherlands, and I will never disown her," she explained to inquirers.

When she left Holland in January 1977 it was for the last time. The remaining six years of her life would be spent in the United States. I wonder if she knew it.

Shalom House

For some months, even before we had to leave America to obtain resident status, Corrie had talked increasingly about having a home in the United States. Her heart was showing signs of slowing down, and she was often tired. I never saw her give in to this, however. She worked very hard, but wanted to find a home in Southern California near her board of directors for "Christians Incorporated," the organization set up some years earlier to handle correspondence, speaking and business arrangements for her. She also wanted to be near World Wide Pictures, with whom she hoped to make several more movies suitable for showing in churches. "So that I do not have to travel much anymore," she explained.

She would have liked to live near the ocean but relinquished that idea as soon as she learned the high prices of coastal property. After a short search, she rented a house in Placentia, about halfway between the ocean, which we visited quite often, and the studios of World Wide Pictures.

On February 28, 1977, 33 years to the day from her arrest in 1944, Corrie moved into her house. She took me by the waist and swung me 'round. *"We hebben een huis! We hebben een huis!"* ("We have a house!") She had no furniture, but when churches in the neighborhood learned of the famous newcomer, several showers were arranged. In a short time her home was furnished.

"The whole atmosphere of the house is one of peace, so I have named it Shalom, the Hebrew word for peace," she told her visitors.

Tante Corrie was extremely happy with her home. It was fairly simple and rather dark inside but was certainly adequate for her needs. It had a bedroom for both of us, a bedroom for visitors and a bedroom that we turned into an office. And it had a garden, with flowers back and front. Somebody even gave her a small lemon tree. With great interest she checked it every day on her walk through her yard. First came buds, then flowers. Would it really bear lemons one day? She was grateful for everything—the birds, flowers, receiving friends, getting to know the neighbors. And what probably made her happiest of all was the fact that she no longer had to travel and could carry out her work in one place with her own desk and books around her.

Corrie's publisher saw her delight and invited her to write a booklet, *A Tramp Finds a Home.* Ever a planner, she wrote:

> The Lord Jesus has the first place in this house. He has given us much important work to do here, and it is because we are doing His will that He blesses the home. Apart from the writing of books and the making of films there is intercession from this house, plus counseling personally and by telephone and letter. Through reading books and magazines that inform us of current events, we keep ourselves up-to-date with local, national and international affairs. We are aware that we are living in a time of crisis in world history. I pray often, "Lord Jesus, come quickly and make all things new." But in the meantime we want to point people to the Lord Jesus Christ, through whom they can live victoriously.[1]

Life with Tante Corrie

It was important to Corrie, however, that we stop work in the evenings. She and I sat together often in the living room on a white semicircular sofa, talked about the day, embroidered—it would not have been my choice, but Tante Corrie never did nothing!—and read books together, sometimes reading to each other. While we were together we shared everything, even the same book. It was *gezellig*. And during the day Tante Corrie took opportunities to read Christian books as she had done in all the decades of her travels and in her youth.

It was not always easy to live with Corrie! Her determination, dogged hard work and stubbornness were often hard to handle. But I am sure it was sometimes equally difficult for Corrie to live with me. "You are as stubborn as a mule," friends have told me more than once.

But we loved each other dearly, and "walking in the light" was part of our daily practice. When tensions came between us, when we needed to forgive each other of anything, it happened before the sun went down.

An example of this had to do with the simple matter of a picture. She asked me to take care of the framing of a copy of a Rembrandt etching. Corrie loved having her own walls. "This is *my* home," she wrote to her friends. "If you come and visit me, you will see the reproductions I had on the walls in earlier days, my portraits and the paintings I like."

Visitors would indeed see her portraits and paintings. Few were valuable, and most were reproductions. She hung them everywhere. People peered down from fading photographs on the mantelpiece. Pictures she had been given graced the most unlikely walls sometimes. It did not matter to her whether frames matched or whether items were hung in a standard order. She knew exactly how she wanted things arranged.

But Tante Corrie did not know the cost of items like framing, and when I arrived back with the etching she was not at all happy with me for spending about $45 on a suitable frame. She was very frugal and let me know she considered it a wasteful purchase. Her displeasure did not last long, though.

A Tramp Finds a Home

One day she told me a story that helped me understand why she was so overjoyed with her rented house, which she made sure I understood was as much mine as hers. We were sitting together on the white sofa. The oil painting of her father—the one that the city of Haarlem presented to him on his eightieth birthday and that Corrie found when she returned home from Ravensbrück—hung behind us on the light beige wall, and a round lamp hanging from a chain shed a golden light from above us. It was peaceful in Shalom House. Each of us had our handwork. She told me the story of the parting of the ways between her and the staff of the Zonneduin rehabilitation center in the mid-'60s. The misunderstanding was caused partly by Corrie's absences from Holland on her long world journeys. Her vision for the house and that of the staff who ran it for her changed as the years progressed and two different ministries emerged. But it was a big blow to Corrie when Zonneduin's staff asked her to leave the house and the room in which she had some items of furniture and other belongings. She wrote in *A Tramp Finds a Home:*

> Once, years ago, I decided to stop the life of a tramp. In Zonneduin, a house in Holland that we had arranged for people who needed to rest, I had one room that I called mine.
>
> To demonstrate to myself that that room would be my home, I opened a drawer where I kept my little pictures and photographs and put them on the walls; here, there and everywhere, almost like a child who arranges his room.
>
> The Lord said no to my desire to stop the life of a tramp and I obeyed, going back to my travels. When I returned to the room after some time, I found that all my little pictures had disappeared, having been removed by people who thought it strange to cover walls with childish pictures. They were right . . . they were fellow workers, and they told me that I was no longer welcome in Zonneduin. I left, and I was wounded.

Corrie forgave her friends, though. She was able to pray:

> Thank You, Father, that Your love in me is victorious over my resentment.
>
> Soon I understood that it was God's will that I went on with my life as a tramp.

Now, in my own home, which was in the Lord's plan for me but at a later date, I put more and more pictures on the walls, and I know I am allowed to do it.[2]

Her Final Works

In the eighteen months between her moving into her home in February 1977 and the stroke that took her powers of communication on August 23, 1978, the former tramp for the Lord was enabled to carry out many of her plans, including the making of filmed messages—a message especially for prisoners called *One Way Door;* a film with American Indians on her 86th birthday; and a film that was in progress at the time of her stroke, later entitled *Jesus Is Victor: A Personal Portrait of Corrie ten Boom.*

Although she mainly "stayed put," as she liked to express it, among other engagements she spoke in San Quentin State Prison, traveled to Tulsa, Oklahoma, for the baptism of Ellen's son, Peter John (who would later be joined by a sister) and took part in Christian Booksellers' conventions in Kansas City and Denver. Six books were published.

Corrie ten Boom's final work was on behalf of prisoners. As well as making a movie for them and writing a book, *He Sets the Captives Free,* she wanted to start an organization that would act as an umbrella for all ministries to prisoners so that one organization could learn from and help another, pooling resources on a national level. In the days leading up to her stroke most of her time was spent on behalf of prisoners.

A Different Kind of Imprisonment

And then on August 23, 1978, life changed radically. Tante Corrie had the first of several strokes that would gradually weaken her through the years that remained.

Many have asked why the Lord allowed His gifted child to spend nearly five years unable to do the work she loved, unable to speak, unable to read, write or comprehend in the normal way. I do not know. Neither did she, I am sure.

In a way it was another kind of imprisonment, but a precious one. The Lord had locked Corrie up with Himself.

At first it was hoped that she would regain some of her faculties of comprehension, but as the weeks turned into months with little improvement, I often thought about a letter Corrie had sent to a lady named Roberta shortly before her stroke. Roberta had written with questions about the reasons for suffering, and I had typed out Corrie's reply:

```
The answer to the question about why there is
suffering in the world is because there is sin
in the world. There will be no end to suffering
until the Lord Jesus comes and makes everything
new. I do not understand, just like you, why He
allows Christians to suffer, but I know that even
then God is the God of love. He makes all things
work together for good to those who love Him. I
did not understand why my nephew and father and
sister died . . . but I see now that their lives
and deaths were used to bless very many thousands
of people all over the world.

When we love God and are trusting the Lord
Jesus, it can be compared to an embroidery. God
is making the embroidery. He sees the top. You
and I see the underside. One day we will see the
top, too. It is beautiful, but now you and I can
know that only by faith in the Lord Jesus.
```

Many stroke patients suffer brain damage and resulting behavioral changes, causing situations that are often very distressing to their families and friends. In many cases the patients are deeply committed Christians. Why the Lord allows this is part of the mystery of suffering. One day we will understand.

As for Corrie, during her very slow decline her personality was not different. Although she became extremely weak physically, she took as large a part in the household as her disabilities allowed, even though she was confined to bed for most of those five years of silence. We worked out a system of communication, we prayed together, and we laughed, too. Many helped me in providing care for her.

She Wanted to "Die in the Harness"

Corrie had always longed to be able to work until the day the Lord came for her. When Miss Henrietta Mears, with whom she had spent time during visits to the West Coast of the United States and whom Corrie greatly respected, died on March 20, 1963, Corrie was in California. She had called to make an appointment to see Miss Mears again, but Miss Mears died before their planned meeting took place. Corrie wrote:

> I am sure that there is much work for her "in higher service," but what a loss it is for the people here. God used her mightily.
>
> Henrietta Mears "died in the harness." What joy to be able to work until the last day of your life! She was of my generation—only a few years older than I am. I may still go on until I pass the torch on to others or until Jesus comes. I pray that God will use me to redeem my time and trust Jesus more.

You may recall that Corrie made the same comment about Abraham Vereide when he died: "No sickness, no suffering," she wrote. "He really died in the harness at 82 years old." Should the Lord Jesus not return beforehand, and she believed He would, Corrie very much wanted to "die in the harness," too.

In those very long years at Shalom House between 1978 and 1983, I often wondered if Tante Corrie's serious brain damage allowed her to ponder the mystery of why she had apparently not been able to work until the last day of her life. Although she could not tell me, I think she did not. For one thing, she was never the pondering type! And I knew from close observation of her life when she was well that if she was still able to think in sequence, Corrie would have surrendered that desire to the Lord and accepted the present moment.

But I believe she *did* work until the last day of her life—and very effectively. She finished the race. She kept the faith. One of the greatest works the Lord did through her in those years, I believe, was her consistent witness to the dark, unseen and evil demonic powers that tried hard to silence her words "Jesus is victor." It was the ultimate test of her character, and the enemy did not succeed.

Still a Victorious Life

In my book *The Five Silent Years of Corrie ten Boom,*[3] written shortly after her death, I describe some of the things I observed in that time when the world of the former "tramp for the Lord" did not extend beyond the four walls of the front bedroom of her Shalom House in California. And yet in another way the world was still wide. We spent hours viewing some of the thousands of slides she had taken on her world travels. And part of each day was spent rearranging the many photographs and pictures on the walls of her own bedroom.

But there was nothing pathetic about her.

Corrie never showed any self-pity. As she had written about her first companion, Conny, years before, it was as if she did not know how to play the role of a patient. She could not speak, so I do not know what she was thinking. All I can tell you is the effect her still victorious life had on me. During those years, which sometimes seemed endless, when no plan could be made by the one who loved planning, she said to me without words: "I served Him in my youth; I will serve Him in my old age. I served Him in strength; I will serve Him in weakness. I served Him in life; and I will serve Him in death."

At 11:00 p.m. on her 91st birthday, April 15, 1983, the Lord undid the harness and took Corrie home.

Tante Corrie's Secret

What made Corrie the woman she was? Why is her story so powerful—even now, more than two decades after her death? Many factors combine. I have written about a few of them in this book—her grounding in the Dutch Reformed Church, her openness to receiving and obeying the Holy Spirit, her willingness to walk in the light, her determination to forgive, her pressing on to know more and more of the riches that are in Christ, and especially her steadfast belief that all her times were in God's very safe hands.

Corrie loved telling stories. *The Hiding Place* is powerful because story itself—the telling of the past course of a person's life for a positive and sometimes life-changing end—is powerful. It cannot be said often or strongly enough that each of us who loves the Lord Jesus has his or her own story without which every other Christian is the poorer. If you and I can learn to tell our stories—not necessarily in writing but in talking about them, in daily living and in worship—we will affect our world in ways that only eternity will tell.

Corrie learned to tell her story, and we can, too. But it will take passion—Corrie's kind of wholehearted passion for the Lord.

What if you and I do not have enough of that passion? How can we obtain it?

In her 1945 letter of forgiveness to the man who betrayed her to the Nazis, Corrie said, "If you find it difficult to pray, ask God to give you His Spirit. He will give faith in your heart." That is the best advice for you and me, too. We can ask God to give us the passion for Himself that we need in these dark days in which He planned for us to live and to tell our own stories about His love. There will be a price to pay, but He will help us to pay it if we ask Him.

All of this contributed to who Corrie was and what made her story so powerful. And yet Corrie herself summed up her secret in one short sentence.

One afternoon while she was still well, she entertained a young neighbor in the back garden of Shalom House. Anna had read *The Hiding Place* and was shy at first, but she soon relaxed when Corrie walked around the backyard with her, pointing to the flowers and to the lemons forming on the small tree.

As they sat down to drink tea, Anna asked, "What is your secret, Corrie?"

The answer was simple, of course. "Well, Anna, you see, one day I just said to the Lord, 'I am Yours from the tip of my toes to the top of my head.'"

Unconditional abandonment to God. Not her own faith. That was Corrie's secret.

Appendix 1

The Influence of Isaac
Da Costa

Taken from *Father ten Boom, God's Man*, pages 29, 31, 32, 33

*C*orrie's passionate words about him and his work, written in the 1970s, show us the strong effect Isaac Da Costa had on the Ten Boom family and their faith:

He was a brilliant lawyer and a famous poet. As a result of the Enlightenment and the French Revolution, Europe had put reason above the Bible. Consequently there was a general relaxing of godly standards in all levels of society. Immediately after his conversion, Da Costa wrote a book titled *Objections Against the Spirit of This Age*. The basic theme was taken from Scripture.

For we are not fighting against people made of flesh and blood, but against persons without bodies—the evil rulers of the unseen world, those mighty satanic beings and great evil princes of darkness who rule this world; and against huge numbers of wicked spirits in the spirit world (Ephesians 6:12, TLB).

Immediately a storm of protest and contempt broke loose upon the courageous young lawyer. He was mocked and scorned in the press. A small circle of Hollanders stood with Da Costa. Among these was the Ten Boom family, including Willem. For these Christians, the clarion call of Da Costa meant the beginning of a new revival movement that left its mark on the whole spiritual atmosphere of nineteenth-century Holland. For many, the Bible was restored to its place of authority as the Word of God.

In 1851 Da Costa attended the World Conference of the Evangelical Alliance in London. Two days were set aside there to discuss the work among Jews in the various countries represented. In the detailed report of this conference I found an address by Da Costa that clearly states the reasons why he founded a number of prayer groups for Israel in various cities of the Netherlands. Here are a few thoughts from his interesting speech:

Brethren, I see you are all rejoicing in the blessings of Christian fellowship. Even so, I have come here to ask for tears. Tears and prayers. Yes, I myself must shed tears in your midst. For there is one nation that has not been represented at this great international gathering. It is God's own beloved people of Israel. Let us remember that our Savior, the Lord Jesus Christ, who is now interceding for us at the Throne of God, was born a Jew in a Jewish family in the nation of Israel. It is true that Israel missed God's target and was, for a time, set aside and dispersed among the nations. But the day will come when they will fall at the feet of their Messiah in true repentance and live!

On this occasion of the Great Exhibition, the Christians of Great Britain have called the nations together on their territory. The time will come when the King of the Jews will call a holy gathering in Jerusalem. This is not human imagination, but God's own Word through the witness of another Jew, the apostle Paul. He expresses this expectation in Romans

11:15:"If their [Israel's] rejection means the reconciliation of the world, what will their acceptance mean but life from the dead?" (RSV).

We all agree that a strong bond ties us to Israel. As to the past, Christianity is a fruit, an offshoot from the old people of God. As to the present, is not Israel's existence among the nations, despite centuries of hostility and persecution, one of the strongest proofs against the world's unbelief? And as to the future, how clearly the fulfillment of God's promises is related to the future of the world and the coming Kingdom of Christ! Well then, brethren! For these reasons I dare come to you with an earnest plea. It is a custom in Israel at certain great feasts to keep an open seat for the prophet Elijah. I request that you reserve an open seat for Israel in our midst today.

You lions of England and Scotland, give full honor to the Lion from the tribe of Judah who has conquered! You morning-watcher of the French people, announce the dawn of the day of His coming! You harp of Ireland, lead us in the song of expectation and longing of God's Church: "Come, Lord Jesus! Amen, come to bless and gather all the peoples of the world, also the long-rejected Israel in their midst! Amen."

Da Costa's work influenced my grandfather Willem to become one of the founders of the Society for Israel. Father often told us, "Love for the Jews was spoon-fed to me from my very youngest years." As a result, deep respect and love for the Jews became a part of our home life. How important childhood impressions are. Over the years we often experienced the truth of God's promise to Abraham, "And I will bless them that bless thee. . . ."

During the second half of the nineteenth century, the Jewish people slowly awakened to the need to return to their homeland. What had seemed an absolute impossibility for nineteen centuries—the establishment of a Jewish state in Israel, the land of the patriarchs—now became the vision of an Austrian reporter, Theodor Herzl. Herzl was not motivated by religious reasons. He thought only of survival for the Jews, but the return of the Jews to

Zion was the beginning of the fulfillment of the Old Testament prophecies concerning Israel's restoration.

Is it presumptuous to think that the small prayer meeting in Haarlem was connected with these events? I believe that God delights to use His children in the fulfillment of His plans for the world. I am sure He loves to use small people to do great things. How honored I am to be part of His plan!

Appendix 2

On Women and Preaching

*I*n 1960, at the age of 67, in her bimonthly publication *It's Harvest Time*, Corrie ten Boom answered some questions put to her on women and preaching:

Question: Have you ever dealt with the difficulty that some people do not like it when women speak in public?

No, because I do not go where I am not allowed to speak.

Question: But do you yourself not have the feeling that you are being disobedient? Paul says in 1 Timothy 2:11–12 and in 1 Corinthians 14:34–35 that women must be silent.

Yes, Paul does say that, but we must understand what these words mean and what they do not mean. We must give them their place, of course, in the present age. Peter gave us a sketch of the present age in the words of Joel: "I will pour out my Spirit on all people. Your sons and daughters will prophesy" (Joel 2:28). Now, what is prophecy? First Corinthians 14:3 says it is "strengthening, encouragement and comfort."

Question: But didn't Peter mean that these things happened at the first Pentecost? (See Acts 2:16–21.)

Yes, they partly happened then. "This that you are now witnessing," says Peter. But in carrying on with the quotation he proceeded to tell about things that were not then happening. "Blood, and fire, and vapor of smoke" have not yet come to pass, and neither has the sun yet been turned into darkness nor the "moon into blood." We know from other Scriptures (e.g., see Matthew 24:29, Revelation 6:12) that these things will happen before the return of the Lord. We live in days past the beginning of the prophecy and before the end of it.

In Acts 2:18 we read, "Even on my servants, both men and women, I will pour out my Spirit in those days, and they will prophesy." There is no distinction of race in this verse; the power is to any devoted servant of Christ, Jew or Gentile, male or female. The 120 on the first Pentecost included certain women, and they all were filled with the Spirit and spoke languages they had never learned (see Acts 2:4–11).

In 1 Corinthians 11:5, we find that women prophesied in the assembly, and this was not forbidden by Paul but merely regulated, the covering of the head being commanded. This verse also tells that women prayed in the Church. In Acts 21:9 we are told about Philip's four daughters who prophesied—not because the prophesying of women was rare, but that it was unusual for four women in one family to do so.

Question: But what about 1 Corinthians 14:34–35, where it is clearly said that women must keep silent in the churches?

I believe that this must be interpreted in the light of these other Scriptures and not in conflict with them. Here is meant silence whilst another is speaking. ("Let them ask their own husbands at home.") Miriam, Deborah, Anna, a prophetess—these are good company for me. And Psalm 68:11 in the original gives them and me the encouragement: "The women that publish good things are a great host." There is one thing that a man or woman cannot do without: the anointing of the Holy Spirit that equips us to speak for God (see Acts 2:18).

"Open your eyes and look at the fields! They are ripe for harvest" (John 4:35).

Appendix 3

Ten Boom Family Resources and Timeline of Corrie ten Boom's Life

I am indebted to researcher and author Emily S. Smith for the following timeline of the Ten Boom family and their family tree. These resources enable the reader to trace many of Tante Corrie's family relationships; to place various members of the family, including the dates of their births and deaths; and to follow the timing of events in Tante Corrie's life and travels in considerable detail.

My warmest thanks go to Emily and to Frits Nieuwstraten, director of the Corrie ten Boom House Foundation in Haarlem, the Netherlands, for granting permission for us to include these meticulous and impressive pieces of work.

This timeline and family tree appear in the book entitled *A Visit to the Hiding Place: The Life-Changing Experiences of Corrie ten Boom*, written by Emily S. Smith and published by the Corrie ten Boom House Foundation. They are reproduced here with permission. This permission covers use in all languages and all editions throughout the world.

For more information about the centuries-old house in Haarlem containing the hiding place, now a museum, visit www.Corrie tenBoom.com

The Ten Boom
Family

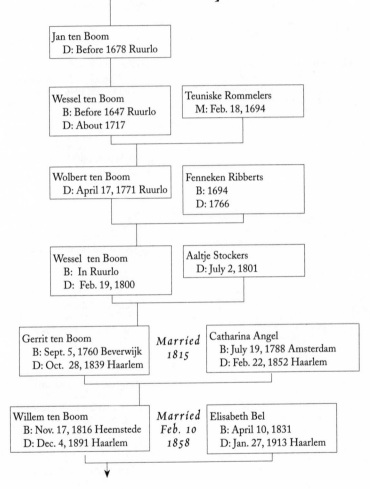

Jan ten Boom
D: Before 1678 Ruurlo

Wessel ten Boom
B: Before 1647 Ruurlo
D: About 1717

Teuniske Rommelers
M: Feb. 18, 1694

Wolbert ten Boom
D: April 17, 1771 Ruurlo

Fenneken Ribberts
B: 1694
D: 1766

Wessel ten Boom
B: In Ruurlo
D: Feb. 19, 1800

Aaltje Stockers
D: July 2, 1801

Gerrit ten Boom
B: Sept. 5, 1760 Beverwijk
D: Oct. 28, 1839 Haarlem

Married
1815

Catharina Angel
B: July 19, 1788 Amsterdam
D: Feb. 22, 1852 Haarlem

Willem ten Boom
B: Nov. 17, 1816 Heemstede
D: Dec. 4, 1891 Haarlem

Married
Feb. 10
1858

Elisabeth Bel
B: April 10, 1831
D: Jan. 27, 1913 Haarlem

All locations in the Netherlands, unless noted.
Van Woerden information verified by Inge van Woerden. Other information provided
by Hendrik ten Boom, Chief of Archives, Rotterdam (nephew of Casper).

APPENDIX 3

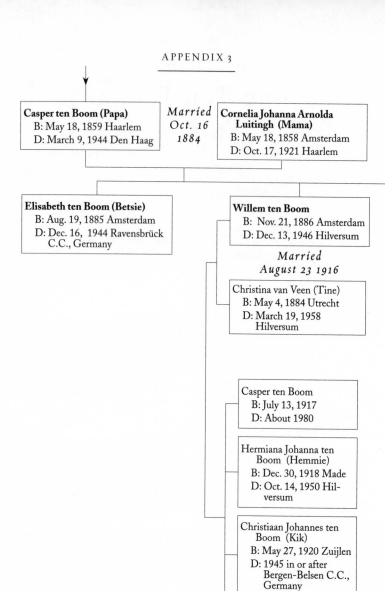

Casper ten Boom (Papa)
B: May 18, 1859 Haarlem
D: March 9, 1944 Den Haag

Married Oct. 16 1884

Cornelia Johanna Arnolda Luitingh (Mama)
B: May 18, 1858 Amsterdam
D: Oct. 17, 1921 Haarlem

Elisabeth ten Boom (Betsie)
B: Aug. 19, 1885 Amsterdam
D: Dec. 16, 1944 Ravensbrück C.C., Germany

Willem ten Boom
B: Nov. 21, 1886 Amsterdam
D: Dec. 13, 1946 Hilversum

Married August 23 1916

Christina van Veen (Tine)
B: May 4, 1884 Utrecht
D: March 19, 1958 Hilversum

Casper ten Boom
B: July 13, 1917
D: About 1980

Hermiana Johanna ten Boom (Hemmie)
B: Dec. 30, 1918 Made
D: Oct. 14, 1950 Hilversum

Christiaan Johannes ten Boom (Kik)
B: May 27, 1920 Zuijlen
D: 1945 in or after Bergen-Belsen C.C., Germany

Cornelia Arnolda Johanna ten Boom (Nolly)
B: Dec. 16, 1921 Zuijlen
D: May 31, 1983 Maarn

APPENDIX 3

Hendrik Jan ten Boom
B: Sept. 12, 1888
Amsterdam
D: March 6, 1889
Amsterdam

**Arnolda Johanna ten Boom
(Nollie)**
B: Sept. 25, 1890 Amsterdam
D: Oct. 22, 1953 Haarlem

**Cornelia Arnolda Johanna
ten Boom (Corrie)**
B: April 15, 1892 Amsterdam
D: April 15, 1983 Placentia,
CA, USA

*Married
July 23, 1919*

Frederik van Woerden
B: Dec. 20, 1890 Den Haag
D: Dec. 27, 1967 Bennebroek

Jacob Frederik van Woerden
B: May 14, 1920
D: 1982

Casper van Woerden (Bob)
B: May 18, 1921

Agatha van Woerden (Aty)
B: July 22, 1922

Pieter van Woerden (Peter)
B: Jan. 7, 1924
D: Sept. 6, 1990

Cornelia Arnolda Johanna
van Woerden (Cocky)
B: Sept. 24, 1926
D: July 28, 1997

Elizabeth Johanna
van Woerden (Els)
B: May 28, 1931

205

Ten Boom Family Timeline

This timeline contains many highlights in the Ten Boom family's life and in Corrie's ministry.

1837

Willem ten Boom (Corrie's grandfather) rents shop space and opens Ten Boom Horlogerie (watch shop) at Barteljorisstraat 19, Haarlem. In 1849, he is able to purchase the house for 1,200 guilders (FtB 27).

1841

Willem marries Geertruida van Gogh. They have thirteen children, but eight die before age four.

1844

Willem begins a prayer group to "pray for the peace of Jerusalem" (FH 15).

1856

Geertruida dies of tuberculosis at age 42 (FtB 26).

1858

Willem marries Elisabeth Bel February 10. They have six children; two die very young.

1859

Casper ten Boom (Corrie's father, the oldest of Elisabeth's children) is born May 18.

1884

Casper and Cornelia (Cor) Luitingh wed October 16. They reside at 28 Korte Prinsengracht, Amsterdam.

1885

Elisabeth (Betsie) is born August 19. Tante (Aunt) Anna (Cor's sister) comes to live with the family.

1886

Willem is born November 21.

1888

Hendrik Jan is born September 12 but dies March 6, 1889.

1890

Arnolda Johanna (Nollie) is born September 25. Ten Booms move to another house in Amsterdam (FtB 47).

1891

Grandfather Willem dies December 4, age 75.

1892

Cornelia Arnolda Johanna (Corrie) is born April 15 on Good Friday, about one month premature. Casper and family move from Amsterdam to a rented house in Haarlem so he can work in Ten Boom Horlogerie (FtB 52-53). Corrie is christened in the Dutch Reformed Church in July (PerL).
(From this point on, Corrie's age appears in brackets after the year. Corrie's birthday is April 15. The age listed for each year is her age following her birthday.)

1895 [3]

Tante Jans (Cor's sister) comes to live with the Ten Booms.

1897 [5]

Elisabeth (Casper's mother) moves from Barteljorisstraat 19, and Casper and family move in. Casper has house remodeled (FtB 55). Corrie prays and gives her life to Jesus (FH 24).

1909 [17]

Papa and Mama celebrate their 25th wedding anniversary. Corrie has completed primary and secondary school and studies at Domestic Science School (FtB 94). Ten Booms begin a missions study group in their home.

1910 [18]

Corrie takes classes at a Bible school in Haarlem for two years. She fails her final exam but receives her diploma eight years later (FH 93–94).

1911 [19]

Corrie works as an au pair (governess). Tante Bep (Cor's sister, who also lived with the Ten Booms) dies of tuberculosis at age 70. Corrie returns home (FH 75). Mama has slight stroke (FH 93).

1914 [22]

World War I begins. Corrie has appendectomy following months of bed rest (PerL).

1916 [24]

Willem is ordained. He is called to a church in Made; the family attends his first sermon. In Made, Corrie's friend Karel (not his real name) talks with her about their future together. They see each other again when Willem marries Tine van Veen August 23. In November, Corrie's heart is broken when Karel introduces her to his fiancée (HP 44–46). Willem pastors in Made four years, then in Zuijlen until 1926.

1918 [26]

Mama has major stroke (HP 48). As World War I ends, Ten Booms take in Willy, Katy and Mrs. Treckmann and her children Ruth and Martha, all from Germany (FH 102–4).

1919 [27]

Tante Jans dies from diabetes at age 71. Nollie marries Frederik "Flip" van Woerden July 23.

1920 [28]

Corrie completes her watchmaking apprenticeship in two factories in Switzerland (PerL).

1921 [29]

Mama dies October 17 at age 63. Corrie works in clock shop full-time; Betsie takes over housekeeping (FH 113).

1924 [32]

Corrie becomes Holland's first licensed woman watchmaker (HP 54).

1925 [33]

Tante Anna dies March 7 at age 64. Ten Booms begin to take in missionary children, three of them from one family: Puck, Hans, Hardy (FH 133), Lessie (FH134), Miep (FH 137) and Marijke (FH 140). In 1925, there are seven foster children total, known as the Red Cap Club. Corrie starts Christian girls' clubs; she works with them until 1940, when the Nazis order no group meetings (FH 125–82).

1926 [34]

Willem starts working with the Society for Israel. He goes to Leipzig, Germany, for one year to study for his doctorate, writes his thesis on racial anti-Semitism, and receives his Doctorate of Philosophy in 1928 (FtB 106).

1937 [45]

The 100th anniversary party of Ten Boom Horlogerie (watch shop) is held.

1940 [48]

Nazis invade Holland beginning May 10. Occupation lasts five years.

1941 [49]

In November, Corrie obtains help from Willem and Kik ten Boom to find a safe house for two Jewish friends (HP 69).

1942 [50]

Early spring, Corrie decides she must help save Jewish people. She becomes involved in the underground. Her nephew Peter van Woerden spends time in prison for showing patriotism to Holland (HP 73–75).

1943 [51]

Many Jews pass through the Ten Booms' home; most are relocated quickly. The names mentioned below are those who spent extended time with the family.

May 13

Ten Booms take young Dutchman Hans Poley into hiding; he becomes involved in the underground (RHP 15).

May 14

Hansje "Thea" Frankfort-Israels (Jew) moves in (RHP 29).

June

Mary van Itallie (Jew), Henk Wessels and Leendert Kip (underground workers) move in.

June 2

First drill for newly constructed hiding place is held (RHP 44).

June 28

Meyer Mossel, "Eusie," (Jew) moves in (RHP 47).

July

Henk Wiedijk (underground worker) moves in (RHP 64). Henk Wessels and Leendert Kip find other places to live, so Mr. de Vries (Jew) moves in (RHP 75).

August 14

Nollie is arrested for hiding a Jew. She spends four weeks in prison. Due to danger of Gestapo searching family members' homes, all in hiding leave Beje (Ten Booms' home) for other safe houses. Mary, Eusie, Henk and Hans return in three weeks. The others remain elsewhere (RHP 81–85). Mirjam de Jong (Jew) moves in (RHP 86).

September 30

All in hiding leave Beje again due to Gestapo worries (RHP 90). Mary, Eusie and Hans return in two weeks (RHP 96). Nel (Jew) and Ronnie Gazan (Jew) move in (RHP 97).

1944 [52]

January

Meta (Martha) and Paula Monsanto (Jews) move in (RHP 118). Paula leaves and moves in with Hans Poley's parents (RHP 120). Willem ten Boom's home is raided by Gestapo; no evidence is found (RHP 121).

February 5

Hans Poley is arrested trying to warn another family of a Gestapo raid (RHP 125). Because of danger, all in hiding leave Beje (RHP 139). Eusie, Mary, Martha and Ronnie return in one week (RHP 140). These are the four Jews living in Beje on February 28.

February 28

Gestapo agents raid Beje at about 5 p.m. (RHP 142). Six people illegally in the house (four Jews and two underground workers) run into the hiding place. About 11 p.m., Casper, Corrie, Betsie and Willem ten Boom and Nollie and Peter van Woerden are taken to the Haarlem jail along with about thirty others (PY 14, RHP 146). Six people remain in the hiding place while Nazis guard the house. Herman Sluring (Pickwick), Corrie's contact in the Dutch National Underground, is arrested elsewhere in Haarlem (HP 122).

February 29

The six family members are transferred to Scheveningen prison near Den Haag (PY 19).

March 1

After over 47 hours, all six in the hiding place are rescued at about 4:30 p.m. Eusie, Mary, Martha and Ronnie (Jews) are taken to new safe houses. Reynout Siertsema and Hans van Messel (underground workers) leave the Beje safely (RHP 160).

March 9

Casper ten Boom dies at age 84 (PY 22).

March 16

Corrie begins solitary confinement in cell 384 (PL 18).

April 15

Corrie spends her birthday in solitary confinement (HP 140).

June 5

Corrie and Betsie find each other as they are transported by train from Scheveningen prison to Vught Concentration Camp in Holland, arriving June 6 (PL 11).

September 4
Corrie and Betsie begin nightmare train ride—three days and three nights jammed into a boxcar. Their destination is Ravensbrück Concentration Camp near Berlin, Germany (PY 85).

September 8
Corrie and Betsie are officially registered as prisoners in Ravensbrück (PY 88).

December 16
Betsie dies in Ravensbrück at age 59 (LST 63).

December 25
After learning she is to be released, Corrie is put in Ravensbrück hospital due to edema (HP 202).

December 30
(or December 28—both dates appear on discharge) Corrie is released from Ravensbrück Concentration Camp (PY 88).

1945 [53]
January 1
As a free person, Corrie arrives in Berlin and finds a train to Groningen, Holland, where she spends ten days in a nursing home. One of her nurses, Truus Benes, is a friend from the YWCA (LST 69). Then Corrie recuperates with Willem and Tine for two weeks before returning to Haarlem (HP 205–8).

May 5
Liberation Day in Holland. Shortly afterwards, Corrie rents and opens part of Schapenduinen (the home of Mrs. Bierens-de Haan) as a Christian rehabilitation center for war victims (HP 212).

May 8
VE Day (Victory in Europe)

June 19
Corrie writes to Jan Vogel, the man who betrayed her family to the Gestapo, and forgives him (PL 81).

June
Corrie's first book, *Gevangene en Toch* ... *(A Prisoner and Yet ...)*, is published in Holland.

1946 [54]
Early in the year, Corrie travels by freighter to the United States (U.S.A.) to share her story. She begins in New York City and receives advice from Irving Harris. Then in Washington, D.C., she is helped by Rev. Abraham Vereide and his daughter Alicia, Marian Johnson, Mrs. Frank McSherry and Kate Cheney. From there, Corrie travels to speaking engagements across the country (HL 149–52). She writes a July prayer letter from Kansas having already worked in New York, Washington, D.C., Pennsylvania, Vermont, Michigan, Illinois and Canada. (Corrie's "work" is evangelism and discipleship.) In Canada, she is helped by Mrs. Bobbie Halliday. She works in California, Utah and Iowa. On December 13, Corrie's brother, Willem, dies at age 60 from tuberculosis of the spine, contracted in prison (HP 218). She returns to Holland after ten months abroad (PrL 6–47).

1947 [55]
Corrie continues work at Schapenduinen (PrL 6–47). She also works in Germany, where she meets a guard from Ravensbrück and forgives him (TfL 82). In September, she works in Canada (CP).

1948 [56]
On her birthday, Corrie speaks in Los Angeles at the University of California (*Contemporary Christian Acts* magazine 4–78). She attends a Youth for Christ conference in Switzerland (HL163).

1949 [57]
Corrie speaks in Germany and works in refugee camps there. With help from the German Lutheran Church, she rents and opens Darmstadt (a former concentration camp) for refugees. The Evangelical Sisterhood of Mary serves the refugees on an ongoing basis until the camp closes in 1960 (CP, HP 218). She also works in Switzerland and the U.S.A. (CP).

1950 [58]
Corrie works in California (HL163–64), Washington, D.C., (CP),

Michigan, Canada and Bermuda. In Bermuda, she speaks twenty times in one week (PerL 3–50). She returns to Holland by freighter and works several months in Germany (CP).

1951 [59]

Corrie works in Germany, England, Canada and the U.S.A. (CP). During this year, she returns to Holland to complete the purchase of the house Zonneduin for the Christian retreat and training center. It moves from its rented house, Schapenduinen (HL 166). She is associated with this work until 1966 (PerL).

1952 [60]

Corrie works in the U.S.A., and then, on her way to Japan, she stops in Hawaii and speaks sixteen times in four days (PerL 4–52). She works in Japan for nine months, partly with missionaries Father and Mother Mitchell (PerL).

1953 [61]

Corrie's second book, *Amazing Love,* is published. It is her first book printed in English. She works in Taiwan and visits leprosy patients with Lillian Dixon (PrL 1–53). She also works in the Philippines, New Zealand, Australia, Israel (CP), South Africa (Reim. 66), Spain and Switzerland (PrL 12–53). On October 22, her sister Nollie dies at age 63. Corrie is greatly affected by her sister's passing (TfL 62). In December, she is in Haarlem where she falls and injures her hip. She is cared for at Zonneduin (PrL 5-54).

1954 [62]

In early January, Corrie is prayed for; she receives the baptism of the Holy Spirit (TfL 62). She works five months in Germany (PrL 5–54). She meets a nurse who was cruel to Betsie in Ravensbrück and leads her to the Lord (HL 160). Corrie also works in the U.S.A. (PrL 10–54), Bermuda and Cuba (PrL 2–54). Her first book, *Gevangene en Toch . . .* , is translated and published in English as *A Prisoner and Yet . . .*

1955 [63]

Corrie works in Canada, Mexico and the U.S.A. (PrL 1–55, 5–55). This trip lasts sixteen months (PrL 1–56).

1956 [64]

Corrie works in Hawaii for one month, where she speaks at 85 meetings (PrL 5–56). Remainder of year she works in New Zealand and Australia with the Revival Fellowship Team of J. Edwin Orr (PrL 1956).

1957 [65]

Corrie continues her work with the Revival Fellowship Team in New Zealand and Australia for this entire year (PrL 1957). Her books *Not Good If Detached* and *Common Sense Not Needed* are published.

1958 [66]

Corrie works in India, Borneo, Korea, Japan and Formosa (IHT 1958). Having been christened as a child, she is baptized by immersion at the William Carey Baptist Church in Calcutta, India, on March 20 (PerL). The name of her personal updates changes from *Prayer Letter* to *It's Harvest Time.*

1959 [67]

Corrie begins the year working in Hong Kong, then in Vietnam and Europe (IHT 1959). She returns to Ravensbrück Concentration Camp to discover her release was a clerical error (HP 219).

1960 [68]

Corrie works in Germany, Spain, England, Switzerland and for three months in Israel (IHT 1960). In Switzerland, she meets Billy and Ruth Graham (LST 106). She begins traveling with a personal companion, Conny van Hoogstraten. They work together seven years (HL 176).

1961 [69]

Corrie works in India for three months, then in Africa for eight months (IHT 1961).

1962 [70]

Corrie works in South America and the U.S.A. (IHT 1962). On April 17, the Netherlands' Queen Juliana makes Corrie a Knight in the Order Oranje-Nassau (LST 102).

1963 [71]

Corrie writes about recent work in Bermuda and Canada (IHT 1–63). She works in the U.S.A. (IHT 3–63). She stays in Buenos Aires, Argentina, in the apartment of Dr. Gwen Shepherd for six weeks. This is the first time in sixteen years she has stayed in the same home that long. She speaks in many meetings and visits patients at Dr. Shepherd's hospital. Then Corrie works in Cordoba, Argentina (IHT 6–63, TfL 102) and Brazil (PerL 7–1963). She returns to Holland for hospitalization due to an infection of the liver (IHT 10–63). She flies to the U.S.A. December 31 (CP).

1964 [72]

Corrie works in the U.S.A. (CP), Germany, Poland and Finland (IHT 1964). Then she is diagnosed with hepatitis. Under doctor's orders, she takes a year off from working. Her sabbatical year begins in September. She spends the first two months receiving medical treatment in Bavaria, Germany; then she stays with her nephew Peter van Woerden and family in Switzerland (IHT 1964–65).

1965 [73]

The remaining months of her sabbatical year are spent with Harry and Evelyn Campbell in Uganda, East Africa (HL 177). During her "year off," Corrie occasionally speaks in prisons and churches in Kenya and Uganda (CP, HL 178). In October, she starts to work again in Tanzania, Kenya, Rwanda, Burundi, Congo and Uganda (CP, IHT 12–65/3–66).

1966 [74]

By the end of January, Corrie finishes four months of work in Africa by speaking in Congo, Kenya and Ethiopia (CP). Then she works in Canada and the U.S.A. (CP). For several months, she works in Russia and Eastern Europe (Hungary, Poland, Czechoslovakia), then Germany and Holland (CP).

1967 [75]

Corrie works in France and Indonesia (CP). She celebrates her 75th birthday in Vietnam. It is wartime, and she is working with missionary Brother Andrew (LST 89). When she returns to Holland, Baroness Elisabeth van Heemstra loans her an apartment to use as a "home base" whenever she is in Holland (HL 186). In the summer, Conny leaves to marry Lykle Hoogerzeil, a Dutch missionary doctor to India (ML 23, 28). Ellen de Kroon becomes Corrie's next personal companion. They work together for nine years. A car Corrie is riding in is involved in a serious accident, and her arm and shoulder are broken. She spends nine weeks in the hospital (HL 186). *Plenty for Everyone* is published.

1968 [76]
On February 28, Corrie is honored by Israel at Yad Vashem (Holocaust Memorial). She is asked to plant a tree in the Garden of the Righteous because of the many Jewish lives she and her family saved during World War II. She works in Israel, Holland, Germany (IHT 5–68), the U.S.A., England and Moscow (CP).

1969 [77]
Corrie begins the year in Switzerland, then works in France (IHT 4–69), the U.S.A. (CP), Moscow (CP), Kazakhstan, Tajikistan, Uzbekistan, Germany (IHT 1–70) and Cuba (CP). Corrie's book *Marching Orders for the End Battle* is published.

1970 [78]
Corrie works in Israel and Cyprus (IHT 5–70). Her former personal companion, Conny, dies of cancer. Corrie speaks at the funeral (HL 179). She returns to Holland for five months' rest—under doctor's orders (IHT 9–70), then works in Alaska and the northern U.S.A. (IHT 12–70). *Defeated Enemies* is published.

1971 [79]
Corrie spends five months in the U.S.A. (IHT 4–71), then works in Holland, the U.S.A. (IHT 8–70) and Canada (CP). *The Hiding Place*, by Corrie with John and Elizabeth Sherrill, is published in November (IHT 8–71).

1972 [80]
Corrie continues to work in the U.S.A. and Canada (IHT 1972).

1973 [81]
Corrie works in the U.S.A. (IHT 2–73). She begins calling her

personal updates *The Hiding Place Magazine,* which is regularly published into 1983. She works in the Netherlands Antilles (HPM Sm 73). In June, she speaks at the Billy Graham Crusade in Atlanta, Georgia (BGCA).

1974 [82]

The Hiding Place movie is filmed from March through June in Haarlem and England. Corrie visits the set (LST 110, HL 202). Corrie works in the U.S.A. and Israel (HPM Sm 74). In July, she speaks at Congress for World Evangelization in Switzerland (MY 122). *Tramp for the Lord,* by Corrie with Jamie Buckingham, is published. In November, she is interviewed at the Billy Graham Crusade in Norfolk, Virginia (BGCA).

1975 [83]

Corrie works in the U.S.A. for several months (HPM Sp 75) and in Bermuda (HPM W 75). The Beje opens as a museum, "The Hiding Place" (LST 98). On September 29, *The Hiding Place* movie is to premiere in Beverly Hills, California. Just as it is to begin, a suspected neo-Nazi group throws a tear gas bomb into the theater. Instead of viewing the movie, hundreds of people enjoy a street meeting with Corrie, Billy Graham, Pat Boone as the master of ceremonies, Bev Shea singing "How Great Thou Art" and Pat and Cliff Barrows leading singing. Newspapers and television carry the story internationally (LST 112). *The Hiding Place* is shown in movie theaters in many countries. In November, a member of the Evangelical Sisterhood of Mary comes to the Beje and presents Corrie with plaques that are hung in the hiding place (LST 98). *Prison Letters* is published.

1976 [84]

In January, Corrie is in Oklahoma (BGCA). In April, Pam Rosewell becomes Corrie's personal companion when Ellen de Kroon leaves to marry Bob Stamps, chaplain of Oral Roberts University (TH 16). Pam works with Corrie seven years. Their first trip is seven months long, working in Switzerland; Toronto, Canada; and the U.S.A. (Honolulu, Hawaii; New York; Wenham, Massachusetts; Charlotte, North Carolina; Williamsburg, Virginia; Knoxville, Tennessee; Tulsa, Oklahoma; Dallas and Waco, Texas; Des Moines,

Iowa; Chicago, Illinois; Miami, Florida; Los Angeles, Anaheim, San Diego, and San Jose, California) (SY 40, 42). On April 23, Corrie receives an honorary degree (Doctorate of Humane Letters) from Gordon College in Massachusetts (HPM Sm 76); then she spends three months in Holland (SY 49). *In My Father's House*, by Corrie with C. C. Carlson, and *Corrie's Christmas Memories* are published. The film *Behind the Scenes of The Hiding Place* is released.

1977 [85]

In January, "The Hiding Place" is closed as a museum because of too many visitors (HPM Sp 77). Corrie is the guest speaker at a Billy Graham Crusade in Gothenburg, Sweden, and then works in Switzerland (HPM Sp 77). Also in January, Corrie and Pam receive resident alien status in the U.S.A. and leave for Florida, where Corrie spends several weeks writing a book (HL 209, SY 50). Then she and Pam go to California to look for a house to rent (SY 49). On February 28, they move into "Shalom" house in Placentia, California (LST 120). Corrie works in New York and Florida (HPM Sm 77). On July 4, in Arizona, she is honored by CHIEF (Christian Hope Indian Eskimo Fellowship), receives a headdress and is welcomed into their tribes. In July, she attends a booksellers' convention in Kansas City and Denver and then goes to Oklahoma for the baptism of Ellen's son, Peter John Stamps. She completes a film made especially for prisoners, *One Way Door* (HPM F 77). On September 25, she speaks at San Quentin Prison, near San Francisco, California (LST 125). In October, Corrie is hospitalized to receive a pacemaker (SY 73). In November, she speaks in Portland, Oregon (HPM Jan 78). *Each New Day; Prayers and Promises for Every Day; He Cares, He Comforts;* and *He Sets the Captives Free* are published.

1978 [86]

On April 15, Corrie spends her birthday in Arizona making a film for American Indians (SY 82). She spends May and June working on the book *This Day Is the Lord's*, which is published in 1979 (ST 156). In the early summer, she works on the film *Jesus Is Victor* (SY 89). In July, she is honored with an evening called "Corrie: The Lives She Touched" (SY 91). On August 23, she suffers her first major stroke

(SY 102) and loses most of her ability to communicate (ST 163). Her books *Father ten Boom, God's Man*; *A Tramp Finds a Home*; and *Don't Wrestle, Just Nestle* are published.

1979 [87]

On April 15, Corrie celebrates her 86th birthday with a small party in the back garden (HPM May 79). In May, she suffers a second serious stroke, losing the use of her right arm and leg (SY 144, ST 169).

1980 [88]

In October, Corrie suffers her third serious stroke and is bedridden (SY 186).

1982 [90]

Corrie's book *Clippings from My Notebook* is published. It is a collection of notes she wrote and photographs she took during her many decades of travel. Corrie's evangelistic film *Jesus Is Victor* is released.

1983 [91]

On her 91st birthday, April 15, Corrie goes to heaven. She dies at approximately 11 p.m. (SY186). Her memorial service is held on April 22, with burial at Fairhaven Memorial Park, Santa Ana, California. Her evangelistic films *One Way Door* and *Corrie: The Lives She's Touched* are released. Her book *Not I, but Christ* is published this year in Dutch, in 1984 in English.

1985

Jesus Is Victor is published. It is a compilation of three of Corrie's books.

1988

On April 15, the Corrie ten Boom House opens as a museum in Haarlem, Holland.

1999

Reflections of God's Glory is published. It contains messages given by Corrie on Trans World Radio.

2002

Messages of God's Abundance is published. This contains additional messages given by Corrie on Trans World Radio.

2003

The Hiding Place movie on DVD is released by World Wide Pictures. It includes four of Corrie's other films: *Behind the Scenes of The Hiding Place, Jesus Is Victor, One Way Door* and *Corrie: The Lives She's Touched.*

Additional tributes given to the Ten Boom family: There is a Corrie ten Boomstraat (street) and a Casper ten Boomstraat in Haarlem, a Ten Boomstraat in Hilversum named for Christiaan ten Boom (Kik), and a Ten Boom School in Maarssen named for Corrie's brother, Willem.

Timeline References

BGCA   From the Corrie ten Boom Collection in the Billy Graham Center Archives, Wheaton College, Wheaton, Illinois.

CP   Corrie's passports, BGCA.

FH   *In My Father's House* by Corrie ten Boom with Carole C. Carlson. Grand Rapids, Michigan: Fleming H. Revell, a division of Baker Book House Company, 1976, 2000. 1976 edition co-published with Christian Literature Crusade, Fort Washington, Pennsylvania. All publications rights held by Baker Book House Company, Grand Rapids, Michigan.

FtB   *Father ten Boom: God's Man* by Corrie ten Boom. Grand Rapids, Michigan: Fleming H. Revell, a division of Baker Book House Company, 1978.

HL   *Corrie ten Boom: Her Life, Her Faith* by Carole C. Carlson. Grand Rapids, Michigan: Fleming H. Revell, a division of Baker Book House Company, 1983.

HP   *The Hiding Place* by Corrie ten Boom with John and Elizabeth Sherrill. Chappaqua, New York: Chosen Books LLC, 1971.

HPM   *Hiding Place Magazine*, a personal update from Corrie ten Boom, in the archives of the Corrie ten Boom House Foundation, Haarlem, Netherlands.

IHT   *It's Harvest Time*, a personal update from Corrie ten Boom, in the archives of the Corrie ten Boom House Foundation, Haarlem, Netherlands.

LST   *Corrie, The Lives She's Touched* by Joan Winmill Brown. Grand Rapids, Michigan: Fleming H. Revell, a division of Baker Book House Company, 1979.

MY   *My Years with Corrie* by Ellen de Kroon Stamps. Eastbourne: Kingsway Publications Ltd and Alresford: Christian Literature Crusade. Copyright: Fleming H. Revell, a division of Baker Book House Company, 1978.

NG   *Not Good If Detached* by Corrie ten Boom. London: Christian Literature Crusade, 1957. Publications rights held by Baker Book House Company, Grand Rapids, Michigan.

PerL   Personal letters from the Ten Boom family, in the archives of the Corrie ten Boom House Foundation, Haarlem, Netherlands.

PL   *Prison Letters* by Corrie ten Boom. Grand Rapids, Michigan: Fleming H. Revell, a division of Baker Book House Company, 1975.

PrL   *Prayer Letter*, a personal update from Corrie ten Boom. in the archives of the Corrie ten Boom House Foundation, Haarlem, Netherlands.

PY   *A Prisoner and Yet . . .* by Corrie ten Boom. London: Christian Literature Crusade, 1954. Publications rights held by Baker Book House Company, Grand Rapids, Michigan.

Reim.   *Het Leven van Corrie ten Boom* by Lotte Reimeringer-Baudert. Hoornaar, Netherlands: Gideon, 1985.

RHP   *Return to the Hiding Place* by Hans Poley. Elgin, Illinois: LifeJourney Books, an imprint of Chariot Family Publishing, a division of David C. Cook Publishing Company, 1993. Copyright: Hans Poley.

SY   *The Five Silent Years of Corrie ten Boom* by Pamela Rosewell. Grand Rapids, Michigan: Zondervan, 1986. Copyright: The Zondervan Corporation.

ST   *Safer Than a Known Way* by Pamela Rosewell Moore.
        Grand Rapids, Michigan: Chosen Books, Fleming H.
        Revell, a division of Baker Book House Company, 1988.

TH   *A Tramp Finds a Home* by Corrie ten Boom. Grand Rap-
        ids, Michigan: Fleming H. Revell, a division of Baker
        Book House Company, 1978.

TfL   *Tramp for the Lord* by Corrie ten Boom with Jamie Buck-
        ingham. Grand Rapids, Michigan: Fleming H. Revell, a
        division of Baker Book House Company, 1974, 2000. 1974
        edition co-published with Christian Literature Crusade,
        Fort Washington, Pennsylvania. All publications rights
        held by Baker Book House Company, Grand Rapids,
        Michigan.

Dates for births, deaths, and marriages were obtained
from official records.

Notes

Chapter 2: Corrie's Early Life and Influences

    1. Corrie ten Boom, *In My Father's House* (Grand Rapids, Mich.: Revell, 1976), p. 17.

    2. Ibid.

    3. Hendrik Marsman (1899–1940), *Herinneringen aan Holland.* This is a free translation by the author. Publisher, if any, is unknown.

    4. Ten Boom, *In My Father's House,* pp. 23–24.

Chapter 3: World War I

    1. Corrie ten Boom with John and Elizabeth Sherrill, *The Hiding Place* (Washington Depot, Conn.: Chosen Books, 1971), p. 45.

    2. Ibid., p. 47.

    3. Ibid.

Chapter 4: The Years between the World Wars

    1. Ten Boom, *In My Father's House,* paraphrased.

Chapter 5: "The Deepest Hell That Man Can Create"

    1. H. R. Wilhemina, Princess of the Netherlands, *Lonely But Not Alone,* trans. John Peereboom (New York: McGraw-Hill, 1960), p. 147.

    2. Ten Boom, *The Hiding Place,* p. 62.

    3. Ibid.

4. Ibid., p. 64.

5. Hans Poley, *Return to the Hiding Place* (Elgin, Ill.: LifeJourney Books, an imprint of Chariot Family Publishing, a division of David C. Cook Publishing Company, 1993), p. 16.

6. Ten Boom, *The Hiding Place*, p. 192.

7. Ibid., p. 195.

8. Ibid., p. 196.

9. Ibid., p. 197.

10. Corrie ten Boom, *A Prisoner and Yet...* (Fort Washington, Pa.: Christian Literature Crusade, 1970), p.162. Similar words are used in *The Hiding Place*.

Chapter 6: Corrie Begins to Tell Her Story

1. Corrie ten Boom, *Tramp for the Lord* (Old Tappan, N.J.: Revell, 1974), p. 40.

Chapter 7: "We Are Able to Live as King's Children"

1. Ten Boom, *The Hiding Place*, p. 215.

2. Grant Colfax Tullar, original source unknown.

Chapter 8: In the Power of the Holy Spirit

1. Ten Boom, *Tramp for the Lord*, pp. 57–61.

2. Ibid., p. 61.

Chapter 10: When Bad Things Happen

1. Corrie ten Boom, *Not Good If Detached* (Grand Rapids, Mich.: Revell, 1966), pp. 40–42.

Chapter 12: I Am Yours!

1. Corrie ten Boom, *A Tramp Finds a Home* (Old Tappan, N.J.: Revell, 1978), p. 51.

2. Ibid., pp. 31–33.

3. Pam Rosewell, *The Five Silent Years of Corrie ten Boom* (Grand Rapids, Mich.: Zondervan Publishing House, 1986).

Index

227

Born near London, **Pam Rosewell Moore** has lived in the United States since 1976. That year she became companion to Corrie ten Boom, the Dutch Christian whose incarceration in a Nazi concentration camp during World War II is known to many through the book *The Hiding Place* and the film of the same name. It was Pam's privilege to live and work with Miss ten Boom from 1976 until her death in 1983.

After seeing the victorious end to Tante (Aunt) Corrie ten Boom's life, Pam wrote her first book, *The Five Silent Years of Corrie ten Boom* (Zondervan, 1986). This describes the last years of the Dutch evangelist's life, when she was crippled and silenced by successive strokes, and it also relates Pam's reactions to those events. *When a person cannot achieve in the normal way, where does his or her value lie?* This is the question the book asks of a society in which a person's worth often seems related to personal achievement.

In 1988 Pam wrote her second book, *Safer than a Known Way* (Chosen), which tells of her growing up in Hastings, Sussex, England, and coming to know the Lord Jesus Christ when she was 21. At that time she surrendered her own will to the will of God. Her previous reluctance to do so had lain in the fact that she thought he might want her to be a missionary—something she was sure she could never do. Missionaries were often required to do three things Pam knew were impossible for her—leave home and family, speak in public and lead a single life. But in the years following her prayer of relinquishment, she was to see the Lord fulfill her through the very things she had feared.

In 1966 Pam left England for a year of volunteer work as secretary to the Archbishop of East Africa in Nairobi, Kenya. In 1968 she joined the mission of Brother Andrew, God's smuggler, in the Netherlands. For more than seven years she saw God work miracles as teams transported Bibles and Christian books across the forbidding borders of Eastern Europe.

After her marriage to Carey Moore in 1986, Pam Rosewell Moore lived for two years in Waco, Texas, before the couple moved to Dallas in 1988. For the next fourteen years she worked at Dallas Baptist University, first as director of that institution's intercessory prayer ministry and then as director of spiritual life. Carey is Government Documents Librarian at Dallas Baptist University.

In 1991 Pam and Carey wrote their first book together. *If Two Shall Agree*, published by Chosen Books, addressed the need for Christian couples to pray together. This book was re-released in 1999 under the title *What Happens When Husbands and Wives Pray Together?* In 2000 a fourth book was published by the same company when Pam wrote *When Spring Comes Late: Finding Your Way through Depression*.

Pam, who speaks often at conferences and other meetings, and Carey Moore and their dogs, Annabelle and Toby, make their home in Waxahachie, Texas, just south of Dallas.

In My Father's House

Also by Corrie ten Boom

In My Father's House

The Years before "The Hiding Place"

Corrie ten Boom
with Carole C. Carlson

Fleming H. Revell
A Division of Baker Book House Co
Grand Rapids, Michigan 49516

Published by Fleming H. Revell
a division of Baker Book House Company
P.O. Box 6287, Grand Rapids, MI 49516-6287

Printed in the United States of America

ISBN:0-7394-4342-9

Unless otherwise indicated, Scripture quotations are from the
NEW AMERICAN STANDARD BIBLE ®. Copyright © The
Lockman Foundation 1960, 1962, 1963, 1968, 1971, 1972,
1973. Used by permission.

Scripture quotations identified PHILLIPS are from LETTERS TO
YOUNG CHURCHES by J. B. Phillips. © Macmillan Publishing Co., 1947, 1957.

Scripture quotations identified KJV are from the King James
Version of the Bible.

When my parents were married, many years ago, they claimed Psalm 32:8 as their "life verse," the promise that they felt was God's assurance for them: "I will instruct thee and teach thee in the way which thou shalt go: I will guide thee with mine eye" (KJV).

. . . this promise became the special directive for my life as well.

Corrie ten Boom
From *Tramp for the Lord*

Contents

Contents

Foreword

Today I know that memories are the key not to the past, but to the future. I know that the experiences of our lives, when we let God use them, become the mysterious and perfect preparation for the work He will give us to do.

Corrie wrote that in *The Hiding Place*, without realizing that it had provided the introduction to this book.

As I worked with Corrie, following her around America and living with her in Holland, I saw her in many different circumstances. It is a constant amazement to me how the Lord uses her. One time my husband, Ward, and I prayed with her in a small room off a large auditorium. She was ashen with pain and weariness. When she walked on the stage before four thousand people, her voice was firm and her message animated. She was—and continues to be— a living example of the way in which the

Spirit of the Lord works through His available servant.

However, as *In My Father's House* began to grow, I became excited to see how this was more than a collection of memories—more than nostalgia from a rich life. Here we had the unique lessons of a family preparing for a future, a future that would demand the power of God's love and strength.

If we are living in the time in which we believe God's plan for planet earth is reaching its completion—when the new beginning Jesus promised will take place—then each individual and family needs the pattern for living in this present age. Never before in human history have guidelines been more important.

The applications of various parts of Corrie's life to modern living were impressed upon me as I savored those wonderful "years before." I've learned so much for my own life and family as I've lived with Corrie *In My Father's House.* Let's visit together . . .

Carole C. Carlson

1
Inheritance

"Remarkable, extraordinary . . . Peter, where did Cook find strawberries in the midst of winter?"

The Dutch merchant summoned his butler and pointed to the luscious fruit in the silver compote. Even in the home of great wealth this was an amazing luxury in the early 1800s.

"It's the gardener, sir . . . ten Boom. He does some miraculous things in that hothouse of his."

"Ten Boom, you say. Hmm, must remember him. Astounding! Bring me some more, Peter, with lots of thick cream."

My great-grandfather ten Boom grew those plump strawberries during the chilling months when ruddy-cheeked children skated over the canals. He was no ordinary gardener, but a master craftsman who caressed the soil into performing miracles. He experimented with plants, manipulating them between an ice cellar and a hothouse, until he produced the fruit that was served at the dinner table of his employer, one of the richest men in Hofstede, Bronstede, Heemstede.

Those simple strawberries saved my great-grandfather from jail!

It was during the time of Napoleon; Europe was trembling from the onslaught of the evil little man from Corsica. Swaggering across the continent, victorious in war, the French emperor conquered country after country and forced men into submission. The government of Holland was ruled by Napoleon's followers and their oppressive regime.

My great-grandfather was an independent man; he had spunk, but not much tact, I'm afraid. He refused to submit to men who denied freedom to other men. However, Hollanders at that time had two alternatives: They were either obedient to those who served the strutting dictator, or they faced what could be very severe punishment.

Tyranny at any time in man's history demands loyalty.

One Sunday Great-grandfather went to his church and heard the minister announce the opening hymn; the theme was from Psalm 21, but as the congregation began to understand the words, one voice after another stopped. They realized it was a pointed description of their political situation. Nobody dared to continue.

But Great-grandfather and the minister sang louder, a defiant duet (translated from the Dutch):

> The evil one considers himself to be free from all bondage, and runs around, while he stirs the people. At the same time, the bad people assume they hold the reins of government, and they are being raised to the summits of honor.

Sad hearts and silent voices were encouraged by the bravery of the minister and the spunky gardener.

When news of ten Boom's traitorous act of defiance reached the authorities, he received a summons to appear at the town hall. He must have been prepared for the consequences, as he addressed the officer in charge.

"What does this Mr. Snotneus [snot-nose] want with me?"

First he challenged the regime; then he hurled that contemptuous name at his accuser!

But where do strawberries fit into all this? Before Great-grandfather had a chance to be sentenced or taken to prison, his boss, who was a very influential citizen, interceded and had him pardoned. (A gardener couldn't grow fruit in jail, could he?)

My father told us this story of Great-grandfather and his personal challenge to the Napoleonic regime with a sense of joy.

"I'm glad he was a real man," Father said.

Over a hundred years later when people said to Father, "Stop having Jews in your house—you will be sent to prison," my father answered, "I am too old for prison life, but if that should happen, then it would be, for me, an honor to give my life for God's ancient people, the Jews."

From Generation to Generation

Willem ten Boom, my grandfather, was not strong like his father, so he chose a work that was not physically difficult. In the year 1837, Grandfather purchased a little house in Haarlem for four hundred guilders and set up shop as a watchmaker.

It was in 1844 that Grandfather had a visit from his minister, Dominee Witteveen, who had a special request. "Willem, you know the Scriptures tell us to pray for the peace of Jerusalem and the blessing of the Jews."

"Ah, yes, Dominee, I have always loved God's ancient people—they gave us our Bible and our Savior."

Beginning with this conversation, a prayer fellowship was started, with Grandfather and his friends praying for the Jewish people. This was an unusual idea among Christians at that time. The Jews were scattered throughout the world, without a country or a national identity; Jerusalem was a city torn by centuries of conflict. The attention of the world was not upon the Middle East, and yet a small group of Dutch believers met in a little Haarlem house, a watchmaker's shop (later called the Beje), to read the Scriptures and pray for the Jews.

In a divine way that is beyond our human understanding, God answered those prayers. It was in the same house, exactly one hundred years later, that Grandfather's son, my father, and four of his grandchildren and one great-grandson were arrested for helping save the lives of Jews during the German occupation of Holland.

Another strutting dictator, more arrogant and insane than Napoleon, had planned to exterminate every Jew in the world. When Holland was controlled by Hitler's troops, many Jews were killed.

For helping and hiding the Jews, my father, my brother's son, and my sister all died in prison. My brother survived his imprisonment but died soon afterward. Only Nollie, my older sister, and I came out alive.

So many times we wonder why God has certain things happen to us. We try to understand the circumstances of our lives, and we are left wondering. But God's foolishness is so much wiser than our wisdom.

From generation to generation, from small beginnings and little lessons, He has a purpose for those who know and trust Him.

God has no problems—just plans!

Beginning with Mama

My mother was a woman with a loving sense of humor and a striking appearance. She had thick, dark, curly hair and brilliant blue eyes—an unusual combination for a Hollander. She came from a large family and was left fatherless just after her mother gave birth to an eighth baby. While she was still very young, her mother and her brothers and sisters were forced to earn their own living.

One of her sisters, Jans, started a kindergarten where Cor (my mother) and another sister, Anna, became her assistants. I'm sure this experience helped my mother later in training her own children.

When Jans added a Sunday school to her kindergarten, she began to work with a young theology student, Hendrik Wildeboer, who became her special boyfriend. Cor caught the eye of a handsome teacher in the Sunday school by the name of Casper ten Boom, and they immediately found something in common: Their birthdays were on the same day, May 18.

Romance grew between Cor and Casper; when Cor journeyed to Harderwijk to visit her grandmother, Casper was so lonely that he followed her the next day.

About fifty years later, I visited the quaint village of Harderwijk on the Zuider Zee with Father. As we walked along the Bruggestraat, Father said, "This is where I proposed to your mother. There were cobblestones instead of pavement at that time, but many of the old houses and the sea gate are still the same."

He paused to remember the youth that had vanished, and his love for the gentle woman with the laughing eyes.

"Did Mother say yes immediately?" I asked.

"No, not until the next day, and I spent a very restless night waiting for that decision!"

When I asked him if he had ever regretted his decision to marry Mama, his voice was firm. "Never! Until the last day of her life, I was just as much in love with your mother as I was on that day in Harderwijk. We didn't have an easy life—we had many sorrows—but God led us by His extraordinary providence."

A Little Jewelry Store

Grandmother died shortly before Casper and Cor were married. By then, Father had started a jewelry store in a small house in the heart of the Jewish section of Amsterdam.

Once a customer arrived who was a pastor from Ladysmith, South Africa. He came into the shop and asked Father to provide a clock and a bell for his church tower. This was a tremendous encouragement to a young merchant. The order was simple to fill; all Father had to do was to go to the factory in Brabant to make the selection; the manufacturer did all the installation. However, the commission from that sale provided enough money for the young Dutch couple to be married.

Uncle Hendrik, Jans's husband, was a minister in a little village near Amsterdam. Mother and Father had to go to the town hall first, to be registered and married in a civil ceremony. The man at the town hall who married them thought they were "high people" because they came from Amsterdam. He tried to be very dignified, in a manner suitable for this distinguished couple, and began the marriage speech with great airs.

"Honored bride and bridegroom . . . you are now . . . you are now gathered . . . you are now gathered here. . . ." He stopped, looked around, and burst into tears.

Father said, "I'm so touched by your speech and tears, but we would like to be married."

The poor fellow finished the ceremony somehow, but Uncle Hendrik conducted the final marriage rites in his church—without tears.

The newlyweds moved into a shabby little house in Amsterdam after their wedding. It's probably just as well that the emotional clerk from the town hall didn't know of their humble means!

Mother had dreamed of a home with a small garden, for she loved flowers and the beauty of color.

"I love to see much of the sky," she often said.

The sky was there, if she stretched far enough to see it in the narrow street outside the old house. Their cramped home had a single room on each story, with worn-out furniture left by my grandmother.

Money was scarce, but happiness was abundant.

The neighborhood of Jewish people made it possible for Father to participate in their Sabbaths and other holy days. He studied the Old Testament, their Talmud, with them and was given opportunities to understand and explain the fulfillment of the prophecies of the Old Testament in the New Testament.

My father's love for the Jewish people was nurtured in the Jewish quarter of Amsterdam during those first years of married life. Father and Mother lived on poverty's edge, and yet their contentment was not dependent upon their surroundings. Their relationship with each other and with the Lord gave them strength.

Plan for Parenthood

When the first baby was expected, Mother was glad she had learned to sew. She had inherited an old sewing machine from her mother, and every moment she could find she stitched little garments for the baby. A Jewess who lived upstairs couldn't contain her curiosity and asked Mother if she was a seamstress.

"No," Mother answered proudly, "but I'm expecting my first baby. See the little dress I've made?" She held up a dainty garment tenderly.

The Jewess was astonished. "You're not sewing the clothes before the baby arrives! That is tempting God!"

Mother was puzzled, but this didn't stop her from preparing for her baby. However, she began to understand why Mary had only swaddling clothes for the baby Jesus. It wasn't lack of money but the Jewish custom not to sew the layette before the birth of the child. I've heard that Portuguese Jews maintain this tradition today.

When Betsie, the first child, was born, Mother became quite ill. She asked her youngest sister, Anna, to come for a few weeks to help with the new baby. Those few weeks stretched into forty years.

Mother and Anna had always been close, but when Mother married, Anna went to live with Jans and Uncle Hendrik. Anna, however, became very lonely for Cor and was delighted when Mother and Father invited her to stay with them in Amsterdam.

Within seven years, four more babies were born, but one didn't live. Father had to look for a cheaper house to accommodate his growing responsibilities.

By the time I was born, they were living on the Korte Prinsegracht, in a house at the end of the canal, where few people passed the shop. Business was at its lowest ebb.

I was a premature baby, with blue skin and pinched features. When Uncle Hendrik saw me he shook his head sadly. "I hope the Lord will quickly take this poor little creature to His home in heaven," he said.

Fortunately, my parents didn't feel the same as Uncle Hendrik. They surrounded me with love and good care. There were no incubators in those days, and one of the greatest problems was keeping me warm. I cried so pitifully from the cold that Tante Anna rolled me in her apron and tied me against her body; then I became warm and quiet.

Many years later while I was in Africa I met a missionary family whose baby could not be comforted, until a native girl bound the child to her back with a piece of cloth. The baby became calm, secure in the closeness to the body of a person who loved him.

I must have felt that same way bound snugly in Tante Anna's apron.

Throughout the first year of my life I was a poor, sickly looking creature. Mother told me that once she was traveling by train with a friend who held a beautiful, plump baby on her lap. The baby's name was Rika, and the people in the coach were giving her many admiring glances and comments. They would look at me in my mother's arms and then turn away, unable to find anything positive to say.

Mother told me this bothered her at first, but then she would hug me and whisper, "I wouldn't exchange you for anyone in the whole world, you darling ugly baby with the beautiful eyes."

When Rika was two years old, she began having epileptic seizures. I played with her all through my childhood, but I remember how aware I was that her little face would change so drastically as the sickness would overpower her. Mother was always ready to care for Rika; throughout her life Mother taught us to be helpful and loving toward those who were weak or abnormal.

Haarlem Inheritance

Grandfather Willem died when I was six months old, leaving Father his shop in Haarlem. We moved into the house, which wasn't very large, and poor Mother still didn't have her garden. She put some flowerpots on the flat roof and called this her yard. She had geraniums in clay pots, hanging fuchsia, and some ivy climbing the brick wall. She developed a roof garden long before the modern penthouse dwellers thought of such a thing.

Even in the "new" house in Haarlem, she could see only a small piece of the sky she loved. The roof became her "outdoors" when she became too weak to take her daily walks in the street.

During those first years of their marriage, the financial situation must have been very serious. Anna worked night and day to nurse Mother when she was ill and to care for four children. She earned the grand sum of one guilder (about thirty cents) a week. Father gave her this magnificent salary each Saturday, but often by the following Wednesday the finances would become so desperate that Father would have to go to the kitchen and ask, "Anna, do you still have your guilder?"

Anna always had the guilder available, and it often bought the food for the family on that day. This was certainly "blessed money."

This was the beginning of my rich inheritance. When I remember my family life, I realize that my parents and my aunts had truly mastered the art of living. They enjoyed life and they loved children.

"We never laughed so much as when you children were small," Tante Anna often said.

In our hearts we must have stored some of the memory of laughter to be brought out in later years, when the sounds of happy voices were scarce in our beloved land.

2

Five Is Not Too Young

In 1892, the year I was born, Holland was entering an exciting and important era. In a few years, Wilhelmina would be crowned queen at the tender age of eighteen. There were signs that the stability of the latter part of the nineteenth century would soon be rocked by the rattling of German swords. Foreign policy was being shaped around lines of power, as young Kaiser Wilhelm II ruled the country that later played such an important part in my life.

History in the making means nothing to a child, but it was a world event for me when Mother or Tante Anna pinched a guilder hard enough to squeeze out some sugar and butter for those fat little cookies I loved. The fragrance of baking would float from the iron

stove into the shop and tantalize the customers just as it put us in a happy mood.

When I was five years old, I learned to
read; I loved stories, particularly those about
Jesus. He was a member of the ten Boom
family—it was just as easy to talk to Him as
it was to carry on a conversation with my
mother and father, my aunts, or my brother
and sisters. He was there.

One day my mother was watching me play
house. In my little girl world of fantasy, she
saw that I was pretending to call on a neighbor. I knocked on the make-believe door and
waited . . . no one answered.

"Corrie, I know Someone who is standing at your door and knocking right now."

Was she playing a game with me? I know
now that there was a preparation within my
childish heart for that moment; the Holy
Spirit makes us ready for acceptance of
Jesus Christ, of turning our life over to Him.

"Jesus said that He is standing at the door,
and if you invite Him in He will come into
your heart," my mother continued. "Would
you like to invite Jesus in?"

At that moment my mother was the most
beautiful person in the whole world to me.

"Yes, Mama, I want Jesus in my heart."

So she took my little hand in hers and we prayed together. It was so simple, and yet Jesus Christ says that we all must come as children, no matter what our age, social standing, or intellectual background.

When Mother told me later about this experience, I recalled it clearly.

But, You're So Little

Does a child of five really know what he's doing? Some people say that children don't have spiritual understanding—that we should wait until a child can "make up his mind for himself." I believe a child should be led, not left to wander.

Jesus became more real to me from that time on. Mother told me later that I began to pray for others, as young as I was.

The street behind our house was the Smedestraat. It was filled with saloons, and many of the happenings there were frightening to me. As I played outside jumping rope, or joined with Nollie, my sister, in a game of *bikkelen* (ball and stones), I saw the police pick up these lurching, incoherent men as they slumped to the ground or slouched in a doorway, and take them into the police station.

I would stand before the *politie bureau* (police station) behind the Beje and watch the drunks being pushed in. It made me shiver. The building was made of dark red brick, and way at the top were turrets with small windows. Were those the cells, I wondered?

It was in that same police station years later that my father and all his children and a grandson were taken after being arrested for helping Jews escape from the German gestapo.

As a child I would be so concerned for those arrested that I would run into the house sobbing, "Mother . . . I'm afraid those poor men are going to be hurt . . . they're so sick!"

Bless Mother's understanding. She would say, "Pray for them, Corrie."

And I would pray for the drunks. "Dear Jesus, please help those men . . . and Jesus, help all the people on the Smedestraat."

Many years later I spoke on a television station in Holland. I received a letter after the program that said, "My husband was especially interested because you told us that you had lived in Haarlem. He lived in a house on the Smedestraat. Three years ago he accepted the Lord Jesus as his Savior."

I read that letter and recalled the prayers of little Corrie. That man whose wife wrote me was one person I had prayed for seventy-six years before.

Does He Listen?

At another time in my later years I was camping with a number of Haarlem girls. Around the campfire one evening, we were talking about the Lord and chatting about the pleasant events of the day.

"Do you know that I am a neighbor of yours?" one of the girls asked me. "I live in the Smedestraat."

"I lived there until five years ago," said another girl.

"My mother lived there," said a third.

We all began to laugh to discover that all eighteen of those girls, who were sleeping in the big camp tent, had lived on that street or their parents had lived there. They found it an amusing coincidence.

"Listen," I said, "I just remembered something that I had almost forgotten. When I was five or six years old, I used to pray every day for the people in the Smedestraat. The fact that we have been talking about Jesus and that God has even used me to reach some of your parents is an answer to the prayer of a little child. Never doubt whether God hears our prayers, even the unusual ones."

How often we think when a prayer is not answered that God has said no. Many times He has simply said, "Wait."

The Future Comes Quickly

When we are very young the future is so hard to grasp. My father had one coming event that he mentioned in every prayer. It baffled me. I didn't want to ask in front of the entire family; I thought they might think I was foolish to ask about something I heard several times a day.

I waited until Father came upstairs to tuck me in; this was a time I could ask him anything.

"Papa, you always pray in every prayer, 'Let soon come that great day when Jesus Christ, Your beloved Son, comes on the clouds of heaven.' Why are you longing for that day?"

"Correman, remember when you saw the men drunk and fighting in the Smedestraat, and they were taken to the police station? The whole world is filled with fighting. You may see worse fighting in your lifetime than what you have seen on the street."

I hoped not. Fighting upset me.

"In the Bible," Papa continued, "we read that Jesus has promised to come to this world to make everything new. The world is now covered with hatred, but when Jesus returns, the world will be covered with the knowledge of God, like the water covers the bottom of the sea."

Thinking of that wonderful day, I knew why Papa prayed for it so often. "Oh, Papa, then everyone will know about Jesus! I'll be very happy when He comes."

Let the Children Come

Decades later I was speaking to a group when I challenged parents to "bring your little ones to the Lord Jesus. He has said, 'Let the children come to me; the kingdom of God is theirs.'" (See Matthew 19:14.)

Then I told how I made a decision for Jesus when I was five years old.

After that talk I left the platform and went into a small room in the building where I found a father with two little boys, all on their knees. The father had an arm around both of those boys, and I moved back quietly while the man told the boys tenderly that they were not too young to ask Jesus to come into their hearts.

What a wonderful heritage those boys have, to know that their father cared enough about them to lead them to a knowledge of their heavenly Father!

Later I received a letter from a lady who told me the results in her life of that evening.

I went home after that meeting and went directly to my little girl, Mary, who was in bed. She knew about the Lord because she had been to a Sunday school, but that night, in her bed, she gave her heart to Jesus.

The next morning she said, "Oh, Mommy, I'm so happy that Jesus is now in my heart. He made me a child of God."

Mary was singing the whole time before she went to school, and I was amazed that she sang many songs about heaven.

My husband went to school to pick her up that day, and as he approached the schoolhouse, he noticed that a great many people were standing around, and there obviously must have been an accident. Then he saw what had happened.

Mary was on the street, her little body crumpled like a rag doll. She was dead.

As I read that letter my eyes were so filled with tears that the words blurred.

Mary had passed behind a big transport truck and had not seen another car, which was coming toward her from the other direction. She was killed immediately.

My husband brought her little body home. He was in deep despair, but then he remembered the songs Mary had sung that morning. I told him what had happened the evening before, and right then, my husband, who had never made a decision for the Lord Jesus, accepted Him as his Savior.

On Mary's burial day many children of her class came to the Lord.

I sat for a long time with that letter on my lap, realizing that I must have a new sense of urgency to talk to parents about the joy of leading their children to the Lord. What a wonderful assurance Mary's parents had to know that someday they would be with her again.

During some of my talks I have often repeated this little poem:

Safe?
Said a precious little laddie,
To his father one bright day,

"May I give myself to Jesus,
Let Him wash my sins away?"

O, my son, but you're so little,
Wait until you older grow,
Bigger folks 'tis true, do need Him,
But little folk are safe, you know.

Said the father to his laddie,
As a storm was coming on,
"Are the sheep all safely sheltered,
Safe within the fold, my son?"

"All the big ones are, my father,
But the lambs, I let them go,
For I didn't think it mattered,
Little ones are safe, you know."

                    Author Unknown

Praying for Crazy Thys

As a child in Haarlem I prayed for a man most people avoided. His nickname was *Gekke Thys* (Crazy Thys), and he was the town tramp, an idiot. I pitied him and when I was five or six years old started to talk about this to the Lord.

How curious the little minds of children are. Was it my mother or one of my aunts who gave me the advice to cast my burden on the Lord in prayer? Or did the Lord Himself give me this motivation?

Every prayer in the evening and in the morning ended with this request: "And Lord, be with all the people in the Smedestraat and also *Gekke Thys.*"

My sister, Nollie, was only a year and a half older than I, but she seemed so much wiser. I remember walking with her through the Smedestraat one day and stopping to watch a crowd of children surrounding someone they were taunting and teasing. As we inched closer to the others, wanting to know what was happening but a bit afraid of getting involved in something that looked so mean, we realized that poor old Crazy Thys was standing in the middle of the circle, confusion and hurt showing in his face.

I was so full of pity for poor Thys and angry at the cruel children that I shouted, "You leave him alone, do you hear!"

The children stopped at my bold challenge. Thys looked for his defender and saw a little girl, less than half his size. Suddenly he walked toward me and stooped down. I could smell the unpleasant odor of his unwashed clothes and matted beard. He put his hand under my chin and kissed me on both cheeks.

Nollie was shocked! She grabbed my hand and pulled me home as fast as we could run. Down the Smedestraat, into the alley that ran beside our house, and through the side door we raced.

"Aunty, someone . . . hurry! That dirty old *Gekke Thys* kissed Corrie. Let's wash her cheeks!"

My face was so thoroughly washed I was afraid my skin would fall off. I heard someone say, "Such dangerous tramps shouldn't be allowed to go so freely in the streets."

Stinging from the rebuke as well as the face scrubbing, I went to my mother. "Mama, why was it so bad that *Gekke Thys* kissed me? He's such a poor unhappy man. Everybody makes fun of him."

Mother took me into her bed and talked quietly with me as I nestled against her soft shoulder. She said, "Correman, it's good that you have pity for this man. The Lord Jesus gives you love for *Gekke Thys* and for the drunken men in the Smedestraat. Jesus loves sinners, but before they are going to love Him, these men can be very bad. It's wise to keep a little distance. But there's one great thing you and I can do—and you are doing that already—pray faithfully for them."

Shortly after that incident *Gekke Thys* disappeared from the streets. I don't know how the Lord worked in his life, but a deep concern for the feebleminded was fostered in me.

Fear No Evil . . . Except

A child is not fearless, contrary to what his parents may think at times. A child is often a bundle of unexpressed fears, unknown terrors, and shadowy worries. I was afraid of the doctor's office, my family's leaving me, and the mystery of death.

Nollie's nightgown was my contact with security. We slept in the same bed, and I can remember clinging to Nollie's nightgown as long as she would allow me. Poor Nollie, when she would try to turn, she would be anchored by my little fist clasping her tightly.

One time Mother took Nollie and me to visit a woman whose baby had died. I wished Nollie had been allowed to wear her nightgown on that journey, because I needed desperately to hang onto it.

We climbed a narrow staircase and entered the poorly furnished room of one of

Mama's "lame ducks" (the name we children had given to her protégés). Although we often did not have sufficient money for ourselves, Mother always found someone who was in greater need.

In that shabby little room was a crib with a baby inside. It didn't move at all and its skin was very white. Nollie stood next to the crib and touched the baby's cheek.

"Feel that," she said to me. "It's so cold."

I touched the little hand and then ran to my mother and buried my face in her lap. I had touched death for the first time, and it seemed that the impression of cold remained with me for hours and hours.

When we returned home, I ran up the narrow stairs to my bedroom and leaned against the antique chest of drawers. There was an enormous fear in my heart—almost terror. In my imagination, I pictured the future in which I saw myself all alone, my family gone, and myself left desolate. My family was my security, but that day I saw death and knew that they could die too. I had never thought about it before.

The dinner bell rang downstairs, and I was so grateful to go to the big oval table and get warm again and feel the security of being with my family. I thought how stupid the grown-ups would think I was if I told them about the fear that was still in my heart.

I ate dinner quietly that night, which was not easy when you are in the midst of such a lively family. Our dinner table spilled over with conversation.

After dinner Father took the Bible, as he always did, and began to read the lines from Psalm 46:2. "Therefore will not we fear, though the earth be removed, and though the mountains be carried into the midst of the sea" (KJV).

I sat up straight in my chair and stared at my father. I didn't know much about mountains, living in flat, flat Holland, but I certainly knew a lot about fear. I thought Papa must have known exactly what my problem was that night.

My faith in Papa, and in the words he read from the Bible, was absolute. If they said not to fear, then God would take care of it. I felt secure again.

3

From Small Beginnings

⚭

My doll, Casperina, and I were going to
have a party! Mama and Tante Anna were
cooking, and I watched their long skirts bus-
tle past me from my perch on the footstool
beneath the table. This was a wonderful
place to play, safe and secure beneath the
red and black tablecloth.

My friend was named after my father, but
the resemblance ended there. I loved her
very much, but dragging her up and down
the stairs of the Beje had left her with a few
fingers missing and a slightly cracked head.
Oh, my, why couldn't she look like Nollie's
doll, who was immaculately dressed and
didn't have a scratch on her china face? Poor
Casperina, she would never be in the same
society with Emma, Betsie's doll, who was
named after the mother of the queen.

41

"Never mind, Casperina," I whispered to her in the shelter of our little house beneath the table, "Jesus loves you, and so do I."

When I was especially happy, I would sing a little song that Tante Jans had composed:

'k Zou zoo graag eens komen, Heiland,
In dat heerlijk Vaderhuis.
(I should just like to come, Savior,
In the beautiful Father-house.)

However, instead of singing *to come* I substituted *to peek,* combining my words with a mischievous look around the fat table leg.

Tante Anna laughed at me. "Corrie, you'd better not let Tante Jans hear you change the words in her songs. When she writes 'I should like to come to heaven,' that's what she means."

Some things grown-ups don't understand, I thought. I meant that it would be great fun just to look around for a moment in heaven, where I knew I would spend my future. I just wanted a little peek; after all, my father-house right here on the Barteljorisstraat was all the heaven I wanted right then.

I clutched Casperina's three-fingered hand in mine and whispered, "We'll just stay in our own secret place, where no one will ever—ever—scold us for anything."

A Time to Uproot

A time comes when all children, even a little Dutch girl with her jaw set and her black-stockinged legs rigid upon the staircase, must leave their father's house for a time. I was born with my feet slightly turned in, a defect that the doctor said would cure itself with time and growth.

"Don't worry," he told Mama and Papa, "when she is about sixteen, she will become vain enough to turn her toes the right way."

However, when I turned my toes in even more and tightened my fingers in a knuckle-whitening grip on the railing, I meant business.

"I'm not going to school. I know how to read; I can learn arithmetic from Papa, and Casperina needs me at home."

There. *That* was settled.

"Of course you're not going to school alone, Corrie. I am going to walk with you."

Papa bent over me, his beard tickling the top of my head, and one by one loosened my fingers on the railing. With the release of each finger, I howled a bit louder. By the time Papa had my hand in his, he was almost dragging me down the street toward school. I thought my hand would break—just like Casperina's—and then it would be impossible for me to go to school.

It must have taken great dignity for Papa, with his immaculate suit and erect carriage, to struggle past the homes and shops of his friends with a red-faced child announcing her objections to the entire world.

I knew Father was not angry, but his will was law. I had to obey.

When we arrived at the school, I saw a little boy being carried into Master Robyns's classroom in his father's arms. (At least I was walking!) He was crying lustily, even louder than I was. He looked so ugly that I felt sorry for him. But what about me? I realized how I must look to others and stopped abruptly.

Papa released my hand; my fingers weren't broken at all—only my heart was slightly injured. However, when Papa kissed me gently on the cheek, bringing the familiar fragrance of cigars and cologne, he assured me that when school was over, he would be waiting at home, and I knew I would find that blessed security I needed in the shelter of his arms.

God was teaching a little lesson in a small life, because sixty-seven years later, He reminded me of my fingers on the railing.

I was in a room of *Zonneduin,* a house in Holland that some friends and I had established first for ex-prisoners who had been in concentration camps, and later for any person who needed nursing and rest. I had been traveling so much and was tired—tired of strange beds and different food, tired of dressing for breakfast, tired of new people and new experiences. I liked this very luxurious house with its large rooms and decided to stay and enjoy the comfortable life in Holland, although I knew that God didn't agree with my decision.

Most of the furniture in the entire house was mine, but there was one room in particular that reminded me of the happy family life of my past. It was a room that held my treasures: photographs of those I loved, mementos of my family during the years before. Every picture was like the railing on the stairs. My hands grasped the past and tried to hold on, but my heavenly Father's hands were stronger.

I left the house for a while for some speaking engagements, intending to return to my old room and settle in for good. However, when I came back to *Zonneduin* some weeks later, my pictures were down and the strange belongings of someone else were on the bed.

My friends had not known of my personal decision to return to this room; my irregular life, my coming and going unexpectedly, was difficult for those who had to manage the big family of patients and staff in an orderly way.

But I decided to stay, and that was settled!

My heavenly Father spoke to me, "Only obey me, Corrie. I'll hold your hand. It is My will that you leave your room. Later you will thank Me for this experience. You do not see it, but this is one of My great blessings for you."

Father's hand was firm, but I knew His love.

I packed up my suitcase again and left for the United States. How the Lord blessed my time there. Meetings began to grow in size, and when I saw people come from darkness into light, from bondage into liberation, I began to see the pattern. I could praise my Father that His hands were stronger than mine.

Blue Stones Can Hurt!

School life did not prove to be as horrible as I thought. I can still remember the sensation of victory when I worked an arithmetic problem and discovered that the final figure was what it was supposed to be. However, my mind was not always so attentive to details. I was a daydreamer, carrying my fantasies into a world where everyone needed an expensive new watch, and every day was a walk on the dunes with the sunshine warming my cheeks.

The headmaster of our school was a strict taskmaster, insisting upon obedience and discipline without question. He had warned all the children not to step on the "blue stone," which was a small square stone slightly higher than the rest in the outer yard. I was not paying attention to his instructions and stepped on the stone. Instantly my face was smarting from a sharp slap on my cheek. I can still feel the shame of it, after all these years, for I don't believe the people at home had ever slapped my face. A color photoplate was impressed upon my mind, which has never faded. The tears covered my face, but I could see the girl who stood in front of me who wore a red dress and a white apron; there was a green door on the garden gate, and the colors all blended with the blazing eyes of Mr. Loran, the headmaster.

I couldn't wait to get home that day. Before I opened the door my cries had overpowered the sound of the bell, which announced any visitors to the shop.

Mama took me on her lap and comforted me; and when I had quieted, Papa held me in his arms as he did when I was a baby. I can still feel the sensation of safety as I put my head upon his shoulder. What a security to have a refuge when life is really hard!

Forty-five years passed after the blue-stone incident. The gestapo had arrested me, and I was being asked the location of the secret room in which I had hidden four Jews and two underground workers. I realized that if I told, it would mean prison and possibly death for the six people who were there, so I didn't tell. The interrogator slapped me on the face, and at the same moment I recalled the backyard of the school, the angry headmaster, and Mother and Father's comforting help.

"Lord Jesus, cover me!" I cried.

"If you mention that name, I'll murder you!" shouted the man interrogating me.

But his hand stopped in midair and he couldn't beat me any longer.

What a security to have a refuge when life is really hard!

In Dat Vaderhuis (In That Father-house)

Our house was not very big, but it had wide open doors. I don't think that many guests who came to the Beje ever realized what a struggle it was to make both ends meet. As Mother said, "We must turn every penny twice before we spend it."

We didn't feel that we were poor, however, and indeed we weren't. The words "we can't afford it" were not a part of our thinking, because as children we knew something about the status of family finances and didn't ask for what we knew was impossible.

Many lonesome people found a place with us, where there was music, humor, interesting conversations, and always room for one more at the oval dinner table. Oh, it's true, the soup may have been a bit watery when too many unexpected guests came, but it didn't really matter.

Mother loved guests. Her lovely blue eyes would brighten, and she would pat her dark hair into place when she knew we would be squeezing another visitor around our table—already bursting with four children, three aunts, herself, and Papa. With a flourish she would place a little box on the table, and spreading her arms wide, she would say to our visitor, "You are welcome in our house, and because we are grateful for your coming, we will add a penny to the blessing box for our missionaries."

Years afterwards on my trips around the world, when I have been dependent upon the hospitality of others, I believe that I have enjoyed the reward for the open doors and hearts of our home. Here on earth I have enjoyed a "house with many mansions."

I often think of the verse that says, "Cast thy bread upon the waters: for thou shalt find it after many days" (Eccles. 11:1 KJV).

Corrie, Stand Still!

Although money was scarce, the outside world thought we were wealthy. Every member of the family dressed neatly and well. At least—almost everyone. Mother made most of our clothes, until the burden became too much, and Miss Anna van der Weyden, the seamstress, came in to help.

Clothes to me were just something to keep me covered and warm. The endless fittings for a new dress and the inevitable pricks from countless pins were torture to my restless body.

"Corrie, come here, dear," Mother would call in the tone I knew was meant to be another torturous session trying on clothes.

"If I don't finish this homework, Mama, Master Robyns will make me stand in the corner."

"Corrie!"

There was no escape. I knew if I didn't subject myself to trying on a new dress that Mama was making, I would probably be assigned next time to Miss van der Weyden, and her clothes didn't fit as well as Mama's. The whole process was such a bore, and there was no way I could look like Nollie or Betsie anyhow. I just preferred to be me. However, I was a ten Boom and must not bring shame to the family name!

Mother had such a marvelous sense of humor, and having been a kindergarten teacher before her marriage, we profited by her practical knowledge of child psychology. She knew that praising my appearance would not provide me with motivation for my self-esteem. However, when she said, "Corre-

man, you are such a bright girl . . . I'm sure
Master Robyns calls on you often in class.
You do want to look nice when you stand up
to recite, don't you?" then she would strike
a responsive chord, for I was eager to learn
and have recognition in school.

I stood still for Mama, but only briefly.
There was so much to do, so many things
to learn, so much to live. I had a built-in
sense of urgency to cram all that life and
love could offer into each precious day.

4

The Many Ages of Love

Children need the wisdom of their elders; the aging need the encouragement of a child's exuberance.

Wisdom and exuberance lived side by side in the Beje, a house filled with the varied personalities of the old and the young.

Tante Bep (Alone in the Crowd)

Children's nurses in the rich houses of Holland were very lonely. They were not at home in the kitchen with the servant girls (who thought the nurses had privileges that they didn't enjoy), and they were not at home in the drawing room with the master and mistress of the house. Consequently, they frequently became bitter with their circumstances of not belonging in any niche of society. Tante Bep was a children's nurse, going from job to job and becoming more unhappy each year.

She was the oldest of Mother's sisters, and one of the reasons (I realize now) that my mother was very skilled in the art of tact. Mother usually had to steer a smooth course in our family with all of the aunts and their individual views on education and discipline; she knew how to bring the ship between the rocks.

When Tante Bep became too weak to work as a nurse, Father and Mother took her in. She had the same big, beautiful eyes like Mother, but the expression was very unhappy. She was quarrelsome about everything. There was the issue of the coffee, for instance. She told Tante Anna, "I'm the only one in this house who can make coffee." Now if there's one thing that was important in our house it was a good cup of coffee. Tante Anna would shift her apron around her ample waist, clear her throat with gusto, and say, "Bep, if you think your coffee is so good, you may just take over all the cooking from now on."

"Anna," Mother would say with her soft smile and gentle persuasion, "we couldn't exist without your fine cooking—and Bep, I know your coffee is excellent too; so perhaps you would like to make it your way on Tuesdays and Thursdays."

It was such a small house, it was impossible to avoid Tante Bep, but I tried because

I didn't like to be compared to the Waller children. The last place she worked before coming to live with us was with the Wallers, and I thought they must have been angels who had their halos polished every day.

The Waller children were always neat. The Waller children never ran in the house. I didn't like to tell Tante Bep anything, because she might say, "The Waller children would never say such a thing."

Mother always soothed my insulted feelings by telling me, "Tante Bep complained about the Waller children when she was caring for them. Love her for what she is, Correman, and remember that she has had a very lonely sort of a life."

Tante Jans (That's That!)

"Corrie, close the door . . . my feet are cold and I'll be sick with all the drafts in this house."

Tante Jans was always concerned about her health and made us very conscious of her needs. She had a diet that was different from the usual fare of the rest of the family; as a child, I sometimes thought it would be interesting to be sick and have my own trays of food and special attention.

Her rooms were special too. Mother and Father had given her more floor space than the rest of the family because Tante Jans had a great deal of furniture to fill the rooms she occupied upstairs.

Her husband had been a well-known minister in Rotterdam, and she had worked faithfully beside him in the church. They had no children, and it was a great loss in her life when he died before she was forty years old. After his death, it was clear that her place was to be in our house.

Tante Jans was not a woman to curl up with grief, and as soon as she had become established in her new quarters, she began all of her many activities that contributed to our buzzing household.

She was a poetess, an authoress, and an unusually good speaker. She started a monthly paper for girls, wrote books with a gospel message, organized clubs for young women, and even began a club for soldiers.

One time Tante Jans swept into the house, pulling the scarf off her mouth, and proclaimed, "There are soldiers wandering around the streets of Haarlem with idle minds and mischievous thoughts. I am going to start a club for soldiers."

That's that! It was settled. When Tante Jans made one of her announcements, the wheels were set in motion. Before we knew what had happened, our house began to look like a military installation. They would come alone or in pairs, young men who disliked the street life and were looking for the simple warmth of a home. One sergeant she met on a streetcar was a great musician. When he saw the harmonium that Tante Jans had against the wall of her room, he sat down and began to play, making the thin walls of the house quiver with each crescendo of volume.

Tante Jans folded her hands and listened intently to the talented soldier. She decided that Nollie and I should have him give us music lessons.

Even if we had not enjoyed music, we would have learned because Tante Jans decreed it. Soon I could play hymns well enough to join in the meetings and accompany the singing. It taught me at a very young age not to be self-conscious in the presence of men—although I don't think that was the intent of Tante Jans.

Some people have the gift of raising money by convincing others of the worth of a project, and this was one of Tante Jans's

special talents. One afternoon she had a tea
and invited some wealthy women she knew
to come to her rooms. We scurried around
rubbing her silver tea set until it glistened
and making sure everything was immaculate for the occasion.

I peeked out the window and watched the
ladies arrive, swishing into the house with
their long dresses underlined with full pet-
ticoats. How could they possibly walk and
maneuver the narrow stairway with all those
skirts? I had a hard time just keeping my feet
in front of me! It must be a burden to be
rich and have to dress in such fancy clothes,
I thought.

Evidently Tante Jans was convincing, for
in a short time she had enough money to
build a military home. When it was finished
and filled with soldiers, she went twice a
week to give Bible studies.

Tante Jans didn't move with the times;
she marched to her own beat. Her outspoken ideas on behavior, clothes, and theology were constant abrasives on the surface
of our family relationships.

When I was a child, I thought Tante Jans
was very rich because she was a minister's
widow and received a small, regular pension. Sometimes she would have an unex-

pected donation, and we would all share her joy. However, when she bought clothing for us it could be embarrassing—especially for Nollie and Betsie who had their own very distinctive tastes.

"Oh, dear," Betsie would say as she turned to give us the effect of a drab gray dress Tante Jans had given her. "Do you think she would mind if I put some lace around the neck—or maybe a pink sash at the waist?"

"Betsie, if you think that's bad, just look at this hat," Nollie would groan as she pulled a bonnet on backwards, sending us all into suppressed giggles. Tante Jans's taste in hats was somewhere between the style of a servant girl and that of a great-grandmother. Nollie was very fashion-conscious, and the gifts of stodgy clothes were a challenge to her ingenuity.

I didn't care about my appearance; I accepted all she gave me and consequently received the most hats and dresses. During the First World War most of Tante Jans's income stopped; it was dependent upon gifts of people who were having a financial struggle themselves. I remember she was surprised by an unexpected gift of fifty guilders (about eighteen dollars) and quickly gathered her muffler and umbrella to go shopping. When she returned, we thought something amazing must have happened, because she had forgotten to button her coat to the top. The sight of Tante Jans with face flushed and scarf loose was as uncommon as seeing the queen riding in a streetcar!

"Come in everyone . . . I have something to show you." We all followed her into her room, and she spread her packages on the sofa and began to distribute them with suppressed excitement. There was a warm blanket for Mother, a coat for me (black and shapeless, but practical), a blouse for Tante Anna, and cakes for the whole family. Any sweets were rare for us, reserved for birthdays and very special occasions.

I found out later that she had spent more than seventy guilders on us. I believe she was one of the richest persons I have known, for she knew how to give to others.

Tante Anna (Sheltering Apron)

Tante Anna, stocky, practical, unsentimental, was our substitute mother whenever Mother was too ill to care for us. She ruled over her little basement kitchen like one of Tante Jans's sergeants over his platoon. She was firm and hardworking, but overflowing with love for Mother, Father, and all the children. When I was very young, I would stand beside her in our basement kitchen and lick the bowl of something she had been making. I watched the legs of the people passing by the kitchen window, for that was all we could see from beneath the street level. I began to wonder about all the people in the gigantic world outside.

"Tante Anna, where do babies come from?" I asked.

She stirred the *alle haphetzelfde* a bit and answered carefully, "Well, Corrie, when a baby is too small and weak to live in the cold world, there is a place underneath a mother's heart where it is kept warm and can grow, until it is strong enough to stand the cold in the big world."

I could understand that. It seemed like a very good plan of the Lord's.

My question answered in a simple manner, I went on to the more important matters of life, such as investigating with my finger the inside of another bowl. This one contained a special treat—*allusion*, which was a dessert made with stiffened egg whites and flavored with lemon and sugar. There was more air than substance, but good for a big family.

Tante Anna was a good cook, stretching a little far. She would cook a stew on the big, black coal stove until most of the vegetables all blended into each other. The *alle haphetzelfde* meant "every bite the same," and I know it was a real surprise and a treat when we encountered a bit of meat.

She had her club work too, and her concern for others reached into the homes of the wealthy who employed servant girls. Every Wednesday and Sunday evening a group of them would come to a club room and bring their sewing and embroidery work. Tante Anna taught them gospel songs and gave them a Bible study. When one of "her girls" went the wrong way, Tante Anna became ill. Her face would become puffy and swell, and we didn't have to ask; we knew that she had received a piece of bad news.

"Tante Anna, who was it this time?" we would ask.

She would take her apron and try to hide her blotchy face. "It was Betty," she would say, dabbing at her eyes. "She wasn't strong enough in the Lord . . . she ran off with Hans . . . he's had two wives before this!" She would become as distressed as any mother would over a wayward child.

"Anna," Father would say, "you must not bear this yourself. Cast your worries upon the Lord."

Nollie (*Mijn Moedertje*)

Nollie was physically the strongest of the three girls in the family. I considered her my elder, although she was only a year and a half older than I. Even when she was a little child, she felt responsible for me; she was my *moedertje* (little mother). As a toddler, whenever she drank water she brought a cup for me too. I had to drink even if I wasn't thirsty. After all, Nollie knew best. I was shy and she was not; she voiced her needs and views. I waited.

One time, when we were very young, Nollie and I were out for a walk when a man on a bicycle knocked us down right in front of our house. Covered with mud and shocked, we ran into the sitting room, loudly declaring our presence.

Nollie screamed and everyone came running, brushing her hair out of her eyes, wiping off the dirt, and kissing away the tears. I stood in the corner, watching all the commotion and wondering when I should take my turn screaming—after Nollie was through, of course. I knew my time to be comforted would come.

Suddenly Mother said, "*Hemeltje!* [Little Heaven!] Come look at Corrie."

Everyone stopped and for the first time realized that I was standing in the corner of the room, big tears making muddy rivers down my cheeks. Finally I was given the attention of the grown-ups.

The little alley beside our house was the locale of many events in our lives. There wasn't much room for playing in our over-crowded house, so the alley was our yard, our recreation room, and our schoolhouse of life. Once Nollie met a little boy named Sammy Staal. I think there must have been some-thing wrong with his heart, for his skin had a bluish color and his nose was always red. He was unable to walk and propelled him-self in a wheelchair. Nollie made friends with him, and encouraged by Mother, she would push him for hours and hours while the rest of the children were playing active games. When he died, Nollie was heartbroken.

Nollie's grief was probably a shared feel-ing. Even when we were very young, we knew that our problems were never too small for the grown-ups; there were many ways and many ages of love under one Dutch roof.

5

Winking Angels

—❦—

Secrets are for children, and promises are like soap bubbles—easy to make, easy to break. The one time I tried to keep a secret from Mama, my little deception was uncovered. I talked in my sleep.

I was very young, perhaps eight or nine, and very flattered that Richard would ask me to go for a walk through the dunes. He was the nephew of our minister and quite grown up—a teenager.

However, I was not prepared for an act of boyish curiosity that surprised and shamed me at the same time. We had reached a valley where we could not be seen, and suddenly he pulled me close to him and started to do very strange things. Even without previous warnings from protective parents, I knew this was wrong.

I pulled away from him, flushing with childish indignation, and stamped my foot.

"Richard, you stop that. Mama would think that's dirty!"

Richard looked frightened but defiant. "She isn't here . . . and you mustn't tell."

"Mama isn't here, but Jesus is, and I'm sure He doesn't think it's right."

Richard was defeated. He stopped immediately and said, "Promise me never to tell anyone what I tried to do, especially your mother?"

I thought this over for a while. After all, he was Richard, and a very important person in my eyes.

"Well, I guess so . . . I promise."

As we walked back home, he told me some very nice stories and I forgot about the incident.

At least I thought I forgot about it!

The next day I was ill and had a fever. I talked about the walk on the dunes but wasn't conscious of what I had said. After the fever was gone, Mama asked me what had happened with Richard.

"A promise is a promise, Mama, and I said I wouldn't tell anybody in the world."

"Correman, never forget that Jesus is always with you. Every morning I ask Him to keep you and all of my children within His constant care. In the evening, I thank

Him that He sent His angels to guard you. Now you and I will pray together."

I remember Mother folded her soft hands around mine when she prayed. I thought how wonderful it was that she asked Jesus to guard me. She prayed, "Thank You, Jesus, that You never leave my Correman alone . . . thank You that You protected her during her walk on the dunes. Please lay Your hand on Richard . . . show him how wrong he was and that You are willing to make him a good clean boy."

How did she know about Richard? I wondered if mothers know everything. Oh, well, never mind . . . Jesus knows, Mama knows, and everything is all right.

Dutch Mischief Makers

I was no little angel. *Mischief* was my middle name, and Dot, my cousin and best friend, was my willing partner. Her father, Uncle Arnold, was the usher, or verger, of St. Bavo's, the magnificent Gothic cathedral that dominates the center of Haarlem. Its cavernous interior provided endless hours of imaginary play. In the banks (or pews) with their enclosed rows of seats, shut off from the aisles by half doors, a child

could have a private house. We could be
pirates, hiding in our caves, or storekeepers
in our offices; we could run a school or own
a sweet shop.

The pulpit was out of bounds. We were
not allowed to go there; that wasn't proper
or respectful. It seemed quite awesome to
a small child, because the chair in the pulpit doesn't stand on the ground. It is held
up by the bronze wings of an eagle. The font
in front of the pulpit is supported by three
brass snakes, and that was enough to keep
us away without being told.

Our voices would echo in the stone interior, adding intrigue to our games. Sometimes Uncle Arnold would have to hush our
exuberance.

"Children, children, there are graves
beneath our feet. Step softly."

The position of usher carried the privilege of living within the cathedral grounds.
Uncle Arnold's family had a cozy little house
just off the side entrance to the church. I
always loved going in through the narrow
passageway surrounded by beautiful blue
Dutch tiles.

Living within the cathedral didn't make
Dot any holier. If I didn't dream up a prank,
she would.

We were in the same grade in school and usually walked together to our classes. I was comfortable with Dot because we were on the same level of academic achievement, which was toward the bottom of the class. Whenever we had difficulty with our homework, we asked Josien van Paassen to help us. She was not only bright but also owned a bicycle. A winning combination. Her father was a minister with a regular monthly income, but the earnings of a watchmaker went up and down like the weights on the grandfather clock.

One morning Dot called for me on the way to school, and she was unusually excited. "Corrie, come here, look what I found."

She handed me a dime that was broken in half; the coin had probably been run over by a carriage, and the two pieces were wedged on the cobblestones just waiting for a little girl to pick them up. A dime was a great deal of money to us; it could buy ten pieces of candy at the sweet shop on the Begynestraat. Such a rare and wonderful treat!

We skipped off to school, neither one of us admitting that we thought we were going to do anything wrong, and ordered our candies from the jolly lady who owned the shop. Dot slipped the two parts of the dime to me and I placed them on the counter, then made a very fast retreat out the door. We were running toward school when we heard the bell of the shop door ring and the owner call, "Girls . . . girls . . . come back . . . !"

I grabbed Dot's hand and we ran a little faster, my feet having their usual problem of keeping up with my own momentum. We felt so guilty and for weeks avoided going by the candy store. The candy didn't taste very good either, and in later years when I read this Proverb I thought about that childish caper. "Bread obtained by falsehood is sweet to a man, but afterward his mouth will be filled with gravel" (Prov. 20:17). Can candy really taste like gravel?

Another time Dot and I made some solid snowballs and put them in our pockets. It was so cold they didn't melt but formed hard balls just the right size for mittened hands to grasp and throw. We were walking through the Kruisstraat behind three dignified men, who were loudly discussing their problems. I winked at Dot, and we reached into our pockets, drew out our ammunition, took aim, and fired. The top hats flew into the snowy streets, and two sweet little girls raced to pick them up.

"Here you are, sir," I said with a serious face and very polite demeanor, as I brushed the snow carefully off the hat. Dot picked up the second hat and handed it to one gentleman who had a very bald, cold head. He fitted the hat on his head and said, "Thank you, young ladies," as he looked around to see who the rascals were who committed such a crime.

Hats Off

Not all my episodes with hats went unpunished, however.

The director of our school was a very strict man, not the type of person who would tolerate misbehavior from his students. Father had helped Mr. van Lyden start the Christian educational institution, and because of this assistance we didn't pay to attend it, a fact that was a great help to the ten Boom family. When the school was new, many of the disciplinary problem children from other areas were sent there, and several times Mr. van Lyden had to send them back to the schools they had attended previously.

I was shocked when a student was expelled. Just imagine how humiliating it was for the parents to have their child sent away from school for bad behavior!

I must have been about ten years old when this occurred. I sat at my desk, gazing out the window, watching the wind swirl the dust on the playground. I was thinking about the new hat Tante Jans had given me, a large blue and white sailor, which I hated just because it was a hat. The teacher stepped out of the room and an idea flashed into my mind.

"Listen, everyone," I said to the class, "I have a brilliant idea. Exactly at two o'clock we'll all put on our hats or caps. We can smuggle them under the desks so Mr. van Ree won't see them. I've got a watch and I'll give the sign."

The room of sixty ten-year-olds crackled with excitement, and I was the leader. The fact that I had a watch made me very important, because I was the only one in the class who had one.

Two o'clock arrived and the classroom was very quiet. We were working out arithmetic problems in silence, and the teacher looked from one to another, distrusting our unusually good behavior.

I was sitting toward the front of the class and, after giving the signal, I took my hat from under my desk and put it on. I didn't hear a thing in back of me. I looked around and to my horror saw that no one else had the nerve to follow my example, except Jan Vixeboxe who sat way in the back of the room. When my eyes returned to the teacher, he was staring right at me, furiously glaring from humorless eyes. There was terror in the atmosphere.

"Go to the headmaster at once, Corrie ten Boom!" he commanded.

Oh, no, not the headmaster! That was Mr. van Lyden, and he expelled students for infraction of the rules.

I slipped from behind my desk, pulling off my hat as I left the room. In the hallway I opened the coat closet and ducked in, hiding myself in a dark corner behind the coats. I don't know how many miserable hours I spent there, but it seemed like an eternity before the bell rang and I ran out ahead of the rest of the students.

I expected to be dismissed, just as the problem pupils from other schools had been. I thought of all the shame I would bring to Mama and Papa, of all they would have to go through because of my misdeed. How I loved them! I thought of all the care they had given me, of the difficulties we had as a result of sickness and lack of money. We were such a close-knit family that we always shared joys and sorrows, and now this! Dismissed from the school my father had helped organize!

At the supper table that night I was so quiet Mama thought I was sick. I went upstairs early and crept into bed, pulling the comforter under my chin. I told Nollie everything that had happened.

"Why don't you ask forgiveness of God?" she suggested.

"I've already done that . . . but do you think He will arrange it so that I won't be sent away from school?"

I asked Nollie the deep questions that were puzzling me, because she was almost twelve! Certainly she would know all the answers.

"I don't know," Nollie replied, "but do you remember that boring psalm that Papa read at the table, where every sixth or seventh verse were the same words? 'Then they cried unto the LORD in their trouble, and he saved them out of their distresses'" (Psalm 107 KJV).

For the first time since the hats-off incident I began to cheer up. "Why couldn't we
do the same?"

We "cried unto the Lord" and then fell
asleep. The next morning Nollie shook me
awake and told me her wonderful idea. We
had a little monthly missionary magazine
that I delivered to several people as my special work in evangelizing the world. Mr. van
Lyden was one of the subscribers. Nollie
suggested, "You must manage in some way
to go to the headmaster and personally bring
him the mission magazine for this month.
It can't do any harm, and perhaps it will do
some good."

That morning, with my heart pounding
right through my best school dress and a
very pious expression on my face, I went to
the headmaster's room and handed him the
paper. He looked at it and then at me. The
pause took a hundred years and the silence
hurt my ears. He didn't have much of a sense
of humor, but I believe the corners of his
mouth turned up just a little bit.

He cleared his throat, tapped the desk
with his pencil, and said, "Corrie ten Boom,
I don't think you behaved as a very good
Christian girl yesterday."

That was all I ever heard about my crime. The Lord saved me from my distress.

Mice in the Manuscript

When I was about twelve, I decided that I wanted to be a writer. I curled up on my bed, pad of paper on my lap, and wove a wonderful fantasy about the adventures of Nollie, Josien, Dot, and all of Dot's brothers and sisters on a holiday without our parents. It was a beautiful story, filled with more adventure than Dickens and more vivid character sketches than Louisa May Alcott. How famous I would be!

Betsie shattered my dreams. She came into the room and asked, "What's that?"

It seemed quite obvious to me. "It's a book I'm writing," I answered as smugly as a sister seven years younger could reply to the ridiculous question of a grown-up.

Betsie seldom voiced any words of discouragement, but this time she said, "How foolish . . . you can't write a book."

I just won't show anyone my book anymore, I thought. So I hid it in the attic and forgot the priceless manuscript for several months.

When I remembered later to take the papers out of their secret niche, there was only one-tenth of this potential best-seller left. The rest was eaten by the mice. I was so disappointed that I decided never to write a book again.

The Shadow of His Wings

My security was assured in many ways as a child. Every night I would go to the door of my room in my nightie and call out, "Papa, I'm ready for bed." He would come to my room and pray with me before I went to sleep. I can remember that he always took time with us, and he would tuck the blankets around my shoulders very carefully, with his own characteristic precision. Then he would put his hand gently on my face and say, "Sleep well, Corrie . . . I love you."

I would be very, very still, because I thought that if I moved I might lose the touch of his hand; I wanted to feel it until I fell asleep.

Many years later in a concentration camp in Germany, I sometimes remembered the feeling of my father's hand on my face. When I was lying beside Betsie on a wretched, dirty mattress in that dehumanizing prison, I would say, "Oh, Lord, let me feel Your hand upon me . . . may I creep under the shadow of Your wings."

In the midst of that suffering was my heavenly Father's security.

Reach as High as You Can

My desire to please my papa was one of the basic motivations of my life. I remember when I was walking home from school, there was a very dirty wall I passed every day. It was full of flies, and during the warm weather one of my games was to run my hand along the wall and try to catch a fly. When the challenge had been met, I would release it and try for the next catch.

One day when I was busy with this messy game, I heard a familiar voice behind me, "Now isn't this a joy to meet my youngest daughter here on the street."

I was suddenly very embarrassed about how dirty I was, for Papa was so immaculate and well dressed that I didn't dare put my hand in his. He never mentioned my appearance, just walked along chatting about the visit to Mrs. de Vries and his talk with the servant girl about the Lord, until we arrived inside the Beje.

"I'm home, Cor," he'd call to Mama. Then he turned to me and said, "And I know, Corrie, that you're going to wash your hands before you see your mother."

Such a small thing, but I remember the shame of being so dirty in Papa's presence.

We were always challenged to do our best. When Papa took a watch apart and put it back together again, it was a task he performed without regard to the owner's social status or wealth. He taught us that it wasn't important what you think, or even what other people think, but what God thinks about the job you have done.

When Nollie and I were teenagers, we decided to take sewing lessons. I made a blouse; it was a very careless job, with crooked seams and poorly fitted sleeves. I pulled it on, knowing that I looked very sloppy but not really caring much until I saw Papa's face. "Corrie, the servant girl may be able to teach you how to scrub a floor, but your mother should teach you how to sew. When you spend your time and money on making something, it should be your best effort."

Achievement and honesty were such basic ingredients in Papa's personality that there were times when we had to hide the giggles

he disliked so much. One of the stories
Mama told about him was, "My husband is
so honest that when the children were
babies, he wouldn't allow me to give them
a pacifier, no matter how loud or how long
they cried. He would say, 'They think they
are getting a drink. That is fooling a child
to put something in her mouth which is a
lie.'"

Mama would sigh with amused resigna-
tion and say, "So my babies never had a pacifier, because my husband is so honest."

Papa was honest about pain too. Whenever we had to go to a dentist or a doctor,
Papa would come along to comfort us. However, he would never say that we would not
have pain. He said that if we had to have a
tooth filled or pulled that we must be brave
and strong. Whenever it was possible, he
went with us. Holding his hand gave us
courage. If the doctor did need his assistance, his strong hands kept our hands or
head from moving.

Perhaps it is wrong to tell this today—in
view of the permissive way in which many
children are being raised—but we were disciplined without spanking. I cannot remember being paddled as a child, but there was

no doubt in our family that we were to obey
Father. His will was law, and we all knew it.

We never spoke about the "line of authority" in our home—it was simply understood.
Father didn't have to stand up and say, "I'm
the head of this family!" He just was. We
never felt any desire to have it any other way,
because the love and security of all our relationships were built upon the established
fact that God was always with us, and He
had appointed Casper ten Boom in charge
of the mansion in Haarlem called the Beje.

6
Around the Oval Table

Can a piece of furniture be important? The oval table in our dining room was the gathering place for hopes and dreams, the listening place for prayers and petitions, and the loving place for joy and laughter.

But Sunday it was something more—it was the special place for family and friends.

Sunday was an important day for us; it was a day when everything—from the clothes we wore to the spoons we used— was distinctive. My Sunday dress was the new one I received for Christmas, so I seldom had a choice about what I would wear to church. Tante Anna could work magic with that dress, adding a colored sash or a ribbon in a way that improved my rather careless appearance. It was another of her small gifts of service that said, "I care."

When we were ready for church, Father would lead the way to St. Bavo's while we trailed along, trying not to scuff our shoes or muss our Sunday outfits.

After church it was good to go home, especially when the weather was chilly, for St. Bavo's was unheated, and there were days when my teeth would chatter through the entire service.

At home I would help with the Sunday dinner, first by smoothing a beautiful white cloth over the oval table. I tried to do this carefully, because I knew that Betsie wanted it to hang evenly, and it was a great desire of mine to meet her standards. Everything about Betsie was neat and I was . . . oh, well—just Corrie.

"Good work, Corrie," she would say, and that was all I needed to encourage me for the rest of the day.

The delicate china, which had been brought from Indonesia by father's older sister, Tante Toos, and Tante Jans's ornate silver service—a gift from wealthy members of her husband's church—were placed on the table. Then Tante Anna would emerge from the kitchen, wiping her hands on the generous apron she used to cover her black silk dress, and ring a little bell.

"Come to dinner, everyone."

When we were seated, Father would remove his fresh Sunday napkin from its holder, place it carefully on his lap, and bow his head.

"Lord, we thank You for this beautiful Lord's Day and for this family. Bless this food, bless our queen, and let soon come the day that Jesus, Your beloved Son, comes on the clouds of heaven. Amen."

Our table talk on Sunday sometimes centered around the sermon we had heard, but usually Father was cautious not to say too much. He attended the cathedral near our home because he felt that God had called him to that place, but he didn't hold any position in the church. His views were not accepted by the liberal thinkers who were in positions of leadership.

Conversations around the dinner table were lively because we all had stories or experiences we wanted to share. I believe that the great enjoyment of a family eating together is having this time when each person can be heard.

Father had a special talent in directing our talks so that no one would feel left out. We loved to tell personal stories but were taught to laugh at ourselves, not to make fun of others.

I remember one time when Nollie was telling about a painting she had done in school.

"I thought the drawing was rather good," Nollie said, "but when Mr. van Arkel walked over to my desk, he held up my picture and looked at it one way and then another, scowling all the time."

"Maybe he just wanted to get a better view," Betsie offered.

"I'm afraid that wasn't his reason," Nollie answered.

(Studies were important in our family, so each one of us received special attention when we talked about school.)

"What did Mr. van Arkel say, Nollie?" Mother asked.

"He said, 'Do you know of which Proverb your drawing reminds me, Nollie ten Boom?'"

"I told him *'Honi soit qui mal y pense.'* [Disgraced is he who thinks wrong of it.] It's from a motto on a badge of knighthood. Boy, did Mr. van Arkel laugh!"

Nollie's eyes twinkled when she told the story. Father really enjoyed a good joke, as long as the girls didn't giggle. Laughter he loved, but giggling was *verboden.*

On Sunday afternoons we frequently had visitors who would stop for a cup of tea and conversation. Sometimes we would go for a walk, but we didn't study, sew, or work on the Lord's Day. The only work allowed was winding the watches that were in the shop for repair.

Father said, "Even on Sunday, I must milk my cows."

Father's Friends

Fellowship around the oval table was more than just a family affair. Throughout the years there were many people, young and old, rich and poor, who contributed so much to the richness of my childhood. I loved to have some of Father's friends visit in our home, because they laughed a lot and always told wonderful stories.

When Father was a young man in Amsterdam he worked in a mission called *Heil des Volks*, which was in a very poor part of the city. There were three other men who gave their time and energy to this particular outreach, and they all became fast friends.

The four men would meet often, sharing their burdens and triumphs, studying the Bible together, and discussing many topics

of interest. As a child, I was always happy
when they came to our house; it was a time
when I loved to listen to the conversations
of these great friends and learn from their
experiences. The children were welcome to
stay during their discussions and encouraged to participate if we had something we
wanted to ask. I can still recall the fragrant
mixture of cologne and good Dutch cigars
that lingered in the room.

Frits Vermeer was a rather round Dutchman who loved to joke. He was "Uncle Frits"
to us, just as the other good friends were
called Uncle Dirk and Uncle Hendrik.

One of the first things Father would do
when his friends arrived was to bring out the
box of cigars from its place in the desk where
the bulky ledger of the shop was kept. From
his pocket, he would take the special cigar
clipper that had keys for winding the clocks
on the other side. It was a very important
tool, and many children over a span of half
a century sat on his lap and played with it.

Uncle Hendrik was considered the theologian of the group and was constantly being
challenged for a Bible verse to meet some
situation or problem. He was seldom at a
loss when asked to quote something appropriate for the occasion.

Uncle Dirk, the fourth member of the group, was the only one who wasn't married. However, he loved children very much and was able to express that love in a special way.

On one occasion, when Father's friends were discussing their concerns, Uncle Dirk was anxious to tell about an orphanage where he was on the board of directors. I sat up and listened carefully, because children without parents bothered me so much. I thought how terrible it would be not to have the love of a mother and father.

"I decided to become the father of the orphanage," Uncle Dirk announced. "I have been on the board of directors, arguing for better conditions for those poor children, but I have not seen any positive results. I must get in there and work myself."

Father was delighted. "Dirk, this is certainly the leading of the Lord for you. He has not given you a wife, but He is going to bless you with many, many children. We will pray about it."

Father would begin to pray with his friends in an attitude that was so easy and natural that the conversation never seemed to stop; it would flow easily from friend to friend to the Lord.

Many times through the years I remember the wonderful moments I had listening to the stories and experiences of Father's friends. There is a Proverb that says, "Do not forsake your own friend or your father's friend" (Prov. 27:10). I have often thought how wise that is.

Bible Study Was a Game

With the dishes cleared off and kitchen duties accomplished, the oval table could be turned into a place for games. We didn't play cards (for that was considered a form of gambling), but we had a lasting enjoyment in the type of games that taught us something.

Different languages were introduced as a game, not as a forced study. When I was in the fourth grade, we began to learn French. As I remember, I loved the melodious sounds of this beautiful language, but it was and remained a difficult language for me. The next year I started English, which was easier, but I wondered as I struggled with all the different English meanings for words if I would ever go to England or America and have an opportunity to use the language.

Father wanted me to learn English well, and he gave me a little Sunday school booklet in English that was called "There's No Place Like Home." I read it over and over again.

The greatest fun in language learning came during our Bible study. The entire family would take part, each one of us having a Bible in a different language. Willem usually had the original in Hebrew and Greek; I would have the English; Mother the Dutch; Nollie the French; and Betsie or Father, German. It was a special and joyous time for us.

Father would begin by asking what John 3:16 was in English. I would answer from my English Bible, Mother from her Dutch Bible, and Betsie would reply in German.

When I was so young, it didn't seem possible that Betsie would ever have a chance to use a Bible verse in German. We didn't know any Germans then! However, God uses such seemingly insignificant ways to prepare us for the plan He has for our lives. Over forty years later, in a concentration camp in Germany, Betsie was able to use that verse— and many more—to speak to the prisoners and the guards about God's love.

When Father Prayed . . .

Every room in our house heard our prayers, but the oval table probably experienced more conversations with the Lord than other places. Praying was never an embarrassment for us, whether it was with the family together or when a stranger came in. Father prayed because he had a good Friend to talk over the problems of the day; he prayed because he had a direct connection with his Maker when he had a concern; he prayed because there was so much for which he wanted to thank God.

When Father talked with the Lord it was serious but unpretentious. He talked to Someone he knew. Once we had a minister in our house, and when his visit was over, Father prayed, "Thank you, Lord, for a good day. We hope everyone goes together in the same way."

The minister left with a puzzled expression on his face. Could this be the Casper ten Boom so many of his parishioners told him had such a deep understanding of God's Word?

Father always prayed before and after each meal. He included two things in his prayer: the queen and the second coming of Jesus Christ.

The knowledge and anticipation of the return of Jesus Christ was given to me by Father during one of the quiet, thoughtful times before I went to sleep as a small child. As for the queen—patriotism and loyalty were an accepted way of thinking in our house, as it was in most Dutch homes. However, I never thought that the prayers of the little ten Boom girl would be answered in such unusual ways.

Me? A Guest of the Queen? Not Me!

It was the year 1956, more than half a century after I first heard Father pray for the queen. I was in Formosa with Dr. Bob Pierce, a man whose outreach of love and concern has spread throughout the world. He said to me one day, "Corrie, I believe it would be a good idea for you to talk with the queen of your country."

Bob is an American, and I forgave him for not understanding about proper protocol with members of royalty. How ridiculous, I thought.

"Bob, you don't know what you're saying . . . I can't go see the queen."

He looked at me gently and said, "Just pray about it." And so I did.

Wilhelmina had been queen through two world wars; her reign had spanned two generations, and now she had abdicated and given the position of monarchy to her only daughter, who is our Queen Juliana. Wilhelmina chose to have the title of *Princess* from that moment on.

When I was back in my homeland, I wrote to Princess Wilhelmina and said that I would like to meet her and bring greetings from Bob Pierce and World Vision International. The day after my letter was delivered, the princess sent her car to pick me up.

I sat in the back seat of the limousine, enjoying every kilometer from Haarlem to *Het Loo Apeldoorn*, where her palace was.

Wouldn't Father have loved this, I thought. *All those years he prayed for the queen and here is his daughter, Corrie, having a visit with Princess Wilhelmina herself!*

One amazing thing after another happened. I was given the opportunity of speaking with the queen and meeting all the people in the palace. After a few hours I had to tell Princess Wilhelmina that I had to leave for some meetings that were planned in Germany.

She looked at me and said, "I expected you to stay several weeks here, and you're just staying a few hours. Why are you going to Germany?"

The war had been over for more than ten years, but its memories were still vivid to many Hollanders.

"I must go to Germany, your Highness, because God has called me to tell them of His love and forgiveness."

She dismissed what I was saying with a wave of her hand, but later when I returned once more to Holland she sent word for me to come and stay in the palace for a long time. I was allowed on that visit one hour each evening with Princess Wilhelmina. She said, "I'm too old for too much, so we may either eat together or talk for an hour." I chose the last part and had my meals with her lady-in-waiting afterward. Princess Wilhelmina knew her Bible very well, and we enjoyed those hours in her lovely private chamber. She gave me the opportunity to tell her of the miracle God had worked in my life to forgive my enemies.

I believe that in some way something of Father's prayers many, many years before were answered when God allowed the daughter of the watchmaker to carry His message of love to the queen.

I had a happy time of fellowship with many people in the palace. I had personal contact with most of them when we talked about the most important person, our Lord Jesus Christ. But the happiest moments of each day were the hours with that great lady who had reigned over our little country in a time when two world wars had wounded Europe.

7
Seventeen, and So Much to Learn

━━━━━━━━━━ ⟨∽∾∽⟩ ━━━━━━━━━━

When Betsie told a story, she wove threads of brilliant color through the word pictures she created. When she moved into a room or dressed for a meeting, it was with a special flair. She knew *levenskunst* (the art of living)!

I wasn't what people would call a "mature" teenager. I was a tomboy during my adolescence—not a "young lady." However, I loved imitating and wanted to learn, but it didn't seem possible to me that I would ever have those soft qualities of womanhood that were so natural to my older sister.

Betsie taught me many things, and one of them was how to tell a story. She had a Sunday school class for many years, starting to teach when she was seventeen. She loved her pupils, and the little gifts and adoring glances she received from those boys and girls proved that her love was returned many times. One day she said to me, "Corrie, you must take a class too."

"What can I teach?" I asked, thinking how embarrassed I would be if someone asked me a question I couldn't answer. There was so much I didn't understand, especially all those kings and judges and battles in the Old Testament.

Betsie's answer was, "Try it! Tell the story of the feeding of the five thousand."

Now there was a story I knew! So I went with her to her class, believing this was a very simple assignment. What an embarrassment! How inadequate I felt when I finished the story in five minutes. The class was thirty minutes long, and I didn't know how to fill the remaining time. Betsie took over, and I listened with amazement as she told the same story over to a spellbound class of kids.

I was rather discouraged; I didn't know how to tell a story, but after that experience I was determined to learn. As I listened to Betsie I realized that you must weave a tale, leading your listeners on a word journey.

A girlfriend of mine, Mina, was a teacher in a Christian school, and she promised to help me. We asked permission of the director of the school to allow me to give the

Bible story in her class every Monday morning. They were pretty drab at first, but gradually I began to learn how to add those
imaginative touches that made them more
interesting.

I used the technique of describing one
picture after another, leading my little class
through the art gallery of the Bible. When
I told the story of the feeding of the five
thousand again, we visualized Jesus with all
the people sitting on the grass around Him.
We would look at these people individually,
imagining where they lived, what sort of
problems they had, and what they might be
thinking about this Man with the divine love
in His eyes. The next picture is of Jesus and
His followers, the disciples, talking about
how the tired, hungry people were going to
be fed. There was no bakery or fish market
within sight, but there was an obvious need
for food. The blue waters of the Galilee
reflected the surrounding green and brown
hills, and the luxuriant grass where the
people sat to listen to Jesus was pressed to
the ground by the crowd.

Then I would carry my listeners with me
to the climax, as Jesus took the five loaves
and two fish offered Him by a boy who had
gone shopping for his mother, and "looking

up toward heaven, He blessed the food and broke the loaves and He kept giving them to the disciples to set before them; and He divided up the two fish among them all. And they all ate and were satisfied" (Mark 6:41–42).

"What a feast we have when we believe Jesus Christ!" I would end.

I had no idea how valuable this lesson was going to be in later life. If Betsie had told me that someday I would be speaking before thousands of people, I'm sure that the fear of such a thing would have silenced my clumsy efforts at storytelling immediately.

From Bach with Love

Music was as much a part of my young life as television is to the children of today. Mother and Tante Anna had taught kindergarten, and I can remember them singing to me the little songs they taught to their schoolchildren. When I was old enough to sit at the organ called the harmonium and pump the pedals with my feet, Tante Jans had arranged for one of her military visitors to give Nollie and me music instruction.

We loved to sing in our house. Nollie had a rich soprano voice, Willem sang tenor, and

I was the alto when we learned to sing the Bach chorale *"Seid froh die Weil."* I grew up loving Bach.

One time Father called us together and said, "We're going to St. Bavo's tomorrow evening for a great treat!"

I couldn't imagine anything that could be better than some of the concerts we had already enjoyed at Uncle Arnold's church. Because of Uncle Arnold's position as care-taker, we were given special permission to listen to the concerts, sitting on the bench beside the door that separated his home from the main sanctuary. Only the people who had money could afford to attend these fine concerts, and without Uncle Arnold, all the members of the ten Boom family would seldom have been able to enjoy such riches.

"Wear your warm clothes," Mama warned, as we were getting ready for the mysterious treat.

St. Bavo's was a vast, unheated building with footwarmers for those who could af-ford to pay, and a hard wooden bench with cold stone at our backs for Uncle Arnold's relatives.

We all lined up, excited over the antici-pation of Father's "great treat," and went to the cathedral, bypassing the front entrance

and going in the side door to our own special reserved seats. The smell of moisture
and dust, smoldering gas lamps, and the
burning coals in the footwarmers was so
familiar, and the excitement began to
build. We sat down, with Father wrapping
a wool blanket around Mother and placing a pillow at her back to make her more
comfortable.

A wiry man with unruly gray hair and a
drooping mustache passed us before going
upstairs to the world-famous pipe organ. I
had explored the area where this impressive
organ stood and wondered how anyone
could learn to play on so many manuals with
sixty-eight stops. We had been told that
Mozart played that organ when he was only
ten years old.

We soon knew why the evening was going
to be such a treat. I held my breath as Albert
Schweitzer began playing a Bach prelude.
He was an authority on organ building and
an organist who could fill the cathedral with
exquisite beauty. During the day St. Bavo's
was a composition in gray, inside and out,
but in the evening—with the gas lamps giving a Rembrandtesque light, the pillars pointing upward in a mysterious glow—the atmos-

phere of harmony was heaven. I thought eternity must contain this kind of beauty.

Albert Schweitzer was a German philosopher, physician, writer, and theologian. He had gone to Africa as a medical missionary and established a hospital and a leper colony. As his fame grew throughout the world, I often thought of the first time I heard him interpret Bach and how much Father's treat contributed to my lifetime love of music.

Impatient to Learn Patience

We are not born with patience, and I believe God began to teach me something of what this means when I was in my seventeenth year. Because I was the youngest of the family, I remained childlike for a long time. I loved life intensely, charged with the desire to cram every available experience into each day. Then came a terrible blow that depressed me so severely I thought I wouldn't survive.

For some weeks I had a slight fever. For a time I managed to disguise how I felt, but soon Mama began to see my listless attitude and called the doctor. He probed and tapped, listened and questioned, and then told me I had tuberculosis.

Death sentence! *So young, I thought . . . why would God want me with Him when there was so much for me to do on earth?*

"You must go to bed, Corrie, until the fever is gone," the doctor pronounced.

In those days tuberculosis was as fearful as cancer is now. I cried and went upstairs slowly, not looking back. It was the middle of the day and it seemed strange to undress and go to bed!

I cried to the Lord, "Why must I be ill, Lord? I will live! I will be healthy!" It took many days before I could surrender and accept the situation. I surely had to learn what it says in Colossians:

> We pray that you will be strengthened from God's boundless resources, so that you will find yourselves able to pass through any experience and endure it with courage. You will even be able to thank God in the midst of pain and distress.
>
> 1:11–12 PHILLIPS

Through my tears and anger, I would thank Him, but I couldn't understand why He wanted me to lie in bed, imprisoned by the walls of my little room.

At first many visitors came upstairs, but after several months had passed, some people forgot me. I began to feel more self-pity and rebellion, but I prayed every day for peace in my heart, and finally the moment came when I could say, "Yes, Lord, you know best."

At that time Willem was a theological student at the University of Leiden. He was going to have an examination in church history and often came home on weekends.

"I get things in my head if I teach them. How about it, Corrie. If I give you some books will you study them?"

It was not the first time I had to assist him in that way. To earn some money in his college time, he gave lessons in Latin to a boy who was a very unwilling pupil. Every morning from seven until eight o'clock he taught him, and I joined the two of them. If the boy didn't listen and was absolutely uncooperative, then Willem taught me Latin. I enjoyed those lessons and knew that my brother was a good teacher.

I gained a great love for church history during those months of confinement, and it took my thoughts away from my illness.

The doctor did not visit me much; rest was the only cure he knew, and he told the family not to allow me to get out of bed until there was no sign of a fever. One day he passed my room after visiting Tante Bep, who was very old and feeble, and I called him.

"Doctor, I have a pain in my abdomen. It's right here," I said, pressing my fist on my right side.

He examined me and found an appendix infection, which was probably the cause of my fever all that time. I don't think anyone has ever been so happy with appendicitis! After five months of confinement I left my bed, had a minor operation, and returned to the wonderful outside world.

In the World, but Not of It

Until that time in my life the outside world was very small. It consisted of the streets and alleys of Haarlem, with only brief excursions with Father to Amsterdam, or an occasional visit to a neighboring village to visit friends.

I began to want to be somebody outside the protection of the Beje—to learn about the world that existed away from the Barteljoristraat. I didn't dream that I could see some of the countries and people that I read about in my geography book, but at least I wanted to experience life outside the shop.

Was I wrong? I struggled with this ambition and decided to ask my Bible teacher, Mrs. van Lennep, who was a very understanding woman who counseled well. She said, "Corrie, it's very natural for you to feel the way you do. You can do something in the world through the power of the Lord."

The first thing I did was launch into an intensive study of many subjects. I received diplomas in home economics, child care, needlepoint, and others. It proved to be a good background for my first job.

My opportunity came to be "out in the world." I heard about a job from one of the girls at school. The Bruins, who had a magnificent home, needed an *au paire* for their little girl. This position was a combination governess and companion. I knew this was what Tante Bep had done in her youth— and she had become a lonely and rather dour old woman—but this didn't quench my original enthusiasm for what I thought would be a new adventure in living.

Father and Mother gave their permission, and I packed my few clothes in a little suitcase and left with great anticipation for

Zandvoort, a village by the sea, about ten miles from Haarlem.

The contrast between my homelife and my new job began with my first glimpse of the home. It was so big! How could just one family live in a house that size?

As I began my job, I tried very hard to please the entire family. At home I had always known fun and laughter, with a large dose of love and affection. Out in the world it wasn't the same. For the first time I was faced with a new way of thinking, a different kind of family life than I had ever experienced.

If this was the way to "be somebody," I wasn't sure it was what I wanted.

Thursday was my day off, and it was such a relief to go back to Haarlem for my catechism lessons. Going home each week only made me realize the contrast between the security of our family and life in the outside world. In some ways, it was disillusioning to me.

I had determined to do my very best as an *au paire*. I wanted to leave often, but I was not a quitter, so I stayed.

One day, however, Willem came to Zandvoort with the news that our oldest aunt, Tante Bep, had died. She had been an invalid in our house for many years, and Tante Anna had the full responsibility of nursing her after I left. Now Willem told me that Tante Anna was very tired and should have a long rest.

I told my employer that I must leave at once because I was needed at home. Freedom at last! In my heart I wanted to rejoice that I was going home, but under the circumstances it really didn't seem the proper thing to do.

As Willem took my little bag and we walked away from that house of luxury, I felt no regret. Willem said, "Let's go down to the beach—it's such a glorious day!" And then he began to sing Bach music very loudly.

Somehow I felt it was all right to rejoice inside, but I didn't think it was right to let it show. "Willem, how can you do such a thing? Tante Bep has died and you shouldn't be acting so happy."

"Of course we would be happy, Corrie. A child of God is a citizen of heaven and the attitude of a Christian must be one of praise when someone has died. Our grief for Tante Bep would just be one of selfishness on our part, of grieving for the sake of ourselves."

I knew he was right, and when we arrived at the Beje, it was with our hearts at peace with the knowledge of the glory of Tante Bep's new home in heaven. How good it was to be home! There was a harmony there that was such a contrast with the rich home of my former employer. I realized then why Tante Bep had the type of personality she had. Just a small taste of the life she had led gave me more understanding. We never know until we walk in someone else's shoes.

The Everlasting Arms

There were so many times when the problems of the moment, whether they were small or large, would overwhelm me. I remember at a time, not long after Tante Bep's death, when Mother became very ill. I was so worried about her, and in addition I knew there was a large bill that had to be paid within the next few days. People were not interested in buying watches at that time, and Father and I were sitting in the dining room talking things over.

I stared at the familiar red and black tablecloth that had seen happy and sad times. I felt so depressed. Everything was wrong, and there didn't seem to be any good thing that could come out of such a discouraging situation.

"Father, what must we do? Everything is so terrible!"

"Don't forget, Corrie—underneath us are the everlasting arms. We won't fall."

I didn't know that expression and I asked, "Is that in the Bible?"

"It certainly is. Moses spoke those words to the sons of Israel."

"How does that help us right now?" I asked rebelliously.

"Girl, it makes all the difference. Moses tells us in the Book of Deuteronomy that God is a dwelling place. We have the promise of security when His arms are beneath us . . . holding us . . . supporting us . . . strengthening us."

Thirty years later I was lying on a dirty mattress in a concentration camp. It was pitch-dark, and in that restless room Betsie lay so close to me that I could feel her heartbeat. It was irregular and feeble.

I tried to think of something comforting to say to her before we fell asleep, and suddenly I remembered the dining room, the red and black tablecloth, and Father saying in his calm voice, ". . . underneath are the everlasting arms."

"Betsie . . . are you asleep?"

"No, not yet," she said weakly.

"Remember what Father told us: 'God is our dwelling place. Underneath are the everlasting arms.'"

I can't be sure, but I believe she must have smiled in that black barracks.

"Oh, yes, Corrie . . . and they will never leave us."

8

The Best Is Yet to Be

Our concerns reached beyond the borders of Holland. We all wanted to know more about other lands, different languages, and people from contrasting cultures. This interest was stimulated by visitors from many countries, and by reading good books.

During my late teen years a man came to Holland who focused our attention on foreign missions. His name was Jan Willem Gunning, and he started a movement for "mission study advice." Betsie, Nollie, Willem, and I became involved in groups that he formed. During the summer we went to a conference in Lunteren, a center in the midst of the woods and heather fields. It was so exciting to meet real missionaries from all over the world.

On the first day of meetings, an elderly missionary led the hundreds of people at the conference in group singing, and our own Nollie was chosen to be a soloist.

"Nollie, isn't it thrilling? Imagine—you're going to sing for all those people," I said.

"Oh, Corrie, don't remind me or I won't be able to utter a sound."

It was a new experience for all of us. We listened to the lectures and then divided into smaller discussion groups. We chose what we wanted to study and later used the material in weekly meetings at home. Mission students from a large school led these discussions, and we became great friends with some of them.

Many girls we knew were interested in more than the study groups; the mission students were as new and different as the subjects we were being taught. Unfortunately, there was very little time for dates. In fact, the only time available was two hours before breakfast. I've never been very alert at an early hour, but I learned to accept the challenge of this discipline for the advantages of the friendships.

I slept with a little rope around my toe. When a boy came to meet me when I was still asleep, he pulled the end of the rope, which hung outside my window, and I would jerk to attention. Soon we would be walking together over the heather fields of Lunteren, talking about mission activities and what we wanted to do with our lives. It was innocent enough—but not the part of the conference I would relate to Tante Jans!

One boy, Albert de Neef, had a girlfriend who was not very strong. She had gone to her doctor for a physical to find out if she was healthy enough to go to Indonesia, but during the conference she heard that she had been rejected. Those two were very sad, so we invited her to come to the Beje for a visit. She had so much fun with us that she almost forgot her disappointment. However, a year later, during another mission study conference, she was reexamined and was given approval to go to the mission field.

Because of that little act of hospitality, we became quite popular among the mission students. A new world opened for all four of us when we started a mission study group at home.

We had such good training at those camps. I never dreamed how much this would mean years later when I became a tramp for the Lord and visited mission fields on five continents.

Beyond the Dikes

My horizons began to stretch. At the camps for missions we met people from all over the world. Then through the YMCA in Haarlem we had further opportunities to know people from other countries and other denominations. The Y was only a building where young men could have meetings, but tourists came from other countries, expecting it to be a hotel. The manager didn't speak English, and many times he brought guests to the Beje, where he knew they would be welcomed. We could exercise our English, broadening our interest in the whole world situation at the same time.

I learned more about Christians who did not have the exact beliefs in some doctrines that we did. As a little girl, I had always thought that the Dutch Reformed Church was the only one that had the right theology. Others could love the Lord, I granted, but they really had a lot to learn!

As my interest in a true ecumenical faith grew, I began to learn about Christians who endured so much for their beliefs. Father once told me of Christians in Russia who were called Stundists. They loved the Lord and were willing to suffer for Jesus. They knew the Bible from cover to cover and were very strict in their behavior.

Father said, "God has given Russia a great blessing by sending these Christians to that country. They live in the vast area of Siberia in a kind of community life where young and old are trained to glorify the Lord."

It seemed so remote to hear about suffering of Christians. We were free in Holland, and it was difficult for me to imagine Christians in another land undergoing persecution.

More than half a century passed after Father told me about the Stundists. Ellen de Kroon, my secretary and companion, and I went to Russia. We traveled all the way to Tadzhik, far inside Russia near to Siberia, and there we found a lively church, so dedicated to the Lord that it was a light in that dreary land. These people were Stundists, and I remembered Father's story.

A very old woman, stooped with age, a lifetime of extreme hardships written on her face, came to me and said, "Corrie ten Boom, I have prayed daily for you for years."

I was astonished. "How did you know about me?"

"Once I got a care package from Germany. One of the boxes was packed with a page from a Christian magazine, and I read about your experiences and the work you do now. God told me to pray faithfully for you."

It never ceases to amaze me the way the Lord creates a bond among believers that reaches across continents, beyond race and color. This spiritual bond is something man has tried to establish with big national or world councils and organized ecumenical movements but always misses when the Spirit of the Lord is not present.

Sadhu Sundar Singh

A person who influenced my life in my late teens was a man from India. As a boy he was taught to hate Jesus. He knew about God, but the Bible of the Christians was a book that he believed was a gigantic lie. Once he took a Bible and burned it, feeling that with this act he could publicly declare his scorn of what he believed were the untruths it contained. When missionaries passed him he threw mud on them.

But there was a terrible unrest inside of him; he longed to know God. He told this story about himself:

"Although I had believed that I had done a very good deed by burning the Bible, I felt unhappy. After three days, I couldn't bear it any longer. I rose early in the morning and prayed that if God really existed, He would reveal himself to me. I wanted to know if there was an existence after death, if there was a heaven. The only way I could know it for sure was to die. So I decided to die.

"I planned to throw myself in front of the train that passed by our house. Then suddenly something unusual happened. The room was filled with a beautiful glow and I saw a man. I thought it might be Buddha, or some other holy man. Then I heard a voice.

"'How long will you deny Me? I died for you; I have given My life for you.'

"Then I saw His hands—the pierced hands of Jesus Christ. This was the Christ I had imagined as a great man who once lived in Palestine, but who died and disappeared. And yet He now stood before me . . . alive! I saw His face looking at me with love.

"Three days before, I had burned the Bible, and yet He was not angry. I was suddenly changed . . . I saw Him as Christ, the living One, the Savior of the world. I fell on my knees and knew a wonderful peace, which I had never found anywhere before.

That was the happiness I had been seeking for such a long time."

When I first heard about Sadhu Singh, the stories seemed to grow, until it was impossible to separate fact from fiction. Then he came to Holland and was asked by some people who were active in mission work to come to a weekend conference at Lunteren. I was so excited about the possibility of hearing him that I went to the conference grounds, although I knew it was booked to capacity.

With a rucksack and a blanket under my arm, I arrived at the entrance to the camp house. A tall student by the name of van Hoogstraten was giving out cards for the rooms. When he came to me I said, "I don't have a reservation, but I can sleep out in the field. I would just like to attend the meetings with the Sadhu."

The student smiled at my determination and said, "Miss ten Boom, there's a room for you. You're welcome here."

This same young student later became a missionary and died in a Japanese prison camp during World War II. The kindness he showed me was one of his characteristics, and years later he was a blessing to his prison guards. One of his daughters, Connie, later became my first companion for seven years as I toured the world.

That weekend, as I listened to the Sadhu, I was amazed but disturbed. He told of the visions he had seen—of how he really saw Jesus—at a time when he didn't believe. We had all read about the apostle Paul's experiences on the road to Damascus, but here was a man who claimed to have had this experience himself.

One boy ventured to ask the question we all wanted to know. "Please, sir, how did Jesus look?"

He put his hand before his eyes and said, "Oh, His eyes, His eyes . . . they are so beautiful." Since then I have longed to see Jesus' eyes.

Nobody moved or spoke. The Sadhu's face was the most Christlike face I've ever seen. It made me happy and sad at the same time.

After the meeting I needed to think, and so I started to walk through the heather by myself, trying to understand all I had heard, questioning my own relationship with God.

As I was walking, I was deep in my own thoughts and almost ran into the Sadhu, who was going for a stroll too. I worked up my courage to ask him some questions but soon found he was very easy to talk to. He put me completely at ease.

"Please, Mr. Sadhu, tell me what is wrong with me? I'm a child of God, I have received Jesus as my Savior, and I know that my sins are forgiven. I know He is with me for He has said, 'I am with you always 'til the end of the world.' But what's wrong with me? I've never seen a vision or experienced a miracle."

The Sadhu smiled at me. "Sometimes people come to me to see a miracle. When they come now I'll send them to Corrie ten Boom. That I know Jesus is alive and with me is no miracle . . . these eyes have seen Him. But you, who have never seen Him, know His presence. Isn't that a miracle of the Holy Spirit? Look in your Bible at what Jesus said to Thomas in John 20:29: 'Blessed are they who did not see, and yet believed.'

"Don't pray for visions; He gives you the assurance of His presence without visions."

It was such a relief to me . . . it seemed as if the Lord had thrown a curtain aside and I could see the light. Yes, it's a tremendous thing that we can know the Lord is with us!

Paul has said, "I know in whom I have believed."

And Peter . . . how beautifully he expressed it:

> And though you have never seen Him, yet I know that you love Him. At present you trust Him without being able to see Him, and even now He brings you a joy that words cannot express and which has in it a hint of the glories of Heaven; and all the time you are receiving the result of your faith in Him—the salvation of your own souls.
>
>   1 Peter 1:8–9 PHILLIPS

Sharing

When I went home after that conference I couldn't wait to tell what I had experienced. It was early in the morning and Tante Anna was still in bed. I woke her up and began to spill out what had happened. I couldn't stop talking.

Betsie and the others heard me and came in, all of us crowding on the bed. I tried to recall everything I had heard and finally, when I paused long enough for anyone to comment, Tante Anna said, "It's just as if you have seen and heard one of the disciples of Jesus."

Father said, "Isn't it wonderful to have such joy here on earth? It's a little foretaste of heaven. Yes, the best is yet to be."

Father often said that after we had shared some particularly rich occurrence.

Years later when Father entered a door of a prison, he said, "Remember, Corrie, the best is yet to be." After ten days Father's spirit stepped out of that prison and into paradise.

The best had arrived.

9

Love and a Sound Mind

───────── ❦ ─────────

It was 1909. The world around us was bursting with change; an American explorer, Robert Peary, had reached the North Pole; the doomed *Lusitania,* one of the largest and most modern ocean liners, was steaming luxuriously across the Atlantic; in Russia the tsar was beginning a program of persecution against the Jews, while in Palestine a young man, David Ben Gurion, was dreaming of a return of God's chosen people to their ancient land.

The early part of the twentieth century was preparing the way for a surge of science and an upheaval of society. In Holland, however, our attention was upon the birth of a baby princess, Juliana, heiress to the throne.

In man's never-ending quest for man-made peace, the leaders of the world were gathering in The Hague, Holland, to make another attempt to form an international body, where nations might try to solve their disputes.

Nollie, Willem, Betsie, and I were young people intensely involved in our own pursuits and yet revolving around each other.

Nollie was a naturally gifted teacher; eventually it became her profession. At one time she taught in Haarlem under a headmaster who was a very narrow-minded, disagreeable man. It was so painful to see our sweet, fun-loving Nollie become depressed on Sunday evening as she thought of the next day, when she would have to face her school superior again. Her face would get longer and longer, but she knew the children loved her so she continued as a first-grade teacher.

Eventually she went to another school in Amsterdam, and this took her away from home for the first time. She met Flip van Woerden, also a teacher, and they were married. The Lord gave her seven children, and she had a better chance to use her motherly gifts than in the classes at school.

My dear, studious brother, Willem, with his precise beard and inquiring mind, provided an intellectual stimulus to our conversations and home life. Although Willem was the natural heir to Father's business, he did not have the inclination toward watch-making, preferring to study theology instead. Father never pushed his children into work that they didn't want, and consequently, Willem did not feel that he was disappointing Father by not following in his footsteps.

We all loved music, but Willem had only one favorite composer—Bach. We learned to sing Bach chorales just as most children learn nursery songs. Nollie sang soprano, Willem, bass, and I, alto. How fortunate we were to have a brother, because Bach with a ladies' trio would have been rather frothy!

Willem did not have any girlfriends, so when he told his friends at the university that he had asked Tine to marry him, Karel, his good friend, said, "I never thought you would marry! You never looked at any girl."

When he had been married ten years Willem was called to be a minister for the Jews. He went to Dresden, Germany, and studied in the Delitcheanum. His thesis was written on racial anti-Semitism, a subject that may not have pleased some of his professors. He wrote that the severest pogrom in the entire history of the world could come in Germany. The amazing fact is that this study was presented by Willem in the year

1930, three years before the birth of Hitler's Third Reich.

I admired my brother very much and sometimes wondered why God hadn't made me an intellectual. Perhaps he could use my simple way of thinking in some way, I thought—but I certainly didn't know how!

When I looked at Betsie, it was usually accompanied by a sigh. Betsie had beautiful curls, my hair was straight. Betsie was neat and lovely, I was put together as an afterthought. How I loved Betsie, who was seven years older than I. She was not able to work hard, because she was weakened by severe anemia, but she managed to accomplish so much.

Betsie could turn a drab room into a place of charm; she could transform a dull happening into a rollicking, amusing story. We were introduced to art at an early age, and Betsie could make an art exhibit a tremendous treat, when she was the guide.

We were so rich in art in Holland and very conscious of our heritage from the masters of the past. When Betsie took me to the Frans Hals museum in Haarlem, she would point out the beauty of each masterpiece.

"Look, Corrie, at the way Hals paints the faces of his subjects. Aren't they marvelous?

And look at their hands—have you ever seen anything more beautiful?"

She would explain to me the exceptional talents of Rembrandt, showing me how he expressed the character of those he painted. Betsie could weave stories through a visit to an art exhibit in such an exciting way that I couldn't wait for the next chapter. It added to the richness of my childhood and the quality of my appreciation for classical art and music.

Betsie didn't promote herself; she remained in the background, always helping and ready with good advice and a sense of humor. Sometimes she assisted Father with his weekly paper, which he wrote for watchmakers, turning an ordinary report on a visit to a factory into an original, humorous story.

The church of our childhood and later years was the *Grote Kerk,* or St. Bavo's, the grand old cathedral that played such an important part in our lives. In the late afternoon there was a service called the "everyday church," which was supposed to last about half an hour. Usually not more than twenty persons attended, but the ministers were obligated to conduct the service for the faithful few. Since it is human nature to forget a job you do not like, sometimes the ministers did not appear.

When I was in my late teens and early twenties, my cousin, Uncle Arnold's son, took his father's job and was usher, or caretaker, of St. Bavo's. He often telephoned me and said, "Corrie, no pastor turned up for the service this afternoon. Please come and help us out."

I remember once when that request came I had a particularly full day at the house and in the shop, and my head was blank of any message I could bring to the small gathering of people. I ran to the kitchen where Betsie was cooking, hoping she would have a suggestion.

"Betsie, what in the world can I tell the people at the cathedral?"

Her answer came without hesitation; it was as if she had prepared it all day. While she told me the sermon, she brushed my coat, fixed my hair, and looked critically at my appearance.

"Keep your coat on, Corrie; your dress isn't too clean. Take Psalm 23 as your subject—'The Lord is my Shepherd.' Sheep can be very stupid, you know. Sometimes they don't see food behind their backs. We

need the Lord just as much as sheep need
a shepherd."

Betsie told me the whole outline of the
sermon while she accompanied me to the
door.

"I'll pray for you . . . I'm sure God will
bless the message."

I was halfway through the little alley
and turned to see her still standing in the
doorway.

"Betsie, I can't think . . . what hymns
should I give them to sing?"

"Just ask them for their favorites."

There was a blessing in the cathedral that
day, while in the kitchen of our house, Betsie prayed.

She was tidy about her person, her possessions, and her thoughts. I remember
years later I passed her cell in the German
prison in Holland where we were political
prisoners of the Nazi regime. The Red Cross
had just sent a food package to the prisoners, and on the little corner shelf stood that
food in neat rows. Over a stool was a handkerchief and a bottle with two tulips, a present from the judge with whom Betsie had
prayed after the hearing. In those stark surroundings was an atmosphere of cleanliness

and order, which was the stamp of Betsie's personality.

Although we had our individual interests, we loved a family project together. Mama and Papa's twenty-fifth anniversary was our chance to plan a real celebration. Nollie had been working as a teacher, and she had to supply the finances for the party. She had saved as much as she could in order to rent the hall of the YMCA. We planned the entertainment, but that was free—except for the personal price of courage I had to pay to perform before all the guests.

Willem came as Johann Sebastian Bach, playing his part with a dignified flourish. He was a musician, and I probably thought it was easy for him. Nollie, who loved to dress up, was Sarah Bernhardt. (Why hadn't I learned those social graces?)

The evening of the party Mother was flushed with excitement; I thought she had never looked more beautiful. Father escorted her to the YMCA as if he were taking the queen herself to a royal ball. Dozens of friends from the rich to the servant class were at the party; merchants on the street; clients whose clocks Father repaired and wound; people to whom Mother had brought soup and comfort—all swarmed into the hall to bring their love and congratulations to the popular watchmaker and his wife.

When the party was almost over, I finally mustered the nerve to contribute my part to the entertainment. I was introduced with a flourish by Willem and stepped forward in a borrowed Salvation Army uniform. I can't remember whether the uniform fit or I sung on key, but I do know that an edge was taken off my shyness in my first public appearance.

The four of us had pooled our money to buy a silver serviette ring for Father and Mother, which Willem had engraved with a Hebrew inscription. It said: THE LORD IS GOOD. HIS MERCY IS FROM ETERNITY AND HIS FAITHFULNESS FROM GENERATION TO GENERATION.

The Lord was faithful in giving me the strength to sing in front of all those people. I don't think I dreamed when I was seventeen that I would be called to speak before thousands some day. His faithfulness is certainly "from generation to generation."

Ethics, Dogmatics, and Bathtubs

In 1910, a Bible school opened in Haarlem. When I saw the program I was so excited. There was so much I wanted to learn. I plunged into this new enterprise, taking seven different subjects at one time. For two years I struggled with ethics, dogmatics, church history, Old Testament, New Testament, story of the Old Testament, and story of the New Testament. Such an undertaking might not be so difficult for a clever student—but that I wasn't.

During this time Mother suffered a slight stroke. Although she became weaker physically, her gentle spirit and positive attitude were an encouragement to all of us.

As my workload at home increased, it became more of a chore to keep up with my studies. Finally the day of judgment arrived—examinations. The first part was practical application; we had to give lessons and answer questions from students. I passed this quite well and was full of confidence when I appeared before the group of ministers who were to give me the second part of the examination.

The ministers gathered to interrogate me in a room that should have held no terror for me. It was a large conference room opening off a familiar corridor in St. Bavo's. Dot and I had played in that room as children, but when I saw the rather formidable-looking gentlemen sitting on both sides of the massive table, my courage began to wither. The fireplace on one side of the room was large enough for me to walk into, but I realized I was no longer a child hiding in the coatroom so the principal wouldn't see me.

The president of the church asked me the first question. "Miss ten Boom, what did you study for ethics?"

"I followed the teaching of Mr. Johnson for two years . . ." I began, but got no further.

St. Bavo's was usually chilly, but the icicles seemed to form on the ceiling. Pastor Williamson, the president, lifted his eyebrows and stared at me. He and Pastor Johnson had been theological students at the same university, and their disagreements were well known among the faculty.

"You studied nothing else?" Pastor Williamson asked disdainfully.

It was tense. I was tense. Suddenly I couldn't remember a thing. Out of seven different subjects I managed to get seven failing grades!

Willem, why didn't I have your brains?

When I returned home with the news of my defeat, Betsie was one of the first to console me. However, I didn't think she gave me the sympathy I deserved because she

said, "You must do it again." Something
about the way she said it made me repress
my objections.

"When you have failed an examination,
Corrie, you know your whole life that you
have failed; when you do it again, then you
know your whole life that you have succeeded and have the diploma."

Eight years later I took the examination
again and passed.

The important lesson I learned from my
Bible school experience was that from these
organized studies we learn the wisdom of
the wise but not much of the "foolishness
of God."

The best learning I had came from teaching. I could serve the church by giving catechism lessons and preparing people who
were to take their confirmation. In the
Dutch Reformed Church you do this when
you are eighteen years or older. I was also
licensed to give Bible lessons in the non-
Christian schools. Parents who sent their
children to secular schools could elect to
have their children take these lessons.

I learned to listen to the Holy Spirit when
I prepared for the lessons, and when I talked
with the children and young people, my
"lessons" were more of a conversation with

them than telling what I knew. It was a joy to learn in this way much of the reality of the gospel. Talking over my experiences with Father and the others was an added training. Besides this important result of that fruitful time, there was the new experience that I received a small amount of money for this and decided to save that special income for a very special project.

When I was growing up there was one luxury I wanted: a flush toilet. Of course we had toilets, one upstairs and one downstairs, but they were the accommodations that necessitated a once-a-month service from the workers in the city sanitation department. As I saved my small salary from the Bible teaching, it was with great anticipation of supplying the Beje with two porcelain pleasures.

Next—a luxury of pure ecstasy—I saved to buy a bathtub! Each room in the house had a bowl to use for washing, but we were very frugal with precious heat during the winter, and there were many mornings when we broke the ice to splash our faces.

When my "bathtub fund" was large enough to buy the splendid fixture, it was a thrilling day at the Beje. The bathtub was equipped with a gas water heater so that it no longer was necessary to be polar bears to get clean. We had a platform built under the tub so the water would drain out.

Somehow all of those hours struggling over ethics, dogmatics, and all the rest of the subjects that enabled me to teach were worth it to achieve such a magnificent material goal. How I enjoyed that tub!

Patriotism and Prayer

Discussing the truths of the Bible was as natural to our family as talking about sports or current events. It was remarkable how Father found so many contrasting people for his Bible study groups. It was this willingness to share his time with others that made him so rich with friends.

For three years we had a prayer meeting every Saturday night in Heemstede, a neighboring village. Father, Betsie, and I went on the streetcar to the meeting, in hot weather and cold, rain or snow; it was a regular part of our life.

In 1914, war swirled around our little country. Each nation had been trying to increase its own wealth and power for decades, and the threat of a clash was becoming a reality. Only five years had passed since The Hague Peace Conference, and yet all the great powers seemed to believe that threats and force were the tactics to use to get what they wanted. The world was engulfed in a terrifying game of fear.

From the time the Austrian crown prince, Archduke Francis Ferdinand, and his wife were assassinated, one after another of the countries of the world issued declarations of war.

Father continued to pray for the queen and the government of Holland, as he always had. We were very patriotic and loyal to Queen Wilhelmina and her prime minister, Abraham Kuyper, who was also a prominent theologian.

A division of purpose developed in our weekly prayer group. "Casper, it's not right to pray for those in government," some of the people said. "The world is evil—Satan is prince of this world and we should only look at the kingdom of God."

But Father said, "As Christians we are in the world, but not of the world. We must not give over our country to the enemy, because then we would be disobeying 1 Timothy 2, which says, 'First of all, then, I urge that entreaties and prayers, peti-

tions and thanksgivings, be made on behalf
of all men, for kings and all who are in
authority, in order that we may lead a tran-
quil and quiet life in all godliness and
dignity'" (vv. 1–2).

As the weeks and months of World War I
went on, the pietists became more uncomfortable as Father, Betsie, and I continued
to pray for our government. The difference
in these basic beliefs drove the group apart.
The others began to draw more and more
into their spiritual shells, until we could no
longer meet together for prayer.

Beyond This World

Father was not quarrelsome about his biblical beliefs, but he stood fast in theological
debates, especially with Tante Jans. They
used to have some rather lively discussions,
which Mother and I didn't enjoy.

Father was a Calvinist, and I heard him
speak frequently about predestination. I
never quite understood what he meant, so
one time I asked, "What is predestination?"

He answered, "The ground on which I
build my faith is not in me, but in the faithfulness of God."

That was an answer I enjoyed, and I repeated it many times in the years to follow.

One of the main points of dissension between Father and Tante Jans came over faith and works. In the Book of Philippians it is written: "So then, my beloved, just as you have always obeyed, not as in my presence only, but now much more in my absence, work out your salvation with fear and trembling; for it is God who is at work in you, both to will and to work for His good pleasure" (2:12–13).

Father talked more about "it is God who is at work in you ..." and Tante Jans emphasized "work out your salvation." I believe the fear she had of death may have been the result of never quite believing she had worked hard enough for God.

The Great Journey

One of the great human mysteries I shared with Father was why Tante Jans, a powerful evangelist, a woman with a zeal to teach and write about the Lord Jesus, had such a dread of dying. When the time came when we knew she didn't have much longer on earth, we didn't know how she would react.

Father loved Tante Jans, as we all did, in spite of her crusty manner and argumentative personality.

"Jans," Father patted her wrinkled hand gently, smiling into the no-longer stern face, "are you ready to make the great journey? The doctor has said that it can't be too long before you have to leave us."

Tante Jans's face lit up. "Jesus said, 'I give my sheep everlasting life.' That's good . . . I can't do anything more . . . I'm safe in the hands of the Good Shepherd who gave His life for us. He prepared a mansion in the house of the Father for me."

When the hour of death arrived, God took away her fear.

On the day of her burial the house was full of people who told how she had been used by the Lord to bring them to Him. We told them about the joy she had and that the fear of death had vanished the moment she knew she had to die. A friend of hers, a nurse, said, "I'm so glad to hear that. I often wonder if in the hour of death the devil will take away my assurance of salvation. I've seen so many Christian people die in agony, attacked by fear, although I knew they were children of God."

Another nurse, who had also come to honor her friend, gave some good advice. "Just tell the Lord that you have this fear . . . then pray that when the hour of death comes for you, Jesus will protect you against any attack of the enemy and that He will give you a clear experience of His presence. He said, 'I am with you always 'til the end of the world.' This prayer will be answered. I've seen many people dying too. All who prayed this prayer beforehand died in great peace and assurance of Jesus' presence and salvation. I could see it on their faces."

When the second aunt in our family died, it made me think more about time and eternity. We are citizens of heaven—our outlook goes beyond this world. I know the truth of the Bible, when it says that God doesn't give us a spirit of fear, but of power, of love and a sound mind.

Her Silent Love

One morning I was talking to Father about a chance to make some attractive magazine advertisements for our business, when I heard the sound of a crash. I ran into the kitchen and saw Mother slumped by the sink; a large kettle had fallen on the floor.

Her left arm hung limply at her side as she struggled to hold on to the counter.

"Mama, sit down, dear." I helped her to a chair and ran to get Father.

"Hurry . . . something's wrong with Mother."

Father rushed in and put his arms around her. She looked up and whispered in a voice that was barely audible, "Oh, Cas, we've been so happy together."

She thought she was going to die right then. We supported her carefully and guided her to her room. When the doctor had examined her, he comforted us by saying that strokes could be dangerous but frequently were not so serious. "One of my patients had a stroke and after that went to Switzerland three times. Your mother can live another eight or ten years."

Mother never fully recovered the use of her body after her next stroke, and for the remainder of her earthly life, her speech was limited to one word: "Corrie." With a word, the nod of her head, the opening or closing of her eyes, we saw a display of love that enriched all of us.

We developed a method of communication in which we would try to guess her thoughts, and she would answer with a motion of her head.

It was such a joy to be with her—and my own attitude improved during the three years God allowed Mother to be with us after her most severe stroke. I began to understand what the verse in Romans meant that says, "For I consider that the sufferings of this present time are not worthy to be compared with the glory that is to be revealed to us" (Rom. 8:18).

God's glory shone through Mother.

10
Reach Out

———— ⫘⫘⫘ ————

Europe was devastated at the end of World War I; there was danger of starvation in war-torn countries, and yet there was also a resurgence of hope in the world. "Make the world safe for democracy" was the slogan of the Allies. The humanitarian compassion of the United States and the victor nations in sending supplies and food prevented millions from going hungry.

In Holland, we were thankful that we were spared from the terrible conflict, but we wanted to reach out with help to those who weren't so fortunate. What could the ten Boom family do?

Germany was a wounded country; many of its children were undernourished and suffering from severe malnutrition. We began to think of ways to provide homes for these children in Holland, building them up with good food and care, before returning them to their own homes. Since Father knew many watchmakers, he discussed with me how we could organize an outreach for children of watchmakers in Germany.

Father was chairman of the international watchmakers, a position he had earned not only because of the respect others in the profession had for him but also because he was willing to work and keep his promises. After the war, he spent many hours contacting watchmakers all over Holland to ask them to take a German child into their homes for a time.

"Why don't you take one yourself, Father?" I asked.

But Father was more realistic. "Just wait, Corrie. Many have promised to take children but not everyone will be faithful. We cannot depend on everyone. There will be children for whom I have no home and we can take them."

When the day came for the children to arrive, Father, Betsie, and I went to the railway station to see that each child went with the proper family. What a scene it was. The children stood on one side, shy, wistful, frightened, and the adults waited expectantly to find out which ones were to be a part of their households. One by one names were called, and someone would step forward to welcome the poor little things. An attempt had been made to match children with families who had girls and boys of the same age. I had to struggle to hold back my tears. Our little Dutch children were so ruddy-cheeked and sturdy beside the pale, undernourished Germans.

Soon everyone was accounted for—well, almost everyone. I had been watching one little girl pushing herself into the corner of the waiting room, as if she hoped to become a part of the woodwork. As each name was called, she tried to make herself less noticeable.

"Father, look at that girl—don't you have anyone left on your list for her?"

"Let's see . . . no, I don't believe so. We shall take her home with us."

My mind began to buzz. She could go to Willem's former room. (He had been married in 1916 to Tine, our doctor's sister.) I must see about some clothes for her—and perhaps we still had some dolls left in the attic.

Then we saw another one. A bedraggled little boy was waiting dejectedly for someone to claim him. Father checked his records and found out that the mother had become ill in the house where he was supposed to go. So we took Willy too.

"Come along, my young friends," Father said. "You need a good meal and a warm bed."

He reached down and held out his hands to two skinny little children, one about ten and the other a year or two younger. What a sight they made. Four spindly legs raced to keep up with Father's stride as we returned home.

Willy was a street urchin from Berlin. The ten Boom home, modest as it was, must have appeared like a palace to him. When the children sat down to the table and Tante Anna brought them soup, they both picked up their bowls and began to slurp, the excess making rivulets down their dirty chins.

"Corrie, these two must have a bath," Betsie announced, although the need was obvious to anyone who could see or smell.

Willy only spoke German, but the word *bath* must have a universal meaning for little boys, because he looked first at Betsie and then at me. There was sheer panic in his eyes.

Father sensed immediately that Willy thought these two funny ladies were going to subject him to the indignity of washing.

"Come along, sir, I will show you the most magnificent invention of our time!"

I'm sure Willy didn't understand what he was saying, but the tone of his voice and the flourish with which he directed him to the bathroom must have assured him that there was a marvelous treat in store.

After we tucked the children between clean sheets, Betsie, Father, and I went to Mother's room to tell her about the additions to our household. She couldn't understand German, but in the following weeks it was such an inspiration to us to see how she managed to love and help those German children. She could quiet a quarrel with the shake of her head or ease a hurt with outstretched hands.

"Isn't it wonderful," Betsie said, "to have children in the house? And what a blessing it is to have Willy. Father has been so outnumbered by females."

The next challenge soon arrived in the person of Mrs. Treckmann and her two little girls. We had known her through our association with the YMCA, and when she wrote from Germany that she was in desperate need of help and that her children were suffering from malnutrition, we started to make up more beds at once.

Mrs. Treckmann was more undernourished than her girls, Ruth and Martha. Her
face was gaunt and lined with the strain of
hardship, which war writes on the bodies
and spirits of human beings. *Oh, Lord,* I
thought, *don't ever put us through that in
Holland. I don't think I would have the personal strength to watch my own family suffer.*

For the weeks their mother was with us
in the house, the two little girls were rather
difficult to handle. Ruth would throw tem-
per tantrums, which threatened not only the
wood paneling on my bedroom door, as she
kicked it uncontrollably, but also the peace
of our house, which was always active—but
not with voices of discord. Her mother
responded to these outbursts with several
solid slaps across her face, which added to
Ruth's rebellion.

Through Mrs. Treckmann's actions we
came in contact with the German way of
discipline. Slapping for the slightest reason
produced rather negative results, for Ruth
responded with more tantrums.

In some way, without words, Mother
taught Mrs. Treckmann that sometimes a
beating on the bottom side of the anatomy
was healthy, but slapping was not wise.

Mrs. Treckmann finally returned to Germany, but we kept Ruth and Martha, along with Willy and Katy, for quite a while. The first time Ruth began her door-kicking, attention-getting tantrums, we ignored her as if she were nothing more than a little fly buzzing around our deaf ears.

No slapping was required. Ruth and Martha became two of the nicest little ladies we ever had.

It was many years later that I received a letter from Ruth. She wrote that she had read some of my books and remembered the time she was in our house. "What a naughty girl I was, and what love I experienced in your home!" she wrote. "My husband and I pray that we can pass on the love we have received to people who need it. The Lord is our strength. How good to know that."

It was twenty-eight years later and I was in Germany. Another World War had engulfed the nations, and by this time I knew from horrible firsthand experience what it was to see my family and thousands of others suffer, even more than those in the First World War.

After a meeting in West Berlin I saw a neatly dressed gentleman smiling at me. Something about him jogged my memory.

Of course—the little street boy with his slang and naughty eyes!

"Tante Corrie, do you remember me? I'm Willy, who lived with your family many years ago."

There was a new light in his eyes, and I wasn't surprised when he told me what had happened to him.

"I had never heard anyone pray in a house before. I knew that people went into the big cathedrals and said prayers, but when I lived with the ten Booms I heard praying before and after meals, and other times during the day. Many years later I accepted the Lord Jesus as my Savior, but I believe it was because you had planted those seeds of love in that skinny, frightened boy who came out of the slums of Berlin."

The Saddest Day

The children from Germany stayed for a while, building their bodies and healing their spirits, before returning to their homeland. Those were growing years for all of us, but weakening years for Mother. Three years after Mother's severe stroke—times in which her love and patience spoke louder than any sermon—her physical life slipped away from us. Father saw the woman he had loved for so many years, the wife who gave him such strength, leave for her home in heaven.

She had taught us so much. She never pushed Father toward greater success in his business; she sustained him with her encouragement, no matter what trials he had. When money was scarce, she stretched what we had; when we met defeats, she taught us to try again.

Father looked at the woman he loved so much, knowing that she was with Jesus and that she was free of pain for the first time in many years.

"This is the saddest day of my life," he said. "Thank you, Lord, for giving her to me."

Father's loss was acute, but he did not engulf himself in self-pity. He knew where Mother was and he also knew that the Lord's work had to go on in this world.

11

In and Out of the Watchmaker's Shop

Five . . . six . . . seven . . . eight . . . the chiming clocks in the shop told me it was eight o'clock in the morning. What a wonderful way to start the day . . . with the graceful Frisian clock singing the hour, the sonorous grandfather clock vibrating its bass melody, and a dozen or more pendulums joining the chorus. I hummed a little tune under my breath as I poked the fire under the coffeepot and brought one slice of white bread and one of brown bread out for Father's breakfast. He would descend the narrow staircase in exactly ten minutes. You could regulate your watch by his arrival in the dining room each morning.

This was the day Father wound the clocks in the homes of his wealthy clients. His breakfast must be prompt, for he was as disciplined as the timepieces he treated.

8:10 A.M. "*Goede morgen,* Corrie. You have been busy already, I believe."

He looked at the sacks lined up against the cupboards and knew that I had been up preparing meals for the day; meat, vegetables, potatoes, and stewed fruit started cooking before breakfast. I would begin the food in boiling water and then remove it from the stove for a special long-cooking method. Each pot would be wrapped in sixteen newspaper pages and then enclosed in a towel, sealing in the heat. It was a very effective and efficient way to cook and store food.

After breakfast and prayers, Father would go to our astronomical clock and check his pocket watch. The clock was impressive, taller than Father, with an accuracy that demanded synchronization with the Naval Observatory clock in Amsterdam. Neither cold nor heat affected the astronomical clock.

"Mmm . . . two seconds fast," Father commented. He adjusted his own timepiece precisely in preparation for the work of the day.

His bicycle was dusted, his hat adjusted, and off he went, pedaling intensely down the narrow Haarlem streets until he reached the homes of his clients in the suburbs of the city. He was an aristocrat and a servant, a gentleman of dignity and a confidante of the most lowly. Class distinction was very strong in Holland, but to him every human being was someone of value.

As he whirred through the streets he waved to many townspeople, endangering the security of his hat in the wind. When he arrived at the first house, breathless but prompt, he would go to the back door, ring the bell, and greet the servant girl who answered his summons.

"Hannah, how delightful to see your shining face this morning," he would say with a manner as gallant as one approaching royalty.

"Oh, Mister ten Boom, I'm so happy to see you. I've been reading the Book of John—just as you told me—and I have so many questions."

"Good, Hannah. I shall come to the kitchen for coffee at eleven o'clock. Perhaps some of the other servants will want to have a little talk too."

Father made everyone feel important, and in a home where there were twelve or fourteen servants, a downstairs maid or cook's helper might not have too much feeling of self-worth. Many of them looked forward all week to the arrival of the watchmaker.

His clients were people of means, many of them in the import business or owners of sugarcane plantations in Indonesia. The mistress of one mansion asked him which dancing school he attended, in order to learn how to bow in such a courtly manner.

Dancing school! Imagine such a thing. Father answered, "I never learned to dance, nor did I attend such a school. My father taught me manners."

Formal training had not been a part of Father's background. He left school when he was fourteen years old to become Grandfather's helper in the workshop. He attended night school for a time, but his training was not of a highly intellectual level. He was self-taught, especially from theological books and magazines. Sometimes when Willem explained to his fellow students at the university Father's answer to a problem, he would be asked, "Where did your father study theology?"

Father's horizon was wide, and he talked with even his most outstanding customers with wisdom and insight. He was equally at home in the kitchen and in the beautiful sitting rooms. He understood all these people because of the love in his heart, received through the Holy Spirit. (See Romans 5:5.)

Among the customers whose clocks he had to wind was a distinguished pastor and philosopher, Dominee de Sopper. Father often asked him probing questions. After some months, the Dominee offered to give a course in philosophy in our home; although Father's beliefs didn't agree with this scholar's liberal views, the disputes between them didn't spoil their warm friendship.

For several winters this pastor, who later became professor of philosophy at the University of Leiden, had a weekly study group in our house. There were agnostics, atheists, fundamentalists, and liberals in this group, all with a quest for knowledge and none able to escape Casper ten Boom's direct answers to complex problems. "The Bible says . . ." he would say when the arguments became involved.

Father had nothing against philosophy, for he believed in a philosophy of living based upon the Word of God. However, he would express his differences when others would base their beliefs in such men as Kant and Hegel. Kant, the eighteenth-century German philosopher, had introduced a way of thinking that influenced many in the intellectual community. He did not believe in absolute right and wrong and questioned whether people could accept things that were beyond their five senses. This would rule out spiritual realities or biblical truths. Hegel pursued the philosophy of relative thinking, which led to the basic political and economic ideas of Karl Marx and Adolf Hitler.

Without formal educational training, Father could debate the most brilliant with the Book he knew so well. He baffled some, converted others, and had the honest respect of all in that unusual study group.

Out of the Frying Pan

When Father returned home after making his clock-winding rounds, I was anxious to hear what had happened.

"What did Mrs. van der Vliet say today? Did you see Pastor de Sopper? What about the cook at the de Boks'—has she been reading the Bible we sent?"

"Oh, Corrie, Corrie," Father laughed, "let's wait until after supper. The thought of the food you prepared this morning sustained me for the last five miles."

My job for many years was to assist Tante Anna in the housekeeping, cooking, cleaning, and nursing. Betsie worked with father in the shop as a bookkeeper, and I pursued the household tasks. I loved housekeeping; I found it challenging and creative. For instance, I tried to beat my own time records in washing and ironing. On Monday my goal was to have the clothes folded and put away by four o'clock. If I could make it by 3:30 or 3:45, I would reward myself with an extra fifteen minutes to half an hour of reading. I learned to bake bread, churn butter, and stretch a little to make a lot.

The division of labor at the ten Booms was suddenly changed by a flu epidemic in Holland. All the members of the family became ill. When Betsie was sick, I had to do her work in the shop; this was something I had never done before. I felt as if I had two left hands. It was a different world: meeting people, remembering their particular likes and dislikes, seeing in facts and figures the precarious balance of the family business.

When Betsie was well again, I made a suggestion. "Why don't we exchange jobs for a few months, so I can learn more about shopkeeping? I'm so terribly ignorant of what goes on in the business."

And so we switched. It was 1920; Willem and Tine had their own family, Nollie and Flip had been married a year, and the little German children had returned home. Time for a change.

I loved the work in the shop. The only thing I thought unpractical was that when a customer brought in a broken watch I always had to ask Father, or one of our watchmakers in the workshop, to look at what repairs were needed or broken parts replaced.

"Father, I believe it would be useful if I learned watch repairing—will you teach me the trade of watchmaking?"

Immediately Father agreed. He had a great trust in my abilities.

"Of course I can teach you—and after some time I will send you to Switzerland to work as an apprentice in a factory. I hope you will become a better watchmaker than I am."

Dear Father, he was one of the best watchmakers in all of Holland; he wrote a book about the exact regulation of watches; he edited a weekly watchmaker's paper; he had been a pupil of Howu, one of the world's best clockmakers in his time. How could Father expect me to become better than he?

Tante Anna overheard his remarks and said, "Cas, I must warn you—Corrie will never give her full time to her trade. She always tries to do six things at a time."

Tante Anna was right. She was a woman with singleness of purpose: the comfort of our family. It must have been difficult for her to cope with the many directions of my attention, those ambitions of my heart that ignored the circumstances of our lives. I knew I was the youngest child of a respected businessman who did not have much money, and I was happy and content as such a person. But I believed there was more for me to do.

"Dear Lord," I would pray in the privacy of my little room, "can You use me in some way?"

Blessed Money and Cursed Money

It took only a week for Betsie and me to know that changing jobs was right for both of us. Betsie, with her natural flair for beauty and order, added a new spark to the household. Cupboards were rearranged more efficiently, flowers appeared on the table and in windowboxes; even the meals seemed to have more imagination.

I loved the store and workshop. It had a very special atmosphere, and gradually I began to overcome my shyness and insecurity in meeting people and enjoyed selling the watches and clocks. There were many ups and downs in the watchmaking business, but Father seemed to have a keen understanding of the economic situation of our times. In his weekly paper, *Christiaan Huygens*, he wrote information and suggestions for others in the business. Since he read all other papers about his trade in German, English, and French, he could adequately fill his paper with important news about trade and business.

However, when it came to making money in his own shop, it wasn't always so simple. He loved his work, but he was not a money-maker.

Once we were faced with a real financial crisis. A large bill had to be paid, and there simply wasn't enough money. One day a very well-dressed gentleman came into the shop and was looking at some very expensive watches. I stayed in the workshop and prayed, with one ear tuned to the conversation in the front room.

"Mmm . . . this is a fine watch, Mr. ten Boom," the customer said, turning a very costly timepiece over in his hands. "This is just what I've been looking for."

I held my breath as I saw the affluent customer reach into his inner pocket and pull out a thick wad of bills. Praise the Lord— cash! (I saw myself paying the overdue bill and being relieved of the burden I had been carrying for the past few weeks.)

The blessed customer looked at the watch admiringly and commented, "I had a good watchmaker here in Haarlem . . . his name was van Houten. Perhaps you knew him."

Father nodded his head. He knew almost everyone in Haarlem, especially colleagues.

"Van Houten died and his son took over the business. However, I bought a watch from him that didn't run at all. I sent it back three times, but it was just a lemon. That's why I decided to find another watchmaker."

"Will you show me that watch, please?" Father said.

The man took a large watch out of his vest and gave it to Father.

"Now, let me see," Father said, opening the back of the watch. He adjusted something and turned it back to the customer. "There, that was a very little mistake. It will be fine now. Sir, I trust the young watchmaker . . . he is just as good as his father. I think you can encourage him by buying the new watch from him."

"But, ten Boom!" the customer objected.

"This young man has had a difficult time in the trade without his father. If you have a problem with one of his watches, come to me, I'll help you out. Now, I shall give you back your money and you return my watch."

I was horrified. I saw Father take back the watch and give the money to the customer. Then he opened the door for him and bowed deeply in his old-fashioned way.

My heart was where my feet should be as I emerged from the shelter of the workshop.

"Papa! How could you?"

I was so shocked by the enormity of what I had seen and heard that I reverted to a childhood term.

"Corrie, you know that I brought the gospel at the burial of Mr. van Houten."

Of course I remembered. It was Father's job to speak at the burials of the watchmakers in Haarlem. He was greatly loved by his colleagues and was also a very good speaker; he always used the occasion to talk about the Lord Jesus.

Father often said that people were touched by eternity when they have seen someone dying. That is an opportunity we

should use to tell about Him who is willing
to give eternal life.

"Corrie, what do you think that young
man would have said when he heard that
one of his good customers had gone to Mr.
ten Boom? Do you think that the name of
the Lord would be honored? There is blessed
money and cursed money. Trust the Lord.
He owns the cattle on a thousand hills and
He will take care of us."

I felt ashamed and knew that Father was
right. I wondered if I could ever have that
kind of trust. I remembered myself as a child,
when I had to go to school for the first time.
My fingers were tight on the railing again,
not wanting to go the direction God wanted,
only to follow my own stubborn path. Could
I really trust Him—with an unpaid bill?

"Yes, Father," I answered quietly. Who was
I answering? My earthly father or my Father
in heaven?

The Trivial Things

As I continued working with Father, we
both realized that our characters were
formed by our job. Watch repairing is a training in patience. How Father helped me
when I had difficulties in the work!

"And who in the whole world should I help with more joy than my own daughter," he often said.

The workshop was opened every morning with prayer and Bible reading. If there were problems, we prayed over them together. Father practiced what Paul advised: ". . . whatever happens, make sure that your everyday life is worthy of the Gospel of Christ" (Phil. 1:27 PHILLIPS).

These simple things kept morale high, but also it was such a joy to experience Jesus' victory. He is a Friend who never leaves us alone.

When my hand was not steady and I had to do a very exact work of putting a frail part of a watch—the balance, for instance—into the movement, I prayed, "Lord Jesus, will You lay Your hand on my hand?" He always did, and our joined hands worked securely. Jesus never fails us for a moment.

I experienced the miracle that the highest potential of God's love and power is available to us in the trivial things of everyday life.

12

All Is Well . . . Until It Rains

I felt a little strange among the people in that room. Most of the women at the meeting of the Christian Union of the Lady Friends of the Young Girl were very dignified, wearing their beautiful black dresses with high collars and long sleeves. *What was I doing here?* I thought. I was suddenly very conscious of my rather low-necked, short-sleeve blouse, which was appropriate for the watchmaker's workshop but a bit out of place for a gathering of the *Union des Amies de la Jeune Fille.*

When one lady began to make her speech, I forgot about myself and listened, as she expressed great warmth and love for girls who needed help and guidance during a time in their lives when there were possibilities for extremes in good or bad.

In Holland, Sunday school classes ended when one was twelve or thirteen years old, and YWCA groups were designed for girls eighteen or older. In those crucial and formative years between the two age groups there was nothing organized for them in the Christian world.

Suddenly I felt a finger punching my back and a whispering voice said, "That's work for you, Corrie ten Boom."

I turned around and looked into the kind eyes of Mrs. Bechtold, a dear old lady who had been a friend of Tante Jans.

"No time," I answered, thinking of the house, the shop, the Bible studies in schools. Oh, dear, I was much, much too busy!

"Talk it over with the Lord," Mrs. Bechtold said.

That was exactly what I did when I went to bed that evening.

Do It

The next day I told Betsie about the meeting and how the Lord had laid it upon my heart to do something about girls in their early teen years. She began to make plans—we had no money, no experience—but we started.

Betsie had taught Sunday school for many years, so it was not difficult for her to get long lists of names of former pupils. She began to talk to her girls about our plans, and in her quiet way she was a tremendous motivator. The first thing we did was to start the Church Walk Club. The youth church on the Bakenessegracht started at ten o'clock Sunday morning, so we met the girls on a bridge at 8:30, had a long walk to the dunes, played there for a while, and then went to church together.

This was a beginning, but we realized that Sunday was not enough. We talked it over with the children and decided that on Wednesday evening we would gather at our usual meeting place on the bridge and walk to Bloemendaal, where some of the wealthy women had said we could use their parks and gardens for games. The grounds of some of those estates were like forest preserves, and it was such a privilege to be able to enjoy them so freely. After each time of fun we would have a talk about the Lord with the girls.

The club grew and grew as girls brought their friends. It began to get around that Tante Kees (my nickname) was "not such a bad sort"—for an adult, that is!

Betsie and I soon realized that we had a serious need for more girls' club leaders.

While Betsie gathered names and addresses of former Sunday school pupils, I found my place for selecting prospects was in the shop. When a young lady bought a watch, or brought one in for repairs, I would find myself looking at her and thinking, "Now I wonder if she's a Christian." As I stood behind the counter and she was sitting in front on a chair, I would start to talk about juvenile delinquency, the need of the gospel's reaching the whole world, particularly girls twelve to eighteen years of age.

When one of these young ladies seemed interested, I invited her to our leaders' club. Within a short time we had forty leaders. Soon some of them dropped out when they realized their responsibilities, but when the chaff left, the wheat remained, and we had an enthusiastic, able group of young women.

Once a week the leaders got together, and everyone had to teach the others the games she knew. I instructed them in giving a Bible message with a short story and a thought they could use that week. Whenever questions came up, we talked them over together to find the answer. We brought up our problems in our prayers and didn't depend on our own resources to work a miracle.

These leaders got together a list of former Sunday school girls and told them about the clubs, where to meet on the bridge, and the name of the park or garden where they would have their game and talk club.

What a beginning we had! It was dynamic—until the rainy month of August started and the entire H.M.C. (*Haarlemse Meisjes Clubs* or Haarlem Girls' Clubs) consisted of dripping-wet leaders who waited in vain on the bridge for the girls who didn't come. We had too many fair-weather girls! We could have given up at that point, but most of us believed if the Lord had directed us into this work, that he wanted us to go on! We were dampened but not drowned!

What we needed was a roof over our heads, and we found a room in a house on the Bakenessegracht. It was close to the Beje, and when supper was over, it took me only a few minutes to run to a meeting. On some Wednesday evenings we had a room jammed with girls, and at other times the place was empty. It was during the "empty" time that our leaders' training club became our leaders' prayer group; we asked the Lord to give us a clubhouse instead of just a club room.

Every city has its famous benefactors, and in Haarlem the name of Teyler was well known. Stories of his wealth, the organizations he had endowed, and his reputation as a promoter of Dutch art were renown. One of the many houses owned by Mr. Teyler had a very large room with many smaller ones around it; from a family viewpoint, it was not a practical home. We asked the regent of the property if we could rent the house—and because we were going to use it for good moral purposes, our offer was quickly accepted. What an answer to prayers!

We had the time of our lives! As we planned together with the girls, they all expressed their different areas of interest. One of the girls, for instance, wanted to learn English. The next week we had an English class started in one of the smaller rooms. The leader of that class was one of our customers in the shop.

The one thing we couldn't do in the Teyler house was the vigorous physical activity that some girls wanted. So for one evening a week we rented a gymnastic hall in Haarlem with all of the equipment we needed. There we started the athletic clubs for the more adventurous.

God blessed the work. Yes, we made mistakes, but in spite of our blunders, the clubs grew in numbers and in strength.

As a result of my association with those women who had given me that first inspiration, we were made a part of the Christian Union of the Lady Friends of the Young Girl, with international headquarters in Switzerland. Our board of directors consisted of dignified ladies, most of them from the upper strata of society and very strict in their opinions. However, they had a healthy sense of humor and astonishing flexibility, considering their background.

One of the areas of real challenge for the board was a young spinster with exploding ideas. Her name was Corrie ten Boom. A doctor's wife, Mrs. Burkens, was given the job of "controlling" Corrie and protecting the larger group from adventures that were considered too dangerous.

Taboo!

Everything went very well with the board, until I came up with an idea that was revolutionary. I wanted to start a club with boys and girls together! Such a thing was unheard-of for a Christian organization; boys belonged in boys' clubs, and girls in girls' clubs, especially during the time of puberty.

Dating had no place in the Christian society; however, a boy and a girl would meet each other in the streets, in secret. After all, I knew a little bit about that—and I will never forget Tante Jans's written tracts after she saw girls flirting in the Barteljorisstraat: *"Jonge Meisjes, Scharrelt Niet!"* ("Young Girls, Don't Flirt!").

The reason we considered having a club for both boys and girls was because the girls themselves were having such fun together that we began to be concerned that we were raising a spinster society. The leaders' group thought if we started a coed club, girls would feel free to invite a boyfriend to the club meeting and wouldn't have to resort to seeing him in secrecy.

I'll never forget the board meeting when I announced that we were starting such a group.

"Corrie, what would some of the parents think?"

"It's never been done before!"

"Corrie, you really surprise us!"

I think I really surprised myself. I pleaded and argued that this was such a good opportunity for real fellowship between the sexes. The only possibility for boys and girls to be with each other was to either meet in the streets, or in the case of bad weather, to meet in the pubs.

I won the battle. However, the board left me with one restriction: For one entire year nobody was allowed to tell about our experiment. At the end of that critical first year, if we didn't have any real problems, we were allowed more publicity. So we started the *Vriendenkring* (The Club of Friends). It may not have been a very clever title, but it was a very popular club. The secrecy of its beginning increased its popularity.

Each evening program of the Friends' Club was unique. My first question was, "Well, what will we do this evening?" Sometimes they discussed rowing on the Spaarne River, but more often the topics centered around politics or the service of the Lord. Somehow young people do not seem to have the same aversion to these topics as their elders.

We had young men of many persuasions; some were communists, while others loved our country and our queen. Many were faithful church members; others were agnostics or atheists. We had no requirements for joining the clubs, and if they didn't like the short Bible talks, they didn't have to listen.

Once the mixed club decided to climb the tower of the cathedral. I'll never forget how I felt as we climbed the highest steps on the outside of the tower and came into the middle of the pinnacle. I looked down upon the *grote markt*, which blossomed with the wares of the farmers and merchants three times a week, and probably wondered what it would be like to land in a bin of onions!

It was the first and last time I ever gathered courage for such an experiment. Going down was almost a greater nightmare than climbing up, and I may have considered (if I had time) the reason why the Lord was putting me through such a test of courage.

Boys and girls found each other in the club, and marriage feasts were high points for all of us. Some were married in churches but later told me, "We have forgotten what the minister said, but the things you taught us in the club feast we understood much better and have remembered them."

Family Leadership

I had an area of concern about the mixed clubs, and that was my own feeling of inadequacy. I knew that the clubhouse needed a director, a substitute father and mother, and I certainly was not equipped for either position. We prayed about it, and out of the *Vriendenkring* came just the right couple.

Wim was a tailor from a family of tailors. His father, brother, and Wim's girlfriend, Fie, worked together in their business. They were such a joy to be around—they loved life and especially liked to celebrate with music. The first days of each week they devoted all of their time to developing their musical interests. The walls of their small tailor shop were covered with musical instruments, such as violins, guitars, and mandolins—even the little nine-year-old daughter joined in the family orchestra.

I had to take one of Father's suits in for alteration one Monday morning and was invited to sit down and listen to their concert. I was their only audience on that day and after almost an hour, I said, "How long do your concerts last?"

"Oh, we play from eight in the morning until eleven at night most of the time on the first four days of the week."

I wasn't used to this lack of work schedule. "But what about your tailoring business?" I asked.

"Most of the time we start that on Thursday . . . sometimes earlier, sometimes later. That depends on . . ."

Their mother finished the sentence, ". . . how much we have to eat in the house!"

My business sense was aroused. "Do your customers agree with this long waiting time when they have ordered a suit or a dress?"

"They don't have to wait long," Wim answered. "When we work, all four of us work together. Fie works with us too." He looked at her with love and pride. "Soon, Tante Corrie, we'll get married and then we are going to live in her room."

I knew Fie's room; it was just an attic in a large apartment house. Not a very pleasant place to begin married life, I thought.

"Well, the room is cheap," Wim said when he saw my concerned face.

"Wim . . . Fie . . . I have an idea. Let's talk about it."

Fie was not only a member of our Friends' Club, she was also a perfect leader of several of the girls' clubs. That Monday morning, in the tailor shop temporarily turned concert hall, we began to dream. If Wim and Fie could live in the big clubhouse and be the directing couple for the H.M.C., not only would some of *their* immediate prob-

lems be solved, but it would also establish
a permanent chaperone on the premises,
which would quiet some of the criticisms
we had heard.

Wim and Fie moved in and faithfully
directed our clubhouse for many years. They
became known as "Uncle Wim and Aunt
Fie," and later their baby daughter became
the youngest member of the H.M.C.

All of my spare time was devoted to the
clubs. Father and I experienced ups and
downs in the watchmaking business, but
each evening I always had one or two clubs
to attend. When I came home, Betsie and
Father were always longing to hear what I
had experienced. They were our prayer partners, and we knew that the Beje was home
base for prayer support for all the work in
the clubs. How we rejoiced together when
people who came to the clubs gave their first
yes to Jesus!

About forty years later I returned to Holland after tramping around the world; in a
church one day I met a man who came to
me and asked, "Don't you know me? In your
Vriendenkring I found the Lord. He has
never failed me."

Another time a minister saw me in his
church and said from the pulpit, "In your

club, Corrie, I learned to appreciate the Bible as the living Word of God."

I praised the Lord and chuckled to myself—it was certainly worth the year of being "on trial" and that terrifying climb up the cathedral tower to hear testimonies like that!

13
The Red Cap Club

The quiet years of the early 1920s in our home were punctuated by the sound of Tante Anna's fading alto voice, singing the great old hymns of the church. As the once-vigorous body became weaker, she stayed in bed most of the time, memorizing verse after verse from her worn hymnal. She knew most of the songs slightly but now learned all the words from the first to the last line. "I've never had time to memorize," she said, "and it's such a joy."

She knew that her time on earth was limited, but she seemed determined to enter heaven with a song on her lips.

When a day in the shop had been particularly difficult, or someone had come to the house burdened with heavy sorrow, it was an encouragement to hear from the little bedroom upstairs the beautiful words:

He leadeth me, O blessed thought!
O words with heavenly comfort fraught!
What e'er I do, where e'er I be,
Still 'tis God's hand that leadeth me.

After a short, severe illness, God led Tante Anna to her new home in heaven. Father, Betsie, and I sat at the big oval table, once so crowded with all the ten Booms, and talked about the past.

"It's a new life now, Corrie; we must remember the past but live in anticipation of the future."

Who could be despondent around Father? His positive attitude enlivened the dullest day. I looked at the empty chairs and began to dream a bit. Mother had always encouraged us in our dreams. I recalled the time Betsie and I had gone to her with an idea we had.

"Mama, when we grow up we want to help children of missionaries. So many of them can't stay with their parents on the mission field, and then they are sent back to Holland to live in those big places where missionary children have their home."

We had recently visited one of those houses, and although the leaders were kind, we felt so sorry for the boys and girls who had to sacrifice because their parents were obeying God by serving in other countries.

I remember how Mother brightened at the thought. She had just left the hospital after a minor operation and told us about a talk she had with the head nurse.

"My nurse had been a missionary for years and when she heard that I had three daughters she said, 'Mrs. ten Boom, I think you should keep one daughter at home, one should be a deaconess in our hospital, and one you should give to the missions.'"

My eyes grew big at the thought. Which one was I to be?

"What was your answer, Mama?"

"I told the nurse—I would not know if I could give a daughter of mine for the mission field!"

Mother explained the reason for her strong feelings. She continued her story: "My own mother was in Indonesia when she was a little child. Her parents lived there, and both died on the same day. There were three small children left without parents. A black woman took them all to her home and cared for them for two years before they could find a ship with a captain who was willing to take the three orphans to Holland on his ship, without grown-ups to supervise them. The kind people who kept my mother and her brother and sister were very good to them, but my mother's childhood was very primitive. If you wish to serve the Lord by educating missionary children, I believe it would be a very worthwhile pursuit, Corrie."

That story and my dream soon leaped into reality. The meanderings of my mind were interrupted by Willem's familiar voice downstairs. "Is anybody home?"

He told us he had something important to tell us, so Betsie, Father, and I gathered in the parlor. Willem began by saying, "As you know, I'm a board member of the Salatiga Dutch East Indies mission."

Oh, dear, was Willem going to go to the mission field?

But that wasn't it at all. His request, I admit, was a strange "coincidence"—coming at that particular time.

"There are three children of missionaries," Willem continued, "who need to have a home on short notice. Their parents must leave for the mission field. They're very clever children, two girls and a boy. Now we can find a home for the boy, but not for the girls. They all need to study, but there isn't much money."

(That was a familiar phrase in our house.)

"This is a faith mission," Willem explained. "When the finances are good the parents can pay; but if there is nothing, then the foster parents must live on faith like the missionaries. I thought perhaps it could be something for you."

"We'll pray about it, Willem," Father replied, pulling on his beard as he did when he was deep in thought.

Willem knew that he couldn't press Father into a decision before prayer; that was the way decisions were made in our family. However, after supper and prayer I cleared the dishes from the table as Betsie poured milk into the steaming cups of coffee and Father lit a cigar.

"One girl could sleep in Tante Bep's room," I suggested.

"So, you are already arranging the house," Father chuckled. "If you two agree, I will not refuse. However . . ." and Father paused, perhaps beginning to think of the foolishness of a man in his sixties with two unmarried daughters taking the responsibility of raising young children. ". . . let's not decide too quickly about this."

The next day the mission director visited us.

"Mr. ten Boom . . . ladies," and he bowed gallantly to us, "the board of the missions met last night and thanked the Lord that you are willing to take the two girls."

Father smiled. "Who told you that? Of course, if you have already thanked God, we cannot refuse. When can the children come that we may see them?"

"Tomorrow."

Betsie and I began to rearrange closets, prepare beds, and plan meals before any of us had a chance to question our decision. It was quite clear to us that the Lord meant for us to take the girls, but we hadn't counted on the added surprise in the missionary package.

The next day three children came: Puck, a spirited little girl of eleven, Hans, a twelve-year-old with great intelligence, and Hardy, their fourteen-year-old brother. We loved them from the beginning, responding immediately to their bright minds and willingness to adapt to a new way of life. When they were small, they were educated in Indonesia, where their parents served on the mission field; but when they grew older they were sent back to their home country to boarding school, or to live with families. Naturally, the children preferred families to the schools, so they were eager to please.

We showed Puck and Hans to their rooms, and they began to unpack their few belongings from the little cloth satchels they brought with them. Hardy stayed in the kitchen, looking down at the floor.

"Come along, Hardy, it's time for us to leave," the mission director said.

"Sir," Hardy said softly, looking from Father to the director, "can't I stay in this house with the bearded old man? I had to say good-bye to Mom and Dad; I don't want to say good-bye to Hans and Puck too."

Father said, "Of course you are staying, young man. You don't think I can run this household full of women all alone, do you?"

And then we were six.

Our quiet, thin little three-story house was suddenly stretching its walls and echoing the activity of three children. The side door swung in and out like the pendulum on one of our clocks, and it was a good sound. Father seemed to increase his productivity with all the chatter and singing going on around him; the entire tempo of our lives picked up.

Betsie and I discussed the division of labor, and it was settled that she would take care of their clothing and food, and I would be responsible for sports and music. I could combine that with my club work. The first thing I did when the children came was to sell my bicycle. I decided to walk a great deal with them, and as long as we didn't have enough money for bicycles for everyone, I intended to train myself and the children to walk where we had to go.

The Alpina watch company had sent us little red caps—the type worn by the Swiss yodelers—and I gave each of the children one of these. The first time we all ventured out on a walk, the conductor of the street car saw us and said, "Well, here comes Corrie and her Red Cap Club."

We bobbed along the streets of Haarlem and out to the dunes for our hikes, but it wasn't long before there were more red caps added to our little "club."

Along Comes Lessie

Just as we had the children of the watchmakers come to live with us after the First World War, we inherited another girl who had been promised a home in Holland and then had been rejected. Lessie was a missionary's daughter, who was on a boat ready to sail from Indonesia to Holland, when a telegram came from the uncle she was going to visit, saying that she was not welcome. Her mother was so upset because Lessie needed a time in Holland to begin the training school for teachers, and all the arrangements had been made.

"The parents of Hans and Puck were at the ship—bidding Lessie good-bye," they said. "They always have room, but if they don't they'll make it."

Consequently, we received a letter announcing the arrival of Lessie within two days. There was no time to write our answer; in fact, there was no alternative.

"We have no room for more beds," Betsie said. Her precise nature of housekeeping was straining with the increasingly crowded and cluttered conditions. However, she didn't complain; she moved things, rearranged furniture, and we made do.

"I can sleep in the tower—the place where the suitcases are kept," Hardy said.

A plan was already forming in my mind. "No, we'll put two beds on top of each other in my room." I invented a type of bunk beds with our old bedsteads.

When Lessie arrived, hurt because she had been refused by her one relative, she was welcomed by us with open arms.

Within a short time the Lord chose to send us two more girls. We experienced that with men there are impossible situations and circumstances, but with God all things are possible.

Our Red Cap Club added more caps, and we began to look like a troop of yodelers!

All the girls went into the training school for teachers, and Hardy went to another school, just for boys. Poor Hardy, he was surrounded by girls, and I'm sure he must have felt overwhelmed at times. He began to disappear for several hours at a time, and one day Betsie marched into the kitchen with a frown on her gentle face.

"Do you know what Hardy is doing?"

Oh, dear. I began to imagine all sorts of evil things, none of which seemed to suit Hardy's basic good character.

"He's going to Charlie Chaplin movies!" Betsie announced indignantly.

"To the movies? You don't say!"

None of us had ever been to the movies, but somehow I didn't hold as scandalous a view of this new invention as Betsie did. We didn't forbid Hardy from this pursuit, but we tried to make the activities for the children so attractive that they weren't too interested in such things.

I loved the physical activities with my foster children. When we walked together, we talked together, and it was more valuable than any "lectures" we might give. We had such great fun on our hikes. Once we walked with one of my clubs from Haarlem to Amsterdam, which was a distance of seventeen kilometers (about ten miles). We carried our lunch and sang whenever our spirits began to droop a bit. My foster children were the most enthusiastic.

We had gymnastic lessons too, although I wasn't a very good pupil myself. My feet never seemed to do what my mind instructed them. We all worked out on the gymnastic bars, with a succession of teachers who taught their individual type of body movements; the German method taught a different style than the French, and both were contrary to the Swedish gymnastics. I learned to do a bird's nest on the bars, but I was certainly an awkward bird compared to my club girls.

In the middle of a gymnastic lesson, I would blow my whistle and we would have a Bible lesson that would last from two to five minutes. The lessons were usually in the form of stories that the children could remember—stories that emphasized a Bible truth.

For instance, I told the story about the old monk. "There was an old monk who sang a Christmas song every Christmas Eve for his brothers in the monastery and for visitors who would come from the village for the special services. His voice was very ugly, but he loved the Lord and sang from his heart. Once the director of the cloister said, 'I'm sorry, Brother Don, we have a new monk who has such a beautiful voice . . . he will sing this Christmas.'

"The man sang so beautifully that everyone was happy.

"But that night an angel came to the superior and said, 'Why didn't you have a Christmas Eve song?'

"The superior was very surprised. 'We had a beautiful song, didn't you hear it?'

"The angel shook his head sadly, 'It may have been very inspiring to you, but we didn't hear it in heaven.'

"You see, the old monk with the raspy voice had a personal relationship with the Lord Jesus, but the young monk was singing for his own benefit, not for that of the Lord's."

"That's a good story, Tante Kees," Puck panted while trying to do a backbend and talk at the same time. (She called me by the nickname that all the club girls used.) "Is that in the Bible?"

"No, Puck, but the Bible does say, 'but if anyone loves God, he is known by Him' (1 Cor. 8:3). Do you think that God knew the young monk?"

The girls were in a training school for teachers, and the quick little Bible studies in story form came in very handy for them.

One day they told us about a student in their class who cried a lot. Hans was especially concerned about her, and at supper time, while everyone was around the oval table, she brought up the subject.

"Remember me telling you about Miep, the girl in our class who cries a lot? Well, I talked to her today during recess and found out that she lives with a cousin. Her parents are in Belgium. She can't seem to eat. Anyhow, her cousin told her that she had to finish her meal before she could leave for school, so she's almost always late. She's miserable with her cousin and doesn't want to go back."

"Please, Tante Betsie, Tante Kees, take Miep into our house," Puck said. "She's really so sweet but so unhappy. We can sleep two in a bed."

The next day, Betsie went to visit the cousin and his wife. They were good people but had very little insight about raising a teenager. They agreed that we should have Miep in our house for a time.

When Miep arrived, Betsie gave her a real welcome. "Look, Miep, no one here has to eat who doesn't want to . . . here is the bread; whenever you are hungry, you can help yourself and make a sandwich."

Miep soon became a happy, relaxed girl, full of humor and a good, normal appetite.

With seven children in the house now, the Beje was an active, noisy place. In the evenings Father sat in the living room, surrounded by his second family, busily writing his weekly paper. He went about his work oblivious to the din surrounding him, looking up occasionally to smile at one of the children.

The girls were always in a hurry to get to one of their clubs or to do their studying. They tried to shorten the devotions at night, but Father, called *Opa* by the children, was aware of their methods.

Puck said once, "Opa, let's just read Psalm 117 tonight."

"Well, now, Puck, I just think I'll read Psalm 119."

A visitor commented to Father that he was astonished at all the noise and laughter in our house. Father said, "Our children are such good kids . . . why they never quarrel and are always ready to help each other. They're just angels."

I sighed and went upstairs to talk to Puck, who had been sent to her room for the "angelic" way she had said, "I hate Lessie!"

She was sitting in the corner of her bed, curled up in that defiant position children take when they know they're going to be punished.

"Puck, don't you know that Jesus says hatred is murder in God's eyes. He told us that we must love our enemies," I said.

"Well, I can't love Lessie!"

"In Romans 5:5 Paul says, '. . . the love of God has been poured out within our hearts through the Holy Spirit who was given to us.' If you give room in your heart for the Holy Spirit, He will give you His love, a part of the fruit of the Spirit—and that love never fails."

Puck looked up, a trace of tears in her eyes, "But, Tante Kees, what must I do? Such hateful thoughts come in my heart."

"John says, 'If we confess our sins, He is faithful and just to forgive us our sins, and to cleanse us from all unrighteousness' (1 John 1:9 KJV). Jesus will cleanse your heart with His blood, and then He will fill you with His love. Shall we go to Him now and tell Him everything?"

Puck relaxed. All the tension in her taut muscles left, and she lowered her head as we prayed together. Puck and Lessie became the greatest of friends. Years later Puck was in a concentration camp in Indonesia, placed there by the Japanese during World War II. The guards were very cruel, and how she needed the Holy Spirit to give her love for her enemies! She was married then, and her husband, Fritz, was in a concentration camp in the Philippines. When she was released she only weighed 79 pounds. Fritz survived the years of imprisonment and was an emaciated 106 pounds when he was freed.

Puck told me after the war, "I always thought if I came out alive, 'I wonder if my parents in Holland will have the strength to stand the hardships of the war—but I know that Opa and Tante Betsie and Tante Kees will be there.' That gave me a feeling of security. When I was beaten, I thought of you and Opa and remembered what you had taught me about love for my enemies."

Puck's parents were still alive when she came back after the war. Opa and Tante Betsie were no longer there, but what they had taught Puck lasted. "The righteous shall be in everlasting remembrance" (Ps. 112:6 KJV).

Although Betsie and I never married, we received such love from all of our children and were able to give them so much of our love! However, a house full of teenagers was not uncomplicated. There were many things to talk over with the Lord. Daily. Sometimes there was not much money. When they needed new shoes they had to wait until the finances were available. Cardboard or newspapers temporarily stuffed in the soles were frequent emergency measures.

We shared our sorrows and joys with all of them. When I sold an expensive clock or watch, I came to the living room, stood in the door, and made an impressive announcement.

"Ladies—and the two gentlemen present—I wish to inform all of you gathered for this important occasion that Mrs. van der Hoeven has just purchased the gold Alpina, and paid cash for it!"

Cheers. Hurrahs.

"Now I can get my shoes."

"And I my petticoat."

When the situation was serious, we prayed about it and didn't forget afterward to thank God together. We lived as a real family.

Betsie was wonderful in contacting the parents; she wrote them every week. When one of the girls got a new dress, she took a snapshot and sent it to the parents together with a piece of material.

Marijke was the only girl who had difficulties in school. She was studying to be a kindergarten teacher and loved children but was terrified of examinations. Once she failed, and it was difficult to persuade her to go back the next time.

She adored Opa—as all the children did. The evening before the crucial day of the examination, he was writing his weekly paper and concentrating so intently that it was almost impossible to stir him, except with something very tempting.

He laid down his pen when Puck brought in the tea. She had made cookies, and everyone had to pay attention to such a treat.

"I'm not going to the examination tomorrow," Marijke stated.

"Why not?" Father asked, immediately concerned over one of his children.

"I'll fail again."

Father smiled. "Listen, Marijke, you have done your best and possibly you can't do it alone. But Paul said, 'I can do all things through Christ who strengthens me.' Do you think He will give you strength if you trust Him?"

"Paul never had to go to examinations," Hardy remarked with the complete assurance of a teenage boy who knows all the answers.

"I think his questioning from Felix was a bit tougher than an exam for a kindergarten teacher," Lessie answered, pleased with herself for making this comparison. (We had been studying the Book of Acts.)

"Can you really pray for everything? Even something as little as an examination?" Marijke asked with renewed interest.

Father leaned back in his chair, warming his hands with the steaming tea, relishing the chance to discuss the Scriptures. "Paul says in Philippians 1:27, 'Whatever happens make sure that your everyday life is worthy of the gospel of Jesus Christ.' When you belong to the Lord, there's not one single thing you have to conquer in your own

strength. The hairs of your head are num-
bered; can anything be more trivial than
that?"

"But, Opa," Puck said, "yesterday I didn't
learn French because I was busy making the
cookies. That was more fun than dull old
French. So this morning I prayed that I
wouldn't be called on. But God didn't help
me. I did get called on—and what a mess I
made of the French words!"

"I'm not surprised," Father chuckled. "If
you didn't learn, you can't expect the Lord
to help you."

Hardy added, with a sudden burst of
understanding that made me very pleased
with him, "I've found out that if I want to
pray for something that is wrong, I simply
can't."

It was years later that I had to learn
another lesson about prayer for something
that was not 100 percent right.

It was in 1945, shortly after the war, that
I went to Switzerland. I had spoken there in
many meetings, but also I visited my former
watchmaker friends from whom I had
learned my trade many years before. I
bought some watches while I was there. In
Holland, there was still a severe shortage of

imported articles and to buy Swiss watches was rather complicated.

When I put my watches in my suitcase, I smiled because of the methods we had learned in the time of the underground work when we saved Jewish people and hid articles in our luggage. Surely nobody should be able to find my three watches!

Before I went to the train, I prayed the way I always do when I start a trip.

"Lord, protect us against accidents, bless the engineer of the train and give him wisdom, make us a blessing for our fellow travelers, and Lord . . . give us success in smuggling . . . in smug. . . ." (I wanted to say, "In smuggling my watches," but I couldn't.)

The moment I started to pray for it, I knew it was a sin. Smuggling to avoid paying money is the same as stealing. I didn't smuggle my watches, and I experienced again that prayer can be a discipline. Praying for something that is wrong is not possible.

As the girls grew older and discovered that boys were more than just a nuisance, it became an increasing challenge to answer their questions. The walks we had together brought a closeness and ease of communication, in spite of our difference in age. Usually we walked on Sunday afternoon, since our week was filled with work and school. I remember when we walked from Haarlem to the dunes near Zandvoort, the sun warm on our faces and the sand inviting us to sunbathe, we would frequently lie on our backs and talk about . . . well, just the things girls talk about.

"Tante Kees, were you ever engaged to be married?"

"Tante Kees, do you long to have a husband? Do you find it difficult to be single?"

Once they started, the girls could ask questions as rapidly as a second hand could move in an accurate timepiece.

"You rascals . . . this is a very important subject to talk about when you are beginning your lives as young women." I had no sadness or regret, only joy in telling the story of Karel.

"There was a time in my life when I expected to marry a boy who loved me and whom I loved. He was going to be a minister and was from a big family where several members were clergymen. They had the usual problems that ministers have with finances.

"His mother did not approve of our getting married. She wanted him to marry a rich girl.

"How I struggled with myself at that time! When he introduced me to the wealthy girl he was going to marry, I had the feeling that my heart would never survive such a blow."

"What did you do, Tante Kees?"

"I went to my room and talked it over with the Lord. From what I can remember it was something like this: 'I want, Lord, to belong to You with my body, soul, and mind. I claim Your victory, Lord Jesus, over that wound which is hurting me. Let Your victory be demonstrated also in my sex life.'

"I didn't quite analyze what I needed, but the joy is that with the Lord, it is not necessary to give Him a clear diagnosis before He knows the cure."

"Did you have an immediate victory?"

"No, there was still a battle—rather severe—but then the Lord healed me and the pain didn't come back. The Lord gave and continues to give me a very happy life. I have the love of all of you—and I love you. My life isn't dull at all. The best thing is that when Jesus restores such a loss, He gives a fulfillment that is a little bit of heaven—a peace that passes all understanding. From our side it is only necessary to surrender."

After I had told this, Puck said, "Now I understand more what Opa said yesterday: 'Our times are in His hands.'"

He Brings You Safely Home

It was the middle of May 1940. By that time the children were all away in their different jobs or married. It was a time of fear and confusion in our land.

Hitler and Goering had ordered a heavy bombing of Rotterdam—and we were bewildered! The Dutch experienced the first large-scale airborne attack in the history of warfare.

We were completely unprepared for such an ordeal. On the morning of May 14, 1940, a German staff officer crossed the bridge at Rotterdam with a white flag in his hand and demanded the surrender of the city. He warned that unless it capitulated, it would be bombed.

While surrender negotiations were actually under way, the bombers appeared and wiped out the heart of our great city. Over eight hundred persons, mostly civilians, were massacred; several thousand were wounded, and seventy-eight thousand homeless. Rotterdam surrendered and then the Dutch armed forces did the same. It was then our dear Queen Wilhelmina and the government members fled to London.

The German juggernaut was on the move. An army of tanks larger in size, concentration, and striking ability than any tank force yet mobilized started through the Ardennes Forest from the German frontier. We read that these tanks stretched three columns wide, for a hundred miles behind the Rhine, and broke through the French armies headed for the English Channel.

Our Hans was married by then and had two children and another one on the way. Her husband was a teacher, and they lived in Rotterdam during that terrible bombardment. They fled to a small suburb of Rotterdam, where her third baby was born in a cellar. For a year they lived in that cellar, which formed a bomb shelter.

Hans told me in later years that over and over again she repeated to her children, "Opa taught us, 'When Jesus takes your hand, He keeps you tight. When Jesus keeps you tight, He leads you through your whole life. When Jesus leads you through your life, He brings you safely home.'"

14

Even the Least of Them . . .

In addition to the work in the business, the club work, and the care for our children, I continued with the Bible lessons in the schools. One of these classes was for children who had learning difficulties. It was such a joy to know that the Holy Spirit doesn't need a high IQ in a person in order to reveal Himself. Even people of normal or superior intelligence need the Lord to understand the spiritual truths that are only spiritually discerned.

God gave me a great love for the "exceptional children." I remember going to these schools and telling Bible stories and being rewarded when their faces lit up with sweet and simple happiness.

Sometimes I asked them questions to see if they understood what I told them. Once a feebleminded girl answered a question of mine that might have baffled a person of normal intelligence. I asked, "What is a prophet and what is a priest?"

She said, "They are both messengers between God and man."

I continued, "Then they are the same—a prophet and a priest?"

She thought a while and then answered, "No, a prophet has his back to God and his face to us—and a priest has his face to God and his back to us."

I wasn't sure if she had learned that by heart, so I asked her, "Well, what was I today?"

She said, "You were both—you told us about God and you were a prophet. Then you prayed. You didn't pray for yourself, but you prayed for us—then you were a priest."

That was a backward child who answered in that manner! When you bring the gospel, it is the Holy Spirit who works.

I tried to teach these children other things with much less success; one time I started to instruct them about the stars. I brought some white beans to school and laid them on the table in the form of constellations. I showed them Orion, and they looked at the formation of the beans, and all of them knew it very well. Then one evening I took them outside and said, "Look, children, there is Orion . . . see it?"

They just shook their heads. "No, Tante Corrie, they are white beans in the sky."

They never understood what I told them about the stars, but the truths of the Lord they seemed to understand well.

Whenever you come in contact with fee-bleminded people, please tell them that Jesus loves them. They often understand God's love better than people who have problems because of their intellectual doubt.

Paul wrote in 1 Corinthians 1:20–21: "Where is the wise man? Where is the scribe? Where is the debater of this age? Has not God made foolish the wisdom of the world? For since in the wisdom of God the world through its wisdom did not come to know God, God was well-pleased through the foolishness of the message preached to save those who believe."

Some Are Forgotten

Father shared my concern, my outreach for the debilitated and the disturbed. Once he heard from a servant girl about a woman in a mental hospital who never received a visit from anyone.

Father, Betsie, and I prayed for this woman, and then I made the trip to the hospital. It took me some hours to go there, and when I finally found the woman, I discovered that she was clear in her thinking, although a bit mentally disturbed. Also her body was sick, and she couldn't leave her bed.

"May I introduce myself? I'm Corrie ten Boom. I've come to visit you," I said.

She looked up at me with tears of joy in her eyes.

"Did God send you?"

"Yes, I'm sure He did . . . and I'm glad too, because I would like you to be my friend. Will you?"

"Oh, yes," she said eagerly. "Will you please visit me sometimes? Can you tell me about Jesus?"

I thought for a moment. How much did this woman know? What Bible story could help her? I prayed for inspiration and then told her about the good shepherd who brought the lost sheep home.

We became real friends, in spite of being such an unequal combination! There I was, a healthy, normal girl, and she was an older woman with a confused mind. I truly believe the Lord brought us together.

Often in the midst of a very busy work-day, with the watch repairs stacked on the counter waiting to be done, Father would say to me, "Why don't you visit Alida today? She's come into my mind . . . perhaps she is lonely."

Dear Papa! It meant more work for him because a visit to this friend of mine took at least four hours of the day.

On one visit we talked at some length about heaven. Two days later the nurse at the hospital called me on the phone. "Alida has died suddenly. Can you give us the address of her relatives?"

I know that tears came to my eyes, but I could thank the Lord that she was now with Him in the beautiful heaven we had so recently talked about. "I'm sorry," I told the nurse, "I don't know anything about Alida's relatives."

"But you were such a close friend," she replied.

"I asked her once if she had sisters and brothers. She told me that years ago they had brought her to the hospital. She had never heard from them again. She didn't know if they were alive, and if so, where they lived."

Father said that evening, "Corrie, I believe that this friendship and the time you gave that poor woman has shown God's loving kindness for the despised and lost more than any other work you have done. I'm sure it was important in God's eyes."

Just a Boy Named Henk

Henk was a boy who was a member of my Bible class for mentally retarded. He came from a family with eleven children, and it was difficult for his poor tired mother to give him much attention.

It was from this simple little boy that I saw again how the Holy Spirit reveals himself in such a marvelous way to low-IQ people.

Once I visited Henk at home, and his mother received me with such a thankful manner. "Henk talks so much about the stories you tell in his Bible class. He never remembers anything about any other class, but when he comes from your class he talks to his brothers and sisters about it."

"Is Henk at home?"

"He's in his room upstairs . . . in the corner of the attic. He's there most of the time . . . he's really my easiest boy. We know he'll never become a professor or anything important, but he does work for a salary—he's in a government workshop where he makes clothespins the whole day. Dear Henk, he's so satisfied, but when he's at home the house is so full of noise that he goes to his attic room."

I went upstairs and found Henk on his knees in front of a chair. Before him was an old dirty picture of Jesus on the cross. I stopped at the door to listen, for Henk was singing. His voice was soft and hoarse.

> Out of my bondage, sorrow and night,
>   Jesus, I come, Jesus, I come;
> Into Thy freedom, gladness and light,
>   Jesus, I come to Thee.
> Out of the depths of ruin untold,
>   into the peace of Thy sheltering fold,
> Ever Thy glorious face to behold,
>   Jesus, I come to Thee.

I've heard Bach played by Schweitzer, and anthems sung by gigantic choirs, but at that moment I felt as if I were in a cathedral with angels surrounding me. I tiptoed back downstairs without disturbing him, praising God again for the love He brings into the lives of "even the least of them."

Some time later I heard that Henk's mother had gone into his attic room and found him before the chair, with the picture of Jesus in his hand. Henk was home with the Lord. When I heard about his death I wondered if he had been singing, "Jesus, I come to Thee" at that last moment.

Thirty Years Later

It was after World War II and I was working in East Germany, teaching the gospel in a huge cathedral. I went into a counseling area to talk with people individually; there were many more who needed help waiting outside in another room. I heard a very noisy discussion; everyone seemed to be talking too loudly at the same time. Suddenly everything was quiet and I heard an unusually tender, beautiful voice singing. It was Henk's hymn in German: "Out of my bondage, sorrow and night, Jesus, I come."

I opened the door into the room where the inquirers were waiting and saw a child of about fourteen years of age. Her face was like an angel, and there was something so moving about her that many in the room were crying. The girl's mother stood beside her and held her hand.

When they came into the inquiry room, I found out that the girl's name was Elsa, and I realized immediately that she was not a normal child.

"Where did you learn that song, Elsa?" I asked her gently.

"In prison . . . a man taught it to me, and I sang it every day."

"Why was Elsa in prison?" I asked her mother.

"My husband is a communist. Elsa is mentally retarded. She loves the Lord Jesus and speaks about Him frequently, but her father is an atheist and a leader in his party, so he had no difficulty putting Elsa in prison. A short while ago we got her out . . . it was so terribly cold in that jail that the guards themselves helped me get Elsa out. They heard and enjoyed her singing, and Elsa was always ready to tell them about her Lord."

My lips quivered as I held Elsa's hands, and I remembered so many things . . . the Bible studies in Holland . . . Henk in his attic room . . . and what Father had often said to me. "Corrie, what you do among these people is of little importance in the eyes of men, but I'm sure in God's eyes it is the most valuable work of all."

15
Leaders and Blunders

I loved the activity—the challenge—the excitement of seeing lives changed. The need in the young people was obvious as the clubs multiplied rapidly.

Once a month we had representatives of every club gather to give suggestions and form plans. We had so many interest groups: handcrafts, sewing, piano, harmonium, choir. As a few girls with other talents expressed the need for another group, we would find a leader and begin another club.

I led the music group myself. Music has always been an important part of my life, and it was such a joy for me to work with these girls. Our club had eight members; seven girls worked at a table on harmony and the study of music, while one went to the piano or organ. Consequently, each member had the lengthy chance of five or ten minutes behind the keyboard.

My, what mistakes I made in that club! If I had taught them watch repair, I would have known exactly what I was doing; but the times that I sent a substitute leader, my lack of real skill in music was glaringly evident! My substitute was Ann, a lady who had many diplomas from the music academy. When she took my organ and piano club, her trained ears suffered—to put it mildly. Dear Ann, I learned so much from her! She never refused to help me. In her humble and shy way, she lovingly told me of some of the horrible mistakes in instruction I had made. However, she didn't have a critical spirit and was able to correct me in such a loving manner. This was a gift that set such an example for me.

I loved this music club, but the few-minute message was the important part of the evening for me. These short talks about the Lord weren't deep theological studies but stories from the Bible and about the lives of other Christians. They were brief on purpose; some of the club members expected this part of the evening, but it wasn't really their cup of tea. They seemed to endure it for the sake of the fun in the clubs.

We had a theme for everything we did: It was "Him in the Midst of the Clubs." This is exactly what we did—put the message in the middle of the meeting. We knew if we gave it at the beginning, some would avoid it by coming late; if we talked of our theme later in the evening, they left early.

However, many seeds fell upon fertile ground, and when club members began to open their hearts and ask questions about Jesus, we decided to start a Catechism Club. In this group, they could learn enough to become a member of the church. Some called it the Confirmation Club.

I especially loved the Heidelberg Catechism (not all of the fifty-two Sundays, but many of them). I translated the old-fashioned and complicated style of expression into everyday language that my girls could understand. It was amazing how they enjoyed it and how much it became a part of them.

My teaching, however, did not always meet with enthusiasm from the pastors of the churches.

To become a member of the Dutch Reformed Church there was an examination by the pastor in the presence of elders and deacons. The first time I had just a few confirmands, so the pastor invited me to come together with the new members he had trained. It was an interesting experience.

First the pastor asked one of his pupils a simple question. "Who was the first man in the world?"

Silence. Embarrassment.

He hinted by saying, "It starts with A."

She replied with a proud smile, "That must be Abram."

The pastor was so humiliated.

My pupils studied the Bible and the catechism very hard. The last few weeks before confirmation, they came several evenings to see me and to repeat what they had learned. One of my confirmands was asked, "Do you know the name of one judge of Israel?"

Without hesitation the boy rattled off the names of Othniel, Ehud, Shamgar, Deborah, and the names of the other judges. The examining board was impressed.

One of my girls was asked to tell the story of one of the judges. She said that Gideon was a very shy and bashful man; and when the angel appeared to him, he told Gideon that because the Lord was with him, he was a mighty man of valor. However, she added, "I would never have chosen him to become a hero. I think he was a sissy. But because the Lord was with him, he was mighty."

Later I heard from the French nanny of the minister's little boy that the pastor came home and declared, "I'll never examine Corrie ten Boom's confirmands and mine together again! I've seldom been so ashamed of the poor results of my teaching."

Later it was more than embarrassment, it became a real collision. I was examining a girl for confirmation and refused to recommend her because she didn't believe that Jesus had died on the cross. She was very unhappy over my decision and said, "I'm not religious like you, but I'd like to become a member of a church. I think it's dignified and I like that. Besides, my mom is going to give me a new dress for the occasion."

I still refused and she went to the minister, who reversed my decision and allowed her to become a church member. He said, "I like the idea of a herd. Some are sheep, some are not—but that doesn't matter."

That minister eventually left the pastorate to become a professor of theology at a university.

Leadership Training

As the clubs and the work increased, it became obvious that we must devote more time to leadership training. When we had our weekly meetings with our leaders, we took turns telling a story from the Bible while the rest of us criticized. The type of questions we asked were:

Was the gospel clear?
How was her first sentence; did it attract attention?
Was there humor?
What help was there for the girls this week?
What importance did the story have for eternity?
Did she describe colors, movements?
Did she draw clear pictures with good illustrations?
Was it an inspiration for action, for faith, for endurance?

Problems were discussed and then there was prayer. All of us did the work because we loved it; we had so much fun ourselves, but we also understood why it was important. It was a humble little piece of building the kingdom of God.

One of the problems we had was that we didn't have enough able leaders. Another serious one was that it was difficult to get rid of the wrong ones. The most impossible of all the leaders was *Kipslang*. The girls gave her that name because she told the Adam and Eve story by saying that the snake had legs like a chicken. After that her name became Kipslang (chicken-snake).

The girls roared with laughter during her story about Adam and Eve, and she cried with holy indignation over their ridicule. Weren't girls supposed to be serious when listening to a Bible story? Kipslang's club was always a sensation. Girls cried often because of her harsh remarks, and she usually answered by crying also. There was always noise and disorder in her club, and on one occasion the girls began to throw chairs at each other. It was quite out of control, but no other club was as popular because something was always happening there!

It was really remarkable: Once we had ten clubs that all formed as a result of split-ups from Kipslang's club! Dear Kipslang—she was often a headache, but club work certainly prepared her for the future. When I last heard of her, she had been married three years and had just given birth to her second set of twins.

Let's Go Camping

During the summer we arranged camps that brought girls and leaders closer together than all the weekly meetings. Most of the time we went to the *Bliscap* (an old word for *joy*), which was a simple log cabin with room for about sixty girls.

The campfires were high spots during our outings. There we talked about the Lord, sang hymns, and prayed. The girls were very strict about our campfire time—they were rascals and "born after the fall," but they always said, "At a campfire you look into the flames and listen to God."

In the camps and conferences, one of the biggest dangers was the gossip. We made a camp law and one of the articles was: "If you must tell something negative about someone else, first tell ten positive qualities about him."

If a gossiping remark was made during a meal, we simply said, "Pass the salt, if you please."

Our foster children enjoyed the club and camp life with me. All of them were such a great help to us as leaders, and the love between us made it possible for me to depend upon them for so many tasks. It was always such a joy to have them together with the other club girls. Most of them had such good training that later they were able to do club work wherever they were, scattered over the world.

My girls learned some of the basic lessons of life and death at the camps. Toddy and Janny, sisters, had several real aunts in Holland with whom they spent a part of their vacations. Once in a camp with me, they received a phone call from an uncle that their most beloved aunt had died. They had known that her life was in danger for she was a hemophiliac. When she had a wound, the bleeding wouldn't stop, and upon the birth of her first baby she died. She was very young, and the girls were brokenhearted. It was the first time that someone they loved had been taken from them by death.

"Would you like to go to be with your uncle?" I asked.

"Yes, we would. We couldn't enjoy camp anymore—perhaps we can help with the funeral."

"Tomorrow I'll take you to the train. There's no connection tonight," I explained.

I saw their sad young faces and suggested taking a walk over the heather fields. When we were alone, I let them talk and talk about their aunt. I have found this is one of the most important things to do for a person who is grieving—have him talk about the loved one who is gone. Toddy and Janny knew their aunt loved the Lord and that she had known there was the danger of dying as soon as she had a wound.

I had my little New Testament in the pocket of my uniform and read from Romans 8:28. "All things work together for good to them that love God. . . ."

Also, "These little troubles (which are really so transitory) are winning for us a permanent and glorious reward out of all proportion to our pain" (2 Cor. 4:17 PHILLIPS).

Toddy and Janny confronted the reality and the glory of death that summer at camp. Some years later Toddy married her uncle, which may seem strange, but he was only nine years older than she. They had several children and a good life together.

Along the River Rhine

One trip (which was unforgettable) was a hiking and camping adventure the club girls had through Germany. All the girls (who could spend the time and money) met each week in our clubhouse to learn the German language. If someone knew a sentence that would be useful when traveling, she would express it to the group, and all the girls would write the sentence in Dutch and in German in their notebooks. Everyone had a little knowledge of the language before we started our trip. I told them the German words and they wrote them down phonetically.

The Rhine River was never so beautiful as it was that summer. I don't believe I've ever enjoyed a trip through a foreign land as much as I did when traveling with girls who had never been outside their country.

Many years later, one of the girls who went on our German trip became seriously ill. In her feverish state she talked about the only foreign country trip she had ever made; it had been the highlight of her life. However, just the recall of that trip didn't help her when she was treading the valley of the shadow of death. There she was not alone, because Jesus was her Savior. She had given her heart to Him in one of the clubs. This was the most important purpose of our club work: to confront each person with Him, who is our only comfort in life and death.

Jesus is the real security in this world, even in the hour we have to leave it.

Blunder Boom

Sometimes I think my middle name is *Blunder*. I made some big mistakes, but I can say that our clubs became a success in spite of me. I loved my girls and shared many of their joys and difficulties.

As the years passed and some of our club girls grew older or others wished to join, some of the teenagers didn't like to belong to a club where "older people" came.

"We must make an age limit for our clubs," some experienced club leaders suggested. "Let's make it twenty-five years."

I protested. I had some fine girls who had already passed that age, and I couldn't stand the idea of being forced to send them away.

"I don't think we should have any limit— let's just consider the ages eight to eighty. Why not?"

No one challenged me. When I had a fixed opinion, it was almost impossible to dissuade me; consequently, the age limit was never changed.

One blunder (which may have turned into a blessing) was when I chose a campsite rather close to soldiers' quarters. In their free time, the men showed a great interest in the girls. Of course, the girls returned that interest. That's understandable.

One day during that camp we marched through the village at the moment the soldiers came off duty. The boys surrounded us on all sides. An officer who had been a daily visitor at the Beje saw our problem. He took his bicycle and rode beside our group, ordering all the soldiers away. Then he escorted us until we reached the camp.

That officer was a blessing to me, but I'm not sure all the girls felt the same way. The campfires became quite a problem. When the girls gathered around the fire, we seemed to have soldiers growing out of the trees. It was very difficult to get any attention from the girls for our talks and singing. I appealed to the officer for help, and he offered. "Every evening I'll send you two trustworthy sergeants to serve as camp watchers. They'll report any soldier who comes within a quarter of a mile of your tents and campfire."

After that two men joined our campfire every evening. They were never the same men, so the rotation system worked very well. They told us later that they enjoyed their "girls' club watch," and there was never a lack of volunteers.

I've sometimes wondered if there was some seed of the gospel sown in the hearts of those men. We never know. God can give a straight blow with a crooked stick. He blesses in spite of our blunders.

16
Safety Pins on Uniforms

———————— ∽∽∽∽ ————————

We used every method we could think of to recruit girls for our clubs. We took lists from school or church, we talked to shop-keepers, we even placed notices in the news-papers. One of our girls, Annie, answered our advertisement when she was only eleven or twelve years old and remained as a club girl for many years. The advertisement was simple, but it brought results. It read: DO YOU LIKE TO GO ON WALKS? IF YOU WANT TO MEET OTHER GIRLS AND HAVE FUN, COME TO THE TEN BOOM SHOP AT BARTELJORISSTRAAT 19.

The gymnastics club was one of the most popular. I worked out with the girls under the guidance of capable teachers, but I certainly wasn't one of the best pupils. Far from it. My girls were much stronger than I, and how they helped me because of my fain efforts to do some of the exercises.

When the gymnastics club needed a slogan, one of the girls suggested that it should be: WE MAKE STRAIGHT WHAT IS CROOKED. What rascals! They looked at my legs and then at my face to see if I understood what they meant. We had such great fun together. The teasing made for an easier relationship. We were friends, and when I blew my whistle, they all sat down to listen. Most of them knew very little about the Lord Jesus, and several of them freely admitted that they came for fun and not for spiritual matters.

One time I flopped on the floor after trying some new trick on the bars and failing miserably. The girls did their best to help Tante Kees accomplish the simple exercises. I spied Greetje sitting cross-legged in the corner and moved wearily toward her. Then I saw that she was crying, and I asked her if she wanted to tell me what was wrong.

"My older sister Betty is dying. I have learned so much here about Jesus, but I know she doesn't know anything about Him."

"Tell her," I said.

"But how, Tante Kees; I don't know as much as you do."

"Tell her about the cross where Jesus died to carry the punishment that we earned. Tell

Betty that Jesus loves her and has said, 'Come to me all'—and that means Betty too."

Greetje began to cry harder, but it was her turn to work out on the bars, so she struggled to get up and wiped away the tears. After she was through she came back to me.

"Then what should I do?"

"Ask Betty if she knows that she is a sinner."

"She knows that."

"Tell her that every sinner may come to Jesus. She must ask forgiveness, and then He will make her heart clear. You know what I told you about that today. She must ask Jesus to come into that clear heart. Let her first say: 'Thank you, Jesus, for dying for me.'"

Greetje went back for another workout. The third time we talked I said, "Tell Betty that Jesus has said, 'In My Father's house are many mansions . . . I go to prepare a place for everyone who belongs to Me.' When Betty gives her heart to Jesus, she surely belongs to Him."

For several gymnasium evenings, I taught Greetje more about the way to bring Betty to the Lord. After a few weeks, I was invited to come to their home. Greetje greeted me at the door and there was no sign of a dis-

tressed little girl. "Tante Kees, come in . . .
I want you to see Betty."

Resting on a small bed against the wall
was a pale young girl, smiling at me with the
radiance only God can give. "Jesus is in my
heart . . . He has forgiven me my sins.
Greetje told me all about it."

Some days later that girl died, and again
I had to speak at a burial. I praised the Lord
that my work in gymnastics with the girls—
even though awkward at times—had been
used to reach someone before it was too late.

Gradually the clubs began to take on more
degree of organization. It was exciting to see
that this wasn't the case of formation of an
organization first, then imposing upon it the
concept of girls' clubs—but of the need coming before the structured format.

Out of the gymnastics club, in particular,
came the Girl Guide clubs in Holland. The
uniforms, slogan, songs, and mottos were
gradually added, but only as there was a
necessity for them. We did discover, however, that there was a healthy difference
between Boy Scouting and Girl Scouting.

One of our gymnast teachers was a scout
leader. I asked him what activities he had
with the boys that week, and he showed me
some games and taught me some knots. *Oh,*

well, I thought, *we can do that.* The next day I taught the knots and played games with my Girl Guides. *This is easy! I'll just ask him each week what he does and copy those activities.*

The next week he told me that he had fastened a strong rope on a tree at the top of a dune and strung the rope to another tree some distance away. The boys had to climb along that rope from one end to the other. I listened to this idea, but that day it dawned on my stupid mind that Boy Scouting and Girl Scouting were two different things!

The End of the World?

One evening I was meeting with a group of pioneers (the older Girl Guides), when Max, one of our faithful members, ran into the room, late and breathless, her voice high with alarm.

"Tante Kees, there's something wrong with the stars! They're running all over the sky, as if they want to see what is happening on the other side of the horizon."

The girls, excitable creatures that they were, jumped up and ran outside. "Why, those are meteors," I said. "Let's go to the Kenaupark and watch from there . . . we can see better."

We ran to the Kenaupark where our beautiful cherry tree The Bride of Haarlem was and watched the exciting display of shooting stars.

Pietje said, "I'm scared . . . is it the end of the world?"

"Girls, those are not stars but meteors, perhaps broken off from other planets. As soon as they enter the earth's atmosphere they are heated and become luminous like a streak of light."

"Pietje, this isn't a sign of the end of the world, although Jesus has told us that when He comes one of the signs of the time will be terrifying things happening in the heavens. Jesus told us to look for these signs. Peter makes it very practical when he tells us, 'Because, my dear friends, you have a hope like this before you, I urge you to make certain that such a Day would find you at peace with God and man, clean and blameless in His sight' (2 Peter 3:13 PHILLIPS)."

We returned to the clubhouse and were seated again in our circle on the floor as the questions began to tumble out. It was an exciting time of sharing, and I was thankful for the shooting stars.

I told about the many signs that Jesus mentioned and that Luke 21:32 tells us that the generation that will see all these signs shall not pass away, until they are all fulfilled.

Jap was one of the girls who was a deep thinker. "I wonder, Tante Kees, if we are living in the generation when all the signs will be fulfilled and Christ will return. We should keep our triangle within the circle and not forget it!"

(The triangle represented the three stages of development: social, intellectual, and physical; the circle meant the spiritual development. We emphasized that when the triangle was within the circle, we were in the proper position in our lives as children of God.)

Milly was puzzled; this was only her second time in our club, and she was hearing us speak of spiritual matters that confused her. "What does that mean, about the triangle and the circle?" she said. "Are you speaking in a secret language?"

For the first time Mien spoke up. "It means . . . stop trying to work things out for yourself and ask God to do it. I tried hard, but it didn't help . . . now I have asked Him to manage me."

On Parade

There was one outstanding yearly occasion when my father took a direct part in working with my girls. This was the important Holland holiday on the queen's birthday.

On August 31, Queen Wilhelmina's birthday, there was a great celebration, with parades and speeches, picnics and fairs. It was an old-fashioned Fourth of July done up in Dutch style. Father, as one of Haarlem's leading citizens, organized the activities of the day and sat on the platform with the mayor.

Since Father was the chairman of the parade committee, my Girl Guides always had a very prominent place in the lineup. We could display our flag, with the triangle inside the circle, and take that opportunity to explain to anyone who asked what the significance was of our symbol.

On one parade route we marched with an elaborate horsedrawn carriage, resplendent with liveried coachmen. It was so elegant that I couldn't resist poking my head out of the coach window and making a funny face. Father, however, was always dignified, in spite of his prankish daughter.

After Wilhelmina was replaced by her daughter, Juliana, as queen, the date for the celebration was changed to April 30. Since the following day was May Day, the occasion for the international communist parade, we always arranged for all the banners to be removed so that the communists couldn't take advantage of our decorations.

Going International

The club work and Girl Guide activities grew each year, until some members of the YMCA in America heard of these efforts and invited me to an international conference in Riga, Latvia. Little Latvia was an independent country then, still able to practice religious freedom. After the communists seized Latvia in 1940, Christian practices were stamped out.

It was in the 1930s when I went to Latvia. On the way to the conference grounds, I was invited to be the guest of two old ladies in their home. Their country had been torn by wars and revolutions and had changed nationalities several times. During a revolution, the house of the old women had been raided, many of their valuable possessions were destroyed, including their antique wall clock. It had been repaired many times but never was able to strike the hours. The chain for the weight was hopelessly tangled, and I worked on the clock for quite some time, although I am a repairer of watches, not

clocks. It was frustrating, so I talked over
the problem with the Lord and He gave me
the solution. I can still see the two ladies
standing hand in hand, tears of joy on their
faces, when they heard their clock strike
again. That night, when one of them heard
the clock, she awakened the other and whispered, "Father's clock is striking."

How glad I was that I was a watchmaker
and could bring some happiness into their
lonely lives.

At the conference I learned that I had a lot
to learn! I heard about the leadership of Girl
Guides in other countries and felt like a real
beginner. The spiritual training, however, was
a bit of a disappointment. There was a lot of
talk about "character building," until finally
I asked, "Don't you think that we miss the
purpose when we tell the girls to be good citizens but fail to bring them to Jesus Christ?"

To my amazement they changed the program because of that question. The talk
about evangelization in the clubs had been
planned for the last day, but it was resched-
uled for the second day.

When I returned home, we decided to
improve our image somewhat and have better uniforms. We made dark-blue uniforms,
but if the girls didn't have enough money

for that, we said that any navy-blue dress was adequate.

With my own homemade uniform, an orange ribbon substituted for the official Girl Guide's scarf, I went to my second international conference on a mountain near Vienna, Austria. There I met the top leaders of the Girl Guide movement in England, and they were very proper. Once we had an official roll call and I couldn't find my belt. I grabbed a belt from another dress and put that around my waist. We were making a horseshoe march in formation and a Dutch Girl Guide whispered to me in agony when she passed me, "You have two belts—one is hanging on your back."

Suddenly I felt very tacky; I compared my dress with the smart uniforms, perfect to the smallest detail. I began to feel like Alice in Wonderland when she grew into a giant. There I was with two belts and that glaring orange ribbon fastened to my front with a safety pin.

One of the Girl Guide officers said to me, "I'm glad that I had the chance to meet you and talk on top of this mountain, but if I meet you in such a uniform in London, I will act as if I have never seen you before."

After that experience I realized that this enterprise was too serious to remain amateurish. When I returned to Holland, we asked some prominent and talented women to help us form a national board of directors. We studied handbooks from other areas and held many conferences. Since there were groups of women interested in this work from many different places in Holland, we chose a central meeting place—the railway station in Amsterdam. We could work in the quiet first-class waiting room until the moment our trains left.

But I became concerned about the direction of the Girl Guides. Coming in contact with leaders from other parts of the country, we discovered that "religious instruction" was not acceptable. It was considered propaganda for a religion. We could have clubs for Christian girls with Christian leaders, but our aim to reach the other girls was made impossible. It seemed that all the club work, Bible studies, conferences, camps were just preparation for something more. Consequently, a new Christian movement was born.

De Nederlandse Meisjesclubs (Netherlands Girls' Clubs) grew out of the Girl Guide movement but added the missing dimension. After a few years, the outreach of these clubs burst beyond the borders of Holland, and we had six thousand members in the Netherlands East Indies and eight hundred in the West Indies. Because of our symbol, the name of our club members was *Triangle Girls*.

The first article of our club law was impressed upon many young minds. It was: SEEK YOUR STRENGTH THROUGH PRAYER.

Years later, in a time when camping and parades, conferences and singing were beautiful memories of peaceful times, I was in a prison cell. Every sound was magnified in the deadly silence of those cubicles; I realized there was a girl crying next door. I called to her and said, "Don't cry, be strong . . . we'll be free soon."

The answer shocked me.

"Tante Kees . . . oh, Tante Kees . . . is that you? I'm Annie."

I recognized her voice. She was one of my faithful club girls, who had been arrested after my family and I had been taken to prison. My heart almost stopped. That poor girl was the last person I expected to be strong in such a terrible spot. I called to her through the barriers of the prison walls. "Annie, do you remember the first article of our club law? 'Seek your strength through prayer.'"

She stopped crying.

17
Opposition!

‎ ‎ ‎

Opposition to lives that are yielded to Jesus Christ takes many forms, some dramatic, some subtle. Satan is a clever angel of light, but sometimes he chooses supernatural ways to frighten us into inactivity.

During a time at camp with the girls, I was singing outside of the cabin after lights-out. The song had the words: "Don't be afraid for whatever is coming, your heavenly Father takes care of you."

Suddenly I heard horrible noises around me. It seemed as if among the trees some sort of beings were trying to make me stop. The noises grew and subsided, sending shivers through my body with their weird tones. While I sang, I pleaded with the Lord: "Cover me and protect me with Your blood, Lord Jesus . . . give me the strength to go on singing and speak through me to reach all these girls."

The noises remained and got louder and more ugly, but I didn't stop. I knew that I stood on the front line of battle, but through Jesus, it was victory ground, not defeat or retreat. As soon as I had finished the song, the noises stopped, just as abruptly as they began.

I went to bed and thanked the Lord for His victory. The next morning I asked the girls if they had heard anything unusual the previous night. They answered that they had never heard me sing so beautifully. Nobody heard anything else.

He Never Fails

Many of the girls in the clubs stand out in my memory. Peggy, for instance, was a member of the gym club who was not able to pay her dues, although it was only a *dubbeltje* (two cents). Unfortunately, we found that she stole from the club money, which was kept in a small box on the windowsill at the clubhouse. I was concerned about Peggy, so I marked a quarter and left it on the windowsill. When it disappeared, I called Peggy aside and asked to see her purse. There was the marked quarter.

Peggy had accepted the Lord as her Savior, but she was still bound to her past and background—a family of so-called down-and-outers. I told her, "Peggy, a child of God is tempted, but the difference from those who are not Christians is that God gives with the temptation a way of escape. He says, 'Confess your sins, God is faithful and just to forgive. . . .'"

Peggy understood and right then confessed what she had done. From that time on, we elected her treasurer of our club and there was never a cent lost. Peggy really meant business when she gave her yes to Jesus; she trusted Him, and I did too—that is why I could trust her. She never failed because Jesus never failed.

The Only Comfort

Pietje was a hunchback, one of our best-liked club girls. Although it was a long time ago, I remember her reactions to the Bible stories. One day we were discussing Exodus 20:5, where God speaks to the Jewish people about the sins of the fathers continuing upon the children, grandchildren, and great-grandchildren. Pietje began to cry, and when I noticed her, I took her into another room to talk over her troubles.

Pietje's face was very dark as she said, "I am a hunchback and that was the punishment for my father who has been an alcoholic."

"But Pietje, did you hear the following verse: 'And showing mercy unto thousands of them that love me, and keep my commandments'? When your father begins to love God he will experience His mercy. You love the Lord, and although you are a hunchback, you are a happy girl, because you experience the mercy and peace in your heart because Jesus lives in you."

When Pietje was in a Bible study group we read Romans 8:34 and I asked, "Who is our Judge?" They answered, "Jesus!" and I said, "Who is our Advocate?" The answer came from Pietje, "Jesus!" Then she almost shouted, "What a joy! Judge and Advocate is the same! Jesus prays for us, so there is nothing to fear."

One day they sent for me to come quickly because Pietje was in a large ward of a hospital, and they told me she was dying. I knew that she had accepted Jesus as her Savior. As I stood beside her bed I said, "It's such a comfort to know Jesus is our Judge, also our Advocate. How He loves you!"

At that moment I saw the transformation on her face from pain to peace. "Pietje, can you hear me?" I said.

She didn't open her eyes. I couldn't reach her anymore; I prayed with her, laying my hand on her feverish head and asking the Good Shepherd to take His lamb in His arms and carry her straight through the valley of the shadow of death into the house of the Father with many mansions.

When I said, "Amen," Pietje opened her eyes for the last time and smiled.

Pietje was still very fresh in my mind and heart when I met the next day with leaders and board members of the YWCA. We talked about club experiences, and then one lady said, "I don't like the method of your clubs in Haarlem. All that preaching you do! I don't think it's right. I believe in Christian surroundings and bringing girls into a Christian atmosphere—that will attract far more girls than just Bible talks will. I preach by my behavior rather than by what I say."

My answer was, "Romans 10:14 says, 'How shall they believe in Him whom they have not heard? And how shall they hear without a preacher?'"

I'm glad that we told Pietje about our Judge and Advocate Jesus in the time we could still reach her. In the twenty-five years that we did club work, there were at least forty girls who died. Accidents, illnesses, even a murder were the causes. When I stood at the deathbed of a club girl, I was so thankful that I had redeemed the time when she was still able to listen to the gospel. Illness, pain, even drugs during the last part of a person's life may make it impossible for him to hear.

When Pietje died, I was the speaker at her burial. Father had conducted so many burial services for his colleagues that he was able to help me in so many ways. His straightforward testimony was not always appreciated, but when death entered a family, Father was a welcome comforter. When someone dies, people are confronted with eternity and there is the right opportunity to speak about the security of eternal life that only Jesus can give.

Father gave me some practical advice for those sad occasions: "When your time comes to speak, Corrie, don't hesitate. Many people are moved and nervous, so look for a place where everyone can hear and see you. Step forward without hesitation. Relatives and friends who are left behind must be challenged to repent of their sins and receive Jesus as their Savior."

Yes, opposition comes in strange places and through unusual vehicles: supernatural sounds from the darkness of a forest and even superficial attitudes from the self-righteous.

Doubt

Opposition also came from within. Has there been doubt in my heart? Has there been dryness in my prayer life? Yes, indeed, there has been.

There was a time when I needed a major operation. For some strange reason, I persuaded the surgeon not to give me a general anesthetic, only a local. I didn't realize that this could be such a severe shock to my system. I didn't suffer pain during the operation, but I did have a great deal of tension. For several months afterward I needed some painful treatments.

In that time my mind and spirit were very low; I couldn't pray; the Bible was uninteresting; church was dull. I remember that my prayers were very short. Most of the time I muttered, "Lord, I can't reach You . . . I can't pray. Lord, I know that You can reach me. Keep me in Your care and help me to be able to pray again soon."

The outward Corrie was the same. I did the club work as I had always done. I worked in the shop, met customers, and carried on all the activities of our busy lives. I don't know if anyone saw what a dark valley I was going through, for I held it inside. I didn't talk over my problems with my family and friends. After all, I thought, they have worries enough. Now I know how stupid that was.

Then a girl, Colly, came to me and asked if she could tell me her troubles. She was a bright girl from a good, hardworking family, and I liked her very much.

"Tante Kees," she said with her head down, "can you help me? For weeks I have been unable to pray. Do you think I'm lost? Do you think I'm no longer a child of God?"

"Colly, you're a child of God and you're not lost. Now sit down and I'll tell you something about myself. I know exactly how you feel, because I'm going through the same problem as you. For several weeks I haven't been able to pray . . . but even though the time has been dark, I know that Jesus is with me and He can reach me. Let's see if there is something in the Bible that can help both of us."

We read Romans 8:26: "The Spirit also helps our weakness; for we do not know how to pray as we should, but the Spirit Himself intercedes for us."

Colly and I both realized that the Holy Spirit helps us with our daily problems and in our prayer problems. When we are totally inadequate, the Spirit is interceding with God the Father for us. The burden of guilt was taken from Colly and me, and together we thanked the Lord that He had forgiven us and restored our communication with Him.

Haarlemsche Meisjesclubs

The H.M.C. (Haarlem Girls' Clubs) had a performance once each year in the concert hall, when each club demonstrated some of its skills and abilities. We opened the program with all of the 250 to 300 girls marching onto the platform. They sang a song, and I gave a five-minute talk to the people in the auditorium.

The mixed club (which had passed the "year's trial" without any serious mishaps) provided the orchestra for the musical part of our entertainment. The first time this group had to play before all of those friends and relatives (about a thousand of them), they were frozen with stage fright. I walked over and picked up a violin and acted as if I were a real virtuoso, but making sure that no one in the audience saw that the bow was turned upside down and not touching the strings. As I "played" the violin, the boys gained confidence and began to perform. The ones who were playing wind instruments probably had trouble stifling their laughter in order to make music.

Tears and laughter, opposition and support—the clubs taught those young men and women preparation for life.

When the war started, we had to close the H.M.C. clubs. I will never forget the evening we were together for the last time. We saluted our flag, with tears running down our cheeks, and then folded it carefully and hid it in a secret closet of the clubhouse.

As we sang the national hymn for the last time together, the girls had a very difficult time. "Girls, we mustn't cry," I said. "We had great fun in the clubs, but it wasn't just for a good time that we have come together. We have learned the important facts of what makes us strong, even in times of disaster. The Lord Jesus gives us security even in the insecurity of wartime."

I looked at those girls and wondered— would they draw on the Lord's strength in the days and years to come? What was in store for them in this world of ours that is filled with hatred and cruelty?

I was so grateful that the time in our clubs
had not been wasted in just building "good
citizens," but that we had the opportunity
to learn the vital message of Jesus' victory,
which would give strength for the suffering
that awaited many of us.

18

"... He Took My Hand"

War. It was early in the morning when we heard the bombs. We knew the sound of the explosions were coming from Schiphol, the airport near Haarlem. I ran to Betsie's room and found her sitting up in bed, pale and shaking. We put our arms around each other and trembled with each blast; the wavering red glow was so eerie in the darkness of our once-peaceful skies.

We were afraid but had learned from childhood how to cast our burdens on the Lord. We prayed like frightened children, running to their father for help and protection.

"Lord, make us strong ... give us strength to help others."

"Lord, take away our fear. Give us trust."

It was a crisis of fear in both of us, but Jesus gave us the victory over it. We were never so frightened as we were during that

253

night, not even when war and occupation destroyed our whole family life and everything we had known for more than a half a century. Was that night the Lord's way of inoculating us in preparation for the future?

In the five days of war that followed, many people came to the house; Father was a pillar of strength for all of them; he prayed with everyone who asked. Sometimes the shock of what was happening would engulf me, and while Father was bringing trust and peace to those in turmoil, I would go to the piano and play Bach. No other music gave me so much rest.

The darkest time during those five days was when our royal family left, our Queen Wilhelmina for England and Crown Princess Juliana for Canada. We knew then that our case was hopeless.

There were not many times that I cried, but when I heard about the royal family leaving the country, I was heartbroken and wept. For the Dutch people, the queen was our security—we loved her.

Then Holland surrendered. I walked in the street with Father, and everyone was talking to everyone else. In that moment there was a oneness that I have never seen before. We were together in the great suffering, humiliation, and defeat of our nation.

Although my heart was aching with misery there was encouragement that people could be so united.

In the millennium we will be like that: The whole world will be covered with the knowledge of God like the waters cover the bottom of the sea. The oneness will not be in misery but in our communion with the Lord.

The German army marched through the Barteljorisstraat: tanks, cannons, cavalry, and hundreds and hundreds of soldiers. The narrow little street where Dot and I had played games, the alley where I had seen the drunks when I was only five and prayed for "all the people in the Smedestraat," the path we had taken on Sunday to St. Bavo's—all were filled with soldiers.

As the conquerors swept in, I noticed some of them were red-faced, shame written in their expressions. After the war a German told me, "With every step I took in Holland, I felt ashamed. I knew I was occupying a neutral nation."

Churches were packed in those days; the psalms, which were written in times of great suffering, gained a new value. Ministers who had never preached about the second coming of Christ now chose their texts from the many places in the Bible on that subject.

In the beginning, we saw little change in our daily life, but gradually the enemy began to impose restrictions. At first the curfew was ten o'clock, which was not difficult for us, but later it was moved back to eight, then six. No one could leave his house; there was absolute blackout, and every window was covered with black paper as soon as the sun was down.

Telephones were cut off; food was rationed; and often after standing in long lines with our ration cards, we would find that the stores were empty.

One beautiful Sunday afternoon, Betsie, Father, and I were walking through our park, south of Haarlem, when the Gestapo descended and took all of the young fathers around us, who were out walking with their families, leaving distraught wives and crying children behind.

All Dutch people have bicycles, and sometimes the Gestapo set up a bicycle blockade. Everyone who rode by was summoned to give up his vehicle. If you were fortunate enough to keep your bicycle, you learned to ride without tires, because they were confiscated and taken to Germany.

We were not even safe in church. Once during a service in the cathedral, the Germans guarded the doors so that nobody could move. Then they opened one door and ordered every man from eighteen to forty to come out. They were sent that same day to Germany—many of these men were never seen again.

The occupation—the underground movement to save Jews—the concentration camps—all of these are documented in *A Prisoner and Yet . . .* , and in my book and the movie *The Hiding Place.*

For more than thirty years since World War II, I have been a tramp for the Lord in more than sixty countries on all the continents of this troubled world. Many people have asked me about my childhood, youth, and the years before *The Hiding Place.* A person doesn't spring into existence at the age of fifty; there are years of preparation, years of experience, which God uses in ways we may never know until we meet Him face to face.

However, from the perspective of over eighty years of living, I have had the marvelous opportunity to discover the sweetness of some of the fruit of His labor. Just recently I have heard from by letter or met in person some of my club "girls." (They are still girls to me!) It has been like a letter from the Lord.

Aukje

One of our faithful club girls was quiet Aukje. She was a peacemaker who could say a few words but make them count. When other girls were unruly and stubborn, I remember Aukje saying, "Don't be so stupid. Why did we come to the club in the first place? Most of us want to have fun and learn something, so if you don't like it then leave and let the rest of us enjoy the club."

To the point—but said with such kindness that most of the time the problems were overcome. When she was about seventeen, Aukje became a club leader herself and led a group of girls who learned handcrafts. She was so quiet and gentle that we didn't expect exciting results from her, but her love for the Lord was very clear.

When the ten Boom family was arrested Aukje came to our house, not knowing that it was a Gestapo trap. She was taken to the police station and spent a week with our oldest Jewish underground girl, Mary, who had been in the hiding place but was later arrested in the street.

Aukje talked to Mary about the Lord Jesus. She told her that Jesus had died on the cross for the sins of the whole world and that He had said, "Come to Me, all who are heavy laden, I will give you rest."

Mary said, "I heard Grandpa ten Boom pray so often when I was in the Beje. He always said to me, 'Mary, you are a Jew; you will not change that if you invite the Lord Jesus into your heart. On His divine side He was the Son of God, but on His human side He was a Jew.'"

Mary received Jesus as her Savior in that cell. Our quiet Aukje had a boldness for the Lord. She told me later that the moment Mary said her yes to Jesus in her prayer of accepting Him, the guards came into the cell and took her away. We heard later that she was sent to Poland where she died.

I heard nothing from Aukje for many years. What a surprise it was for me when she came to my room in Haarlem thirty years later. She told me that she was working in a small village where there was no minister; she preaches every Sunday for the little congregation. She said, "What I learned in your clubs I still use when I teach the children and have my Bible study groups."

Poes

Poes was an outgoing little rascal; wherever she was in a club there was laughing and fun. At camp she was the happy note, even when it was raining and attitudes were down. When there were weaker girls who needed help in hikes or gymnastics, Poes was always ready to help.

I remember one time she was walking behind me and was quite outspoken in her ideas about my legs. She said, "If I had such legs, I should decide to march beside them." She married an older boy and moved to South Africa. I met them there once after the war, but only briefly. He called himself an atheist but did not object when Poes and I shared with him our love for the Lord Jesus. I promised to pray for him, but in later correspondence Poes never mentioned that he was interested in spiritual affairs.

Then a strange thing happened—one of those "coincidents," which are such a marvelous part of God's plan. Poes and her husband were walking in the streets of Johannesburg when a boy asked them to buy a raffle ticket to raise money for a house for a boys' club. Poes said, "Sure, I enjoyed clubs when I was a girl—I hope you have a lot of fun in your new cabin."

Later she found out that they had the ticket that won the first prize in the raffle—it was a round-trip plane ride for two to the

Netherlands! And so it happened that one day they stood in my room in Holland. What memories we shared! Poes told me she had become a member of a church, and Henk, her husband, listened with amusement as we talked about the clubs. He declared very strongly that he didn't believe in God. I knew I had only one chance to bring him the gospel, so I said, "Henk, I'll probably only have this one time to talk with you. There are two ways to live: You can go your way or God's way; you can accept Jesus Christ as your Savior, and He will make you a child of God. Then you can bring Him all your sins and ask and get forgiveness. He makes sure you're a child of God, and He will put your name in the book of life."

After I prayed with them, Henk said, "I believe it's time that I gave my heart to Jesus. I've seen much of Him in the life of Poes, and He must be a reality. I know I'm a sinner and you said that Jesus accepts sinners. So I'll tell Him all that I have done and I have been and believe that He will make me a child of God."

They returned to South Africa, and Henk became a member of a lively church. Some months ago Henk died, but he said, "Tell

Tante Kees that God has used her to bring me to the Lord."

God began working years before in a mischievous little girl, Poes, in a gymnastics club in a little Dutch town.

The Golden Tea Party

What would they be like? Would the years have changed them? What joys and sorrows, trials and triumphs would they have seen in the decades since we had last met?

I was so excited, as that younger Corrie had been when she introduced her club girls at the yearly performance in the Haarlem concert hall. Now in my eighties, I had returned to Holland for a visit and had invited those women who had been in clubs in years past—and were still in the vicinity of Haarlem—to my house for tea.

No uniform with two belts and a safety pin this time! I wore my best red and white silk summer dress and made sure that not one thing would mar my appearance.

They arrived at the front door at the same time. Some came on their big old-fashioned bicycles, some drove little cars, and others walked from the bus stop. There was no need for protocol, for they began to laugh and talk all at once.

What an afternoon we had! Each girl told a little of her story, ending on the same theme, which added so much joy to my heart.

Ariapja, whose nickname was *Jap*, bubbled with her enthusiasm about the club work. She told how she first became a part of our group and her mother had said, "You may not have a uniform!"

So she went to her first camp feeling a bit ashamed, because she wasn't dressed like the rest of the girls. It was the most important issue in her life then. Hank, who had also come for tea that afternoon, was the one who gave Jap her uniform; that unselfish act was remembered by Jap all her life. When she went home she asked her mother if she could be a Girl Guide. Her mother told her that it was all right, if she didn't wear the uniform on Sunday.

Girl guiding became Jap's life, and she told us that sunny afternoon in my living room in Holland that much she learned as a young girl in the clubs had prepared her for her total life experiences.

Stien had gone to one of my clubs when she was sixteen to learn the catechism. I had been her teacher, and after she was received into the Dutch Reformed church I said, "Now, Stien, you must lead a club."

After Stien had been one of our club leaders she took the initiative and began a club for feebleminded children. She told me later, "You had taught me, Tante Kees, to love those less fortunate, and I truly did love those children." For Stien going to the clubs was the best part of her young life. Her home was never open to others, and she spent many evenings at the Beje. Fortunately, she had stayed at home on that fateful day in February 1944 when the Gestapo paid us an unwelcome visit.

Annie, who had answered a newspaper advertisement to join a club, said that she came for fun and not for all those "spiritual things." And she did have fun! She joined the singing club, the English club, and the gymnastics club, and when she told about the latter, she reminded all of us about the club slogan. (I knew someone would bring that up—the rascals!) The gymnastics club slogan—WE MAKE STRAIGHT WHAT IS CROOKED—was not very good—too long to put on a program. (I had to pretend not to notice the laughter every time it was mentioned.)

Annie told how she fell in love with the gym teacher. However, when his girlfriend came, Annie became very jealous and out of spite sewed his pants together and put water in his shoes.

(Tea cups almost fell off laps when this story was recounted.)

As a punishment, I told Annie that she would not be allowed to go to the club for three weeks. She reminded me, however, that she returned in one week, proving that Tante Kees's discipline was sometimes a little lax.

When Annie was seventeen, she was at the camp at Bliscap, feeling very low. She had just split up with her current boyfriend and thought it was the end of the world. She remembered that we were sitting outside looking at the stars and I had told her, "When you're in need and don't know the answer, tell the Lord about it. He has your past, present, and future in His hands." It was then that Annie accepted Jesus Christ as her Savior; she said that every time she was in need in years to come she remembered that moment.

"I know the Lord is willing to take your life in His hands when you're small," Annie said.

Nellie was born in Germany and didn't come to Holland until she was fourteen years old. She came into the clubs when she was eighteen, not as a believer in Jesus Christ, but found Him during one of the camps. When Nellie remembered the outstanding experiences of her club time, she talked about the campfires—the time of deep discussions together. She thought a while when we asked what club work had prepared her for. Then she remembered one of the articles in the club law, which was to give help to others. She said that even today people know there is help in her home. "Let's go over to Nell's—she always has the soup on."

As the girls began to share more and more of their memories and their later life experiences, one story after another spilled out. Reina told how she loved the circle and the club song. It was difficult for Ellen de Kroon, my secretary, and Carole Carlson to contain themselves as we all stood up and joined hands to repeat our motto and sing our song after almost forty years of separation! The voices may have changed a bit, but the fervor was still there!

Reina said she had come from a Christian family, but the club work had inspired in her the personal desire to bring the gospel to other girls.

"Did you know," she said, looking around the room, "that the last time the Girl Guides wore their uniforms was at my wedding?"

Hank was in at the start of the clubs and remembered the first camp experience she had. One of the girls had trouble with sleepwalking, and she told how Tante Kees had been so concerned about her and had walked her gently back to bed. However, it was also discovered that the so-called sleepwalker had a sweet tooth, for the following morning the chocolate bars, which had been left out for campfire treats, had been strangely consumed by someone in her sleep.

Julie had been rather quiet but finally began to bring the conversation back to the present. "I want so much to give our young people some of the love, the experiences, the strength in knowing the Lord that we learned in your clubs, Tante Kees. Our children have so much—and yet they're so poor. They're so free today—much more so than we were—and yet they face many more dangers from the world."

It became very still in the room. Everyone had her own thoughts about children, grandchildren—our youth, who face the "wars and rumors of wars" that exist in a world racing toward self-destruction.

I looked through my small living room into the dining room, where Papa's portrait hangs. I could see him at the oval table, head bowed, praying: "Lord, bless the queen; we thank You for this beautiful Lord's Day and for the promise of Your soon coming. Thank You for this food and for this family. In the name of Jesus Christ, Amen."

How grateful I am to have lived in my Father's house! Yes, Lord, I thank You for this family. I looked at my friends, gathered for an afternoon of tea and memories, and thanked the Lord for the family of believers all over this globe. How the love of God stretched in and out of the watchmaker's shop to all parts of the world—to mansions in California and hospitals in Kenya, from queens to prison guards.

As the "golden tea party" ended and the club girls left, we broke some of our Dutch restraint and hugged each other. Many of them had suffered much through the years, and yet they had remained strong in the Lord. I realized that all we do through our own strength has to be cleansed, but what we do through the Lord has value for time and eternity.

This is no time to look back. What challenges we have today! I remember what

Father often said: "When Jesus takes your hand He keeps you tight. When Jesus keeps you tight He leads you through life. When Jesus leads you through life He brings you safely home."

Corrie ten Boom was imprisoned by the Nazis during World War II for harboring Jews. Upon her release, she began a world-wide ministry of preaching and teaching. *The Hiding Place* is the best-known book about her life.

Tramp
for the
Lord

Also by Corrie ten Boom

Amazing Love
Clippings from My Notebook: Writings and
    Sayings Collected by Corrie ten Boom
Common Sense Not Needed: Some
    Thoughts about an Unappreciated
    Work among Neglected People
Corrie's Christmas Memories
Corrie ten Boom's Prison Letters
Don't Wrestle, Just Nestle
Each New Day
Father ten Boom: God's Man
He Cares, He Comforts
He Sets the Captives Free
The Hiding Place
In My Father's House: The Years before
    "The Hiding Place"
Jesus Is Victor
Not Good if Detached
Not I, but Christ
The End Battle
Plenty for Everyone
Prayers and Promises for Every Day
A Prisoner and Yet . . .
This Day Is the Lord's
A Tramp Finds a Home

Tramp
for the
Lord

Corrie ten Boom
with Jamie Buckingham

Revell
Grand Rapids, Michigan

Contents

6

Foreword

My wife, Jackie, and I met Tante (Aunt) Corrie and her pretty, blond secretary, Ellen de Kroon, at the airport in Melbourne, Florida. Ellen had called the night before saying they were flying in but that Corrie had been having some severe heart pains. At eighty years of age, that's serious business.

We met the plane and whisked them to our house, which is just minutes from the airport. "I'm very tired," Tante Corrie said. "I like to rest a while."

Moments later she was stretched out on our daughter's lavender bedspread. I opened the window so the soft, tropical breeze could blow in from the lake behind the house. Gently closing the door, I cautioned the children to speak in whispers and tiptoed into the kitchen to join Jackie and Ellen.

Ellen had brought us some Gouda cheese and we sliced it, reminiscing over my first meal in Corrie's house in Holland. Ellen couldn't wait to tell Jackie about the expression on my face when Corrie had informed me I had a choice of two dishes for lunch: raw mullet dipped in onion, or smoked eel.

Talking softly and munching on cheese and crackers, I glanced up to see Tante Corrie coming down the hall, her eyes sparkling.

"Aren't you going to rest?" I asked.

"Oh, I have already a good sleep," she answered in her thick, Dutch accent. "Ten minutes is all you need when God gives the sleep."

It is this remarkable power of recuperation that has allowed Tante Corrie, at more than eighty years of age, to tramp the world for the Lord. I saw that same power at work in her life a year later in Pittsburgh. We were both on the program for a Bible conference at the Pittsburgh Theological Seminary. She had spoken three times that day to a congregation made up of everybody from bearded Jesus People to university professors. I was out late that night and, when I returned to the dormitory, I saw Ellen running down the hall. "Tante Corrie is having a heart attack," she said.

I raced to Corrie's room. She was stretched out on her bed, her face gray from the pain. "God has told me my time is not yet up," she whispered. "I have sent for a minister to pray that I may be healed."

Moments later, as the young minister arrived and laid his hands on her, I saw her features relax and the color return to her cheeks. "Thank You, Lord," she said softly, "for taking away the pain." Then, signifying she was ready for us to leave, she said, "I go to sleep now."

The next morning at eight o'clock she was behind the pulpit speaking to a thousand persons in the great auditorium—as though nothing extraordinary had happened.

I am convinced that the secret of Tante Corrie's great recuperative power, as well as the secret of her popularity as a speaker, lies in her childlikeness. As a little girl believes her Daddy can do anything, so Corrie ten Boom trusts in God—even more. She is living proof of what happens when a woman—when *any* person—is filled with the Holy Spirit.

Jamie Buckingham

Introduction
The World Is My Classroom

I will teach you, and guide you in the
   way you should go.
I will keep you under my eye.
                    Psalm 32:8 NEB

The school of life offers some difficult courses, but it is in the difficult class that one learns the most—especially when your teacher is the Lord Jesus Himself.

The hardest lessons for me were in a cell with four walls. The cell in the prison at Scheveningen, Holland, was six paces in length, two paces in breadth, with a door that could be opened only from the outside. Later there were four barbed wire fences, charged with electricity, enclosing a concentration camp in Germany. The gates were manned by guards with loaded machine guns. It was there in Ravensbruck that more than ninety-six thousand women died.

After that time in prison, the entire world became my classroom. Since World War II, I have traveled around it twice, speaking in more than sixty countries on all continents. During these three decades I have become familiar with airports, bus stations, and passport offices. Under me have been wheels of every description: wheels of automobiles, trains, jinrikishas, horse-drawn wagons, and the landing gear of airplanes. Wheels, wheels, wheels! Even the wheels of wheelchairs.

I have enjoyed the hospitality in a great number of homes and have slept in many times more than a thousand beds. Sometimes I have slept in comfortable beds with foam rubber mattresses in the United States, and sometimes on straw mats on dirt floors in India. There have been clean rooms and dirty rooms.

One bathroom in Hollywood had a view of exotic plants and flowers from the sunken Roman bathtub, while a bathroom in Borneo was simply a mud hut equipped with nothing but a barrel of cold water. Once, while staying with a group of young Jewish girls in Israel, I had to climb over a mountain of building materials and walk through a junk-filled field to make my way to a tiny outhouse that was nothing more than a hole in the ground. Such a place would have been impossible to find at night.

Always in my travels, even now that I am in my ninth decade of life, I have carried in my hand and in my heart the Bible—the very Word of Life, which is almost bursting with Good News. And there has been plenty for everyone. I often feel as the disciples must have felt as they fed more than five thousand with five loaves and two fishes. The secret was that they had received it from the blessed hand of the Master. There was abundance for all and twelve basketfuls of fragments left over.

There has been plenty for the dying ones in the concentration camps—plenty for the thousands gathered in universities, in town halls, and in churches all over the world. Sometimes I have spoken to a few men in prison who stood behind bars and listened hungrily. Once to a group of six missionaries in Japan who offered me hospitality during a twenty-eight-hour rainstorm in which more than a thousand persons perished around us. Groups of hundreds and crowds of thousands have listened under pandals in India and in theaters in South America. I have spoken to tens of thousands at one time in the giant stadiums of America and retreated to the mountains of North Carolina to spend time with a small group of girls in a summer camp.

"God so loved the world . . ." (John 3:16) Jesus said. And that is why I keep going, even into my eightieth years, because we've a story to tell to the nations, a story of love and light.

God has plans—not problems—for our lives. Before she died in the concentration camp in Ravensbruck, my sister Betsie said to me, "Corrie, your whole life has been a training for the work you are doing here in prison—and for the work you will do afterward."

The life of a Christian is an education for higher service. No athlete complains when the training is hard. He thinks of the game, or the race. As the apostle Paul wrote:

In my opinion whatever we may have to go through now is less than nothing compared with the magnificent future God has in store for us. The whole creation is on tiptoe to see the wonderful sight of the sons of God coming into their own. The world of creation cannot as yet see reality, not because it chooses to be blind, but because in God's purpose it has been so limited—yet it has been given hope. And the hope is that in the end the whole of created life will be rescued from the tyranny of change and decay, and have its share in that magnificent liberty which can only belong to the children of God!

It is plain to anyone with eyes to see that at the present time all created life groans in a sort of universal travail. And it is plain, too, that we who have a fore-taste of the Spirit are in a state of painful tension, while we wait for that redemp-tion of our bodies which will mean that we have realised our full sonship in him.

Romans 8:18–23 PHILLIPS

Looking back across the years of my life, I can see the working of a divine pattern, which is the way of God with His children. When I was in a prison camp in Holland during the war, I often prayed, "Lord, never let the enemy put me in a German con-centration camp." God answered no to that prayer. Yet in the German camp, with all its horror, I found many prisoners who had never heard of Jesus Christ. If God had not used my sister Betsie and me to bring them to Him, they would never have heard of

Him. Many died, or were killed, but many died with the name of Jesus on their lips. They were well worth all our suffering. Faith is like radar that sees through the fog—the reality of things at a distance that the human eye cannot see.

> My life is but a weaving,
>   between my God and me,
> I do not choose the colors,
>   He worketh, steadily,
> Oftimes He weaveth sorrow,
>   and I in foolish pride,
> Forget He sees the upper,
>   and I the underside.
> Not till the loom is silent,
>   and shuttles cease to fly,
> Will God unroll the canvas
>   and explain the reason why.
> The dark threads are as needful
>   in the skillful Weaver's hand,
> As the threads of gold and silver
>   in the pattern He has planned.
>   Anonymous

Although the threads of my life have often seemed knotted, I know, by faith, that on the other side of the embroidery there is a crown. As I have walked the world—a tramp for the Lord—I have learned a few lessons in God's great classroom. Even as I share these things with those of you who read this book, I pray the Holy Spirit will reveal something of the divine pattern in God's plan for you also.

1
A Strange Place to Hope

Consider it all joy, my brethren, when you
encounter various trials, knowing that the
testing of your faith produces endurance.
James 1:2–3 NASB

Rank upon rank we stood that hot September morning in 1944, more than a thousand women lining the railroad siding, one unspoken thought among us: Not Germany!

Beside me my sister Betsie swayed. I was fifty-two, Betsie fifty-nine. These seven months in a prison and concentration camp since we had been caught concealing Jews in our home had been harder on her. But prisoners though we were, at least till now we had remained in Holland. And now when liberation must come any day, where were they taking us?

Behind us guards were shouting, prodding us with their guns. Instinctively my hand went to the string around my neck. From it, hanging down my back between my shoulder blades, was the small cloth bag that held our Bible, that forbidden book that had not only sustained Betsie and me throughout these months, but given us strength to share with our fellow prisoners. So far we had kept it hidden. But if we should go to Germany . . . We had heard tales of the prison inspections there.

A long line of empty boxcars was rolling slowly past. Now they clanged to a halt and a gaping freight door loomed in front of us. I helped Betsie over the steep side. The dark boxcar grew quickly crowded. We were pressed against the wall. It was a small European freight car; thirty or forty people jammed it. And still the guards drove women in, pushing, jabbing with their guns. It was only when eighty women were packed inside that the heavy door slid shut and we heard the iron bolts driven into place outside.

Women were sobbing and many fainted, although in the tightly wedged crowd they remained upright. The sun beat down on the motionless train; the temperature in the packed car rose. It was hours before the train gave a sudden lurch and began to move. Almost at once it stopped again, then again crawled forward. The rest of that day and all night long it was the same—stopping, starting, slamming, jerking. Once through a slit in the side of the car I saw trainmen carrying a length of twisted rail. Maybe the tracks were destroyed. Maybe we would still be in Holland when the liberation came.

But at dawn we rolled through the Dutch border town of Emmerich. We were in Germany.

For two more incredible days and two more nights we were carried deeper and deeper into the land of our fears. Worse than the crush of bodies and the filth was the thirst. Two or three times when the train was stopped the door was slid open a few inches and a pail of water passed in. But we had become animals, incapable of plan. Those near the door got it all.

At last, on the morning of the third day, the door was hauled open its full width. Only a handful of very young soldiers was there to order us out and march us off. No more were needed. We could scarcely walk, let alone resist. From the crest of a small hill we saw it—the end of our journey—a

vast gray barracks city surrounded by double concrete walls.

"Ravensbruck!"

Like a whispered curse, the word passed
back through the line. This was the notorious women's death camp itself, the very
symbol to Dutch hearts of all that was evil.
As we stumbled down the hill, I felt the little Bible bumping on my back. As long as
we had that, I thought, we could face even
hell itself. But how could we conceal it
through the inspection I knew lay ahead?

It was the middle of the night when Betsie and I reached the processing barracks.
And there, under the harsh ceiling lights,
we saw a dismaying sight. As each woman
reached the head of the line she had to strip
off every scrap of clothes, throw them all
onto a pile guarded by soldiers, and walk
naked past the scrutiny of a dozen guards
into the shower room. Coming out of the
shower room she wore only a thin regulation prison dress and a pair of shoes.

Our Bible! How could we take it past so
many watchful eyes?

"Oh, Betsie!" I began—and then stopped
at the sight of her pain-whitened face. As
a guard strode by, I begged him in German
to show us the toilets. He jerked his head

in the direction of the shower room. "Use the drain holes!" he snapped.

Timidly Betsie and I stepped out of the line and walked forward to the huge room with its row on row of overhead spigots. It was empty, waiting for the next batch of fifty naked and shivering women.

A few minutes later we would return here stripped of everything we possessed. And then we saw them, stacked in a corner, a pile of old wooden benches crawling with cockroaches, but to us the furniture of heaven itself.

In an instant I had slipped the little bag over my head and, along with my woolen underwear, had stuffed it behind the benches.

And so it was that when we were herded into that room ten minutes later, we were not poor but rich—rich in the care of Him who was God even of Ravensbruck.

Of course when I put on the flimsy prison dress, the Bible bulged beneath it. But that was His business, not mine. At the exit, guards were feeling every prisoner, front, back, and sides. I prayed, "Oh, Lord, send your angels to surround us." But then I remembered that angels are spirits and you can see through them. What I needed was an angel to shield me so that the guards could not see me. "Lord," I prayed again, "make your angels untransparent." How unorthodox you can pray when you are in great need! But God did not mind. He did it.

The woman ahead of me was searched. Behind me, Betsie was searched. They did not touch or even look at me. It was as though I was blocked out of their sight.

Outside the building was a second ordeal, another line of guards examining each prisoner again. I slowed down as I reached them, but the captain shoved me roughly by the shoulder. "Move along! You're holding up the line."

So Betsie and I came to our barracks at Ravensbruck. Before long we were holding clandestine Bible study groups for an ever growing group of believers, and Barracks 28 became known throughout the camp as "the crazy place, where they hope."

Yes, hoped, in spite of all that human madness could do. We had learned that a stronger power had the final word, even here.

2
Witnesses unto Me

❦

You shall be My witnesses both in Jerusalem, and in all Judea and Samaria, and even to the remotest part of the earth.
Acts 1:8 NASB

It was a week after Betsie had died in Ravensbruck that I took my place in the ranks of women prisoners standing together in the icy cold of the early morning.

"66730!"

"That is my number," I said weakly as we took our place for roll call.

"Ten Boom, Cornelia."

"That is my name." I thought how strange that they would call me by name when they always addressed us by number!

"Come forward."

We were falling in line for the roll call. Ten in a line, every one hundredth woman,

one step forward. My friends looked at me
sadly.

   What does it mean? I asked inwardly. *Punishment . . . freedom . . . the gas chamber . . .
sent to another concentration camp?*

   There was but one thought that comforted me. What a joy that Betsie is in
heaven. No matter what terrible things now
happen, she will not have to bear it.

   The guard, a young German girl, shouted
at me. "Nr. 66730!"

   I stepped forward, stood at attention, and
repeated the necessary words. "Schutz-
haftling ten Boom, Cornelia, meldet sich."

   "Stand on number 1 on the roll call."

   I went to the place to the far right, where
I could overlook the entire square of the
bleak camp. Standing in the crowd I could
not feel the draft, but now, standing in the
bitter cold, the wind whipped through my
ragged prison dress. Another girl, young and
frightened, was sent to stand beside me.
Roll call took three hours and we were
almost frozen. She saw how cold I was and
rubbed my spine when the guards were not
looking.

   "Why must I stand here?" I asked through
chattering teeth.

Her answer was barely audible as it came from her blue lips. "Death sentence."

I turned back to the Lord. "Perhaps I'll see You soon face-to-face, like Betsie does now, Lord. Let it not be too cruel a killing. Not gas, Lord, nor hanging. I prefer shooting. It is so quick. You see something, you hear something, and it is finished."

I looked back at the young girl beside me. "Lord, this is perhaps the last chance I will have to bring someone to You before I arrive in heaven. Use me, Lord. Give me all the love and wisdom I need."

"What is your name?" I asked her softly, glancing always to see if the guards were looking.

"Tiny."

"I am Corrie," I whispered. "How long have you been here?"

"Two years."

"Did you ever read the Bible?"

"No, I never did."

"Do you believe God exists?"

"I do. I wish I knew more about Him. Do you know Him?"

"I do. Jesus, His Son, came to this world to carry our punishment. He died on the cross, but He rose from the dead and has promised to be with us always. My sister died here. She suffered so much. I, too, have suffered. But Jesus is always with us. He did a miracle in taking away all my hatred and bitterness for my enemies. Jesus is willing to bring into our hearts God's love through His Holy Spirit."

Tiny listened. For almost three hours we talked while the guards completed the roll call. It was miracle, for I had a chance to explain many things about Jesus. The prisoners behind us listened too. I felt happy. Perhaps this was my last chance in life, but what joy!

I continued. "Jesus wants to live in your heart. 'Behold, I stand at the door and knock,' He says. 'If anyone opens the door, I'll come in.' Will you open the door of your heart and let Him come in and change you?"

"I will," she said.

"Then talk to Him. Tell Him whatever you think. Now you have a Friend who never leaves you alone."

The siren sounded, and the guards shouted at the prisoners. "Get to work!"

Thousands of women prisoners were running to their places where they had to march to their work. Tiny disappeared from sight. Only I was left standing in my place, where I had been ordered not to move. I still did not know what fate awaited me.

I did know, however, that the God who never slumbers nor sleeps was now with Tiny. And Tiny knew it too. Neither of us knew at that time how important that was going to be to her in the next few days. But above the din of the concentration camp, I thought I heard the singing of the angels.

Then I heard my name called. Was it death? Oh, thank God, no. It was life. I was being released. I later learned it was through an administrative blunder, but even then I knew it was not the end of an era—it was just the beginning. Ahead of me was the world.

3
Release!

_____ ∽∽∽∽∽ _____

Then he turned my sorrow into joy! He
took away my clothes of mourning and
gave me gay and festive garments to
rejoice in.

Psalm 30:11 TLB

When you are dying—when you stand at
the gate of eternity—you see things from
a different perspective than when you think
you may live for a long time. I had been
standing at that gate for many months, living in Barracks 28 in the shadow of the crematorium. Every time I saw the smoke
pouring from the hideous smokestacks I
knew it was the last remains of some poor
woman who had been with me in Ravensbruck. Often I asked myself, *When will it
be my time to be killed or die?*

But I was not afraid. Following Betsie's
death, God's presence was even more real.

Even though I was looking into the valley of the shadow of death, I was not afraid. It is here that Jesus comes the closest, taking our hand and leading us through.

One week before the order came to kill all the women of my age, I was free. I still do not understand all the details of my release from Ravensbruck. All I know is, it was a miracle of God.

I stood in the prison yard—waiting the final order. Beyond the walls with their strands of barbed wire stood the silent trees of the German forest, looking so much like the gray-green sets on the back of one of our theater stages in Holland.

Mimi, one of my fellow prisoners, came within whispering distance. "Tiny died this morning," she said without looking at me. "And Marie also."

"Tiny! Oh, Lord, thank You for letting me point her to Jesus, who has now ushered her safely into Your presence." And Marie. I knew her well. She lived in my barracks and had attended my Bible talks. Like Tiny, Marie had also accepted Jesus as her Lord. I looked back at the long rows of barracks. "Lord, if it was only for Tiny and Marie— that they might come to know You before they died—then it was all worthwhile."

A guard spoke harshly, telling Mimi to leave the yard. Then he said to me, "Face the gate. Do not turn around."

The gate swung open, and I glimpsed the lake in front of the camp. I could smell freedom.

"Follow me," a young girl in an officer's uniform said to me.

I walked slowly through the gate, never looking back. Behind me I heard the hinges squeak as the gate swung shut. I was free, and flooding through my mind were the words of Jesus to the church of Philadelphia:

> Behold, I have set before thee an open door, and no man can shut it.
>
> Revelation 3:8

First that door directed me back to Holland. The train ride took three days. Another prisoner, Claire Prins, had been released with me. Her leg was alarmingly swollen, and of course both of us were mere skin and bones. But we were *free!*

Arriving in Groningen, we made our way to a Christian hospital called the Deaconess House, where I asked to speak to the superintendent. Perhaps they would help us until I could return to Haarlem, I thought.

"Sister Tavenier cannot come at the moment," the attendant said. "She is helping conduct a Christian service in one of the wards. I'm afraid you will have to wait."

"Would you mind," I said, looking at the attendant, "if I attended the service also?"

She looked at me tenderly, sensing, perhaps, some of my suffering. "Why, of course. You may rest in the waiting room until it starts. I'll come after you."

"Nurse," I hesitantly asked, "have you anything for me to drink?"

Again the look of compassion crossed her face. "I'll bring you some tea," she said gently.

A few minutes later she placed it before me, saying, "I have not put butter on the toast for I see you are sick. The dry toast and tea will be good for you."

I was deeply touched by this tiny show of consideration. A moment later I was lying in a comfortable chair with my legs outstretched on a bench. A wonderful feeling of rest descended on me. I was in the Netherlands, among good people. My suffering was over.

A nurse came for me to take me to the ward where the service was to be held. Chairs had been arranged in a semicircle between the beds, facing a table. An elderly minister walked in, and a hymnal was handed to me. I could see the nurses and patients glancing stealthily at me. My clothes were ragged and filthy, hanging from my gaunt body like rags on a scarecrow. Yet I was so thankful to be free I cared not.

The minister spoke in a well-modulated voice. Then we joined in singing. I could not help but make comparisons: the dirty prison dormitory, infection-ridden and filthy, the beds full of lice, and now this. Clean sheets and pillowcases and a spotless floor. The hoarse voices of the slave drivers and the mature, melodious voice of the minister. Only the singing was the same, for we had sung at Ravensbruck. Singing was one of the ways we kept up our courage.

Following the service the nurse took me to the superintendent's office. "Miss Prins has been taken care of," she said, "and is already in a fresh bed. You both must have had a horrible experience. But now, what must be done with you?"

I sat in a chair across from her desk. For more than a year I had not been allowed to make a decision. All I could do was follow orders. It was difficult even to think. "I don't know, Sister," I said. It was enough just to be surrounded by people who were not angry with me.

"I know what," she said, as she touched a bell. "First we'll give you a warm dinner."

A young nurse appeared and took my arm, guiding me down a hall toward the dining room. "I understand you have just been released from Ravensbruck," she said. "Where are you going? Where is your home?"

"I am going to Haarlem," I replied.

"Oh, Haarlem," she said with excitement. "Do you know Corrie ten Boom who lives there?"

I looked at her. She was one of the YWCA leaders I had worked with before the war. "Truus Benes!" I exclaimed in delight.

"Why, yes, that is my name," she said, bewildered. "But I don't believe I know you."

"I am Corrie ten Boom."

The nurse stopped abruptly in the hall, staring at me. "Oh, no, that is impossible. I know Corrie ten Boom very well. I have been in girls' camps with her several times. She is much younger than you."

"But really, I am Corrie ten Boom," I argued. Then I thought of how I must have looked. My face was thin and pale, my mouth wide, like skin stretched across a skull. My hair fell queerly about my face. My eyes were hollow. My coat was dirty, for I had at times slept on the floor of the train as we traveled out of Germany. The belt of my dress sagged, for I had not had the energy to fasten it.

The nurse reached out tenderly and touched my chapped hand. "Yes . . . yes . . . it is you. It *is!*" And then we both broke into laughter.

In the dining room we sat opposite each other at a small table, and I asked about our mutual acquaintances. Was Mary Barger still living? Jeanne Blooker and . . . ? It was ridiculous to ask such questions, but I wanted to know everything. The world, for me, had stopped while I had been in the concentration camp. Now it was beginning to turn again, and I had so much catching up to do.

Then I was eating. Potatoes, brussels sprouts, meat and gravy, and for dessert, pudding with currant juice and an apple!

"I have never seen anyone eat so intensely," one of the nurses from a nearby table commented. I cared not. With every mouthful of food I could feel new life streaming into my body. I had once said to Betsie in camp, "When we get home we shall have to eat carefully, taking only small amounts at a time until our stomachs are ready."

"No," Betsie had said, "God will see to it that we shall be able to retain all sorts of food right from the start."

She was right. How wonderfully good that food did taste. I shall remember that meal as long as I live.

Then came a warm bath. They could hardly get me out of it. My poor sick skin, damaged by lice, seemed to grow softer the moment I slipped into that warm tub.

Afterwards they dressed me. Several of the ex-leaders of the Netherlands Girls' Clubs were among the nurses—girls that I had known before the war. They dressed me up as if I were a doll. One of them had lingerie, another shoes, another a dress and pins for my hair. I felt so happy that I laughed for sheer joy. How sweet they were to me.

These young women had been trained in kindness. How opposite from the concentration camp, where men had been trained in cruelty.

I was then taken to a cozy bedroom so I could rest. How lovely was the combination of colors. I was starved for color. In the concentration camp everything was gray. But here in Holland the colors were vivid again. My eyes could not seem to get enough to satisfy them.

And the bed! Delightfully soft and clean with thick woolen blankets. One of the little nurses brought an extra pillow and tucked it under my swollen feet. I wanted to laugh and cry at the same time.

On a shelf was a row of books. Outside I heard the whistle of a boat on a canal and the merry sound of little children calling to one another as they skipped down the street. Far in the distance I heard the sound of a choir singing and then, oh, joy, the chimes of a carillon. I closed my eyes and tears wet my pillow. Only to those who have been in prison does freedom have such great meaning.

Later that afternoon one of the nurses took me up to her room where, for the first time in many months, I heard the sound of a radio. Gunther Ramin was playing a Bach trio. The organ tones flowed about and enveloped me. I sat on the floor beside a chair and sobbed, unashamedly. It was too much joy. I had rarely cried during all those months of suffering. Now I could not control myself. My life had been given back as a gift. Harmony, beauty, colors, and music. Only those who have suffered as I, and have returned, can fully understand what I mean. I knew my life had been given back for a purpose. I was no longer my own. This time I had been ransomed and released. I knew that God would soon be sending me out as a tramp for the Lord. But right now, He was letting me enjoy the luxury of thanksgiving. I was drinking from a fountain I knew would never run dry—the fountain of praise.

One of the first places I visited after my release from the concentration camp was the Grote Kerk in Haarlem. Since it was so close to where I had grown up in the Beje, I counted it as much of an old friend as I did the watchmaker's shop.

"May I show you through?" the old usher said as he met me at the door.

"If it is all right," I said, "I would like to be alone."

He nodded understandingly and disappeared into the shadows of the sanctuary. I walked over the gravestones that formed the floor of the ancient building. My shoes made a strange scraping sound that gave forth a hollow echo in the empty cathedral. I remembered the many times I had played here as a child.

My cousin Dot was my closest friend. She was the youngest daughter of my Uncle Arnold, who was the previous usher—the caretaker—of the Grote Kerk.

Dot and I did everything together, but our favorite pastime was to play hide-and-seek in the big church. There were many wonderful places to hide: pews, old doors giving entrance to spiral staircases, and many closets. There was a world-famous pipe organ in the cathedral, and sometimes when there was a concert, Uncle Arnold would allow members of his family to come into the church, sit on a wooden bench without a back, and lean against the cold, moist stone wall to hear the magnificent music.

The cathedral was a symphony in gray tones during the day, both inside and outside. In the evening, when the gas lamps were lit on the side transepts, we could see the pillars and ceilings pointing upward, as the shadows danced about in a mysterious glow.

Only one place was absolutely off-limits as we played hide-and-seek. That was the old pulpit. We never went there, but for the rest—what a playground that old church was! When we shouted, the echo would ring from transept to transept, and our laughter never, never seemed to be sacrilegious. Unlike some of the stern adults who sometimes frowned on our frolic, I had always thought that the laughter of little children in an empty cathedral was the most beautiful of all hymns of praise. And so we grew up, knowing only a God who enjoyed our presence as we skipped, ran, and played through this building, which was built for His glory.

One afternoon we played very late, and before we knew it, the darkness of the cathedral swallowed us up. I looked around. Through the beautiful stained glass windows I saw a little light coming in from the streets around. Only the silhouettes of the Gothic pillars stood out in the darkness as they reached upward and upward.

"Let's go home," whispered Dot. "I'm scared."

I was not. Slowly I went to the usher's door that opened out to where Uncle Arnold lived. There was a presence that comforted me, a deep peace in my heart. Even in the darkness, smelling the dust and dampness of the church building, I knew that the Light of the World was present. Was the Lord preparing me for some time in the future when I would need to know that His light is victorious over all darkness?

It was forty-five years later. Betsie and I walked to the square where roll call was being held in the concentration camp. It was still early, before dawn. The head of our barracks was so cruel that she had sent us out into the very cold outdoors a full hour too early.

Betsie's hand was in mine. We went to the square by a different way from the rest of our barracks-mates. We were three as we walked with the Lord and talked with Him. Betsie spoke. Then I talked. Then the Lord spoke. How? I do not know. But both of us understood. It was the same presence I had felt years before in the old cathedral in Haarlem.

The brilliant early morning stars were our only light. The cold winter air was so clear. We could faintly see the outlines of the barracks, the crematorium, the gas chamber, and the towers where the guards were standing with loaded machine guns.

"Isn't this a bit of heaven!" Betsie had said. "And, Lord, this is a small foretaste. One day we will see You face-to-face, but thank You that even now You are giving us the joy of walking and talking with You."

Heaven in the midst of hell. Light in the midst of darkness. What a security!

4

A Song in the Night

Behold, God is my salvation; I will trust and not be afraid: for the LORD JEHOVAH is my strength and my song; he also is become my salvation.

Isaiah 12:2

The war was over. Even before I left the concentration camp, I knew I would be busy helping those who had lost their way. Now I found myself starting just such a work in Bloemendaal. It was more than a home for the homeless; it was a refuge for those who had lost their way, spiritually as well as physically.

Yet, because I had lived so close to death, looking it in the face day after day, I often felt like a stranger among my own people—many of whom looked upon money, honor of men, and success as the most important issues of life. Standing in front of a crematorium, knowing that any day could be your day, gives one a different perspective on life. The words of an old German motto kept flashing in my mind: "What I spent, I had; what I saved, I lost; what I gave, I have."

How well I understood the feeling of the artist who painted the picture of the corpse of a once wealthy man and entitled it *Sic transit gloria mundi*—So passes the glory of this world. The material things of this world no longer excited me—nor would they ever again.

It was during this time that I visited Haarlem, the town where I had spent more than fifty years of my life. It was late in the evening as I walked through the streets. Waiting before a traffic light, I had a strange feeling that the people should fall in line, five by five, as in the concentration camp. Instead, they chatted about insignificant things, and when the light changed, they moved on without anyone shouting at them.

Walking the streets that night, however, I felt growing in me a tremendous desire to tell all men, especially those in bondage to material things, of the One who can set us free from all prisons: Jesus.

It was after midnight when I finally made my way to the Barteljorisstraat. There were few streetlights, but the moon and many stars were visible above the ancient rooftops of the familiar houses on the short street. I paused in front of the Beje on the corner of the small alley that came out in the midst of the street. I let my fingertips run across the door of the watchmaker's shop. Even though the Beje was no longer my home, it was still part of my heart. Little did I dream that one day it would be set aside as a museum to commemorate my family and the hiding place of those precious Jews who had been saved from certain death at the hands of the Nazis.

I stood alone in the darkness, allowing myself the sweet luxury of remembering. How often had I put the shutters before the show window. Through this door I had walked on my first day of school, almost fifty years ago. Oh, what an unwilling pupil I had been, crying in fear of leaving the dear old house whose warmth in winter had protected me, whose windows had kept out the rain and mist, whose cheery fire had welcomed me and others in the family each night after the dinner dishes had been put away. Yet my father, knowing my fear, took

me by the hand and led me through this
door out into the world of learning, into an
unknown world of teachers and classrooms.

Now Father was dead. Only my heavenly
Father remained. I ran my hand over the door,
letting my fingers explore the cracks. It was
no longer my hiding place. Others lived here
now, and the world was my classroom, and
my only security came in knowing that underneath were the everlasting arms. How thankful I was for my heavenly Father's strong
hand around mine.

I looked into the small alley. It was almost
pitch dark. I strained my ears, and in the
far-off recesses of my heart could imagine
the voices of Father, Betsie, and the others.
Had it been only a year ago? It seemed like
centuries. "What an honor," Father had
said, "to give my life for God's chosen
people, the Jews."

I felt the wall with my hands, then gently pressed my face against the cold stones.
No, I was not dreaming. It was reality. The
old Beje, the old hiding place, was no longer
mine. Ravensbruck had taught me much I
needed to learn. My hiding place was now
in Jesus alone. Even though I was wandering the streets at midnight in a town that
used to be my home but was now only a

town, I knew the presence of the heavenly Father.

Suddenly the cathedral started to play its nostalgic chimes. Day and night through my lifetime I had heard the beautiful music from the Grote Kerk. It was not a dream, as I had often experienced in the concentration camp. It was real. I walked out of the shadows of the alley and made my way down the Barteljorisstraat to the Grote Markt. I paused to look at the cathedral, which was silhouetted against the dark sky, framed into place by a million twinkling stars.

"Thank You, Jesus, that I am alive," I said.

In my heart I heard Him reply, "Lo, I am with you alway, even unto the end of the world" (Matt. 28:20).

I stayed there for long minutes as the hands on the face of the great clock moved toward the hour. Then the chimes in the cathedral tower pealed forth once again, this time with the sounds of Luther's famous hymn "A Mighty Fortress Is Our God." I listened and heard myself singing the hymn, not in Dutch, but in German: "Ein' feste Burg ist unser Gott."

"How like You, Lord," I half chuckled, "that You would remind me of Your grace by letting me hear a German hymn."

A policeman passed, looked at me, and spoke a friendly word. I said, "Good-night, Policeman. A mighty fortress is our God."

I was free.

5
A Great Discovery

—— ✺ ——

By faith Abraham, when he was called to go out into a place which he should after receive for an inheritance, obeyed; and he went out, not knowing whither he went.

> Hebrews 11:8

When my parents were married, many years ago, they claimed Psalm 32:8 as their "life verse," the promise that they felt was God's assurance for them. "I will instruct thee and teach thee in the way which thou shalt go: I will guide thee with mine eye."

Now that Father and Mother were gone, this promise became the special directive for my life as well—God's pledge to guide me in all my journeys. It was especially needed as I set out for my first trip to America.

50

The war had only been over a short time, and many Europeans wanted to go to America. However, few, if any, wanted to go for the same reason I did—to carry the gospel as a missionary to the Americans. For all of us, however, it was the same story when we applied for passage to America: "It is impossible to obtain papers."

I prayed, "Lord, if it is Your will that I go to America, then You must provide the necessary papers."

I soon discovered that man's importunity is God's opportunity. He uses our problems as building materials for His miracles. I began to understand that this was my first lesson in learning to trust Him completely, my first steps on the path to complete dependence on, and obedience to, His guidance. How much I had to learn!

At last all my papers were approved, except the final one—the most important one. I sat alone on a hard wooden bench in the hall of the Immigration Office in The Hague. Everyone coming out of the office warned those of us waiting in the hall, "That fellow in there is as hard as flint. He passes no one."

"Lord," I prayed silently, "I am willing to go or stay. It is up to You."

"Hello, there! Don't we know each other?" It was the voice of a middle-aged woman in front of me. I looked up into her face, trying vainly to recognize her.

"You're Corrie ten Boom," she laughed. "I'm one of your cousins, and this is Jan, my husband. I haven't seen you for years, and of course, Jan has never seen you since we were married only six years ago."

"Are you trying to go to America also?" I asked.

"Oh, no," she laughed. "I'm visiting Jan. He has his office in this building."

"Then perhaps you can help me," I said, shaking his hand. I told him my story.

He was polite but said, "I'm sorry. I would like to be of service to my brand-new cousin, but that's not my department. However, if you have trouble, ring me up." He gave me his telephone number and we shook hands again as he left.

I continued to wait. The "man of flint" left the office for coffee and a young clerk took his place. Then it was my turn.

"You had better wait until my boss returns," the clerk said when I told him where I wanted to go and why.

My shoulders sagged. "I cannot wait any longer. Won't you please call this number?"

I handed him the card that Jan had handed me earlier.

I prayed while he placed the call. Moments later he hung up. "All is arranged. I am approving your passport. You may make your trip to America."

From there I traveled to Amsterdam to try to arrange passage on a ship of the Holland-America Line. However, another mountain loomed before me. The agent told me they would only put my name on the waiting list. "We will notify you in about a year," he said.

"A year! But I must go now." The agent just shrugged his shoulders and returned to his work.

Disappointed, I returned to the square in the center of the city. God had told me to go to America—of that I was certain. All my papers were in order. God had seen to that also. Now it was up to Him to move this mountain. Glancing across the street I noticed a sign: "American Express Company." Stepping into the office, I inquired, "Have you passenger accommodations on any of your freighters to America?"

The old clerk looked over his glasses and said, "You may sail tomorrow, Madam, if your papers are in order."

"Oh, tomorrow is too sudden," I said, hardly believing what I heard. "What about next week?"

"That, too, can be arranged," he said. "We don't have very many women your age who ship out on freighters. But if you are willing, so are we."

Several weeks before I had met an American businessman who was visiting relatives in Holland. When I told him of my plans to visit America he tried to discourage me. "It's not easy to make one's way in America," he said.

"I believe you," I told him. "But God has directed me, and I must obey."

He then gave me two checks, one small and one larger. "If you need it, use it," he said. "You can repay me later." I tucked them away for safekeeping.

So I arrived in New York as a missionary to America. I was only allowed to bring in fifty dollars, and of course I knew no one. However, I found my way to the YWCA, where I found a room and a place to leave my bags.

I had the address of a group of Hebrew-Christian immigrants who were meeting in New York. I made a phone call, and they invited me to come speak. Since they were

German, I could not use the English lectures I had prepared on board the ship but had to speak to them in their native language. It was better, perhaps, for my English was rather hard to understand.

At the end of the week, after wandering around the city in a rather helpless daze, I went downstairs in the YWCA to pay my bill. The clerk looked at me sympathetically. "I am sorry, but our accommodations are so restricted that we cannot allow you to stay here any longer. One week is our limit. Do you have a forwarding address?"

"Yes. I just don't know what it is yet."

"I don't understand," she said, perplexed.

"God has another room for me," I explained. "He just hasn't told me what the address is. But I am not worried. He led me through Ravensbruck; He will surely see me through America as well."

Suddenly the clerk remembered. "By the way, a letter came for you."

Strange, I thought, as she handed me the envelope. *How could I receive a letter? No one knows where I am staying.* But there it was. I read it hurriedly and then turned to the clerk. "My forwarding address will be this house on 190th Street."

"But why didn't you tell me that before?" she asked.

"I didn't know. It was in this letter. A woman I do not know writes, 'I heard you speak to the Jewish congregation. I am aware that it is almost impossible to get a room in New York City. My son happens to be in Europe, so you are welcome to use his room as long as you are in New York.'"

The lady at the desk was more amazed than I. However, I reasoned, perhaps she had not experienced miracles before.

I rode the subway to 190th Street. The house at the address was a large, multistoried building occupied by many families. I found the correct apartment at the end of a hall, but no one was home. Certainly my hostess did not expect her invitation to be an eleventh-hour answer to my problem. I arranged myself among my suitcases on the floor, and leaning against the wall, soon began to drift off to sleep.

In those last moments before sleep took over, my mind drifted back to Ravensbruck. I could feel Betsie's bony hand touching my face. It was pitch-black in Barracks 28, where seven hundred other prisoners were asleep. Each day hundreds of women died and their bodies were fed to the ovens. Bet-

sie had grown so weak, and we both knew
that death was always moments away.

"Are you awake, Corrie?" Her weak voice
sounded so far away.

"Yes, you wakened me."

"I had to. I need to tell you what God has
said to me."

"Shhh. We hinder the sleep of the girls
around us. Let us lie with our faces toward
each other."

The cot was so small. We could only lie
like spoons in a box, our knees bumping
against the knees of the other. We used our
two coats as covers, along with the thin
black blanket provided by the Nazis.

I pulled the coat over our heads so we
could whisper and not be heard. "God
showed me," Betsie said, "that after the war
we must give to the Germans that which
they now try to take away from us: our love
for Jesus."

Betsie's breath was coming in short gasps.
She was so weak, her body wasted away
until there was nothing but her thin skin
stretched over brittle bones. "Oh, Betsie,"
I exclaimed, "you mean if we live we will
have to return to Germany?"

Betsie patted my hand under the blanket. "Corrie, there is so much bitterness.

We must tell them that the Holy Spirit will fill their hearts with God's love."

I remembered Romans 5:5. Only that morning some of the women in the barracks had huddled with us in the corner while I read from our precious Bible. But I shuddered. Germany. If I were ever released from this horrible place, could I ever return to Germany?

Betsie's weak voice whispered on. "This concentration camp here at Ravensbruck has been used to destroy many, many lives. There are many other such camps throughout Germany. After the war they will not have use for them anymore. I have prayed that the Lord will give us one in Germany. We will use it to build up lives."

No, I thought. *I will return to my simple job as a watchmaker in Holland and never again set my boot across the border.*

Betsie's voice was quivering so I could barely understand her. "The Germans are the most wounded of all the people in the world. Think of that young girl guard who swore in such filthy language yesterday. She was only seventeen or eighteen years old, but did you see how she was beating that poor old woman with a whip? What a job there is to do after the war."

I found a place where I could put my hand. It was such a stupid problem, I thought, yet it was a small cot and it was difficult to position my hands and arms. My hand rested on Betsie's left side, just on her heart. I felt her ribs—only skin and bones. How long would she be able to live? Her heart was fluttering inside of the rib cage like a dying bird, as though it would stop any moment.

I rested and thought. How close to God's heart was Betsie. Only God could see in such circumstances the possibility for ministry in the future—ministry to those who even now were preparing to kill us. Most of all, to see in such a place as Ravensbruck an opportunity to bless and build up the lives of our enemies. Yes, only the Lord Jesus could have given Betsie such a vision.

"Must we live with them in Germany?" I whispered.

"For a while," Betsie answered. "Then we will travel the whole world bringing the gospel to all—our friends as well as our enemies."

"To *all* the world? But that will take much money."

"Yes, but God will provide," Betsie said. "We must do nothing else but bring the gospel, and He will take care of us. After all, He owns the cattle on a thousand hills. If we need money we will just ask the Father to sell a few cows."

I was beginning to catch the vision. "What a privilege," I said softly, "to travel the world and be used by the Lord Jesus."

But Betsie did not answer. She had fallen asleep. Three days later she was dead.

Going to bed the night after Betsie died was one of the most difficult tasks of my life. The one electric lightbulb was screwed into the ceiling toward the front of the room. Only a feeble ray reached my narrow cot. I lay in the semidarkness—thinking—remembering—trying to reconstruct Betsie's vision.

There was a shuffle of feet near my bed and I looked up. A Russian woman, thin and gaunt, was shuffling down the aisle between the beds looking for a place to sleep. The Russians were not received kindly, and everyone turned away. As she neared me I saw the haunted look in her eyes. How awful to be in prison and not have even a place to sleep!

Betsie's place beside me was vacant. I motioned to the woman and threw back the blanket for her. She crept in, gratefully, and stretched out beside me. We were sharing the same pillow and with our faces so close I wanted to speak. But I did not know her language.

"Jesoes Christoes?" I asked softly.

"Oh!" she exclaimed. Quickly making the sign of the cross, she threw her arms about me and kissed me.

She who had been my sister for fifty-two years, with whom I had shared so much of weal and woe, had left me. A Russian woman now claimed my love. And there would be others, too, who would be my sisters and brothers in Christ all across the world.

I was awakened by a gentle hand shaking my shoulder. It was after midnight, and I realized I had fallen asleep in the midst of my suitcases, sitting on the floor and leaning against the wall of the hallway.

"Come," my new friend said softly as she opened the door, "the floor is no place for a child of the King." I rose from my cramped, huddled position and entered her apartment. I was her guest for the next five weeks.

As the weeks passed, however, I realized I was running out of money. Jan ten Have (the publisher of my little book in Holland) was visiting New York. He helped me as much as he could, and I spent most of my time looking up addresses given me in Holland. The Americans were polite and some of them were interested, but none wanted me to come to speak. They were all busy with their own things. Some even said I should have stayed in Holland.

As the weeks slipped by, I found more and more resistance to my ministry. No one was interested in a middle-aged spinster woman from Holland who wanted to preach. "Why did you come to America?" people began to ask.

"God directed me. All I could do was obey."

"That's nonsense," they answered. "There is no such thing as direct guidance from God. Experience proves we must use our common sense. If you are here and out of money, then it is your fault, not God's."

I tried to argue back in God's defense. "But God's guidance is even more important than common sense. I am certain He told me to bring His message to America. I can declare that the deepest darkness is outshone by the light of Jesus."

"We have ministers to tell us such things," was the reply.

"Certainly, but I can tell from my experience in a concentration camp that what such ministers say is true."

"It would have been better for you to have remained in Holland. We don't need any more preachers. Too many Europeans come to America. They should be stopped."

I was growing discouraged. Perhaps the Americans were right. Perhaps I should return to Holland and go back to my job as a watchmaker. My money was gone, and all that remained was the second check given me by the American businessman. Yet I was hesitant to cash it without his approval. I found his address and arrived in an imposing business office in Manhattan. Only this time his face was not as friendly as it had been in Holland.

"Do you mind if I cash your second check?" I asked.

"How do I know if you can return the money?" he asked. "You've been in America five weeks and have found there is no work. I think it would be better if you simply returned the check."

Mustering all my courage, I said, "I am sure God has work for me here. I am in His will and will somehow return all your money."

He snorted, tore up the check, and then wrote out another—for a much smaller amount.

I was embarrassed and humbled. I had money in Holland—a balance left from my first book and a small income from the business I had sold. But these funds could not be brought to America. I returned to my room and closed the door. It was time for a long consultation with my heavenly Father.

Kneeling beside the bed, I prayed, "Father, You must help me out. If I must borrow money to return to Holland, people will say, 'There, you see, the promises of the Bible are not real. Direct guidance does not exist.' Father, for Your honor's sake, You must help me out."

I fell weeping across the bed. Then, slowly, like a deep realization that dawns in a person's heart, the answer came: "Do not worry about My honor. I will take care of that. In days to come you will give thanks for these days in New York."

A great ocean separated me from my homeland. I had no money. Nobody wanted to hear my lectures. All I had was an inner word from God that He was guiding me. Was it enough? All I could do was press on—and on—and on—for His name's sake.

Before going to sleep I opened my Bible, my constant companion. My eyes fell on Psalm 147:11. "The LORD taketh pleasure . . . in those that hope in his mercy." It was a thin web—a tiny filament—stretching from heaven to my little room on 190th Street in New York. I fell asleep holding on to it with all my strength.

The next day I attended a Dutch service in a New York church. Dr. Barkay Wolf was the speaker, and many Hollanders were present, meeting afterward for coffee in the vestry. The Reverend Burggraaff, who had baptized our Canadian-born princess, was presented to me.

"Ten Boom," he mused when he heard my name. "I often tell the story of a nurse by that name. She experienced a miracle in a concentration camp with a bottle of vitamins that never ran out. I tell it to prove that God still performs miracles today, as in Bible times. Do you happen to know that nurse? Is she related to you?"

I felt joy springing in my heart. "She is not a nurse," I replied. "She is a watchmaker. And you are looking at her. It was I who had that experience in 1944."

"Then you must come with me to Staten Island and tell your story to my congregation," he exclaimed.

I spent the next five days in this pleasant parsonage with Rev. and Mrs. Burggraaff. What a joy to eat good Dutch food again. I had been trying to find out how long one could exist on Nedick's ten-cent breakfast, which consisted of a cup of coffee, a doughnut, and a small glass of orange juice, eaten while standing at a counter. Now God was resupplying me, not only with food, but with new hope. I could see that the Lord does take pleasure in those that hope in His mercy!

A week later I returned to Manhattan. Walking down the street I saw a church with a notice on the door. Drawing closer I saw it was an invitation to attend the Lord's Supper next Sunday morning, Easter.

Following the service, the minister gave me the address of Irving Harris, the editor of a Christian magazine called *The Evangel*. He encouraged me to go by and see him.

I did. In fact, the very next morning I went up to his office and talked to him. "I know I am walking in the way God has led me," I told him, "but so many declare there is no such thing as direct guidance."

"Pay no attention to them," Mr. Harris advised. "The Bible contains many promises that God will lead those who obey Him. Have you ever heard of a good shepherd who does not lead his sheep?"

Mr. Harris asked if I had any material that he might use in his magazine. I gave him a copy of one of my lectures and told him to use as much as he could.

"There is one drawback," he explained. "We cannot pay. This paper exists only to spread the gospel, not for financial profit."

"Wonderful!" I exclaimed. "I am in the presence of an American who sees money in its proper perspective."

Mr. Harris gave me a name and address in Washington, D.C. He strongly urged me to make an appointment and go down to see Mr. Abraham Vereide. I knew nothing of Mr. Vereide at the time, although I later discovered he was one of the great Christian leaders of America. I was suspicious, afraid I was being shrugged off again. But I felt I could trust Mr. Harris and followed through, taking a chance and making a phone call to Washington.

Mr. Vereide received me graciously, inviting me to Washington as his guest. At dinner three other guests were present, all professors who plied me with questions throughout the evening. I felt like a schoolgirl who had been invited out by her headmistress. My English was crude and my mistakes seemed more glaring than ever before. How could I compete with such learned men?

The next afternoon, however, I was asked to address a group of women. They asked specifically that I share my prison experiences with them. This time I felt at home. Certainly I could tell them what the Lord had done in my life.

They received me warmly—enthusiastically—in fact. "Corrie," one of the ladies said afterwards, "this is your message. Share it wherever you go." She then handed me a check that enabled me to return all the money I had borrowed in New York.

Suddenly the tables were turned. Instead of no work, I had to guard against overwork. Abraham Vereide's recommendation brought in calls from everyplace, asking me to come and share my testimony. The calls came from villages and towns, as well as from the big cities. I spoke in churches, prisons, universities, schools, and clubs. For almost ten months I traveled America, everywhere telling the story that Jesus Christ is reality, even in darkest days. I told them that He is the answer to all the problems in the hearts of men and nations. I knew it was so, because of what He had done for me.

As the year drew to a close I began to sense that God wanted me to return to Europe. I was homesick for Holland, but this time I felt Him leading me in another direction—Germany. The one land I dreaded.

When I left the German concentration camp I said, "I'll go anywhere God sends me, but I hope never to Germany." Now I understand that was a statement of disobedience. F. B. Meyer said, "God does not fill with His Holy Spirit those who believe in the fullness of the Spirit, or those who desire Him, but those who obey Him." More than anything I desired to be filled with God's Spirit. I knew I had no choice but to go to Germany.

6

Music from Broken Chords

❧

I will sing of the mercies of the LORD for
ever: with my mouth will I make known
thy faithfulness to all generations.

Psalm 89:1

The Germans had lost face in defeat.
Their homes had been destroyed and when
they heard the enormity of Hitler's crimes
(which many Germans knew nothing
about) they were filled with despair. As they
returned to their Fatherland they felt they
had nothing to live for.

Friends in Darmstadt helped me rent a
former concentration camp to use as a
home for displaced persons. It was not big,
but there was room for about one hundred
sixty refugees, and soon it was full with a
long waiting list. I worked closely with the
refugee program of the Lutheran Church
(das Evangelische Hilfswerk) in the Darm-

stadt camp. Barbed wire disappeared. Flowers, light-colored paint, and God's love in the hearts of the people changed a cruel camp into a refuge where people would find the way back to life again.

Marienschwestern, the Lutheran Sisterhood of Mary, whose members had dedicated their lives to serving the Lord and spiritually hungry people, assisted with the children's and women's work. Pastors and members of different churches helped by building homes. I was traveling and helping raise money for the work.

The camp was crowded. Some rooms were jammed with several families. Noise and bedlam were everywhere as families, many without men because they had been killed in the war, tried to carry on the most basic forms of living. Often I would walk through the camp talking with the lonely, defeated people and trying to bring them hope and cheer.

One afternoon I spotted an elderly woman huddled in the corner of a big room. She was obviously new to the camp. She had been put in the big room along with three other families and was told she could set up housekeeping in the corner. There she crouched like a whipped child, her faded, worn dress pulled tightly around her frail, wasted body. I could sense she was distressed by the bedlam of all the crying children, but most of all she was defeated by life itself.

I went to her, sat beside her on the floor, and asked who she was. I learned she had been a professor of music at the Dresden Conservatory before the war. Now she had nothing.

I asked her to tell me about her life, knowing that sometimes it helps just to have someone willing to listen. She told me that a minister in a nearby town had given her permission to play his piano. She had also learned of several farmers' children nearby who wanted to receive music lessons. But the minister's home was miles away, and the only way to get there was on foot. It all seemed so hopeless.

"You were a professor of piano?" I asked excitedly. "I am a great lover of Germany's master musician, Johann Sebastian Bach."

For an instant her eyes lighted up. "Would you care to accompany me to the minister's home?" she asked with great dignity. "I would be most happy to play for you."

It was a great privilege, and even though we had to walk many miles, I sensed God was doing something special.

She seated herself at the battered piano. I looked at the instrument. Even though it had been saved from the bombing, it had not been protected from the rain. The strings were exposed through the warped frame and I could see they were rusted. Some were broken and curled around the others. The pedals had long been broken off and the keyboard was almost entirely without ivory. If any of the notes played it would be a miracle.

Looking up, the old woman said, "What would you like me to play?"

Silently I prayed, knowing that failure at this moment could crush her forever. Then, to my own amazement, I heard myself saying, "Would you please play the 'Chromatic Fantasy' of Bach?"

I was aghast. Why had I picked one of the most difficult of all piano pieces for this old woman to play on such a ruined instrument? Yet the moment I said it, I saw a light flicker behind her eyes and a slight, knowing smile played across her tired face. She nodded, and with great finesse, put her fingers on the broken keyboard.

I could hardly believe my ears. From that damp, battered old piano flowed the beautiful music of Bach as her skilled fingers raced up and down the broken, chipped keys. Tears came to my eyes and ran down my cheeks as I thought of wounded Germany, left with only the remnants of the past, still able to play beautiful music. Such a nation will survive to create again, I thought.

As the notes of Bach faded from the air, the words of an old gospel song, written by the blind composer Fanny J. Crosby, came to mind:

> Down in the human heart, crush'd by
>   the tempter,
> Feelings lie buried that grace can
>   restore;
> Touched by a loving heart, wakened by
>   kindness
> Chords that were broken will vibrate
>   once more.

As we walked back to the former concentration camp, my companion had a new spring in her step. "It has been many years since I played the 'Chromatic Fantasy,'" she said. "Once I was a concert pianist, and many of my pupils are now outstanding musicians. I had a beautiful home in Dresden that was destroyed by the bombs. I had to flee and was not able to take one thing with me."

"Oh, no, you are wrong." I said. "You took with you your most prized possession."

"And what is that?" she asked, shocked.

"Your music. For that which is in your heart can never be taken from you."

Then I told her of what I had learned in Ravensbruck, of Betsie's vision, and that God's love still stands when all else has fallen. "In the concentration camp they took all we had, even made us stand naked for hours at a time without rest, but they could not take Jesus from my heart. Ask Jesus to come into your life. He will give you riches no man can take away from you."

We returned to the camp in silence, but I knew the Holy Spirit was pricking her heart, reminding her of the things that man cannot snatch from us. Soon it was time for me to leave the camp and move on to other fields. The day I left she was sitting in that same corner of the room. A boy was playing his mouth organ, a baby was crying, there were the sounds of shouts and the pounding of a hammer against a wooden crate. The room was full of discord and disharmonic noises, but her eyes were closed and there was a faint smile on her face. I knew God had given her something that no one could ever take from her—ever again.

After the war, Germany was filled with wounds and scars—not all of them on the surface. In one tiny cubicle in the camp at Darmstadt, I found a German lawyer. He was sitting miserably in a wheelchair, the stumps of his legs poking out from under a lap blanket. He was filled with bitterness, hatred, and self-pity. He told me he had once been an active member of his Lutheran church and as a boy had rung the church bell in the village where he lived. Now the horrible injustice of war had taken his legs, and he was bitter against God and man.

I felt attracted to him since some of his experiences were similar to mine. One morning I made a special trip to his room to tell him something of my life.

I found him sitting in his wheelchair, staring at a blank wall. His face was gray, his eyes lifeless. I never was one for introductions so I got right to the point of my visit.

"The only way to get rid of bitterness is to surrender it," I said.

He turned slowly and looked at me. "What do you know about bitterness?" he asked. "You still have your legs."

"Let me tell you a story," I said. "In Holland, during the war, a man came to me begging me to help him liberate his wife. I felt compassion for him and gave him all my money. I also convinced my friends to do the same. But the man was a quisling, a traitor. The only reason he came to me was to trap me so he could have me arrested. Not only did he betray me, but he betrayed my entire family and my friends. We were all sent to prison where three members of my family died. You ask me about bitterness and hatred. You only hate circumstances, but I hated a man. Sitting in the prison in my homeland, waiting to be transferred to a concentration camp in Germany, hatred and bitterness filled my heart. I wanted that man to die. I know what it is like to hate. That is why I can understand you."

The lawyer turned his chair to face me. He was listening. "So, you have hated also. What do you suggest I do about my hate?"

"What I have to say is of no importance. Let me tell you what the Son of God had to

say. 'For if ye forgive men their trespasses,
your heavenly Father will also forgive you:
But if ye forgive not men their trespasses, neither will your Father forgive your trespasses'
[Matt. 6:14–15]. If we forgive other people,
our hearts are made fit to receive forgiveness."

The lawyer shifted uneasily in his wheelchair. I could see the muscles in his neck
stand out as he pushed with his hands to
change position. "When we repent," I continued, "God forgives us and cleanses us.
That is what I did, believing that if I confessed my sin God would be faithful and
just to cleanse my sin and forgive me from
all unrighteousness" (1 John 1:9).

The lawyer looked at me and shook his
head. "That is easy to say, but my hatred is
too deep to have it washed away."

"No deeper than mine," I said. "Yet when
I confessed it, not only did Jesus take it
away, He filled me with love—even the ability to love my enemy."

"You mean you actually loved the man
who betrayed you and who was responsible
for the death of your family?"

I nodded. "After the war, when that man
was sentenced to death, I corresponded
with him and God used me to show him the
way of salvation before he was executed."

The lawyer shook his head. "What a miracle! What a miracle! You mean Jesus can do that to a person? I shall have to give this much thought."

Since I have learned not to push a person beyond where God has left him, I bade my friend good-bye and returned to my room.

A year later I was in Darmstadt again. My friends had given this man a car with special fixtures so he could drive without legs. He met me at the train station to bring me to the camp. As I got in the car, he laughed at my startled look.

"You taught me that Jesus is Victor," he said. "Now surely you are not afraid to drive with a man who has no legs."

"You are right," I answered. "I shall not be afraid. I am so glad to see you again. How are you?"

"Fine. I must tell you at the very beginning that I have surrendered my bitterness to God. I repented and the Lord did just as you said. He forgave me and filled my heart with His love. Now I am working in the refugee camp and am praising God that He can use even a legless man if he is surrendered."

He paused, and then continued. "But there is something I must know. After you forgave your enemies, was it settled once and for all?"

"Oh, no," I answered. "Just this month I had a sad experience with friends who behaved like enemies. They promised something but did not keep their promise. In fact, they took great advantage of me. However, I surrendered my bitterness to the Lord, asked forgiveness, and He took it away."

We were bouncing over a bumpy road but the lawyer was more intent on me than his driving. "Was the bitterness gone for good, then?"

"No, just the next night, at four o'clock I awoke, and my heart was filled with bitterness again. I thought, *How could my dear friend behave as she did?* Again I brought it to the Lord. He filled my heart with His love. But the next night it came back again. I was so discouraged. God had used me often to help people to love their enemies, and I could always give my testimony about what He had done in my life; but now I felt defeated.

"Then I remembered Ephesians 6:10–20 where Paul describes the 'armor of God.' He said that even after you have come to a standstill, still stand your ground. I was at a standstill, so I decided to stand my ground and the bitterness and resentment fell away before me.

"Corrie ten Boom without the Lord Jesus cannot be victorious. I need the Lord every moment. And I have learned that I am absolutely dependent on Him. Because of this He has made me rich."

We were just arriving at the refugee camp, and my lawyer friend parked before the building, turned off the motor, and looked at me with a grin. "I am glad to hear that," he said. "For sometimes my old bitterness returns. Now I shall just stand my ground, claim the victory of Jesus over fear and resentment, and love even when I don't want to."

My friend had learned well the secret of victory. It comes through obedience.

7

Love Your Enemy

We feel this warm love everywhere within us because God has given us the Holy Spirit to fill our hearts with his love.

Romans 5:5 TLB

It was in a church in Munich that I saw him—a balding, heavyset man in a gray overcoat, a brown felt hat clutched between his hands. People were filing out of the basement room where I had just spoken, moving along the rows of wooden chairs to the door at the rear. It was 1947, and I had come from Holland to defeated Germany with the message that God forgives.

It was the truth they needed most to hear in that bitter, bombed-out land, and I gave them my favorite mental picture. Maybe because the sea is never far from a Hollander's mind, I like to think that that's where forgiven sins were thrown. "When we confess our sins," I said, "God casts them into the deepest ocean, gone forever. And even though I cannot find a Scripture for it, I believe God then places a sign out there that says, 'NO FISHING ALLOWED.' "

The solemn faces stared back at me, not quite daring to believe. There were never questions after a talk in Germany in 1947. People stood up in silence, in silence collected their wraps, in silence left the room.

And that's when I saw him, working his way forward against the others. One moment I saw the overcoat and the brown hat; the next, a blue uniform and a visored cap with its skull and crossbones. It came back with a rush: the huge room with its harsh overhead lights; the pathetic pile of dresses and shoes in the center of the floor; the shame of walking naked past this man. I could see my sister's frail form ahead of me, ribs sharp beneath the parchment skin. *Betsie, how thin you were!*

The place was Ravensbruck, and the man who was making his way forward had been a guard—one of the most cruel guards.

Now he was in front of me, hand thrust out: "A fine message, Fraulein! How good it is to know that, as you say, all our sins are at the bottom of the sea!"

And I, who had spoken so glibly of forgiveness, fumbled in my pocketbook rather than take that hand. He would not remember me, of course—how could he remember one prisoner among those thousands of women?

But I remembered him and the leather crop swinging from his belt. I was face-to-face with one of my captors, and my blood seemed to freeze.

"You mentioned Ravensbruck in your talk," he was saying. "I was a guard there." No, he did not remember me.

"But since that time," he went on, "I have become a Christian. I know that God has forgiven me for the cruel things I did there, but I would like to hear it from your lips as well, Fraulein." Again the hand came out. "Will you forgive me?"

And I stood there—I whose sins had again and again to be forgiven—and could not forgive. Betsie had died in that place—could he erase her slow terrible death simply for the asking?

It could not have been many seconds that he stood there—hand held out—but to me it seemed hours as I wrestled with the most difficult thing I had ever had to do.

For I had to do it—I knew that. The message that God forgives has a prior condition: that we forgive those who have injured us. "If you do not forgive men their trespasses," Jesus says, "neither will your Father in heaven forgive your trespasses."

I knew it not only as a commandment of God but as a daily experience. Since the end of the war I had had a home in Holland for victims of Nazi brutality. Those who were able to forgive their former enemies were able also to return to the outside world and rebuild their lives, no matter what the physical scars. Those who nursed their bitterness remained invalids. It was as simple and as horrible as that.

And still I stood there with the coldness clutching my heart. But forgiveness is not an emotion—I knew that too. Forgiveness is an act of the will, and the will can function regardless of the temperature of the heart. "Jesus, help me!" I prayed silently. "I can lift my hand. I can do that much. You supply the feeling."

And so woodenly, mechanically, I thrust my hand into the one stretched out to me. And as I did, an incredible thing took place. The current started in my shoulder, raced down my arm, sprang into our joined hands.

And then this healing warmth seemed to flood my whole being, bringing tears to my eyes.

"I forgive you, brother!" I cried. "With all my heart."

For a long moment we grasped each other's hands, the former guard and the former prisoner. I had never known God's love so intensely as I did then. But even so, I realized it was not my love. I had tried, and did not have the power. It was the power of the Holy Spirit as recorded in Romans 5:5, "The love of God is shed abroad in our hearts by the Holy Ghost which is given unto us."

8

In the Power of the Spirit

And Jesus being full of the Holy Ghost
returned from Jordan, and was led by the
Spirit into the wilderness. . . . And Jesus
returned in the power of the Spirit into
Galilee: and there went out a fame of him
through all the region round about.

Luke 4:1, 14

As I stood in the railroad station in Basel,
Switzerland, waiting for my luggage, I suddenly realized that I did not know where I
was supposed to go. For ten years, after my
release from prison, I had been traveling
all over the world at the direction of God.
Many times I did not know why I was to go
to a certain place until I arrived. It had
become almost second nature not to make
my plans and then ask for God's signature.
Rather, I had learned to wait for God's plan
and then write my name on the schedule.

But this time was different. Suddenly I was in Basel and had no idea why, or whom I was to contact. Besides, I was tired. Sleeping each night in a different bed and always living out of a suitcase had worn me down. I felt a sensation of panic in my heart and sat down, trying to remember to whom I was going. At sixty-three years of age could it be that I was so overworked that I was losing my memory? Or even worse, had God withdrawn His conscious presence from me and was letting me walk alone for a season?

Inside my suitcase I found an address. It had no meaning to me, but it was all I had to go on. I took a taxi to the place, but the people at that address were complete strangers and had never heard of me. By now I was desperate—and a little bit frightened.

The people told me of another man I might contact. Perhaps he would know who I was and why I had come to Basel. I took another taxi but this gentleman, too, was unfamiliar with my work.

For ten years the Lord had guided me step by step. At no time had I been confused or afraid. Now I was both—unable to recognize the presence of God. Surely He was still guiding me, but like the pilot who flies into the clouds, I was now having to rely on instruments rather than sight. I decided to turn around and go back home to Holland, there to await further orders.

Because of a severe storm the planes were not flying. I had to travel by train. Arriving in Haarlem, I started toward the phone near the station to call Zonneduin, the house where I was to stay in the outskirts of the city in Bloemendaal.

But on the way to the phone booth I slipped on the wet pavement, and before I knew it I was sprawled in the street. A sharp pain shot through my hip, and I was unable to stand.

"Oh, Lord," I prayed, "lay Your hand on my hip and take away this horrible pain."

Instantly the pain disappeared, but I was still unable to get up. Kind people assisted me to a taxi where a policeman asked if he could help.

"What is your name?" he asked.

"Corrie ten Boom."

He looked surprised and questioned me further. "Are you a member of the family of that name whom we arrested about ten years ago?"

"That is right."

During the war many of the good Dutch policemen had been in the service of the Gestapo, remaining there for the express purpose of helping political prisoners. This man had been on duty that day my family was arrested.

"I am so sorry about your accident," he said sympathetically, "but I am glad to see you again. I will never forget that night in the police station. You were all sitting or lying on the floor of the station. Your old father was there with all his children and many of your friends. I have often told my colleagues that there was an atmosphere of peace and joy in our station that night, as if you were going to a feast instead of prison and death."

He paused and looked at me kindly as if trying to remember my face. "Your father said before he tried to sleep, 'Let us pray together.' And then he read Psalm 91."

"You remember!" I exclaimed. After ten years that policeman had remembered which psalm my father had read.

For a fleeing moment, sitting in that old taxi on a Haarlem street while the rain pelted the roof, I allowed myself that pain of looking backwards. It was in this same city that we had been arrested. In fact, the prison was only a short distance from where I was now sitting. That was the last time our family had been together. Within ten days Father was dead. Then later Betsie. All gone. Now, ten years later this policeman still remembered.

> He that dwelleth in the secret place of the Most High shall abide under the shadow of the Almighty.
>
> Psalm 91:1

Now the message was clear. Although there was no light to guide me, I was still in God's will. Actually, when one is abiding under the shadow of the Almighty there will be no light, but that is only because God's presence is so near.

I leaned back in the seat. "Dear God, when this shadow came over me I thought You had departed. Now I understand it was because You were drawing closer. I eagerly await whatever You have planned for me."

Eager I was, but not so patient. An X ray showed my hip was not broken, only badly bruised. The doctor said I would have to remain in bed for several weeks for it to heal. I was taken from the clinic to Zonneduin, where I was put to bed, unable to move or turn over without the help of a nurse.

I was a very impatient patient. I had only five days to get to a student conference in Germany, and as the days slipped by and I realized my hip was not healing fast enough to make the conference, I grew irritable.

"Is there not a Christian in all Haarlem who can pray for me to be healed?" I asked.

My friends sent for a particular minister in the city who was known to have laid hands on the sick for healing. That same afternoon he came to my room.

Standing beside my bed he said, "Is there any unconfessed sin in your life?"

What an odd question, I thought. I understood he had agreed to come pray for my healing, but was it his job to get so personal about my sins and attitudes? However, I did not have far to look. My impatience and demanding attitude, which I had displayed toward my nurse, had been wrong—very wrong. I asked her to come to the room, and I repented of my sin, asking both her and God to forgive me.

Satisfied, this gentle man then reached over and laid his hands on my head. Only

the year before, my sister Nollie had died.
Ever since, my heart had been broken with
mourning. I had the feeling of being left all
alone and knew that the insecurity I had
experienced had contributed to my being
here in this bed, rather than in Germany
with the students. Yet as this tall, handsome
man laid his hands on me and prayed, I felt
a great stream of power flowing through
me. Such great joy. The mourning left and
I wanted to sing with David:

> Thou hast turned for me my mourning
> into dancing: thou hast put off my sack-
> cloth, and girded me with gladness.
> Psalm 30:11

I felt the presence of the Lord Jesus all
around me and felt His love flowing through
me and over me as if I were being immersed
in an ocean of grace. My joy became so
intense that I finally prayed, "No more,
Lord, no more." My heart felt it was about
to burst, so great was the joy. I knew it was
that wonderful experience promised by
Jesus, the baptism in the Holy Spirit.

I looked at the man who had prayed for
me. "Can I walk now?" I asked.

He smiled. "I do not know. All I know is you asked for a cupful and God gave you an ocean."

Ten days later I was on my way to Germany, late but still filled with joy overflowing. Only after I arrived did I realize why God chose this particular time to fill me with His Holy Spirit. In Germany, for the first time, I came face-to-face with many people who were demonized. Had I gone in my own power I would have been consumed. Now, going in the power of the Holy Spirit, God was able to work much deliverance through me as we commanded demons to be cast out in the name of the Lord Jesus Christ.

Jesus specifically warned His followers not to try to minister in His name without His power. As I found out from my experience in Basel, trying to do the Lord's work in your own strength is the most confusing, exhausting, and tedious of all work. But when you are filled with the Holy Spirit, then the ministry of Jesus just flows out of you.

It was the beginning of a new spiritual blessing that each day brings me into a closer walk with the Lord Jesus. Now, whether I am walking in the bright light of

His presence or abiding under the shadow of the Almighty, I know that He is not only with me, He is in me.

> Greater is he that is in you, than he that is in the world.
>
> 1 John 4:4

9
Conny

Though I walk through the valley of the
shadow of death, I will fear no evil.
Psalm 23:4

After twelve years of traveling alone,
someone joined me in my worldwide travels. The Lord saw and supplied my need in
the person of Conny van Hoogstraten, a
beautiful, young, Dutch woman who became my first constant traveling companion. I met her on one of my visits to England. We worked well as a team (not to
say we did not have difficulties—as always
happens when people work so closely together). However, those hard moments
were used to bring us closer to Jesus as we
learned to walk in the light with each other.
Yes, 1 John 1:7–9 became a reality, and the
Lord used Conny in the lives of countless

people all over the world to show and teach them the joy of walking in the light.

We laughed much together, for the Lord had given Conny an infectious sense of humor and a happy laughter. One of Conny's special gifts was the ability to change a house into a home. People always found an open door and quickly became friends. We were so different, but the Lord molded us into a team fit to do His work. I will never forget the day, now almost eight years ago, that Conny told me of the someone else who had come into her life and that we would have to pray for a new partner. That was one of those very difficult days, and the best thing I could do was to go for a long walk. I experienced more than ever before that I was so dependent upon Conny and that I loved her like a sister. I could not understand the Lord's purpose, but during that walk I surrendered Conny to the Lord, and I also surrendered myself in a new way and entrusted my whole being to Him who knew best. Conny was in good hands so why not trust Him for the future? Those last years together were so different from all other years.

In that final year together, the Lord made it clear to me to go to Viet Nam. Conny and

I talked it over, and Conny shared with me that her fiancé was not in favor of her going there, so we had to look around for someone else. It was early spring, and I happened to meet a good brother in the Lord who shared that he had been called to go to Viet Nam also. I rejoiced and thanked the Lord as we made plans to go together. The young man was Brother Andrew, and he proved to be a very good traveling companion. In Viet Nam, the Lord gave me a very nice nurse who worked with the W.E.C., and she took care of me when I traveled while Brother Andrew was away on other trips to very dangerous places.

I will never forget the tremendous needs I saw in the hospitals and other places I visited, but instead of taking all those needs to Jesus, I kept them in my heavy and overburdened heart. How silly I could be! With that heavy heart and aching body I had to go on to Indonesia. Oh, the Lord worked in spite of me, and the people were very kind to me and helped me in many ways, but the happiest moment came when we landed in Amsterdam. We quickly drove to Soestdijk where a very dear friend, Elisabeth van Heemstra (who was working in Jerusalem at that time), had made her apartment available to me. That was a great gift from the Lord! I had no place I could really call home but now I had one—and what a haven it was! Beautiful surroundings in a quiet section of town. There Conny and I spent our last months together, and it was a precious time. Conny was busy with marriage preparations and the new house she and her husband would move into. Many old-time friends came by to say hello. We talked and prayed much and we trusted that the Lord would supply a new partner before Conny's marriage.

How marvelous are His ways! The Lord answered our prayers and gave me another Dutch companion, Ellen de Kroon, a registered nurse who loves the Lord very much. I will never forget the first time Ellen visited me. Conny and her fiancé were there also. It was a nice day in June, and we decided to sit outside on the balcony. After talking for some time, Ellen noticed that I was getting cold, so she got up, asked me where she could find a shawl and put it around my shoulders. I noticed that Conny's face was beaming, and her eyes seemed to say, "See! You prayed for that 'someone' who would take care of you and love you and here she is." It was a testimony for Conny as well, knowing that Ellen would take her place.

On Conny's wedding day, September 1, 1967, the Lord filled the empty place left behind by Conny with Ellen, the tall, fair-haired nurse. Conny and her husband lived not far from us, and she took much time to help Ellen with the work. Almost a year after Conny was married, her husband had to go to India for several weeks. During that time, Conny accompanied me to the United States to start the work on the book *The Hiding Place*, while Ellen took care of the work in Holland. Yes, it was Conny who started to type that book, which has already blessed so many lives all over the world. I knew that she loved the work we were doing, but she also missed her husband. It was so good to bring him daily before the Lord. Our prayers were answered and Conny's husband returned safely to Holland while I continued my travels with my new companion, Ellen.

Two years had passed when we learned that Conny had been taken ill. We returned to Holland and were on our way to visit Conny in the hospital. I knew that she was very ill, because she had received treatment that would indicate terminal illness unless the Lord would perform a miracle. When we entered Conny's room, it was like stepping into a flower garden and in the midst of it was Conny, almost asleep. Her husband was sitting beside her. That day, her specialist had informed her of her illness and that there was no hope. Conny was prepared to go and be with her Lord and Savior, but to take that trip all by herself was so difficult for her. Would Jesus ask that of her?

Slowly she said, "I have taken many trips in my lifetime but there was always someone with me. Mother was there when I was small, Corrie was with me during many of them, and now my husband is with me. But on this trip, who is going to go with me?"

Her husband gently took her hand and said, "Conny, here is my hand and as soon as Jesus comes for you, I will surrender your hand to Him!"

Conny did not answer but her face looked content. Suddenly she turned to us and asked us to sing Psalm Twenty-Three for her. I swallowed the lump in my throat and asked the Lord to help me in joining the others in the singing, but the phrase we left out was, "though I walk through the valley of the shadow of death . . ."

When we finished Conny said, "You forgot one phrase—please sing it!"

So we sang, "though I walk through the valley of the shadow of death" while the tears rolled down our cheeks. Then Conny thought of all the friends all over the world whom we had come to know and love, and she asked me to greet them. We began to pray and Conny laid her hands on Ellen's head and said, "Be . . . faithful unto death, and I will give thee a crown of life" (Rev. 2:10).

Conny died a victorious death. Her life bore much fruit, and she prepared many people to meet the Master, our Lord Jesus Christ, who came to call her home to be with Him forever.

10
Authority over Demons

∮

And these signs shall follow them that
believe; In my name shall they cast out
devils.

Mark 16:17

For weeks I had been traveling through
Eastern Europe—Russia, Poland, Czechoslovakia—speaking in many home groups
and even, on occasion, in a church. Many
churches were still open in Eastern Europe,
although the communists were very strict
about who could speak—and what they
said. However, as a harmless old Dutch
woman I was allowed to sometimes speak
in one of the churches.

As if by a miracle, I was invited to speak
in a series of meetings in a great cathedral
in a large communist city. I found that the
pastors loved the Lord and had a heavy burden for lost souls.

The first several nights I spoke about the abundant life in Jesus Christ—the joy, the unspeakable love, and the peace that passes all understanding. It was as though I was carried by the Holy Spirit through the joyful storehouse of abundance that we possess when we know Jesus. I described in great detail the precious promises made available to us in Christ.

But something was wrong. Although some of the people rejoiced, most of them simply sat rooted to their benches. They were like chained animals, dying of hunger but unable to reach the food. And the more I tried to give them, the more I was aware their hearts were shackled so they could not taste the food I was offering them.

Each night I would return to my room with a heavy heart for I knew that although these dear people wanted to receive what I was giving them, they could not. "It is as if the devil keeps a fence around these people that you cannot reach them," my traveling companion said.

"Could it be that demons keep them in bondage?" I wondered.

I opened my Bible and read, "In my name shall they cast out devils" (Mark 16:17).

"Lord, what must I do?" I cried out.

"Obey Me!" came the answer.

"But how, Lord? There are so many who are bound by demon powers, and I cannot meet with each of them individually."

"Where did I say that you can deal only with individuals?" He asked.

I was confused and returned to His Word. It became apparent that the Lord wanted me to send all the evil spirits away in His name. Yet I knew this type of ministry was forbidden in communist lands.

That night was the final night of the meetings. The great cathedral was crowded with people, but it was the same as on all the other nights. They were not able to receive what I was giving them. I spoke again of Jesus the Victor. "In the world ye shall have tribulation: but be of good cheer; I have overcome the world" (John 16:33). They sat like stone images, unable to grasp the joy of the Lord.

I knew God was calling on me to act. I trembled, but I had no choice. "I must interrupt my message for a moment, friends," I said. "Many of you cannot grasp the richness the Lord offers us this evening. The servants of Satan are keeping you in bondage."

Then I obeyed. Taking a deep breath and offering one last quick prayer, I said in a loud voice, "In the name of Jesus I command all dark powers keeping people from the blessings of God to disappear. Go away! Get out of the hearts of these people. Get out of this church. Go to the place where God sends you."

Then, closing my eyes I raised my hands upward and prayed, "Lord, will You now protect us with Your precious blood. Amen."

I was afraid, but I felt secure. I knew God had told me to do it. Then, as I opened my eyes and looked out over the huge congregation, I saw a miracle happen. The people who had been in bondage came alive. They began to rejoice, and as I continued my message I could sense their eager hearts drinking in the living water as I poured it out before them.

After the service I was scheduled to meet with a large group of local pastors who had attended the meeting. By the time I was able to break away from the crowd of people who came forward to speak to me and get to the back room, the pastors were already meeting. Their conversation was very serious.

"How could you do that?" one pastor asked as soon as I entered the room. "Communists do not allow people to speak about demons!"

"I had to obey God," was my only answer.

The pastors resumed their discussion about the meeting. They, too, had seen the bondage. They had also sensed the release when the demons were cast out. But there were some who had studied psychology and others who had studied demonology. They entered into a heated argument about the subject. I had studied none of these. All I knew was God had told me to use my authority in the name of Jesus. So I sat back while the argument swirled around me.

At last one of the pastors said, "We know God's promises and God's command, but who among us has ever been willing to obey Mark 16:17: 'And these signs shall follow them that believe; In my name shall they cast out devils'?"

There was a long, uncomfortable silence. When the Bible interferes with man's theology, it always causes a strain. The pastor then continued, "God has this evening given Corrie the grace to take the authority of Jesus and in His name cast out devils. We should be thankful instead of all this arguing."

That was the end of the pastors' meeting, but, oh, what a lesson I learned that night. It is tragic to be around people, especially men of God, who do not recognize the fact that we are surrounded, not only by angels but also by the powers of darkness.

Someone once asked my opinion of the missionaries in a certain country. My answer was, "They have given all, but they have not taken all. They have given homeland, time, money, luxury, and more; but they have not taken all of the boundless resources of God's promises. Many do not know about two precious weapons: the power of the blood of Jesus—and every Christian's legal right to use the wonderful name of Jesus to cast out demons."

In *War on the Saints*, Mrs. Jessie Penn-Lewis wrote, "When the existence of evil spirits is recognized by the heathen, it is generally looked upon by the missionary as 'superstition' and ignorance; whereas the ignorance is often on the part of the missionary, who is blinded by the prince of the power of the air to the revelation given in the Scriptures, concerning the satanic powers."

We need to recognize the enemy in order to overcome him. But let us beware of the mistakes that C. S. Lewis described in

Screwtape Letters. He says, "There are two equal and opposite errors into which our race can fall about the devils. One is to disbelieve in their existence; the other is to believe and to feel an unhealthy interest in them! They themselves are equally pleased by both errors, and they hail a materialist or a magician with the same delight."

We have a good safeguard and guide—the Bible, God's Word. Here we find not only the necessary information about Satan and demons but also the weapons and the armor that we need for this battle.

God wants and expects us to be conquerors over the powers of darkness—not only for the sake of personal victory and the liberation of other souls—but for His glory, so that His triumph and victory over His enemies may be demonstrated!

First, then, let us see what the Bible says about the powers of darkness. The devil (or Satan) is introduced to us as a person who opposes God and His work. He is the "god of this world" who blinds the minds of the people to the truths of God's Word. Having rebelled against God, he was cast out of heaven; then, he caused man's fall in paradise. Jesus calls him "the father of lies, a liar, a murderer" (John 8:44). He works often as an "angel of light," seeking the ruin of the elect. But he was cursed of God. Jesus triumphed over him at the cross of Calvary and in His resurrection. He has been condemned and will finally be destroyed.

There are many kinds of demons, and they afflict people in various ways. They also bring false doctrine, trying to seduce the elect by oppressing, obsessing, and possessing. They know Jesus, recognize His power, and tremble before Him. For them, hell is the final destination, as it is for Satan.

Second, the Bible gives us direction concerning the stand we have to take against these powers. It is most important to realize that ours is the position *in Christ*. We are called to resist the devil in the "whole armor of God," by virtue of the blood of Jesus, by faith, prayer, and fasting.

I remember in Ravensbruck, for instance, when we had very little to eat, my sister Betsie said, "Let us dedicate this involuntary fast to the Lord that it may become a blessing." Almost immediately we found we had power over the demons that were tormenting us and were able to exercise that power to cast them out of our barracks.

Let us remember that God's Word stands forever and that His commandments mean for us today exactly the same as for His disciples twenty centuries ago. Those who act on them, in obedience, will in the same way prove God's almighty power. Yes, Jesus said, "In my name shall they cast out devils." And that means us today.

Our fight is not against a physical army, a political party, an atheistic organization—or anything like that. Our fight is against organizations and powers that are spiritual. Demons may come in as a result of occult sin, even from years back. This includes contact with hypnotism, astrology charts, fortune-telling, Ouija boards and other forms of occultism, sometimes entered into "just for fun." These demons will remain until they are cast out in Jesus' name.

We are up against the unseen power that controls this dark world and the spiritual agents are from the very headquarters of evil. Therefore, we must wear the "whole armor of God," that we may be able to resist evil in its day of power, and that even when we have fought to a standstill, we may still stand our ground.

Conny and I had traveled throughout Poland. Conny was then my constant companion, and we met many wonderful Christians in that Iron Curtain country. It encouraged us to know that God was using us to bring comfort and strength to the men and women of God. However, the longer we stayed in Poland, the more exhausted we became.

"I do not understand it," Conny said one morning as we were getting up. "I have just wakened from a full night's sleep, but already I am weak and tired."

I, too, felt the same way. We thought perhaps it was some kind of sickness we had picked up; yet neither of us seemed to be really sick.

Then in Warsaw one day we happened to meet an old friend from Holland. Kees was in Poland with his wife, traveling with his camping trailer.

"What a joy to meet you," he said. "How are things going?"

I looked at Conny and she looked at me. "You know, Kees, we both feel so tired. It is as if our legs are heavy, like when you have the flu. Yet we are not ill, just tired."

Kees looked at us intently. "Is this your first time to work in Poland?"

"Yes," I answered. "But what does that have to do with it?"

"Let me explain," Kees said. "Your tiredness is nothing less than an attack of the devil. He does not like your work in Poland, for the antichrist is busy here, arranging his army."

Reaching out, he put his hand on my arm. "Corrie and Conny, you must remember you have the protection of the blood of Jesus. Whenever you experience these attacks from the dark powers, you must rebuke them in the name of Jesus."

I knew what Kees was saying was right. We sat in his car while he read from the Bible. "They overcame him by the blood of the Lamb, and by the word of their testimony; and they loved not their lives unto the death" (Rev. 12:11).

Then Kees prayed with us, laying his hands on us in the name of Jesus and rebuking the dark powers that would attack us. Even as he was praying I felt the darkness leave. By the time the prayer was over, we both felt covered by the blood of the Lamb and all our tiredness had disappeared.

God had taught us a valuable lesson that we would remember in many other areas of the world. We learned that in a country where a godless philosophy reigns, that only by claiming the blood of Jesus can you stand

and not fall. The same is true in a city, or school, or even a church building. If Jesus Christ is not recognized as supreme, then darkness rules.

Since then we have traveled in many countries and felt this same tiredness coming over us. Often I have felt it in American cities. Now I know it simply means that I am in a place where Satan rules. But praise the Lord! I can be an overcomer when I stand in the power of the blood of the Lamb.

11
Lights from Darkest Africa

❧❦❧

But I say unto you, Love your enemies, bless them that curse you, do good to them that hate you, and pray for them that despitefully use you, and persecute you.

Matthew 5:44

Thomas was a tall black man who lived in a round hut together with his big family in the middle of Africa. He loved the Lord and loved people—an unbeatable combination.

Thomas's neighbor, who lived across the dirt street, hated God—and hated men like Thomas who loved God. The hatred grew stronger and stronger until the man began sneaking over at night and setting fire to the straw roof on Thomas's hut, endangering his small children. Three nights in a row this happened, and each time Thomas was able to rush out of his hut and put out the flames before they destroyed the roof and the walls. The fact that he never said an unkind word to his neighbor, only showing him love and forgiveness, made his neighbor hate him even more.

One night the neighbor sneaked across the street and set fire to Thomas's roof. This night, however, a strong wind came up, and as Thomas rushed to beat out the fire, the sparks flew across the street and set the neighbor's house on fire. Thomas finished putting out the fire on his roof and then rushed across the street to put out the fire on his neighbor's roof. He was able to extinguish the flames, but in the process he badly burned his hands and arms.

Other neighbors told the chief of the tribe what had happened. The chief was so furious that he sent his police to arrest the neighbor and throw him into prison.

That night Thomas came to the meeting where I was speaking (as he had done each night). I noticed his badly burned hands and asked him what had happened. Reluctantly he told me the story.

"It is good that this man is now in prison," I said. "Now your children are no longer in danger, and he cannot try again to put your house in flames."

"That is true," he said. "But I am so sorry for that man. He is an unusually gifted man, and now he must live together with all those criminals in a horrible prison."

"Then let us pray for him," I said.

Thomas dropped to his knees, and holding up his burned and bandaged hands, he began to pray. "Lord, I claim this neighbor of mine for You. Lord, give him his freedom and do the miracle that in the future he and I will become a team to bring the gospel in our tribe. Amen."

Never had I heard such a prayer.

Two days later I was able to go to the prison. I spoke to the prisoners about God's joy and God's love. Among the group who listened intently was Thomas's neighbor. When I asked who would receive Jesus in his heart, that man was the first one to raise his hand.

After the meeting I told him how Thomas loved him, how he had burned his hands trying to put out the fire to save his house, and how he had prayed that they might become a team to spread the gospel. The man wept big tears and nodded his head, saying, "Yes, yes, that is how it shall be."

The next day I told Thomas. He praised
God and said, "You see, God has worked a
miracle. We never can expect too much
from Him." He left, running off down the
path, his face beaming with joy.

I had been in Africa for three weeks when
I finally got to visit the prison on the out-
side of the city. I inquired of the warden if
I could talk to the prisoners.

"Impossible," he said. "The prison is on
restriction for an entire month due to an
uprising that has broken out among the
prisoners. Nobody is allowed in to see the
men, much less give a sermon."

I felt discouraged but knew that God had
brought me to that place for some reason.
So, I just stood—looking at the warden.

He grew very uncomfortable (having me
stand and look at him). At last he said,
"There are some political prisoners who
have been sentenced to death. Would you
like to speak to them?"

"Certainly," I said.

The warden called three heavily armed
soldiers who escorted me down a long hall
past many barred doors and into a cell
where one man was sitting on a low bench,
which was also his bed. There was abso-

lutely nothing else in the cell. The only light came from a small window high above the floor that let just a little spot of sunlight fall on the hard-packed dirt floor in that dreary place.

I leaned against the wall. He was a young man with black skin and very white teeth. He looked up, his eyes filled with sadness. What could I say? "Lord, give me some light to pass on to this man who sits in such darkness."

Finally I asked him a question. "Do you know about Jesus?"

"Yes," he said slowly, "I have a Bible at home. I know that Jesus died on a cross for the sins of the world. Many years ago I accepted Him as my Savior and followed Him for some time until political affairs absorbed all my time. Now I wish I could start again and live a surrendered life, but it is too late. This week I die."

"It is not too late, my friend," I said. "Do you know the ones responsible for your death sentence?"

"I could give you the entire list of those who have put me here," he answered, gritting his teeth. "I know all their names and hate them."

I opened my Bible and read, "But if you do not forgive men their trespasses, neither

will your Father forgive your trespasses."
Then I closed the Bible and looked at him.
"Do you want your Father to forgive you
before you die?"

"Of course I want that," he said. "More
than anything else in the world. But I cannot meet the conditions. I am not able to forgive. I am young, strong, and healthy. I have
a wife and children. These men have
wronged me, and now this very week they
will take away my life. How do I forgive that?"

The man looked at me with eyes full of
despair and hopelessness. I felt such a great
compassion in my heart, yet I knew I must
be stern for much depended on it.

"Let me tell you a story," I said. And then
I told him of my experience in the church in
Munich when my former guard from the
concentration camp asked me to forgive him.

"That moment I felt a great bitterness
swelling in my heart," I said. "I remembered
the sufferings of my dying sister. But I knew
that unforgiveness would do more harm to
me than the guard's whip. So I cried out to
the Lord, 'Lord, thank You for Romans 5:5:

The love of God is shed abroad in our
hearts by the Holy Ghost which is given
unto us.

'Thank You, Lord, that Your love in me can do that which I cannot do.'

"At that moment a great stream of love poured through me, and I said, 'Brother, give me your hand. I forgive all.'"

I looked down at the African man sitting on the bench. "I could not do it. I was not able. Jesus in me was able to do it. You see, you never touch so much the ocean of God's love as when you love your enemies."

The man listened as I told him more of Jesus. Then, promising to meet him on the other shore, I prayed with him and left.

The next day a missionary friend came by the place where I was staying. He told me that as soon as I left the prison the prisoner had sent a message to his wife saying, "Don't hate the people who brought me here and who will cause my death. Love them. Forgive them. I cannot, and neither can you, but Jesus in us can do it."

I slept well that night, knowing why God had brought me to Africa.

I had spoken in many prisons in my travels across the world, but the prison in Ruanda, Africa, was the dreariest, darkest prison I had ever seen. The men were all black, their uniforms were black, and they were sitting in the mud on the ground.

I had just entered the prison gate with my interpreter, a missionary lady. Steam (the aftermath of a hard tropical rain) was rising from the mud. The men were sitting on pieces of paper, branches, banana leaves, their legs caked with mud up to their knees.

"Why don't we go into the building?" I asked my interpreter.

"Impossible," she whispered, obviously afraid of the men. "There are so many prisoners that even during the night only half of them can go inside."

I looked at their faces. Like their skin, their eyes were dark. It was the look I had seen so many times in Ravensbruck—the look of those whose hope had died. Unhappiness. Despair. Hopelessness. Anger. How could I speak to them? What could I, an old Dutch woman, say to these miserable men that would help their lives?

"Lord," I prayed, "I am not able to overcome this darkness."

"Take my promise of Galatians 5:22," I heard an inner voice say.

Quickly I took my Bible and opened it to that passage. "But the fruit of the Spirit is love . . ."

"Thank You, Lord," I whispered. "But I have a great love for these men already or I would not be here."

I read on. "But the fruit of the Spirit is love, joy . . ."

"Joy?" I asked. "In these surroundings?" Then I remembered what Nehemiah said. "The joy of the Lord is my strength."

"Yes, Lord," I cried out. "That is what I need. That is what I claim. I claim the promise of joy."

Even as I spoke the words I felt a wonderful, lifting sensation in my heart. It was joy—more joy than I had ever felt. It poured like a river out of my inner being; like the rising tide it covered the salt flats of my depression and turned the ugly mud of despair into a shimmering lagoon of blessedness. Moments later I was introduced to the prisoners, who all sat, staring at me in hatred. The steam rose around them and the stinging insects swarmed their mud-coated ankles and legs.

I began to talk of the joy that is ours when we know Jesus. What a Friend we have in Him. He is always with us. When we are depressed, He gives us joy. When we do wrong, He gives us the strength to be good. When we hate, He fills us with His forgiveness. When we are afraid, He causes us to love.

Several faces changed, and I saw that some of my joy was spilling over on them. But I knew what the rest were thinking. *After your talk you can go home, away from this muddy, stinking prison. It is easy to talk about joy when you are free. But we must stay here.*

Then I told them a story.

"Morning roll call at Ravensbruck was often the hardest time of the day. By 4:30 A.M. we had to be standing outside our barracks in the black predawn chill, in blocks of one hundred women, ten wide, ten deep.

"Names were never used in the concentration camp. It was part of the plan to dehumanize the prisoners—to take away their dignity of life—their worth before God and man. I was known simply as Prisoner 66730.

"Roll call sometimes lasted three hours, and every day the sun rose a little later and the icy-cold wind blew a little stronger. Standing in the gray of the dawn I would try to repeat, through shivering lips, that verse of Scripture that had come to mean so much to me:

Who shall separate us from the love of Christ? shall tribulation, or distress, or persecution, or famine, or nakedness, or peril, or sword? As it is written, For thy sake we are killed all the day long; we are accounted as sheep for the slaughter.

Romans 8:35–36

In all this there was an overwhelming victory through Jesus, who had proved His love for me by dying on the cross.

"But there came a time when repeating the words did not help. I needed more. 'Oh God,' I prayed, 'reveal Yourself somehow.'

"Then one morning the woman directly in front of me sank to the ground. In a moment a young woman guard was standing over her, a whip in her hand.

"'Get up,' she screamed in a rage. 'How dare you think you can lie down when everyone else is standing!'

"I could hardly bear to see what was happening in front of me. *Surely this is the end of us all,* I thought. Then suddenly a skylark started to sing high in the sky. The sweet, pure notes of the bird rose on the still, cold air. Every head turned upward, away from the carnage before us, listening to the song of the skylark soaring over the crematorium. The words of the psalmist ran through my mind: 'For as the heaven is high

above the earth, so great is [God's] mercy
toward them that fear Him' (Ps. 103:11)."

I looked out at the men who were sitting
in front of me. No longer were their faces
filled with darkness and anger. They were
listening—intently—for they were hearing
from someone who had walked where they
were now walking. I continued.

"There in that prison I saw things from
God's point of view. The reality of God's love
was just as sure as the cruelty of men.

O love of God, how deep and great,
Far deeper than man's deepest hate.

"Every morning for the next three weeks,
just at the time of roll call, the skylark
appeared. In his sweet song I heard the call
of God to turn my eyes from the cruelty of
men to the ocean of God's love.

"A Jewish doctor, Viktor Frankl, who went
through far more suffering in the concentration camps than I, wrote a book. He ends
the book with these words: 'We have come
to know man is that being who has invented
the gas chambers of Auschwitz; however,
he is also that being who has entered those
gas chambers upright with the Lord's Prayer
or the Shema Yisroel on his lips.'"

Although I was speaking through an interpreter, God's Spirit was working through both of us. I saw joy appearing on the faces of nearly all the men sitting before me.

"Say, men," I said, "do you know Jesus is willing to live in your hearts? He says, 'I stand at the door, and knock: if any man hear my voice, and open the door, I will come in' [Rev. 3:20]. Just think: That same Jesus loves you and will live in your heart and give you joy in the midst of all this mud. He who is willing, raise his hand."

I looked around. All the men, including the guards, had raised their hands. It was unbelievable, but their faces showed a joy that only the Holy Spirit could produce. As I left the prison and returned to the car, all the men accompanied me. The guards did not seem worried or anxious that they swarmed around me. In fact, they did not even prevent them from going out the gate to stand around my car. As I opened the door and got in, the men began to shout and chant something, repeating the same words over and over.

"What do they shout?" I asked my interpreter. She smiled and said, "They shout, 'Old woman, come back. Old woman, come back and tell us more of Jesus.'"

The missionary turned to me as we drove off. "I must confess to you that I thought this place was too dark for the light of the gospel. I had been here once before and was so frightened I said I would never come back. Now, because I had to come interpret for you, I have seen what the Holy Spirit can do. The joy of the Lord is available, even for such a place as this. From now on I shall return every week to tell them about Jesus."

Months later I received a letter from her in which she said, "The fear is gone. The joy remains."

12
God Will Provide

Carry neither purse, nor scrip, nor shoes:
and salute no man by the way. . . . And in
the same house remain, eating and drinking such things as they give: for the la-
borer is worthy of his hire.

Luke 10:4, 7

The people in America seem to feel I
should not hesitate to ask for money for my
ministry, which supports other ministries
such as Bible and book translations in many
parts of the world. However, from the very
beginning of my ministry, I have felt it was
wrong to ask for money—even to ask for
travel expenses. I did not want to be paid
for "services rendered." I simply wanted to
preach the gospel and let the Lord provide
for me.

I learned this lesson very early in my traveling ministry. I was in England and spoke,

among other things, about the former concentration camp where I helped refugees in Germany. My hosts had asked me to do this, saying they knew the American people would like to help support it. After the meeting a dignified, well-dressed lady came up and handed me a check for a rather large sum of money. It was designated to my work in Europe.

"It was so very interesting to hear about your work," she said.

"What did you think about the other things I said?" I asked. "Did you find them important also?"

She gave me a quizzical look. I continued. "Of course it is a very good thing to give money for evangelistic work, but today I also spoke about conversion. God does not want a little bit of your money; He wants all of your heart. He wants to possess you completely. God will not let me take your check." I handed it back to her.

As I was speaking I noticed a haughty, proud look come into her eyes. Very deliberately she pulled her fur cape around her neck. Then, without answering at all, she arrogantly walked away.

When I got back to my room I looked sadly at the other checks that had been given to me. Was God speaking to me? Was it wrong to speak of my own work while at the same time I urged people to be converted or to forgive their enemies? Was it wrong to listen to these Americans who were urging me to receive collections for my ministry? I dropped to my knees in prayer. God knew my needs.

The answer was very clear from the Lord. "From now on you must never again ask for money."

Great joy entered my heart, and I prayed, "Heavenly Father, You know that I need more money than ever before. But from this day on I shall never ask for a penny. No guarantees before I come speak. No travel expenses. Not even a place to stay. I will trust in You, believing that you will never forsake me."

That very day I received two letters. One was from a woman in Switzerland. "Corrie, God told me that from now on you must never again ask for money."

The other letter was from my sister in Holland. She wrote, "When I prayed for your work this morning God made it clear to me that you should not ask anybody for financial support. He will provide everything."

I thought of the night in the concentration camp when my sister Betsie had talked with me about our plans for the future. "Corrie, we should never worry about money," she said. "God is willing to supply our every need."

Many years later, when I faced a severe hardship, I was forced to remember this principle. I felt I had received a direct command from the Lord to go to Russia. The price of our tickets and expenses would be five thousand guilders. However, when I looked at my checkbook I found we had only three thousand guilders in the bank.

"Lord," I prayed, "what must I do? You have commanded me to go to Russia, but I need two thousand more guilders."

I thought that this time God would let me write a few wealthy friends, telling them of my need and asking them to send the money for the plane ticket. Instead I heard a very clear directive from God: "Give away two thousand guilders."

"Oh, no, Lord," I said, as I sat at the table in my apartment in Baarn, Holland. "You did not understand. I did not say I wanted to *give* away two thousand guilders. I said I needed someone to give *me* that amount so I could go to Russia."

However, God seldom listens to my arguments. He waited for me to get through with my objections, and then repeated His original command. This time, though, it was even more specific. I was to give two thousand guilders to a certain mission group that had an immediate need.

I could not understand how anyone's need could be more immediate than my own, but foregoing the "wisdom of the wise," I sat down and wrote a check to this mission group, depleting my bank account down to one thousand guilders.

Later that day I went back down to see if I had received any mail. Among the letters was one from the American publishing company that was to publish *The Hiding Place*. For some months I had been writing back and forth, and only two weeks before I had finally signed the contract. I brought the letter back upstairs and opened it. As I pulled it out, a check fluttered to the floor. It was an advance from the publisher, money I did not think I was going to get until the manuscript was completed. I looked at the figure. It amounted to more than I needed!

God takes His prohibition of asking for money very seriously, just as He means it seriously when He says He will care for and protect us. However, if we seek to raise our own money, then God will let us do it—by ourselves. Many times we will be able to raise great amounts of money by human persuasion or downright perseverance in asking. But we will miss the greater blessing of letting Him supply all our needs according to His own riches. And, as I found out in the case of the guilders needed for the trip to Russia, God has more for us than we would think of asking.

I would much rather be the trusting child of a rich Father than a beggar at the door of worldly men.

Yes, the Lord is not only my Shepherd; He is my Treasurer. He is very wealthy. Sometimes He tries my faith, but when I am obedient, then the money always comes in just in time.

My last stop on my first trip to the Orient was Formosa. It was time for me to move on, so I went to the travel agency in Taipei and gave the girl a list of all the places I needed to go on the next leg of my journey. Hong Kong, Sydney, Auckland, then back to Sydney, on to Cape Town, Tel Aviv, and finally to Amsterdam.

The travel agent wrote it all down and then asked, "What is your final destination?"

"Heaven," I answered simply.

She gave me a puzzled look. "How do you spell that?"

"H-E-A-V-E-N," I spelled out slowly.

After she had written it down she sat looking at the paper. At last she looked up. "Oh, now I understand," she said with a smile. "But I did not mean that."

"But I meant it," I said. "And you do not need to write it down because I already have my ticket."

"You have a ticket to *heaven?*" she asked, astonished. "How did you receive it?"

"About two thousand years ago," I said, noting her genuine interest, "there was One who bought my ticket for me. I only had to accept it from Him. His name is Jesus and He paid my fare when He died on the cross for my sins."

A Chinese clerk, working at the next desk, overheard our conversation and joined in. "What the old woman says is true," he told his companion.

I turned and looked at the Chinese man. "Have you a reservation for heaven?" I asked him.

His face lit up in a smile. "Yes, I have," he said, nodding enthusiastically. "Many years ago, as a child on the mainland, I received Jesus as my Savior. That makes me a child of God with a place reserved in the house of the Father."

"Then you are also my brother," I said, shaking his hand. Turning back to the other clerk I said, "When you do not have a reservation for a seat on the plane and try to get aboard, you face difficulty. But when you do not have a place reserved for you in heaven, and the time comes for you to go, you end up in far greater difficulty. I hope my young brother here will not rest until you have made your reservation in heaven."

The Chinese clerk smiled broadly and nodded. I felt confident he would continue to witness to his fellow worker now that I had opened the door.

I left the travel agency with a good feeling in my heart. Surely God was going to bless this trip since I was already off to such a good start. However, when I arrived in my room and checked my ticket, I found the girl had made a mistake in the route. Instead of sending me from Sydney to Cape Town to Tel Aviv, as I had requested, she had routed me from Sydney to Tel Aviv and then to Cape Town. I went immediately to the phone and called her.

"Why have you changed my schedule?" I asked. "My Chief has told me I must go first to Cape Town and after that to Tel Aviv. However, you have changed the sequence. God is my Master, and I must obey Him."

"Then God has made a mistake," she said, half-seriously. "There is no direct flight from Australia to Africa since there is no island in the Indian Ocean for the plane to land and refuel. That is why you must first go overland to Tel Aviv and then down to Cape Town."

"No," I argued. "I cannot follow that route. I must do what my Chief has told me. I'll just have to pray for an island in the Indian Ocean."

We both laughed and hung up. "Lord," I prayed, "if I have made a mistake in hearing Your direction, please show me. But if I heard correctly, then open the way."

An hour later the girl called back. "Did you really pray for an island in the Indian Ocean?" she asked, incredulous. Before I could answer she continued, "I just received a telegram from Qantas, the Australian airline. They have just begun to use the Cocos Islands for a refueling station, and beginning tomorrow will have a direct flight from Sydney to Cape Town."

I thanked her and hung up. It was good to know that God does not make a mistake in His plans.

However, I am stubborn and never seem to learn my lessons well. Just a few days later, after I got to Sydney and was to make a short trip to Auckland, New Zealand, and back, I ran into another situation that would have been much easier on me had I remembered the lesson I should have learned back in Formosa.

Since I was only going to be in Auckland for four days before returning to Sydney and then on to Cape Town, I packed all my essential items into one suitcase I would carry with me. I left the other suitcases with my friends in Sydney, planning to pick them up when I came back through on my way to Africa. Besides my essential clothing, I also took with me my notebooks, Bibles, literature, and colored slides. My slides, taken in many lands, and the manuscripts of my sermons are all very valuable to me. Although I seldom read from my notes when I speak, I feel more comfortable when I have them before me. I have been accused by my friends of ascending the platform with three Bibles and five notebooks. I think it is hardly that bad, but I have met so many people and jotted down so many ideas that I cannot remember them all. So I try to carry all my notes with me.

As I started to leave the Sydney Airport for the plane, one of the pilots spotted me struggling along with my heavy suitcase. He volunteered to help me. "I have to stop by the radio room first," he said, "but then I shall bring your bag directly to your seat."

I hesitated to turn loose my bag, however, since it was filled with everything I needed for the rest of my journey, not to mention a lifetime of treasures.

"You can trust me," he insisted. "I will arrive at the plane before you and shall leave your bag on your seat."

Reluctantly I parted from my suitcase and watched the pilot as he walked out the door. Several minutes later we boarded the plane, and I rushed to my seat. The bag was not there. Alarmed, I called the stewardess. She assured me that the bag had been stowed with the rest of the luggage and was perfectly safe. I tried to settle back in my seat as we took off, yet I had an uncomfortable feeling inside.

The plane made a stop in Melbourne before heading out over the Tasman Sea for New Zealand. However, when we landed in Melbourne there was a radio message waiting for me. Like Job, the thing that I greatly feared had come upon me. The message was from Sydney. A bag, belonging to Corrie ten Boom, had been left in the radio room.

I was frustrated—and angry. "Can they send it to me?" I asked the ticket agent.

"I'm sorry," he said, shaking his head. "The only way we can get it to you is to send it on our next plane to London. From there it will go to Rome, then Tel Aviv, and then . . ."

"Oohhh," I groaned, waving him quiet. "It will never make it. It contains all my earthly treasures, and it is not even locked. Tell them just to hold it for me in Sydney. I shall pick it up when I return in four days. In the meantime, I have nothing, not even a toothbrush."

I reboarded the plane and slumped in my seat, dejected, angry, and full of resentment. On the flight from Sydney to Melbourne I had witnessed to the stewardess about my faith in Jesus Christ. I had told her that Jesus was Victor in every situation and that

He gave us the power to praise Him in all situations. Now, however, I did not feel very much like praising Him at all.

I looked up, and the stewardess was bending over me. "How wonderful it must be to be a Christian at a time like this," she said. "Most people would be full of anger and resentment."

I forced a smile and said, "Well, it must be for some reason; nothing happens by chance to a child of God."

Even though I was speaking the truth, I was not walking in the victory. Victory would mean that I had no resentment at all, and at that moment I was overflowing with it.

It was late evening as the plane took off from Melbourne. It would be a night flight to Auckland, and I tried to make myself comfortable. Below us was the sea, with only the engines of the plane to hold us in the sky. I dozed, fitfully, and then woke to the smell of smoke in the cabin. The other passengers were awake also, and some of them were up in the aisle, expressing alarm. Moments later the stewardess was at my seat.

"I have good news for you," she said softly. "We are returning to Sydney to pick up your bag."

"Yes, indeed, good news for me," I said. "But tell me, are we not in great danger?"

"No," she said, smiling sweetly and patting my pillow, "we are just having some hydraulic difficulties. There is no danger."

I followed her with my eyes as she went from seat to seat, assuring all the passengers that there was no danger. I leaned across the aisle and asked the man in the next seat what was meant by hydraulic difficulties.

"It is bad news," he said. "All the mechanisms on the plane depend on the hydraulic system. The wing flaps, the steering mechanism, even the landing gear is controlled by the hydraulic system. Since the fire is in that system, it means the pilot could lose control of the plane at any moment."

I sat back in my seat and tried to look out the window. Below was the blackness of the Tasman Sea. The smell of smoke was still very strong in the cabin. I was not afraid of death. Often, as a prisoner I had faced it. I remembered the words of Dwight Moody, "The valley of the shadow of death holds no darkness for the child of God. There must be light, else there could be no shadow. Jesus is the Light. He has overcome death."

Yet I knew I was not right with God because I was not right with man. I still held resentment in my heart and knew it had to be removed before I could even pray. I leaned back in my seat and opened my heart to God, confessing my resentment over my suitcase (which was worthless to me now that we might crash into the sea) and asking Him to forgive me. Then I prayed, "Lord, perhaps I shall see You very soon. I thank You that all my sins have been cleansed by the blood of the Lamb."

I opened my eyes and looked around me. "What of the others?" I wondered. "Are they prepared to die?" No one was sleeping. All were sitting alert in their seats. I noticed a woman busy applying lipstick and shook my head. How silly to feel you have to enter eternity with painted lips! I had the strongest urge to stand up and say to the people around me, "Friends, perhaps in a few minutes we shall all enter eternity. Do you know where you are going? Are you prepared to appear before God? There is still time to accept the Lord Jesus. . . ."

But I could say nothing. I wanted to stand and urge them to come to Jesus, but I could not. I was ashamed of the gospel of our Lord

Jesus Christ. And not only that, but there was fear in my heart.

We finally made a landing—a safe landing—in Sydney. My bag was returned to me, but there was no joy in my heart. Even though I had been forgiven of my resentment, I had been ashamed of the Lord Jesus. I found a seat in the lounge and sat with my head bowed, my eyes closed.

"Dear Lord, I am not fit to be a missionary. I stood before the very portals of eternity and warned no one."

I opened one of my notebooks and read on the margin of a page a note I had made many years before. "To travel through the desert with others, to suffer thirst, to find a spring, to drink of it, and not tell the others that they may be spared is exactly the same as enjoying Christ and not telling others about Him."

"Oh, Lord," I moaned. "Send me back home. Let me repair watches. I am not worthy to be Your evangelist."

As I sat there, like Jeremiah, trying to resign my commission, I saw a man coming toward me. He introduced himself as a Jewish doctor who had been aboard my flight. "I watched you all through those hours on the plane when our lives were

great danger," he said. "You were neither afraid nor anxious. What is your
secret?"

A ray of light. Perhaps God was giving me
another chance. "I am a Christian," I said
joyfully. "I know the Messiah, Jesus, the
Son of God. He died on the cross for my
sins, and yours also. If our burning plane
had fallen into the sea, I had the assurance
of going to heaven."

We sat and talked for a long time before
he excused himself. But a few minutes later
he was back again. "I must hear more about
this Jesus who gives you such peace," he
said.

Four times he got up and left, and yet
he kept coming back. Each time his
request was the same. "Tell me more about
Jesus."

I told him how Jesus gives us authority
over Satan, how Jesus has promised us
mansions in heaven, how He gives to all
who believe the power to become the sons
of God.

The Jewish doctor drank it all in and
finally left saying I had given him much to
think about. I sat back in my chair. The
Lord, my treasure, had given me just
enough of His wealth that I might share it

with one of His hungry children. I had been found worthy to evangelize after all. And in the process I had learned another valuable lesson in the school of life. When I am weak, then am I strong (2 Cor. 12:10).

13
A Place to Be

⊰⊱

He shall feed his flock like a shepherd: he shall gather the lambs with his arm, and carry them in his bosom.

Isaiah 40:11

Everyone needs a place to be. One of the great joys of heaven is that it is a place, a prepared place. I am thankful that there I will have a special house that is reserved just for me.

When I was born, Father and Mother were living on the Korte Prinsegracht, a typical Amsterdam canal. I was born prematurely, and my skin was blue. Uncle Hendrik, Tante Jans's husband, looked at me and exclaimed, "I hope the Lord will quickly take this poor little creature to His home in heaven."

But my parents and Tante Anna did not agree with him. They surrounded me with love and care. However, since there were no incubators in those early days, I cried much from the cold. Tante Anna, knowing I missed the warmth of the special place under my mother's heart from which I had come, rolled me in her apron and tied me against her stomach. There I was warm and quiet.

Many years later I was in a primitive house in Africa. The bathtub was made from an old oil drum that had been sawed in half. Missionaries lived there, and they invited me in to eat with them. Walking into the kitchen, I saw an African woman with the white missionary child strapped tightly to her back.

"Hey, how nice she has your baby on her back," I said to the missionary mother.

The white mother smiled and said, "The baby was so fearful this morning. All she would do was cry. When the African cook came to the house she took one look at the baby and said, 'Ah, Missee, give me the baby. I will keep her quiet.' So she strapped her on her back, and the baby has slept all morning while the cook has been busy around the kitchen."

I could understand that feeling of having a place—of belonging. I was often afraid as a small child. Sleeping beside my sister Nollie, who was a year and a half older than me, I begged to be able to hold her hand at night. She refused, and instead gave me the hem of her nightgown. By and by she did not even like me holding on to that, but told me to hold on to the hem of my doll's nightgown.

Then, when I was five years old, the Lord Jesus became a great reality to me. My mother told me how He loved little children and was even willing to live in my heart if I asked Him in. I did, and a feeling of peace and security took the place of the fear I had so often felt. From then on I could go to sleep at night and not be afraid.

As a child I prayed a nursery rhyme:

> Ik ga slapen, ik ben moe;
> 'k Sluit mijn oogjes beiden toe.
> Heere, houd ook deze nacht
> Weder over mij de wacht.
>
> (I'm going to sleep, I am tired;
> I close both my little eyes.
> Lord, watch over me again
> The whole night long.)

In all these years that I have been a "tramp for the Lord," I have often been afraid. But in those moments I have always reached up and touched the hem of Jesus' garment. He has never failed to wrap me close to Him. Yet I still long for that time when I shall have a mansion in heaven.

Here on earth, at the age of seventy-seven, for the first time I found a place of my own—a beautiful apartment in Baarn, Holland. Even though I am seldom there (for I intend to keep on traveling until I die in harness), it is still a place to hang up my pictures on the walls and put the few sticks of furniture that I have saved from my days in the Beje. Yet, even with this "home" here on earth, I still long most of all for my heavenly mansion.

When I was a child, Tante Jans composed a children's song. I remember two lines:

'k zou zoo graag eens komen, Heiland,
In dat heerlijk Vaderhuis.

(I should just like to come, Savior,
In that beautiful Father-house.)

As a child, however, I always got the words mixed up when I sang the song. Instead of singing, "to come," I would sing "to peek." The older people laughed at my mistake, but I thought they were very stupid. With all my heart I meant what I was singing. As a little child I did not want to go to heaven; I just wanted to peek for a moment. Now, though, that my days have grown long, I no longer sing as I did as a child. Now my greatest desire is to come for all eternity into the beautiful Father-house.

14
Obedience

⚜

Behold, to obey is better than sacrifice.
1 Samuel 15:22

Obedience is easy when you know you are being guided by a God who never makes mistakes.

Conny and I were in Africa, and one day during my quiet time I began to feel that God was telling me it was time to leave Africa.

"Lord, where do You want us to go?" I asked.

"Argentina," came the answer deep in my heart.

Argentina? I had never been to Argentina. I could not speak a word of Spanish. In those days air travel was sometimes poor in Africa, and to fly across the Atlantic Ocean to Buenos Aires would be a trying ordeal. Yet as I sat before the Lord, the word *Argentina* became even stronger.

"Yes, but . . . ," I started to answer Him. Then I remembered that obedience never says, "Yes, but . . ." Rather it always says, "Yes, Lord!" Some months before, a missionary by the name of Breson had written me, asking if I would be willing to speak in his church if I ever came to Argentina. I did not know Breson very well, so I had not thought much about the invitation. Now, however, with God speaking to me so strongly, I sat down and wrote Mr. Breson a letter, asking if he could meet us in Buenos Aires and arrange some meetings for me to speak.

We waited almost a month, but there was no answer. "Are you sure it is the Lord's guidance for us to go to Argentina?" Conny asked. "Perhaps this man Breson no longer lives in Buenos Aires. What if we go and there is no one to meet us? Then what will we do?"

I reached out and touched Conny's hand. "Yes, I know it is God's will for us to go to Argentina. Some years ago God spoke to me and told me to go to Japan. I had no money. I knew no one in Japan. I could not speak the language. Yet I knew God had led me. I finally saved up enough money to fly to Tokyo and stepped off the plane on a dark, rainy night in that strange land and said, 'Lord, here I am. Now what?' I remembered that David Morken was there with Youth for Christ. He found me a room, and because of my obedience God opened many doors of ministry. I was alone on that trip, but this time I have you. No, I know we should go to Argentina."

The plane flight was much longer than we expected. Connections were very bad, and we had to spend one whole day in a hot, dirty African airport awaiting a connecting flight that would take us on to West Africa for our flight across the ocean. It was almost midnight when we caught our last plane, and I could sense Conny's anxiety. However, I was sure of God's guidance.

We finally arrived in the busy Buenos Aires airport. I looked out across the hundreds of hurrying people, hoping I might see Mr. Breson's face. There was no one.

Conny and I struggled with our luggage, and at the ticket desk a man asked us, in broken English, if he could send our bags to our address.

"I do not yet know my address," I said. Conny looked worried. I knew her thoughts. *Do you know for sure it is Argentina where*

God would have you work? We were both exhausted from all-night plane rides that had been added to the ordeal of waiting in all those African airports. We carried our suitcases to the curb, and I sat down. "See if you can find a taxi," I said to Conny. "Perhaps there is a YMCA hotel nearby."

But there were no taxis. The air was heavy and hot. I finally asked a man, "Do you know where there is a YMCA hotel?"

The man gave me a blank stare and moved on. I could speak Dutch, German, and English, but none of those languages helped me here. We sat on our suitcases, looking at the streams of traffic passing down the street.

"Aunty, Tante Corrie, are you sure that God's guidance brought us to Argentina?"

I looked at Conny. Her face was dirty and creased with lines of exhaustion. I, too, was hot and tired and unhappy. But I was also sure of God's leadership. "Yes," I said wearily. "I am sure."

"I don't like Argentine mosquitoes," Conny said, slapping her arm. "They are just as cruel as African mosquitoes."

We looked at each other and laughed. Here we were in a strange country with a strange language. Holland was far, far away, yet we were laughing.

Then I heard a man's voice from the other side of the street shouting, "Bent u Corrie ten Boom?" ("Are you Corrie ten Boom?")

My name. My language. What joy! I could barely see the man on the far side of the streaming traffic, but he was waving his arms as he shouted.

"Ja, dat ben ik," I shouted back.

The man had to wait for the traffic to thin before he could run across the street. Finally, after dodging cars, he stepped onto the curb. "I am Reverend Mees," he said, extending his hand. "I did not think you would be here but felt I should come and check just the same."

"Do you know Mr. Breson?" I asked. "I had hoped he would meet us."

"Did you not receive Breson's letter?" Reverend Mees asked. There was a look of alarm on his face.

"No, we heard nothing from him."

Reverend Mees put his hand on his forehead and looked toward the sky. "Oh, this is too bad. He wrote you a letter telling you not to come. He could not arrange any meetings and is now on a mission tour in the jungle. He will not be back for two months."

I sat back down on my suitcases, feeling even more tired than before.

"Do you know if there is a YMCA hotel in the city?" I asked, as if this would solve all our problems.

Reverend Mees smiled, "No, I do not know of a YMCA hotel, but a dear friend of mine, a woman doctor, knew about the possibility of your coming. She asked me to bring you to her hospital, and from there she will take you to her home. She has a spare bedroom and a little apartment where you can be very comfortable."

Dr. Gwen Shepherd received us graciously at the hospital. I knew at once that she was one of God's precious children and therefore my sister also. She took us to her car, and for the first time I experienced what traffic in Buenos Aires is like. Traveling in the jungles of Africa was nothing to the streets of Buenos Aires. There were no traffic lights. At every intersection the cars came racing together, four abreast. Those who arrived first were the first ones through. I never saw an accident (but perhaps that was because I kept my eyes closed most of the time!). However, after bouncing and speeding down the streets, we finally reached her home, where she provided wonderful hospitality. That night she invited a number of youth group leaders to her home, and I had an opportunity to share with them. The next day another invitation came for me to speak, and before long I was even busier than I had been any other place on the earth. Dr. Shepherd had a wonderful gift of administration and arranged much ministry for me. It was indeed God's guidance for me to come to Argentina. What a joy I would have missed had I disobeyed.

Perhaps the greatest joy of the entire trip, however, happened one afternoon in Dr. Shepherd's hospital. I was allowed into a ward where polio patients were being treated. One room was filled with people in iron lungs. I had never seen the wheezing, gasping iron lungs before, and they scared me.

"Do you wish to talk to some of the patients?" a kind nurse asked me.

I looked around and said, "No, I think I am unable to talk. I just want to go off somewhere and cry."

Always when I say that I am not able, I get the same answer from the Lord. He says,

"I know you can't. I have known it already a long time. I am glad now you know it for yourself, for now you can let Me do it."

"All right, Lord, You do it," I said. And surely the Lord did. I went from one iron lung to another, telling the men and women about the Lord Jesus Christ who breathes into each one of us His Holy Spirit.

Then I came to a man on a rocking bed. He had a different kind of polio, and instead of being in a lung, he was on a bed that rocked up and down. When his head was up he could breathe in. When his head went down he breathed out. The nurse told me he was Jewish.

"Ah," I said, "I am happy to meet one of God's chosen people. My old father, my dear sister, and some others in my family died in concentration camps because we loved the Jews. I, too, was in prison for helping Jews. But tell me, do you know the Jew, Jesus, as your personal Messiah?"

The bed rocked up and down, and he shook his head, for he could not speak. He had a long tube in his nose and could only move one hand slightly to write tiny notes.

"Then is it all right if I tell you about Him?" I asked.

He picked up his stubby pencil and scribbled on a small notebook on the side of his moving bed. "I am ready to listen."

I stayed beside that rocking bed and told my Jewish friend about the great Messiah, the one whom the prophet called "Wonderful, Counsellor, The mighty God, The everlasting Father, The Prince of Peace" (Isa. 9:6).

I finished speaking and from my bag took a small embroidery. On one side was stitched a beautiful crown. The other side was quite mixed up. "When I see you on this bed," I said, "not speaking, not moving, I think of this embroidery. I held up the back side of the embroidery. "Your life is like this. See how dark it is. See how the threads are knotted and tangled, mixed up. But when you turn it around, then you can see that God is actually weaving a crown for your life. God has a plan for your life, and He is working it out in beauty."

He picked up his pencil and wrote again, "Thanks God I am already seeing the beautiful side."

What a miracle. He understood God did not want him to become a Gentile. Rather he would become a completed Jew. I prayed and thanked the Lord with him. Then it was time to go, and Dr. Shepherd once again took me to her beautiful home.

The next day I returned to the polio ward and asked the nurse if I could speak with my Jewish friend.

"I am sorry," she said, "but your Jewish friend on the rocking bed is no longer with us. Just five minutes after you left he beckoned me to come to his side. There was a wonderful light shining in his eyes, and he wrote on a little paper, 'For the first time I prayed in Jesus' name.' Then he closed his eyes and died."

"Then I am not sorry," I answered. "I am glad. I know he has his own crown of life. Praise God."

God has a divine pattern for each of His children. Although the threads may seem knotted—as they did when we were sitting outside the airport in Buenos Aires—on the other side is a crown.

15

The Real Corrie ten Boom

For my thoughts are not your thoughts,
neither are your ways my ways, saith the
LORD.

Isaiah 55:8

While in Havana, Cuba, I was asked to
speak at a youth rally in the Salvation Army
hall. Of course this was before the communist takeover, so there was still freedom
to talk openly about the Lord Jesus Christ.

It was a hot June night, and the hall
was small and stifling. The meeting was
scheduled to begin at seven o'clock, but
more and more groups continued to arrive
from other parts of the city, so no one
seemed to be in a hurry to start. As in
most Latin American countries, everything was "Mañana, mañana," even the
church services.

Finally, I was seated on the platform between two men with huge drums. One of them, an old Negro with white hair, tried to show his love for the Lord by vigorously beating one of the drums. The sound was almost unbearable. The captain had a very sharp voice and led the singing by shouting, waving his hands, and pounding on the top of the pulpit. The young Cubans sang loudly, with much clapping of hands and stomping of feet. By nine o'clock I was already worn out, and all I had done was sit and listen. There was a terrific ringing in my ears, and my head was splitting with a headache from the crashing sounds of the drums. Finally, though, I was called on to speak, and the hall grew silent. I was grateful for the few moments of peace.

After I spoke, the captain introduced a missionary who had brought his slides. The lights were turned out, and we all sat in the miserable heat while the missionary began his long slide presentation. Like many missionaries, he had been called upon to do some medical work in the field, so many of his slides dealt with that. He had photograph after photograph of drugs and medicines that had been given him by various doctors. "This particular bottle of pills was given to me by Dr. Smith," he droned on. Then flipping to his next slide he said, "And this box of medicines was sent to me by Dr. Jones."

The young people in the hall were not the least bit interested in seeing those boxes, bottles, and jars. The noise grew louder and louder and finally reached such volume that the missionary had to shout to make himself heard. It was ten-thirty when he finally finished his presentation and the lights came back on.

Now the room was filled with flying bugs, moths, insects, and some kind of huge flying beetle that buzzed around the exposed lightbulbs and then dropped to the floor or in people's laps. The young people were climbing over the backs of the benches, babies were asleep on the floor, and everyone was sweating profusely. I did not think I could stand much more.

Then the captain came to the front again and began to preach. A flying insect went in my ear, and another was caught in my hair. I looked for some way to escape, but I was boxed in by the huge drums on either side. Finally the captain gave an invitation for people to come forward and be saved.

Surely no one is in a mood to do anything but go home, I said to myself. Then I thought, *I hope nobody comes to the front. I long to get out of here and go to bed.*

Yet, to my surprise, people began getting up from their seats and coming to the front. They were kneeling around the altar rail. Twenty of them. I saw tears in the eyes of some of the young Cubans and listened as the captain spoke with great persuasion, his voice full of love.

A startling realization swept over me. I was selfish. I had hoped nobody would be saved because of my own weariness. My sleep was more important than the salvation of sinners. Oh, what a terrible egotist I was. Suddenly my bed was no longer important. I was willing to stay up all night if God was working. But what could I do with my guilty feeling for having been so selfish?

Then I began to praise God, for I had learned what to do with my sin. I confessed it to the heavenly Father in Jesus' name and I claimed His forgiveness. With joy I was able to get up and pray with the twenty young people who had made the important decision to commit their lives to Jesus

Christ. It was eleven-thirty when the meeting finally came to a close.

The next morning, Sunday, I spoke in a beautiful church that was filled with the most prominent people in Havana. As I entered the imposing building I was given a copy of the parish magazine, which had been handed to all the other people. In it I read an introductory article about my ministry. It said, "Corrie ten Boom is a most popular world evangelist. . . . She is tireless and completely selfless in her absolute dedication to the cause of the gospel."

Oh, Lord, I thought, *if only these people knew who the real Corrie ten Boom is, they would not have come out this morning to hear me.*

"Tell them," the Lord answered immediately.

By that time I was seated on the platform looking out over the sea of faces before me. "But Lord, if I tell them, they will reject me."

"Can I bless a lie?" the Lord asked me in my heart. "I can only bless the truth. You do want My blessing, don't you?"

Then it was time for me to speak. The gracious minister gave a flowery introduction and asked me to come to the pulpit.

Before I could give my message, however, I knew what I had to do.

Reading first from the parish paper, I then said, "Sometimes I get a headache from the heat of the halo that people put around my head. Would you like to know what Corrie ten Boom is really like?" Then I told them what happened the evening before—how my own sleep had been more important in my eyes than the salvation of young people. "That," I said, "was Corrie ten Boom. What egotism! What selfishness! But the joy is that Corrie ten Boom knew what to do with her sins. When I confessed them to the Father, Jesus Christ washed them in His blood. They are now cast into the deepest sea, and a sign is put up that says 'NO FISHING ALLOWED.' Corrie ten Boom is lazy, selfish, and filled with ego. But Jesus in Corrie ten Boom is just the opposite of all these things."

Then I waited. Surely now that the congregation knew what kind of person I was, they would no longer want to hear me. Instead, I sensed them all leaning forward, eager to hear what I might say. Instead of rejecting me, they accepted me. Instead of a beautiful church with prominent members and a popular world evangelist, we were all sinners who knew that Jesus died to lift us out of the vicious circle of ego into the light of His love.

God had blessed the truth!

16

Checkpoint Charlie

━━━━━━━ ∽∾∽ ━━━━━━━

For the Son of man is come to seek and
to save that which was lost.

Luke 19:10

Conny and I stood in line with other
people outside Checkpoint Charlie, the
gate for foreigners into East Berlin. Many
of those in line were Dutch, and I saw they
were being passed without difficulty. Everything seemed routine: Hand your passport
to a guard, walk down the line, and receive
your passport back with a stamp that
allowed you to spend the one day in East
Berlin. I hoped it would be as easy for us
when it was our turn to be checked.

Finally we were in front of the window.
The guard looked at our passports, looked
in a book, and then turned and said something to another man behind him.

"Is there a problem?" I asked the man.

He turned and gave me a stern look. "Come with me," he said, motioning for Conny and me to follow him into a small room to one side. We were questioned and they opened my handbag. There they found two books. One of them was one of my books, which had been published in East Germany. The other was a copy of Billy Graham's *Peace with God,* which had also been translated into German.

The officer picked up Billy Graham's book and shouted, "What? A book by that machine gun of God!"

I laughed. "I like the name you give to Billy Graham. I will tell him what you called him the next time I see him—'God's Machine Gun.' However, if I am not allowed to take the books with me into East Berlin, I will just give them to you, and you can let us go on."

"Oh, no," he said sternly, "it is not that easy. First we have to write up your deposition."

He searched me to see if I had hidden more books before he began his inquisition. I did not like his rough, crude manner and told him so.

"I really feel as if I am in the hands of the Gestapo again," I said.

"No," he said, abashed, "I am no Gestapo."

"You surely have the same manners," I said bluntly.

He softened his approach but still kept us in the inquisition room for more than three hours. A woman typist copied everything I said and wrote it into a "protocol." I learned that my name was on the blacklist for East Germany, which was the reason I was being so thoroughly questioned. However, I was primarily upset because we had only a few hours to visit the Christians in East Berlin, and our time was being wasted here in the guard station.

"Lord," I complained silently, "why are You keeping us here when we need to be about Your business in East Berlin?"

Then slowly it came through my stubborn Dutch mind that God had us in the guard office for a purpose. He not only loved the Christians in East Berlin, but He loved these communist guards also—the officer and the uniformed typist. What a sad mistake we sometimes make when we think that God only cares about Christians. Although God desires that all people become Christians, He does not love one group more than another. In fact, it was for the world that God gave His only begotten Son, and Jesus Himself said "I am not come to call the righteous, but sinners to repentance" (Matt. 9:13). I remembered the words of Jesus when He said, "Ye shall be brought before governors and kings for my sake, for a testimony against them and the Gentiles. But when they deliver you up, take no thought how or what ye shall speak: for it shall be given you in that same hour what ye shall speak" (Matt. 10:18–19).

Suddenly my attitude toward the officer changed. Instead of an enemy, I saw him as one of those for whom Christ died. Now I answered every question testifying of my faith in Jesus. It became almost a kind of game.

I asked the officer, "Do you ever read the Bible?"

"No, I am a Marxist," he said stubbornly.

"The Bible was written especially for Marxists," I said. "It says that God so greatly loved the Marxists that He gave His only begotten Son so that any Marxist who believes in Him shall not perish, but have eternal life."

Both the officer and the woman typist were listening with serious faces. I went ahead to talk about the two problems of the human race—sin and death—and stated that the Bible gives us the answer to these problems by telling us about Jesus.

"Why don't you keep my books and read them?" I said. "I will be glad to autograph my book for you, and the book by Billy Graham will answer many of your questions."

"Must I read it?" the officer said.

"It will not do you any harm," I laughed.

The officer laughed too, but then, catching himself, became very serious and businesslike again.

"I see, Fraulein, that you are carrying chocolate with you? What is your reason?"

"I am taking it for the minister's children in East Berlin. Don't you bring chocolate with you when you visit a family with children?"

"No, I take flowers with me," he said seriously.

"Flowers are nice for parents, but children prefer chocolate. Besides, I often preach about chocolate."

"What crazy people we have here today," the officer said. "You carry books by a man who talks like a machine gun, and then you tell me you preach about chocolate. Tell me, what kind of sermon do you get from a chocolate bar, old woman?"

"Several years ago," I answered, "I spoke to a group of Germans who prided themselves on being intellectuals. They would not receive me because they felt that they were more profound in their theology than I. So, my last time with them I brought them all some Dutch chocolate. Since chocolate was very rare after the war, they eagerly accepted my gift. Later, when I stood to speak to them, I told them, 'No one has said anything to me about the chocolate.'

"They disagreed, saying that they had all thanked me for it.

"'I did not mean that,' I said. 'I mean no one questioned me about it. No one asked whether it had been manufactured in Holland or Germany, what quantities it contained of cocoa, sugar, milk, or vitamins. Instead of analyzing it, you just ate it.'

"Then I picked up my Bible and said, 'It is the same with this Book. If you try to analyze it as a book of science or even a book of theology, you cannot be nourished by it. Like chocolate, it is to be eaten and enjoyed, not picked apart bit by bit.'"

I stopped talking and noticed, once again, that the officer and the typist were deeply interested in what I was saying. Then the officer straightened up, cleared his throat, and said to the typist, "Please type Fraulein ten Boom's protocol, and we will let her pass." With that he stood and left the room, never looking back.

I sat quietly while the typist finished typing her report. Moments later the officer was back. He pulled the paper from the typewriter and read aloud. "When in prison Corrie ten Boom received from God the commission to bring the gospel of Jesus Christ over the whole world. Her church has taught her to bring chocolate when she visits families with children."

The officer nodded and excused himself, saying he had to read it to his superior officer before I could be approved for entrance into East Berlin. While he was gone I talked with the typist, urging her to accept Jesus as her Lord. She listened intently, reading through some of the pages in my book. However, when the officer returned she straightened up and returned to her typewriter.

I handed Billy Graham's book to the officer. "Sir, be sure and take this book by 'God's Machine Gun' home with you. It will change your life."

He tried to look severe, but behind his eyes I could sense both hunger and thirst. Without saying a word he took the book and slipped it into his briefcase. He handed my book to the typist and motioned her to put it in her purse. Then he opened the door and pointed in the direction of East Berlin. "I am sorry to have detained you so long, Fraulein," he said. "But what we have been doing here is even more important than your visit to your friends."

I shook his hand, and Conny and I entered the communist city, wondering if the officer actually realized the truth of his last statement. What we had to do in East Berlin was important, but even more important was bringing the Good News of Jesus to those who walk in darkness.

17
Facing Death

———— ❧ ————

If you are reproached for being Christ's followers, that is a cause for joy, for you can be sure that God's Spirit of glory is resting upon you.

1 Peter 4:14 PHILLIPS

Watchman Nee once said, "When my feet were whipped my hands suffered pain." Christians all over the world are bound together as the body of Christ. Many Americans, in particular, do not realize it, but a part of that body is suffering the most terrible persecution and tribulation in the history of mankind. If we are members of that same body—and we are—then we must suffer with them, pray for them, and where it is possible, help them.

I remember hearing of a missionary—a single woman—who turned her back on all her possessions at home and went to

177

China. "Are you not afraid?" a friend asked as she prepared to board the ship.

"I am afraid of only one thing," she said, "that I should become a grain of wheat not willing to die."

How much more like Christ that is than the churches who gather at Thanksgiving to sing: "Let thy congregation escape tribulation!"

Several years ago I was in Africa in a little country where an enemy had taken over the government. There was great oppression against the Christians by the new government. The first night I was there some of the native Christians were commanded to come to the police station to be registered. When they arrived they were arrested, and during the night they were secretly executed. The next day the same thing happened with other Christians. The third day it was the same. By that time the entire district realized that the Christians were being systematically murdered. It was the intent of the new government to eradicate them all—men, women, and children—much as Hitler tried to eradicate all the Jews.

I was to speak in a little church on Sunday morning. The people came, but I could see fear and tension written on every face. All during the service they looked at each other, their eyes asking the same questions: "Will this one I am sitting beside be the next one to be killed? Will I be the next one?"

I looked out on that congregation of black and white faces. The room was hot and stuffy. Moths and other insects came through the screenless windows and swirled around the naked lightbulbs hanging over the bare, wooden benches upon which the natives sat. They were all looking at me, expecting, hoping that I could bring them a word from God for this tragic hour.

I opened my Bible and read 1 Peter 4:12–14.

> And now, dear friends of mine. I beg you not to be unduly alarmed at the fiery ordeals which come to test your faith, as though this were some abnormal experience. You should be glad, because it means that you are sharing in Christ's sufferings. One day, when he shows himself in full splendour, you will be filled with the most tremendous joy. If you are reproached for being Christ's followers, that is a cause for joy, for you can be sure that God's Spirit of glory is resting upon you (PHILLIPS).

I closed the Book and began to talk, simply, as an aunt would talk to her nieces and nephews. "When I was a little girl," I said, "I went to my father and said, 'Daddy, I am afraid that I will never be strong enough to be a martyr for Jesus Christ.'

"'Tell me,' Father said, 'when you take a train trip from Haarlem to Amsterdam, when do I give you the money for the ticket? Three weeks before?'

"'No, Daddy, you give me the money for the ticket just before we get on the train.'

"'That is right,' my father said, 'and so it is with God's strength. Our wise Father in heaven knows when you are going to need things too. Today you do not need the strength to be a martyr; but as soon as you are called upon for the honor of facing death for Jesus, He will supply the strength you need—just in time.'"

I looked out at my African friends. Many of them had already lost loved ones to the firing squad or the headsman's ax. I knew that others would surely die that week. They were listening intently.

"I took great comfort in my father's advice," I said. "Later I had to suffer for Jesus in a concentration camp. He indeed gave me all the courage and power I needed."

My African friends were nodding seriously. They, too, believed God would supply all their needs, even the power to face death bravely.

"Tell us more, Tante Corrie," one grizzled old black man said. It was as though they were storing up all the truth they could so they could draw on it in the day of trial.

I told them of an incident that had taken place in the concentration camp at Ravensbruck. "A group of my fellow prisoners had approached me, asking me to tell them some Bible stories. In the concentration camp the guards called the Bible "das Lügenbuch"—the book of lies. Cruel death punishment had been promised for any prisoner who was found possessing a Bible or talking about the Lord. However, I went to my little cot, found my Bible, and returned to the group of prisoners.

"Suddenly I was aware of a figure behind me. One of the prisoners formed the words with her lips, 'Hide your Bible. It's Lony.' I knew Lony well. She was one of the most cruel of all the aufseherinen—the women guards. However, I knew that I had to obey God who had guided me so clearly to bring a Bible message to the prisoners that morning. Lony remained motionless behind me while I finished my teaching, and then I said, 'Let's now sing a hymn of praise.'

"I could see the worried, anxious looks on the faces of the prisoners. Before it had been only me speaking. Now they, too, were going to have to use their mouths to sing. But I felt God wanted us to be bold, even in the face of the enemy. So—we sang.

"When the hymn was finished I heard a voice behind me. 'Another song like that one,' she said. It was Lony. She had enjoyed the singing and wanted to hear more. The prisoners took heart, and we sang again—and again. Afterwards I went to her and spoke to her about the Lord Jesus Christ. Strangely, her behavior began to change until, in a crude sort of way, she became a friend."

I finished my story and stood silently while the words took their effect on my African friends. "Let me tell you what I learned from that experience," I told them. "I knew that every word I said could mean death. Yet never before had I felt such peace and joy in my heart as while I was giving the Bible message in the presence of mine enemy. God gave me the grace and power I needed—the money for the train ticket arrived just the moment I was to step on the train."

The faces before me broke into broad grins. Gone were the wrinkles of fear and anxiety. Once again their eyes were flashing with joy and their hearts were filled with peace. I closed the service by reading a poem of Amy Carmichael.

> We follow a scarred Captain,
> Should we not have scars?
> Under His faultless orders
> We follow to the wars.
> Lest we forget, Lord, when we meet,
> Show us Thy hands and feet.

The meeting was over, and the Africans stood to leave. Then softly, in the back of the room, someone began singing an old gospel song.

> There's a land that is fairer than day,
> And by faith we can see it afar.
> For the Father waits over the way,
> To prepare us a dwelling place there.
> In the sweet by and by, we shall meet on
>   that beautiful shore,
> In the sweet by and by, we shall meet on
>   that beautiful shore.

I don't know how many were killed that week, but someone told me that more than half of those who had attended that service met a martyr's death—and thus received a martyr's crown. But I know that God's Spirit of glory had been resting upon them (1 Peter 4:14).

18

Saved by a Newborn Infant

———— ✦ ————

. . . and a little child shall lead them.
Isaiah 11:6

One of my greatest privileges is visiting
with missionaries all over the world. Those
of us who live in the comfort and security
of our homes cannot begin to imagine what
the life of a missionary is like. Many of
them have no fresh water and only simple
food. They constantly face the threat of
sickness and infection. Some live in primitive places where their very lives are in danger. Much to my sadness, yet to the glory
of God, the list is growing longer each day
of men and women who are literally laying
down their lives for Jesus' sake on the mission field. These men and women stand on
the front lines, often in lonesome places,
but knowing that their Master, who has

placed them there, will also stand with them.

Once in a primitive spot in Africa I visited a missionary couple. Their small home was located in a delightful spot that gave a beautiful view of lakes and mountains. They had very little of this world's goods but were rich in God's grace and had been given a homesite that many wealthy people would pay thousands of dollars to have as their own. Crowded into this tiny shack were six children, the youngest just a few months old.

"Come with me," the missionary wife said as she picked up the baby and walked outside. "I want to tell you a story."

We sat on a bench overlooking an awesome scene of grandeur. Spreading before us was a mighty view of the mountains, covered with deep jungle and spotted with lakes and waterfalls.

"To have many little children can be a burden for a missionary," she said. "There comes a time when you have to send them to the homeland because there are no good schools here. But while they are small you try to enjoy them."

She paused and looked down at the sweet baby asleep in her arms. Her voice was tense with emotion as she continued. "But when I learned I was going to have another baby, I rebelled against God. We already had five small children, and it did not seem fair that we should have to bear another. My health was not good, and I looked upon having another child with great sorrow and unhappiness."

Tears were streaming down her face as she talked. "Was it not enough to have five children? Oh, how my heart cried out at God, and there were times when I wished He would take the baby from me.

"The time for the birth was here. I was very weak and there were no doctors nearby. We had no one to leave the other children with, so my husband put us all in the car and drove us into a town where there was a good mission hospital. There we stayed until the baby was born."

The tiny child stirred in her arms, stretched her little arms, and yawned. How precious she looked! The mother's voice grew soft. "When we returned to our home with the new baby we learned that in the short days we had been gone the dreaded Mau Mau had come. They had murdered every white person in the entire area. Had we been home we would have all been killed."

She hugged the little baby to her breast, tears flowing down her face. "This little darling was sent by God to save all our lives. Never again shall I rebel against His ways for our lives."

19
Miracles Every Day

My times are in thy hand.
Psalm 31:15

It was my first time in India, and I was to speak at a conference of missionaries in Vellore. However, when my plane arrived in Bangkok I was told the next plane to Vellore did not leave for three days.

"But this means I will have to miss the first three days of the conference," I said.

"We are sorry, but there is no way," the man at the ticket counter told me. However, the airlines did make arrangements for me to stay at a hotel until the next plane left.

Arriving at the hotel, I asked the kindly Indian man who was in charge of my arrangements, "Is there no possibility that I can catch another plane to Vellore?"

"The airlines are making every effort," he assured me.

"Then we must pray that God will help them," I said.

"Do you *profess* to be a Christian?" he said with a startled look on his face.

"Yes, I do," I answered. "I am a *professor* of Jesus Christ. And what about you?"

He hung his head. "I have been, but I am what you call a lost sheep."

"Hallelujah!" I said. "Then you are just the one sheep for whom the Shepherd left the ninety-nine to find."

We talked a long time in the lobby of the hotel. Finally I asked the man if he would be willing to come back to Jesus. "Oh, yes," he said. "For I believe God kept you here just for this reason."

We prayed together in the hotel, and then I said to him, "Now that God has used me for this miracle, will you pray with me for another miracle—that I might arrive in Vellore in time for the conference?"

The man leaped to his feet. "While you pray I must run an errand. I'll be back shortly." With that he was out the door, leaving me sitting among my suitcases.

Half an hour later he was back. "Make quickly ready for the plane," he said. "I think God has performed your miracle. We have discovered another plane going by a different route to Vellore."

"Did you arrange that?" I asked.

"I did," he smiled as he hoisted my bags to his back. "But don't thank me. I must thank you for bringing me back to the Shepherd."

We rushed madly to the airport, and I found the plane was supposed to have left long before. However, they were holding it just for me. Panting, I climbed the steps to the plane.

"Ah, Professor," the stewardess said as she closed the door behind me, "we were afraid we would have to leave you."

"Professor?" I asked. "What's this?"

"Oh," she smiled sweetly. "We know all about you. Our hotel agent told us you are an important *professor* from Holland who has to give significant speeches in Vellore. That is why we have held the plane on the ground until you arrived."

I took my seat near a window. Outside, the once-lost sheep was grinning and waving. I waved back. *Surely,* I thought, *God not only had a special reason for keeping me in Bangkok, but He must have an equally important reason for wanting me in Vellore.*

I was right. My first talk to the missionary conference in Vellore was the next morning. I spoke on the reality of God's promises in the Bible. After the service I slipped away from the crowd and strolled in a beautiful garden near the conference center. It was alive with color: Green and red crotons mixed their rich colors with the dark orange of the copper plants and the rainbow hues of the flowering shrubs. *How wonderful,* I thought, *to be in the center of God's will.*

"Excuse me," a shy voice said from behind.

I turned and recognized one of the English missionary ladies. Her body seemed weak. She hesitated to speak but at last said, "Do you really believe in God's promises?"

"Yes, I do," I said.

"Do you believe the Lord still heals the sick?"

"Of course," I answered. I motioned for her to sit with me on a stone bench near a flowering hibiscus. First I read to her from the Bible where Jesus said we would lay hands on the sick and they would be healed (Mark 16:18–20). Then I told her of a recent experience in Indonesia.

"I was staying in the house of a dear Chinese pastor and his wife," I said. "Since we were so busy, the wife had no time to cook, so a member of their church, another Chinese lady, came every day in a ricksha to fix me a good Chinese meal.

"One morning I was sitting in the house and looked out the window. I saw this dear woman stumbling up the pathway. Her head was bleeding and her dress badly torn. I rushed out to meet her and helped her into the house. Her ricksha had collided with another ricksha, and she had been badly injured, hitting her head against a metal part of the primitive vehicle. Since Chinese people were not popular in Indonesia at that time, no doctor would come to see her. Instead, they just brought her to the house and let her out.

"I knew her condition was serious and also knew that the doctor would not come to the Chinese pastor's house either. Therefore, I just laid my hands on her and prayed in Jesus' name that she be healed. She was restored instantly."

The missionary lady was listening intently. "Must you know a person's type of sickness before you pray for them?" she asked.

"No, I'm not a doctor. I do not heal. It is the Lord who heals."

"I am very ill," she said quietly. "Will you lay hands on me and pray?"

"I will," I said. She slipped off the bench and knelt in that beautiful garden while I put my hands on her head and prayed for her to be healed in the name of Jesus Christ.

She rose slowly to her feet. "Now I will tell you my sickness," she said. "I have leprosy."

I had been in leper colonies, and suddenly I was filled with a great fear. *Oh,* I thought, *this is far too difficult for the Lord. I wish now she had told me ahead of time so I would have known not to pray for her.*

Then I felt ashamed and asked forgiveness for my small faith and unbelief. After all, it was not I who said He would heal the sick—but He who had said it.

Some years passed, and I lost the name and address of the lady missionary, although many times I remembered that time in the garden and continued to pray for her. Five years later I was back in India, staying with friends of the Pocket Testament League. One afternoon there was a knock at my hotel door. "Do you remember me?" a beautiful lady asked.

I looked at her and said, "I have seen you before, but I do not remember who you are."

"Do you remember a time in Vellore when you laid hands on a leper patient and prayed in Jesus' name that she be healed?"

"Oh, yes," I exclaimed. "I surely remember you. But you are a different person."

She smiled. "The Lord wonderfully healed me. The doctors say I am absolutely healed from leprosy."

"Thank You, Lord," I said aloud. "Your name be glorified! You are always ready to meet our needs, even when our faith is small."

20

God's Word, the Sword— God's Perfect Weapon

The grass withereth, the flower fadeth: but the word of our God shall stand for ever.

Isaiah 40:8

It had been a hectic half year. I had flown from New Zealand to Korea, where I had spoken in more than two hundred and fifty meetings in a three-month period. I then returned to Hamilton, New Zealand, for a brief visit before continuing to India.

In New Zealand I had stayed with a family that was memorizing verses of Scripture, using the Navigators' system. I was thrilled to find so many of the new converts in New Zealand studying this course. Since I knew less Scripture in English than I did in Dutch, I, too, determined to start memorizing Scripture. I knew that once the Word of God was hidden in my heart it would be with me always.

Leaving New Zealand full of new zeal, I arrived in the state of Kerala, India, where I was to speak in a series of small conferences far back in the jungle. My Indian companion met me at the airport and took me to a small place on the river where a canoe was waiting. We climbed in and started our slow trip down the peaceful river. Slowly our little craft glided over the shallow waters. Except for the rhythmic sound of the paddle and the occasional murmur of the soft wind in the trees, there was nothing to be heard.

My Indian companion was the leader of a home group. Twice a year the home groups in the area come together in a conference to study the Bible, pray, and plead for revival. I was to speak three times a day in several such conferences, which would be held in a pandal—a wide roof protecting the congregation from the hot sun. There are no walls so the breeze can pass through, and the people sit on the grassy floor.

As the coolie paddled our canoe down the river, my Indian companion told me of the great longing in his heart to win souls for Jesus Christ.

"Yet I am not successful," he said. "I always give my testimony, but I am not able to persuade people to make a decision."

"Do you use the sword of the Spirit, the Word of God?" I asked him.

"I fear I am not very adept at handling that sword," he admitted. "Just at the critical moment I am never able to find a text that fits the situation."

"Yes, I can understand that," I confessed. "I sometimes have the same problem. However, I am now memorizing certain verses of Scripture, which I call my 'first-aid course.' These are emergency Scriptures I apply to the wound until I can look up the rest of the Scriptures, which will bring further healing."

My Indian companion brightened, and then I told him of a recent experience in Canada where I had learned that it was not me, but the Word of God coming through me, that won people to Christ anyway.

"I had just finished speaking to a class of university students," I told him as the canoe glided down the quiet river. "I was relaxing on the veranda of one of the dormitories when a very educated woman, who had attended my lectures, sat down with me.

"'What you just told the students was very interesting,' she said. 'But you are too narrow. I am an expert on world religions. I have traveled to many countries and have had long discussions with the leaders of many religious groups. I have discussed the road of life through time and eternity with Muslims, Brahmins, Shintoists, and many others. All of them know God, even though they do not believe in Jesus Christ. I am sorry to have to disagree with your talk this afternoon, but you put too much emphasis on Jesus Christ and do not allow that other religions are just as good as Christianity.'

"I was embarrassed," I told my Indian companion. "Then I remembered something a friend had once told me. 'You are not called to convince anyone,' he had said. 'You are simply called to be an open channel for the Spirit of God to flow through. You can never be anything else, even though you may think so at times. Follow the pathway of obedience, let the Word of God do its own work, and you will be used by God far beyond your own powers.'

"Therefore, I said to the woman, 'Your argument is not with me, but with the Bible. It is not I who say these things, it is the Word of God. Jesus said that no man can come to the Father but by Him (John 14:6). If you wish to dispute someone, dispute Him.'"

I looked at my Indian friend. His eyes were fixed on my face as he drank in what I was saying. I continued with the story. "Some time later a reception was held in Ottawa, Canada, for all who wished to meet Prince Bernhard of the Netherlands. It was a pleasure to see so many Hollanders together. The prince looked tired, but he was cheerful and kind to us all. I met many old acquaintances and then, suddenly, I was face-to-face with this same lady who had so adamantly disputed me some time before.

"'I am glad to see you,' she said genuinely. 'I have never been able to forget what you said when you spoke at our university when you quoted Jesus, "No man cometh unto the Father but by me." I have tried to argue with that from every angle but am unable to get away from the fact that Jesus said it. I can argue with you, but I am having a difficult time arguing with Him.'

"'How wonderful,' I told her. 'Now you are listening to the voice of God. Keep listening. He has much more to say to you.'

"'Yes,' she said. 'I believe He does.'

"We parted, and I have not seen her since, but I know the sword of the Spirit is still doing its work in her life."

I turned and looked at my Indian friend. He was nodding his head in understanding. "If we diligently read the Bible, the Holy Spirit will give us the right words and Scripture references," I said. "If we depend on Him, we are like the branches of these vines along the river that bear fruit. However, if the branches are broken off, then no fruit will appear."

By this time the forest had thinned out on either side of the river. We could see narrow paths that permitted the people to tread single file through the trees. It was almost dark, and I saw, coming down the paths, files of Indian people carrying torches of lighted palm leaves in their hands. The white clothes they wore gave the scene a strange, ethereal appearance, as though they were pilgrims walking to heaven. Many had gathered already in the pandal, away in the distance, and were singing a gospel song in a monotone, chanting it over and over as the white-robed pilgrims made their way to the meeting place.

After the meeting that night I lay in my little thatched hut praising God for the power of the Word of God, which had not only drawn these people together but which had won them to the Lord Jesus Christ. In my mind I listed five reasons why I believe the Bible is inspired:

1. It says so. "Holy men of God spake as they were moved by the Holy Ghost" (2 Peter 1:21).
2. The effect it has upon all who believe and follow it.
3. Though some of it was written more than two thousand years before Jesus arrived on earth, all the writers agree.
4. The authors do not offer any excuses for their own faults or sins.
5. The writers record some of the most harrowing scenes that affected them greatly, yet they never express one word of emotion. The Holy Spirit wanted the facts recorded and not their feelings about the facts.

Many persons make the mistake of thinking they can measure the certainty of their salvation by their feelings. It is the Word of God that is their foundation, and therefore, it is essential for the new convert in Christ to have a practical knowledge of the Bible.

More than anyone else, it is the new convert who will come under the fire of the enemy. He needs the knowledge of the sword of the Spirit. As the Lord Jesus used this sword to overcome the evil one in His temptation experiences, so we must learn to defend ourselves against every sort of attack.

21

Where Is Heaven?

But lay up for yourselves treasures in heaven. . . . For where your treasure is, there will your heart be also.

Matthew 6:20–21

Happiness is not dependent on happenings but on relationship in the happenings. My father taught me this when I was just a child. He often told me of the early days of his marriage. He had opened a small jewelry store in a narrow house in the heart of the Jewish section of Amsterdam. Poor Mother! She had dreamed of a home with a little garden. She loved beautiful things and spacious views. "I love to see the sky," she often said. Instead, she found herself on a narrow street in an old house—the kind with only a single room on each story—with worn-out furniture that they had inherited from Grandmother. Yet they were both happy, not because of the circumstances but because of the relationships in the circumstances.

There in Amsterdam in that narrow street in the ghetto they met many wonderful Jewish people. They were allowed to participate in their sabbaths and in their feasts. They studied the Old Testament together and, on occasion, even the New Testament.

I have remembered many times the lessons I learned from my father about happiness and happenings. But never was it so clear as when I was in Korea, many, many years later.

I had been in the Orient for three months, spending much of the time in Korea. While there I spoke in many meetings in schools, orphanages, children's homes, and churches. One day, after I had spoken in a university, a theology student came to me. I had never seen such gloom on the face of a man who said he wanted to be a minister of the risen Christ.

"Why is it that you are so full of unhappiness?" I asked.

"I have lost my way," he said sadly. "When I first became a Christian my pastor taught me the Bible is true. In those days I had great happiness. But now I am studying the famous scholar Rudolph Bultmann, who says our Bible is full of myths and fables. I have lost my way and no longer know where heaven is."

I was angry. It did not seem right that the simple boys of Korea had to struggle through this horrible theology. They studied many hours at the universities, going to school twice as long as students in America, yet because of what they studied, they often lost their faith. I answered his question about heaven by telling him what I had just seen and heard the day before while driving through the countryside.

There I saw the poorest shack I had ever seen. It was a tiny lean-to, made from materials collected from the garbage heap— pieces of cardboard, tin cans that had been smashed flat, old boards. . . . As we drove past, though, I heard the beautiful voice of a woman singing. Seldom, even in the concert halls of Europe, had I heard such a sweet voice. We stopped the car and listened, for it was like the song of a skylark.

I said to the missionary who was traveling with me, "Do you know that song?"

"Yes," she said, "it says, 'Where Jesus is, 'tis heaven there.'"

Oh, how my heart leaped for joy as I heard this beautiful song coming from such a poor place. It is one thing to hear such a song in a dignified church, or pouring through the speakers of an expensive stereo set. But when one hears it coming from the poorest shack in the midst of such poverty, then it means something else.

I looked at the young theological student before me. "Jesus said, 'The kingdom of God is within you' (Luke 17:21). Bultmann is wrong, and Jesus is right. Heaven is not a myth or fairy story: Heaven is a prepared place for prepared people. Theology in the hands of the Holy Spirit is a beautiful science. But in the hands of unbelievers it is death. If you want to find where heaven is, get out of your stuffy classroom and go back out into the countryside. Listen to the simple faith of those who read only the Bible and trust only in God, not in material things. What do they care if some theologian says that heaven is a fable? They have found Jesus, and where Jesus is, 'tis heaven there."

22
When You Are Tempted to Quit

And how shall they preach, except they be sent?

Romans 10:15

The enemy tries to make everything work out for the worst. Usually it is not the big problems that depress me but the multitude of inconveniences that stack up like small rocks to form an immovable mountain. A series of such small incidents almost caused me to resign my commission from the Lord.

In my journeyings I often have to cross borders between countries. Knowing that smuggling is sin, I do not do it. My first irritation came through an encounter with a customs official.

"Do you have anything to declare?" he asked rudely.

"Yes," I replied. "Nylon stockings."

I had put them on top of my luggage to show him, for I knew that at that time it was necessary to pay duty on such items.

"There are four pair here," he said. "You told me one pair."

"No, I did not!" I answered.

But he did not believe me. For the next hour he searched my baggage. He tried all the little boxes to see if they had false bottoms. He squeezed my toothpaste tube to see if it contained diamonds. He checked my shoes for false heels that might contain drugs. He felt the hem of my dresses to see if I had sewn pearls into them. He almost pulled the lining out of my suitcases. Of course he found nothing at all and finally allowed me to pass—after paying the duty on the four pair of stockings. I was both offended and unhappy.

Later I understood why this incident had made me so upset. I had not surrendered my self-righteousness. I was so sure of my own honesty that I suffered from the consequence of wounded pride. It is easier to surrender one's sins than one's virtues!

Unaware of the reason for my depression, I then discovered that I had missed my plane connections due to the delay in the customs office. I was forced to sleep on a couch in the ladies' room at the airport. However, I am a good sleeper and enjoyed a sound slumber. When I awoke, the amazed cleaning woman (who was sweeping the floor around my couch) said with admiration, "How wonderful to be able to sleep so soundly with so much noise going on around you."

Eventually the plane on which I was traveling flew into a storm, making me feel airsick. Then the night following my arrival there was an earthquake. I hate earthquakes, for they remind me of the bombs that fell during the war.

Then the kind people who should have arranged my meetings greeted my arrival with, "We thought you needed a holiday and rest, so we have not organized anything." Sometimes this is God's plan, but more often it is just a sign of people's laziness to make preparations. So I did not appreciate the fact they had not arranged any meetings for me.

The final inconvenience—the one that caused me almost to give up completely—had to do with my room. My hosts put me in a small room that had no writing table. Ordinarily this would not have disturbed me, for I am used to writing on my knee, but on top of everything else that had happened, I crumpled like the camel loaded with straw. I blew up.

The reason was not hard to find. Self-pity had come into my heart. Self-pity is a nasty sin, and the devil uses it and always starts his talks with "Poor Corrie."

This time he began by saying, "Why must you always live out of your suitcases? Stay at home, and then you won't have trouble with customs officials, passports, luggage, plane connections, and other things. Every night you will be able to sleep in the same comfortable bed, and there are no earthquakes in Holland. After all, you are no longer young. You've lived like a tramp for many, many years. It is time to hang up your harness and retire into a nice green pasture. Let someone else do the work. You've earned your reward."

By this time I was nodding. "Yes, yes, Satan, you are right." So having listened to his advice I wrote a friend in Holland who managed an international guest house where at the time I had a room kept for me with my own few pieces of furniture.

"I believe the time has now come for me to work in Holland," I wrote. "I am tired of all this traveling, and I cannot stand having wheels beneath me any longer. Will you arrange to have a desk—a big one—put in front of the window in my room, and an easy chair—a very easy one—on the right. . . ." In my fantasy I had worked out a lovely dream of heaven here on earth, and me in the middle of it!

That afternoon I posted the letter and then came back to my room to look over my calendar. I jotted down all the names of people I would have to write, canceling my appointments. Everyone would understand. Had not many said, "My, you must be tired at your age!"?

Everything would have gone all right (or perhaps I should be truthful and say "all wrong") had I not picked up my Bible. This old, black Bible has been my guidebook in times of light and in times of darkness. I began to read, asking, "Lord, what would You have me do?"

I opened to the Book of Romans, chapter 10. "How shall they call on Him in whom they have not believed? and how shall they believe in Him of whom they have not heard? and how shall they hear without a preacher? . . . As it is written, How beautiful are the feet of them that preach the gospel of peace, and bring glad tidings of good things" (vv. 14–15).

I remembered the words of a paratrooper instructor. He said that when he had his men in the plane and they were over the battlefield, he gave four commands:

> First, "Attention!" *Lift up your eyes* (John 4:35).
>
> Second, "Stand in the door!" *Look on the fields; for they are white already to harvest* (John 4:35).
>
> Third, "Hook up!" *Be ye filled with the Holy Spirit* (John 20:22).
>
> Fourth, "Follow me!" *I will make you . . . fishers of men* (Mark 1:17).

I sat for a long time—thinking. It is not our task to give God instructions. We are simply to report for duty.

I laid my Bible on the bed and picked up pen and paper. Balancing the pad clumsily on my knee, I wrote my friend in Holland. "Forget about that last letter," I wrote. "I am not coming home to Holland. I refuse to spend the rest of my life in a pasture when there are so many fields to harvest. I hope to die in harness."

23

I'll Go Where You Want Me to Go, Dear Lord ... but Not up Ten Flights of Stairs

━━━━━ ⟆⟆⟆⟆⟆ ━━━━━

And so, dear brothers, I plead with you to give your bodies to God. Let them be a living sacrifice, holy—the kind he can accept. When you think of what he has done for you, is this too much to ask?

Romans 12:1 TLB

I had spoken that Sunday morning in a church in Copenhagen, Denmark, urging the people to present their bodies as living sacrifices to the Lord. I had said even though I was an old woman that I wanted to give myself completely to Jesus and do whatever He wanted me to do, go wherever He wanted me to go—even if it meant dying.

214

After the church time, two young nurses approached me. They invited me up to their apartment to have a cup of coffee. I was very tired. At almost eighty years of age I found that standing on my feet for long periods of time was beginning to be exhausting. The cup of coffee sounded good, so I accepted their invitation.

But I was not prepared for the walk up to their apartment. Many of the houses in Copenhagen are old, high houses with no elevators. The nurses lived on the tenth floor of such a house and we had to walk up the steps.

"O Lord," I complained as I looked up at the high building, "I do not think I can make it." But the nurses wanted me to come up so badly that I consented to try.

By the time we reached the fifth floor my heart was pounding wildly, and my legs were so tired I thought they could not take another step. In the corridor of the fifth floor I saw a chair and pleaded with the Lord, "Lord, let me stay here a time while the nurses go on up the stairs. My heart is so unhappy."

The nurses waited patiently as I collapsed into the chair, resting. "Why, O Lord, must

I have this stair climbing after this busy day of speaking?"

Then I heard God's voice, even louder than my pounding heart. "Because a great blessing is waiting you, a work that will give joy to the angels."

I looked up at the steps, towering above me and almost disappearing into the clouds. Perhaps I am leaving this earth to go to heaven, I thought. Surely that will give joy to the angels. I tried to count the steps. It seemed there were at least one hundred more to climb. However, if God said that the work would give joy to the angels, then I had to go. I rose from my chair and once again started trudging up the long flights of stairs, one nurse in front of me, the other behind me.

We finally reached the apartment on the tenth floor, and on entering I found a room with a simple lunch already prepared on the table. Serving the lunch were the mother and father of one of the girls.

I knew there was only a short time and also knew that a blessing of some kind was waiting us. So, without many introductions, I started asking immediate questions.

"Tell me," I asked the nurse's mother, "is it long ago that you found Jesus as your Savior?"

"I have never met Him," she said, surprised at my question.

"Are you willing to come to Him? He loves you. I have traveled in more than sixty countries and have never found anyone who said they were sorry they had given their hearts to Jesus. You will not be sorry either."

Then I opened my Bible and pointed out the verses about salvation. She listened intently. Then I asked them, "Shall we talk now with the Lord?"

I prayed, then the two nurses prayed, and finally the mother folded her hands and said, "Lord, Jesus, I know already much about You. I have read much in the Bible, but now I pray You to come into my heart. I need cleansing and salvation. I know that You died at the cross for the sins of the whole world and also for my sins. Please, Lord, come into my heart and make me a child of God. Amen."

I looked up and saw tears of joy on the face of the young nurse. She and her friend had prayed so much for her parents, and now the answer was given. I turned and looked at the father, who had sat quietly through all this.

"What about you?" I asked him.

"I have never made such a decision for Jesus Christ either," he said seriously. "But I have listened to all you have told my wife, and now I know the way. I, too, would like to pray that Jesus will save me."

He bowed his head, and from his lips poured a joyful but very sincere prayer as he gave his life to Jesus Christ. Suddenly the room was filled with great rejoicing, and I realized the angels had come down and were standing around, singing praises unto God.

"Thank You, Lord," I prayed as I walked back down the long steps, "for making me walk up all these steps. And next time, Lord, help Corrie ten Boom listen to her own sermon about being willing to go anywhere You tell me to go—even up ten flights of stairs."

24

To All the World—Beginning with One

For the earth shall be filled with the knowledge of the glory of the LORD, as the waters cover the sea.

Habakkuk 2:14

To give a tract to someone in Russia is always a risk. If the person you are talking to is alone, then there is a little more freedom. However, if a third person is present, both are always uneasy—each afraid the other might turn him over to the secret police.

Conny and I had been in a Leningrad hotel for about a week when one morning, on our way down to breakfast, I handed the cleaning woman a tract. It was a simple tract, written in Russian, called "The Way of Salvation." It used only Scripture verses with no commentary.

She glanced at it and then glanced at the other woman cleaning the hall. She pushed the tract back to me, motioning with her hand as if to say, "That is nothing for me."

I felt sorry for her. The answer no hurts when you want to help someone. Conny and I continued on down the hall to the elevator, heading to the dining room for breakfast. We were the only ones on the elevator, and on the way down I cast this latest burden on the Lord. "Father, I can't reach this woman. Do bring her in contact with someone who can tell her the gospel in her own language. Lord, I claim her soul for eternity."

I was shocked by the boldness of my prayer. Never in all my life had I prayed that way. Was it proper? Could I actually claim the soul of someone else? In a kind of postscript I asked, "Lord, was this wrong or right? May I say such a prayer?"

Then, even before I could receive His answer, I heard myself praying a prayer that frightened me even more. "Lord Jesus, I claim all of Russia for You."

The elevator stopped, and Conny and I walked through the huge corridor to the dining room. I was bewildered. My cheeks were red and hot. "Lord, was this right? Was this too much? But no, Lord, Your Word says, 'The earth is the LORD'S . . . the world, and they that dwell therein' (Ps. 24:1). Surely that means Russia too."

Still confused, we entered the dining room. It was crowded, and the waiter came up and said, "There are only two of you. You cannot eat breakfast here since all the tables are reserved for big groups."

We looked around. A Japanese man had heard the waiter and motioned for us to come to his table, where there were two empty places. "Just come," he said. "We will act as if you belong to our group."

But the waiter saw what had happened and refused to wait on us. I felt unhappy and unwelcome. Turning to Conny, I said, "At dinner yesterday I took some white buns up to my room in my purse. They are still there, and we have some Nescafé. Why should we sit here and wait? Let us go to our room."

It was quiet and peaceful upstairs. Our breakfast tasted good, although it was only dry buns and Nescafé without any cream.

Suddenly there was a knock at the door. Conny opened it, and there stood the cleaning woman, the one who had refused the tract. Her hair was pulled back in a tight bun, and I noticed her heavy leather shoes squeaked when she walked. She closed the door behind herself. From her lips poured a stream of Russian words, not a single one of which we could understand. Then she pointed a finger at my brown bag.

"Conny, she wants to have a tract," I almost shouted.

Conny gave her one, but it was not the same one as we had given her the first time. She looked at it, shook her head, and pointed again at the bag.

"Conny, she wants to have 'The Way of Salvation.'"

I got up, rummaged through my bag, and found the original tract. I smiled and handed it to her. She looked at it, and her face burst into the great light of joy. Smiling and nodding in appreciation, she backed out of the room.

I was beaming with joy too, for God had answered my prayer. I had not claimed too much after all. The first prayer had already been answered, and now I was sure that the second prayer, the one the Holy Spirit had prayed through me without my first thinking up the words, was going to be given a yes answer too.

Conny, who was as excited as I, took her Bible and read, "For the earth shall be filled with the knowledge of the glory of the LORD, as the waters cover the sea" (Hab. 2:14). What a promise—the whole of Russia under the waters of God's glory!

There was another knock at the door. There stood our cleaning woman again. She entered and put a long loaf of fresh white bread on the table. Her face was still wreathed in smiles as she refused payment for it. It was her thank offering to God.

I had never had such a good breakfast in all my life.

25
Leaving My First Love

━━━━━━━━━━ ❧ ━━━━━━━━━━

But I have this against you, that you have
left your first love.

Revelation 2:4 NASB

After twenty years of wandering the
world as a tramp for the Lord, I was ill. At
seventy-three years of age my body had
grown tired. A doctor examined me and
said, "Miss ten Boom, if you continue at
the same pace, you cannot possibly work
much longer. However, if you will take a
furlough for a year, then perhaps you can
work for another few years."

I consulted my Lord. He said very clearly
that this advice of the doctor was in His
plan. It came to mind that I could live during that "sabbath year" in Lweza, a beautiful house in Uganda, East Africa. Several
years before I had contributed to this place
so it could be used as a house of rest for

missionaries and other workers in God's kingdom. Now the bread I had cast upon the waters was coming back to me. I made my plans, and soon Conny and I were safely ensconced in Africa.

Lweza was a paradise. Built on a hill in the midst of a garden that must surely resemble Eden, it looked southward out over Lake Victoria. The climate was ideal. Since there were many universities, churches, prisons, and groups in Kampala, the nearby town, I was able to speak in two or three meetings a week. So, while my body rested, my spirit remained active.

The greatest pleasure was to sleep every night in the same bed. During the last twenty years I had slept in more than a thousand different beds, always living out of my suitcases. This year I rested. I put my clothes in a drawer, hung my dresses in a closet, and best of all, each night I laid my head on the same pillow.

In November the sabbath year ended. Conny and I took a map of the world and stretched it out across my bed, following our usual method of making plans for the next year—the same method I had used for the last twenty years. First we listened to God's plan, then we signed it. This was unlike the method I once used when I made my own plans and then asked God to sign them. Our desire was to be "planned" by the Holy Spirit.

God's plan looked very good to Conny. There would be three months in different countries in Africa, two months in America, and then three months in Eastern Europe behind the Iron Curtain. "Thank You, Jesus," Conny said. But inside I was not so thankful. Conny was young, much younger than I. She loved to travel, but I was getting old and was still rather tired.

After Conny left I turned to the Lord. "I prefer to stay here," I said stubbornly. "There is so much to do in Kampala and Entebbe, the two nearest cities. I will work for You. I am willing to have meetings every day, counseling, writing books; but please, let me sleep every night in the same bed. Everyone can understand that at my age I should take it a bit easier."

I got up rejoicing. This new plan of mine made me really happy.

Then Conny called. An African minister from faraway Ruanda had come to visit. He started immediately to welcome me: "We are so glad that you are willing to come to Ruanda again. Five years ago you helped us so marvelously when you told what the Lord had been to you in your great need. You said that it was not your faith that helped you through three prisons, for your faith was weak and often wavering. You said it was the Lord Himself who carried you through and that you knew from experience that Jesus' light is stronger than the deepest darkness."

The African brother continued, "Five years ago, however, that was just theory to us. None of us had ever been prisoners. Now there has been a civil war in our country. Many of us have been in prison. I, myself, was in prison for two years. It was then that I remembered everything you had said. I did not have the faith of Corrie ten Boom. I did not even have faith for myself, but I knew to look to the same Jesus who gave you faith. He has also given it to me, and that is why we are so happy that you are coming again to Ruanda."

But I was not happy at all. His words were different from what I wanted to hear. I knew that in such situations I could change the subject by asking a question. Perhaps this would make God stop reminding me of His plans and leave me alone so I could follow mine.

"How is the church in Ruanda?" I asked. "What kind of message do they need now?"

Without hesitating one moment, the brother opened his Bible and began to read:

> Write this to the angel of the Church in Ephesus: These words are spoken by the one who holds the seven stars safe in his right hand, and who walks among the seven golden lampstands. I know what you have done; I know how hard you have worked and what you have endured. . . . I know your powers of endurance—how you have suffered for the sake of my name and have not grown weary. But I hold this against you, that you [have lost your first love]. Remember then how far you have fallen.
>
> Revelation 2:1–5 PHILLIPS

This arrow penetrated my heart. Not only Ruanda needed that message, but also Corrie ten Boom. I had lost my first love. Twenty years before I had come out of a concentration camp, starved, weak, but in my heart there was a burning love, a love for the Lord who had carried me through so faithfully, a love for the people around me, a burning desire to tell them that Jesus is a reality, that He lives, that He is Victor.

I knew it from experience. For this reason I went to Germany and lived in the midst of the ruins. For this reason I had tramped the world for twenty years. I wanted everyone to know that, no matter how deep we fall, the everlasting arms are always under us to carry us out.

And now? Now I was interested in my bed. I had lost my first love. I asked my African brother to continue to read.

> Repent and live as you lived at first. Otherwise, if your heart remains unchanged, I shall come to you and remove your lampstand from its place.
>
> Revelation 2:5

Suddenly joy came in my heart. I could bring my sin, my cold heart, my weary body to Him who is faithful and just. I did it. I confessed my sins and asked for forgiveness. And the same thing happened that always happens when I bring my sin to God in the name of Jesus: He forgave me. Jesus cleansed my heart with His blood and refilled me with the Holy Spirit.

As God's love—the fruit of the Holy Spirit—was poured out into my heart, I set

out again on my journeys—a tramp for the
Lord.

What a great joy it was to experience the
love of God, who gave me rivers of living
water for the thirsty world of Africa, America, and Eastern Europe. Of course, it might
be the will of God that some old people
retire from their work. In great thankfulness to the Lord, they can then enjoy their
pensions. But for me, the way of obedience
was to travel on, even more so than ever
before.

Jesus warned us in Matthew 24:12 that
the love of most men waxes cold because
iniquity abounds. It is very easy to belong
to the "most men." But the gate of repentance is always open wide. Hallelujah!

26
Walking in the Light

But if we walk in the light, as he is in the light, we have fellowship one with another, and the blood of Jesus Christ his Son cleanseth us from all sin.

1 John 1:7

Our last few weeks in Lweza proved to be the most fruitful of our entire time spent there, for it was in these weeks that I learned another valuable lesson—the lesson of walking in the light.

One afternoon Conny and I were sitting in the garden looking at the monkeys jumping from one tree to another. The trees and shrubs were a mass of color and sound, causing my heart to be filled with the glory of God's grace.

Yet Conny was discouraged. She had started a girls' club in the YWCA in Kampala and had spent many hours' work with it. However, the girls were not interested. I was concerned about her discouragement, feeling it went far deeper than the problems she was having with her class.

I started to ask her about it when we were interrupted by a man walking toward our hill. Conny squinted her eyes in the sun and then shouted, "It is William Nagenda!"

What a joy it was to meet that dear African saint again. I never met an African with whom I could laugh so much and yet learn so much at the same time.

After we exchanged greetings, William said, "When I saw you sitting here together a question came to my mind, 'Do they walk in the light together?'"

We answered almost simultaneously, "Oh, yes, we do walk in the light together. We are a team."

Just at that moment a boy from the house called that there was a telephone message for me. I excused myself while Conny and William remained behind to talk.

Conny was sitting in a cane and wicker chair, while William squatted on his haunches beside the path, his brown knees poking up beside his face.

"I have something to confess to you," Conny said to William.

"And what is that?" he answered gently.

"Your question gripped my heart. I must tell you that I do not really walk in the light with Tante Corrie."

William's face broke into a wide grin, and his eyes began to sparkle. "So, that is why God had me ask that strange question."

Conny was serious. "Tante Corrie is so much more mature than I," she continued. "She has walked with Jesus for so many years. She has suffered much for Him in many ways. Thus when I see things in her life that are not right, I hesitate to speak them out to her."

"Oh," William said, startled. "That is not right. The Lord wants you to be very honest with Tante Corrie. That is one reason He has put you with her. Since she is walking in the light, then when you also walk in the light, you will help shed light for her path as well as yours."

That night, after we had gone to our room together, Conny sat on the side of the bed and said, "Tante Corrie, this is very difficult for me to say, but I now realize I must walk in the light."

I turned and looked at her. Her face was drawn and solemn. One by one she began listing the things in my life that bothered her—the things I did that she believed did not glorify God. It was not easy for me to hear the things I had done wrong—things that had caused a shadow to come in Conny's heart. But how wonderful it was that Conny was being completely honest with me. I apologized for the things she had listed and then thanked her for bringing them into the light. "Let us always walk in the light together," I said seriously.

But it was still hard for Conny. She was much younger than I and felt she was still learning. Even though I wanted her to continue to correct me, she found it very difficult. The final breakthrough came after we left Africa and flew to Brazil.

We had been in Rio de Janeiro, one of the most beautiful cities of the world, for a few weeks. As we prepared to leave—to fly south to Buenos Aires—we discovered our suitcases were overweight. The kind people in Rio had given us so many presents we were more than twenty kilograms overweight. It was going to cost us a great deal of extra money to go on to Argentina.

I unpacked my luggage and made three piles: one to send to Holland by sea, one to give away to the poor in Rio, and the smallest one to go back in my suitcase to carry on to our next destination. Finishing my repacking I hurried next door into Conny's room and unpacked her suitcase also. I went through the same procedure, sorting her belongings into three heaps and then repacking only her necessary items. I was in too much of a hurry to notice that Conny said nothing.

A week later, after a beautiful time in Buenos Aires, we were walking along a lonely stretch of beach near our cabin. I was enjoying the beautiful view over a quiet bay when Conny began to talk. Her voice was strained. "I promised God I would walk in the light," she said, "and that means that I must get something settled with you. When you repacked my suitcase and decided what things to send to Holland and what to leave with me, I was not happy about it."

How stupid and tactless I had been to rush in and interfere with Conny's life! I reached out and took her hand. "How thoughtless I have been," I said. "Forgive me for not leaving it up to you."

"I do forgive you," Conny said. Like myself, she had learned not to play lightly with sin, but to hear another's apology and then, instead of passing it off, to forgive it.

We walked on for a long time in silence and then Conny spoke again.

"Are you unhappy, Tante Corrie? You are so quiet."

Now it was my time to walk in the light. "There is something hindering me," I said. "Why did you not tell me immediately that you were disturbed? That way it could have been settled on the spot, and you would not have had to carry this darkness for all these days. From now on let us both 'speak the truth in love' and never let the sun go down on our misunderstandings."

It was a good lesson. From then until Conny married in 1967 and went to live with her husband, we walked all over the world—always trying to walk in the light.

27

Secure in Jesus

I say therefore to the unmarried and widows, It is good for them if they abide even as I.

1 Corinthians 7:8

It is Satan who tries, in every way, to spoil the peace and joy that God's servants have in their work.

Ellen, my new traveling companion, had gone with me to a lonely mission field in Mexico. Our hostess was a lady missionary, unmarried, in her forties. One evening while we were alone in her little adobe, she confessed her bitterness and resentment over being unmarried.

"Why have I been denied the love of a husband, children, and a home? Why is it that the only men who ever paid any attention to me were married to someone else?" Long into the night she poured out the poison of her frustration. At last she asked me, "Why did you never marry?"

"Because," I said, "the Lord had other plans for me than married life."

"Did you ever fall in love and lose someone, as I have?" she asked bitterly.

"Yes," I said sadly. "I know the pain of a broken heart."

"But you were strong, weren't you," she said in biting tones. "You were willing to let God have His way in your life?"

"Oh, no, not at first," I said. "I had to fight a battle over it. I was twenty-three. I loved a boy and believed he loved me. But I had no money, and he married a rich girl. After they were married he brought her to me and, putting her hand in mine, said, 'I hope you two will be friends.' I wanted to scream. She looked so sweet, so secure and content in his love.

"But I did have Jesus, and eventually I went to Him and prayed, 'Lord Jesus, You know that I belong to You 100 percent. My sex life is yours also. I don't know what plans You have for my life, but Lord, whatever it may be, use me to realize Your victory in every detail. I believe You can take away all my frustrations and feelings of unhappi-

ness. I surrender anew my whole life to
You.'"

I looked across the little table at the bitter woman in front of me. Her face was fur-
rowed, her eyes hard with resentment. I
sensed she had been trying to run away
from her frustrations. Perhaps that was
even the reason she was on the mission
field. Sadly, there are some of God's children who go to the mission field to escape
the pain of not having a husband. I know
others, back home, who spend every
evening away from their families, attending Christian meetings, because they are
unhappy and frustrated in their marriages.
Work—even mission work—can become a
wrong hiding place.

"Those called by God to live single lives
are always happy in that state," I said. "This
happiness, this contentment, is the evidence of God's plan."

"But you loved and lost," she exclaimed.
"Do you believe that God took away your
lover to make you follow Him?"

"Oh, no," I smiled. "God does not take
away from us. He might ask us to turn our
backs on something or someone we should
not have. God never takes away, however;
God gives. If I reach out and take someone

for myself and the Lord steps in between, that does not mean God takes. Rather it means He is protecting us from someone we should not have because He has a far greater purpose for our lives."

We sat for long minutes in the semidark room. Only a small kerosene lamp gave its flickering light, casting faint shadows on the walls and across our faces. I thought back— remembering. I had always been content in the Lord. Back when I was in my thirties God gave me children—the children of missionaries—whom I raised. Betsie, my sister, fed and clothed them while I was responsible for their sports and music. We kept them in our home in Holland, and I found deep satisfaction in seeing them grow to maturity. I also spent a great deal of time speaking and sharing in various clubs for girls. But it was not the work that brought balance to my life, for work cannot balance our feelings. It was because my life was centered in the Lord Jesus that I had balance. Many people try to lose their feelings in work, or sports, or music, or the arts. But the feelings are always there and will eventually, as they had done tonight in this missionary, come boiling to the surface and express their resentment and discontent.

I turned to Ellen, my companion. Ellen was a tall, blond, beautiful Dutch girl in her early thirties. Single, she had learned the secret of living a balanced life. While I believe God set me apart before I was born to live a single life, Ellen was different. She did not feel that God had called her to a single life; rather she felt that one day, in God's time, she would marry. However, until that time arrived—one year or thirty years from then—I knew she was secure in Jesus and was not looking to a husband or children for her security.

I spoke to the missionary. "There are some, like me, who are called to live a single life," I said softly. "For them it is always easy, for they are, by their nature, content. Others, like Ellen, are called to prepare for marriage, which may come later in life. They, too, are blessed, for God is using the in-between years to teach them that marriage is not the answer to unhappiness. Happiness is found only in a balanced relationship with the Lord Jesus."

"But it is so hard," she said, tears welling up in her eyes.

"That is so," I said. "The cross is always difficult, but 'ye are dead, and your life is hid with Christ in God' (Col. 3:3). Dear girl, it cannot be safer. That part of you which would cling to a husband is dead. Now you can move into a life where you can be happy with or without a husband—secure in Jesus alone."

I do not know if she really understood me, for often we set our minds on some one thing we think will make us happy—a husband, children, a particular job, or even a "ministry"—and refuse to open our eyes to God's better way. In fact, some believe so strongly that only this thing can bring happiness that they reject the Lord Jesus Himself. Happiness is not found in marriage, or work, or ministry, or children. Happiness is found by being secure in Jesus.

28

I Have Much People in This City

───────── ✎ ─────────

After these things the Lord appointed other seventy also, and sent them two and two before his face into every city and place, whither he himself would come.

Luke 10:1

My second trip to Cuba was much different from the earlier one because this time Cuba was in the hands of communists. Ellen was with me, and we had come from Mexico with our bags loaded with books. Friends had told us that the communists in Cuba were burning Bibles and confiscating Christian literature, so I was not at all sure we would be allowed to bring all these books in with us. We had also heard that most of the churches were closed and many of the Christians were in prison—some of them for passing out literature. Thus we were very cautious.

At customs in Havana, the officer pointed to my suitcases. "What are these books?" he asked.

"They are written by me," I said. "I am going to give them to my friends."

I saw him scowl as he picked one of them up. My heart began to beat rapidly. "Oh, Lord," I prayed inwardly, "what must I do?"

Then I heard myself saying brashly, "Would you like to have one of my books? Here, I will autograph it especially for you."

The customs officer looked up. I took the book from his hand and wrote my name in the front and then handed it back. He grinned broadly and thanked me. Then, glancing once more at my suitcase filled with books, he nodded and motioned us through the line. I closed the suitcase and stepped out on the streets. Hallelujah! The miracle had happened.

But why were we here? What kind of plans did the Lord have for us on this island? Had all our former friends been put in prison? Were any of the churches still open? These and many other questions pounded at my mind as we turned our faces toward the city.

An Intourist limousine brought us into the heart of Havana, where we found a hotel room. After washing up we went out onto the streets, hoping to find some Christians. But how do you find Christians in a strange city when you cannot even speak their language? We walked up and down the sidewalks, hoping God would show us someone to speak to, but we received no guidance whatsoever.

I finally approached an old man who was leaning against the side of the building. He had a kindly face, I thought. I asked if he knew where there was a church.

He shrugged his shoulders but then, motioning us to wait, went to one of the free telephones along the street. Ellen and I stood praying. Was he going to call the police? Had we broken a law, and would we be put in jail? Then we realized he was calling some of his friends, asking if they knew the whereabouts of a church. No one knew anything, and he returned, saying he could be of no help.

We were discouraged, and to make matters worse, it started to rain. Neither Ellen nor I had a raincoat, and soon we were soaked to the skin. We had been walking for hours, and I was exhausted.

"Ellen, can we try to get a taxi?" I asked.

"Well, Tante Corrie, we will need a miracle. However, we know that all things are possible with God."

I found a little stool and sat down while Ellen walked on down the street, hoping to find a taxi. I looked out over the sea and felt as if I had just waded out of the surf, so wet was I. I thought of the words of the driver of the Intourist limousine as he brought us from the airport. "This is the hospital," he had said as we drove by. "Everyone who is ill can go there, and it does not cost a penny. Here is a cemetery. When you die, we bury you, and even that does not cost your relatives anything."

I had been in many countries, but this was the first place they had offered to bury me!

We knew that the Lord had sent us to Cuba, but we had no idea of our mission. Where were the churches? We had seen some, but they were closed. Some even had trees growing in front of the doors. We had tried to call some Christians, but the ones we knew were no longer living in the area. I sat, waiting, while the water poured down my face. Then I heard a car stopping in front of me. Looking up, I saw Ellen's face in the rear window of the ancient, rusted vehicle.

"Tante Corrie," she called above the sound of the rain, "here I am again." I hobbled to the taxi and got in the back door. "Be careful where you put your feet," Ellen laughed, "or you will touch the street."

The taxi took us to our hotel, and soon we were in dry clothes, our wet garments hung across the fixtures in the bathroom, where the steady drip, drip of water reminded us of our failure out on the street. I love to walk with Jesus, but after eight decades I realized I was not as young as I used to be. It was in such moments that I started to feel old.

Ellen could not sleep that night. We were supposed to stay in Cuba for two weeks, but if we could not find any Christians, then what would we do? She arose in the middle of the night and prayed, "Lord, give me a word so I may know we aren't in vain in this country."

Sitting on the side of her bed, she reached for her Bible, which was on the small table. She began to read where she had stopped the night before. She had learned that God does not want His children to be fearful, and the best way to overcome fear is through the Word of God.

She read Acts 18:9–10.

Then spake the Lord to Paul. . . . Be not
afraid, but speak, and hold not thy peace:
For I am with thee, and no man shall set
on thee to hurt thee: for I have much
people in this city.

What an answer!

The next morning Ellen could not wait
to find all those people, and neither could
I. She had one address we had not con-
tacted. It was the address of a small house
on a side street where some Christians we
had once known used to live. Walking from
the hotel, she finally found the street and
made her way to a dingy door, weather-
beaten and cracked. She knocked boldly.

A small man, deeply tanned and with
wrinkles around his eyes, cautiously opened
the door. Ellen could speak no Spanish, but
she held up her Bible and one of my books
(*Amazing Love*), which had been translated
into Spanish.

The man glanced at the books and then
back to Ellen. Ellen smiled and pointed to
my name on the book, then pointed back
toward the city. Suddenly his whole face
came alive. He threw open the door and

shouted, "Corrie! Corrie ten Boom està aquì. Ella està en Havana!"

Ellen walked in and found the room was filled with men, all kneeling on the floor. They were pastors who met each week to pray for God's help and guidance in their difficult ministry. Ellen hurried back to the hotel, and soon I was meeting with these wonderful men of God. We distributed all our books and made many new friends among God's people. Indeed, God did have "much people" in that city.

29
The Blessing Box

Cast thy bread upon the waters: for thou shalt find it after many days.

Ecclesiastes 11:1

Many times, on my trips around the world, I am dependent on the hospitality of Christians. From the time of my first trip to America, when I was befriended by God's people in New York, and later by Abraham Vereide in Washington, D.C., I have known the love and generosity of others in the body of Christ.

It was on one of those continual trips, when my only home was my suitcase (that big red one), that I was invited to stay with friends in Colorado. I didn't feel well and needed rest. My hostess escorted me to her lovely house with tall white columns. Taking me up the carpeted stairs she showed me to a beautiful room. From the windows

I could see the clear, blue sky, which framed the snowcapped Rocky Mountains. She then put her arms around me and said, "Corrie, this is your room. It will always be here for you."

"This room! For me?" I could hardly believe it was true. A place for me to unpack my suitcase! To hang up my clothes! To spread out my writing papers and put my Bible on a desk! Since that gray time in the concentration camp I had longed for bright colors as a thirsty man yearns for water. This room, and the scenery outside, was filled with color. I wanted to cry, as a child cries when she is happy. But I have learned to control my tears (most of the time, anyway) and was content just to tell the Lord of my deep thankfulness. The Lord is so good, for He has given me so many friends, just like this, all over the world.

It was during one of my visits in this Colorado home that I received an early-morning telephone call. I was already awake, since we intended to leave that afternoon to fly to Washington to speak in a series of meetings arranged by Mr. Vereide.

The phone call was from Alicia Davison, Mr. Vereide's daughter. "Oh, Alicia, I cannot wait to see you today. I am looking forward to it and the meetings in your fellow-ship house."

There was a pause, then Alicia said, "Tante Corrie, Dad is with the Lord."

"Oh, Alicia . . ." I tried to speak, but nothing else would come out.

"It is all right, Tante Corrie," she said calmly. "I am calling to ask you to please come on to be with all of us. We will not have the meetings, but so many people are coming, and we want you to be with us."

"I shall be there this afternoon," I said. After a brief prayer over the phone, I hung up.

I hurried to finish my packing, remembering all the kindnesses that had been poured on me by this wonderful family and their many friends. I have faced death many times, but there is always an empty place in my heart when someone I know and love leaves to be with the Lord. Nor did it ever occur to me that almost two years later I would once again fly to Washington to sit in that same Presbyterian church, not to attend a memorial for Abraham Vereide but to attend the meeting in honor of Alicia. Although still young and beautiful, she would die in Hong Kong while making a mission tour with her husband, Howard Davison.

I was warmly received by my friends in Washington. Although sad, they were rejoicing in the Lord. That night after I had gone to my room, I prayed, "Lord, why are people so kind to me? I am just a simple old Dutch woman. Why am I treated so graciously and shown so much hospitality?"

Then the Lord reminded me of my mother's blessing box.

Our house in Haarlem was not really big, but it had wide open doors.

I do not suppose that the many guests who were always coming to the Beje ever realized what a struggle it was to make both ends meet. Yet many lonesome people found a place with us and joined in our music, humor, and interesting conversation. There was always a place at the oval dinner table, although perhaps the soup was a bit watery when too many unexpected guests showed up. Our entire home was centered in the ministry of the gospel. All people who came to us were either workers in the kingdom of God or people who needed help.

Mother loved all her guests. She often showed her love by dropping a penny in the "blessing box" when they arrived.

The blessing box was a small metal box that sat on the sideboard near the oval dinner table. Here money was collected for the mission that was so close to our hearts. Every time our family was blessed in a particular way, Mother would drop money in the blessing box as a thank offering to God. This was especially true if Father sold an expensive watch or received extra money for repairing an antique clock.

Whenever visitors came, Mother would spread her arms wide and welcome them, and then to show how she really appreciated their presence would say, "A penny in the blessing box for your coming." If it were a special visitor she might even put in a dime.

Then, at the dinner table, Father would always bless our visitors, thanking God that our house was privileged by their presence. It was always a special occasion for us all.

I well remember the sister-in-law of a minister who spent the night with us. The next morning Tante Anna went to her room and found her sheet twisted into a rope and lying across the bed.

"What is this?" Tante Anna asked.

The woman broke down in tears. "I must confess. Last night I wanted to commit suicide. I made my sheet into a rope and tied it around my neck to jump from the window. But I could not forget the prayer at the dinner table, as Mr. ten Boom thanked God that I could come and share in this hospitality. God spared my life through that prayer."

After a few days in Washington I continued my traveling as a tramp for the Lord. However, fresh on my mind was the hospitality of my dear friends. And I remembered Mother's blessing box and Father's prayers. Often I am dependent on the hospitality of Christians. God's people have been so generous to open their homes to me, and many times when I lay my head on a strange pillow, which has been blessed by the love of my friends, I realize that I am enjoying the reward for the open doors and open hearts of the Beje.

Heaven will be blessed, but here on earth I already am enjoying a "house with many mansions."

30
Closing the Circle

If we confess our sins, he is faithful and just to forgive us our sins, and to cleanse us from all unrighteousness.

1 John 1:9

It would seem, after having been a Christian for almost eighty years, that I would no longer do ugly things that need forgiving. Yet I am constantly doing things to others that cause me to have to go back and ask their forgiveness. Sometimes these are things I actually do—other times they are simply attitudes I let creep in that break the circle of God's perfect love.

I first learned the secret of closing the circle from my nephew, Peter van Woerden, who was spending the weekend with me in our little apartment in Baarn, Holland.

"Do you remember that boy, Jan, that we prayed for?" Peter asked.

I well remembered Jan. We had prayed for him many times. He had a horrible demon of darkness in his life, and although we had fasted and prayed and cast out the demon in the name of the Lord Jesus Christ, the darkness always returned.

Peter continued, "I knew God had brought this boy to me, not only so he could be delivered but to teach me some lessons too."

I looked at Peter. "What could that boy, Jan, so filled with darkness, teach you?"

"I did not learn the lesson from Jan," Peter said with a smile, "but from God. Once in my intercession time for Jan the Lord told me to open my Bible to 1 John 1:7–9. I read that passage about confessing our sin and asked the Lord what that had to do with the darkness in Jan's life."

Peter got up and walked across the room, holding his open Bible in his hand. "God taught me that if a Christian walks in the light, then the blood of Jesus Christ cleanses him from all sin, making his life a closed circle and protecting him from all outside dark powers. But," he turned and emphatically jabbed his finger into the pages of the Bible, "if there is unconfessed sin in that life, the circle has an opening in it—a gap—and this allows the dark powers to come back in."

Ah, I thought, *Peter has really learned a truth from the Lord.* "Tante Corrie," Peter continued, "even though I was able to cast out the demon in Jan's life, it always crept back in through the opening in the circle— the opening of Jan's unconfessed sin. But when I led Jan to confess this sin, then the circle was closed, and the dark powers could no longer return."

That same week the wife of a good friend came to me for counseling. After I had fixed her a cup of tea she began to tell me about all the people who had prayed for her, yet she was still experiencing horrible dreams at night.

I interrupted her conversation and drew a circle on a piece of paper. "Mary," I said, "do you have unconfessed sin in your life? Is this the reason the circle is still open?"

Mary said nothing, sitting with her head down, her hands tightly clasped in her lap, her feet together. I could see there was a strong battle going on in her life—a battle between spiritual forces.

"Do you really want to be free?" I urged.

"Oh, yes," she said.

Suddenly she began telling me about a strong hatred she had for her mother. Everyone thought she loved her mother, but inside there were things that caused her actually to want to kill her. Yet, even as she spoke, I saw the freedom coming into her eyes.

She finished her confession and then quickly asked Jesus to forgive her and cleanse her with His blood. I looked into her eyes and commanded the demon of hatred to leave in the name of Jesus.

What joy! What freedom!

Mary raised her hands in victory and began to praise the Lord, thanking Him for the liberation and forgiveness He had given her. Then she reached over and embraced me in a hug so tight I thought she would crack my ribs.

"Dear Lord," she prayed, "I thank You for closing the circle with Your blood."

Having thus learned to close the circle by confessing my sins, I wish I could say that ever since then the circle has remained closed in my life. It is not so. For since Satan comes against us so often, then it is necessary to confess often also. Regardless of how old a person may be, or how long he has ministered in the name of Jesus Christ, that man still needs to confess his sins again and again—and ask forgiveness.

This truth became painfully clear to me recently when I was invited to Washington, D.C., to speak to a luncheon of business-men and women. I love to talk to busi-nessmen and was very excited about the meeting. When I arrived, however, I found only women present. This upset me, for I felt that men needed to hear the message of forgiveness also.

After the meeting a fine-looking lady came up to me. "I am in charge of arrang-ing the program for the world convention of our ladies' group," she said. "Some of the most influential women in the world will be present. Would you come speak to us in San Francisco?"

I was still miffed that no men had been present for the luncheon. It's not that I dis-approve of women's meetings. But I am concerned when men leave the spiritual activity to the women. God is calling men. Thus, I gave her a short, discourteous answer. "No, I will not. I must speak to men also. I don't like this business of all women."

She was very gracious. "Don't you feel that you are the right person?" she asked.

"No," I said, "I am not the right person. I do not like this American system where men go about their business, leaving the women to act like Christians. I will not come." I turned and walked away.

Later that afternoon I was in my room, packing to catch the plane. The Lord began dealing with me. "You were very rude to that woman," He told me.

I argued with the Lord: "But Lord, I feel that Your message is for all people, not just the women."

"You were very rude to that woman," He said again, gently.

He was right, of course. He always is. I had been speaking on forgiveness but was unwilling to ask forgiveness for myself. I knew I was going to have to go to that gracious woman and apologize—confess my sin. Until I did, the circle would be open in my life, and Satan would be pouring in many other dark thoughts as well.

I looked at my watch and saw I had only enough time to finish my packing and get to the airport. It made no difference. If I left Washington without closing the circle, I would be no good anywhere else. I would just have to miss my plane.

I called the front desk and found which room the woman was in. Then I went to her room. "I must ask your forgiveness," I said as she opened the door. "I spoke to you rudely."

She was embarrassed and tried to pass it off. "Oh, no," she said, "you were not unkind. I understand perfectly. I, too, feel that men should be the spiritual leaders, not women."

She was returning my unkindness with kindness, but that was not what I needed. I needed for her to admit that I was wrong about not speaking to women and forgive me. I know it is often more difficult to forgive than to ask forgiveness, but it is equally important. To withhold forgiveness often leaves another person in bondage, unable to close the circle and thus open to further attacks from Satan. It is as important to forgive as it is to ask forgiveness.

This sensitive woman understood. Reaching out and tenderly touching my hand, she said, "I understand, Tante Corrie. I forgive you for your remarks about women's groups, and I forgive you for being unkind to me."

That was what I needed to hear. In the future I would indeed speak to women's groups. I would also keep a watch on my lips when tempted to speak unkindly. I missed my plane, but the circle was closed.

31
One Finger for His Glory

And there came a certain poor widow, and she threw in two mites . . . and [he] saith unto them, Verily I say unto you, That this poor widow hath cast more in, than all they which have cast into the treasury: For all they did cast in of their abundance; but she of her want did cast in all that she had, even all her living.

Mark 12:42–44

We arrived at her apartment by night in order to escape detection. We were in Russia (in the region of Lithuania, on the Baltic Sea). Ellen and I had climbed the steep stairs, coming through a small back door into the one-room apartment. It was jammed with furniture, evidence that the old couple had once lived in a much larger and much finer house.

The old woman was lying on a small sofa, propped up by pillows. Her body was bent and twisted almost beyond recognition by the dread disease of multiple sclerosis. Her aged husband spent all his time caring for her since she was unable to move off the sofa.

I walked across the room and kissed her wrinkled cheek. She tried to look up, but the muscles in her neck were atrophied so she could only roll her eyes upward and smile. She raised her right hand slowly, in jerks. It was the only part of her body she could control, and with her gnarled and deformed knuckles she caressed my face. I reached over and kissed the index finger of that hand, for it was with this one finger that she had so long glorified God.

Beside her couch was a vintage typewriter. Each morning her faithful husband would rise, praising the Lord. After caring for his wife's needs and feeding her a simple breakfast, he would prop her up into a sitting position on the couch, placing pillows all around her so she wouldn't topple over. Then he would move that ancient black typewriter in front of her on a small table. From an old cupboard he would remove a stack of cheap yellow paper. Then, with that blessed one finger, she would begin to type.

All day and far into the night she would type. She translated Christian books into Russian, Latvian, and the language of her people. Always using just that one finger—peck . . . peck . . . peck—she typed out the pages. Portions of the Bible, the books of Billy Graham, Watchman Nee, and Corrie ten Boom—all came from her typewriter. That was why I was there—to thank her.

She was hungry to hear news about these men of God she had never met, yet whose books she had so faithfully translated. We talked about Watchman Nee, who was then in a prison in China, and I told her all I knew of his life and ministry. I also told her of the wonderful ministry of Billy Graham and of the many people who were giving their lives to the Lord.

"Not only does she translate their books," her husband said as he hovered close by during our conversation, "but she prays for these men every day while she types. Sometimes it takes a long time for her finger to hit the key, or for her to get the paper in the machine, but all the time she is praying for those whose books she is working on."

I looked at her wasted form on the sofa, her head pulled down and her feet curled back under her body. "Oh, Lord, why don't You heal her?" I cried inwardly.

Her husband, sensing my anguish of soul, gave the answer. "God has a purpose in her sickness. Every other Christian in the city is watched by the secret police. But because she has been sick so long, no one ever looks in on her. They leave us alone, and she is the only person in all the city who can type quietly, undetected by the police."

I looked around at the tiny room, so jammed full of furniture from better days. In one corner was the kitchen. Beside the cupboard was her husband's "office," a battered desk where he sorted the pages that came from her typewriter to pass them on to the Christians. I thought of Jesus sitting over against the treasury, and my heart leaped for joy as I heard Jesus bless this sick old woman who, like the widow, had given all she had.

What a warrior!

When she enters the beautiful city
And the saved all around her appear,
Many people around will tell her:
It was you that invited me here.
                    Author unknown

Ellen and I returned to Holland, where we were able to obtain a new typewriter and have it shipped to her. Now she could make carbon copies of her translations.

Today we got a letter from her husband. In the early morning hours last week she left to be with the Lord. But, he said, she had worked up until midnight that same night, typing with that one finger to the glory of God.

32
The Ding-Dong Principle

Haven't you yet learned that your body is the home of the Holy Spirit God gave you, and that he lives within you? Your own body does not belong to you. For God has bought you with a great price. So use every part of your body to give glory back to God, because he owns it.

1 Corinthians 6:19–20 TLB

In Holland we have many churches with belfries. The bells in the steeples are rung by hand with a rope that is pulled from the vestibule of the church.

One day a young Flemish girl, who had repented and received deliverance from lust and impurity, came to me while I was speaking in one of these churches.

"Even though I have been delivered," she said, "at night I still keep dreaming of my old way of life. I am afraid I will slip back into Satan's grasp."

"Up in that church tower," I said, nodding toward the belfry, "is a bell that is rung by pulling on a rope. But you know what? After the sexton lets go of the rope, the bell keeps on swinging. First ding, then dong. Slower and slower until there's a final dong and it stops.

"I believe the same thing is true of deliverance. When the demons are cast out in the name of the Lord Jesus Christ, or when sin is confessed and renounced, then Satan's hand is removed from the rope. But if we worry about our past bondage, Satan will use this opportunity to keep the echoes ringing in our minds."

A sweet light spread across the girl's face. "You mean even though I sometimes have temptations, I am still free, that Satan is no longer pulling the rope that controls my life?"

"The purity of your life is evidence of your deliverance," I said. "You should not worry about the dings and the dongs. They are nothing but echoes."

Demons seldom leave without leaving behind their vibrations—dings and dongs. It is as though they give the clapper one big swing on the way out, scaring us into think-ing they are still there. They know that even though they have to flee at the name of Jesus, if we grow fearful over the remain-ing echoes, other demons can come in and take their place.

The same is true of forgiveness. When we forgive someone, we take our hand off the rope. But if we've been tugging at our grievances for a long time, we mustn't be surprised when the old angry thoughts keep coming up for a while. They're just the ding-dongs of the old bell slowing down.

The Bible promises that after we confess and denounce our sins, God cleanses us from them by the blood of Jesus. Indeed, He says, "[Your] sins and iniquities will I remember no more" (Heb. 8:12). However, we can do something God cannot do. We can remember our old sins. These are the dings and the dongs of our past life. When we hear them we need to remember that through Jesus' sacrifice on Calvary, Satan can no longer pull the rope in our life. We may be tempted. We may even fall back occasionally. But we have been delivered from the bondage of sin, and even though the vibrations may still sound in our lives, they will grow less and less and eventually stop completely.

Once Satan has been cast out of the house of your life, he cannot return as long as you walk in obedience. Your body is the temple of the Holy Spirit. However, that does not prevent him (or his demons) from standing outside the house and shouting through the windows, saying, "We're still here!"

But, hallelujah, we know Satan for who he is—the prince of liars. He is *not* still here. He has been cast out. So whenever you hear one of those old echoes in your life—one of the dings or dongs—you need to stop right then and say, "Thank You, Jesus. You have bought me with Your blood, and sin has no right to sound off in my life."

33
The Blacks and Whites of Forgiveness

And when you stand praying, if you have a grievance against anyone, forgive him, so that your Father in heaven may forgive you the wrongs you have done.

Mark 11:25 NEB

I wish I could say that after a long and fruitful life traveling the world, I had learned to forgive all my enemies. I wish I could say that merciful and charitable thoughts just naturally flowed from me and on to others. But they don't. If there is one thing I've learned since I've passed my eightieth birthday, it's that I can't store up good feelings and behavior—but only draw them fresh from God each day.

Maybe I'm glad it's that way, for every time I go to Him, He teaches me something else. I recall the time—and I was almost seventy—when some Christian friends whom I loved and trusted did something that hurt me. You would have thought that, having been able to forgive the guards at Ravensbruck, forgiving Christian friends would be child's play. It wasn't. For weeks I seethed inside. But at last I asked God again to work His miracle in me. And again it happened: first the cold-blooded decision, then the flood of joy and peace. I had forgiven my friends; I was restored to my Father.

Then why was I suddenly awake in the middle of the night, rehashing the whole affair again? *My friends!* I thought. *People I love.* If it had been strangers, I wouldn't have minded so.

I sat up and switched on the light. "Father, I thought it was all forgiven. Please help me do it."

But the next night I woke up again. They'd talked so sweetly too! Never a hint of what they were planning. "Father!" I cried in alarm. "Help me!"

Then it was that another secret of forgiveness became evident. It is not enough to simply say, "I forgive you." I must also begin to live it out. And in my case, that meant acting as though their sins, like mine,

were buried in the depths of the deepest
sea. If God could remember them no
more—and He had said, "[Your] sins and
iniquities will I remember no more" (Heb.
10:17)—then neither should I. And the reason the thoughts kept coming back to me
was that I kept turning their sin over in my
mind.

And so I discovered another of God's
principles: We can trust God not only for
our emotions but also for our thoughts. As
I asked Him to renew my mind, He also
took away my thoughts.

He still had more to teach me, however,
even from this single episode. Many years
later, after I had passed my eightieth birthday, an American friend came to visit me in
Holland. As we sat in my little apartment
in Baarn, he asked me about those people
from long ago who had taken advantage of
me.

"It is nothing," I said, a little smugly. "It
is all forgiven."

"By you, yes," he said. "But what about
them? Have they accepted your forgiveness?"

"They say there is nothing to forgive!
They deny it ever happened. No matter
what they say, though, I can prove they were

wrong." I went eagerly to my desk. "See, I have it in black and white! I saved all their letters and I can show you where . . ."

"Corrie!" My friend slipped his arm through mine and gently closed the drawer. "Aren't you the one whose sins are at the bottom of the sea? Yet are the sins of your friends etched in black and white?"

For an astonishing moment I could not find my voice. "Lord Jesus," I whispered at last, "who takes all my sins away, forgive me for preserving all these years the evidence against others! Give me grace to burn all the blacks and whites as a sweet-smelling sacrifice to Your glory."

I did not go to sleep that night until I had gone through my desk and pulled out those letters—curling now with age—and fed them all into my little coal-burning grate. As the flames leaped and glowed, so did my heart. "Forgive us our trespasses," Jesus taught us to pray, "as we forgive those who trespass against us." In the ashes of those letters I was seeing yet another facet of His mercy. What more He would teach me about forgiveness in the days ahead I didn't know, but tonight's was good news enough.

Forgiveness is the key that unlocks the door of resentment and the handcuffs of hatred. It breaks the chains of bitterness and the shackles of selfishness. The forgiveness of Jesus not only takes away our sins; it makes them as if they had never been.

34
Getting Ready for the End

❧

Even so, come, Lord Jesus.
Revelation 22:20

Some time ago, I was with a group of students in the Midwest. Some of them were new Christians, but most of them did not know the Lord. They were interested in all kinds of other things, and a Christian professor had organized weekly meetings to answer their questions. So it was, that at the last evening meeting of that semester the professor said, "Now you can hear something about Christianity in practice."

First I spoke to those who were Christians. "How long have you known Jesus?" I asked.

One said, "Two weeks." Another said, "Three years." And still another answered, "I met Him only yesterday."

Then I said to them, "Well, I have good news. I have known Him seventy-five years, and I can tell you something, men. He will never let you down."

Next I told the other students about Jesus Christ and what He had done for me, and the great miracles also. When He tells you to love your enemies, He gives you the love that He demands from you. They were listening intently, and I was led by the Holy Spirit not to go into any doctrines or teachings other than the reality of Jesus Christ. I told them of the joy of having Jesus with me, whatever happened, and how I knew from experience that the light of Jesus is stronger than the greatest darkness. I told them of the darkness of my prison experiences, realizing that only those people who were in a German concentration camp could ever fully understand. However, I wanted these students to know that, even though I was there where every day six hundred people either died or were killed, when Jesus is with you the worst can happen and the best remains.

Afterwards the students came up and we had coffee. One said to me, "I would love to ask Jesus to come into my heart, but I cannot. I am a Jew."

I said, "You cannot ask Jesus into your heart because you are a Jew? Then you do not understand that with the Jew (Jesus) in your heart you are a double Jew."

He said, "Oh, then it is possible?"

"On the divine side He was God's Son. On the human side He was a Jew. When you accept Him you do not become a Gentile. You become even more Jewish than before. You will be a completed Jew."

With great joy the boy received the Lord Jesus as his Savior.

There is a great new surge of interest in spiritual things. Many are interested in Jesus Christ who have never shown any interest before. Churches—which have been dead and cold like mausoleums—are coming to life. All across the world many are being saved and being filled with the Holy Spirit.

At the same time, however, many others are turning away from God. They are openly worshiping Satan. Many others are calling themselves Christians but are involved in the occult, fortune-telling, astrology, mind science, and other things of Satan.

I see over the whole world that there are two huge armies marching—the army of

the Antichrist and the army of Jesus Christ.
We know from the Bible that Jesus Christ
will have the victory, but now the Antichrist
is preparing for the time that will come
before Jesus returns. The Bible says there
will be a time of tribulation, and the
Antichrist will take over the whole world.
He will be a very "good, religious" man, and
he will make one religion for the whole
world. After it has been arranged, he will
proclaim himself as its god. The Bible
prophesies that the time will come when
we cannot buy or sell unless we bear the
sign of the Antichrist; that means that world
money is coming, and people know this
today. If I did not believe in the Bible before,
I should believe in it now. Because what
was foretold in the Bible you can now read
in the newspapers.

At a student meeting in California, a theological student approached me saying,
"What's all this talk about Jesus coming
again? Don't you know that men have been
prophesying for years that He would come,
and He never has. Even the early church
could not live their religion because they
were too busy looking for Christ to return.
He is not coming back. It is all foolishness."

I looked at the young man. He was so smug, so full of scoffing, and I felt sorry for him.

"Indeed, Jesus is coming again, and soon," I said. "And you have just proved it to me."

He blinked his eyes. "How did I prove it to you?"

"Because the Bible talks about it in 2 Peter 3:3, that in the last days there shall come scoffers walking after their own lusts, and they will say, 'Where is the promise of His coming? Ever since the early church men have been looking for Him, and He has not come.' So you see, my young friend, you are one of the signs of His coming."

I am not afraid when I think about the coming of the Lord Jesus. Instead I welcome it. I do not know whether it would be better for me to die and be among the great host of saints who will return with Him, or whether it would be better to remain here and listen for the sound of the trumpet. Either way, I like the words of the song that says:

> God is working His purpose out,
> As year succeeds to year:
> God is working His purpose out
> And the time is drawing near—

Nearer and nearer draws the time
The time that shall surely be,
When the earth shall be filled with
    the glory of God,
As the waters cover the sea.
                A. C. Ainger

I find that when communists speak of the future of the world, they show a pattern for peace through communism. But when I ask them, "What about when you die?" they say, "Then everything is ended. There is no life after this life." The Bible tells us that the Antichrist can imitate much, even the gifts of the Spirit. But there is one thing he cannot imitate, and that is the peace of God that passes all understanding.

But there are *good* things to tell about the future of the world. For instance, the Bible says the Tree of Life will be used for the healing of the nations. This means that there will be *nations* to heal, and there will be *healing*. I am so thankful that we have the Bible and can know the future of God's plan.

As the end times draw closer and closer, so does the power of God grow greater and greater. One day, on a trip to Russia, I approached the customs officer with a suitcase full of Russian Bibles. I stood in the line and saw how carefully the customs officers checked every suitcase. Suddenly a great fear swept over me. "What will he do when he finds my Bibles? Send me back to Holland? Put me in prison?"

I closed my eyes to shut out the scene around me and said, "Lord, in Jeremiah 1 it is written that 'God watches over his word to perform it' (v. 12). Lord, the Bibles in my suitcase are Your Word. Now, God, please watch over Your Word—my Bibles—so I may take them to Your people in Russia."

Now I know that is not what Jeremiah meant, but I have found that if I pray with my hand on the promises of the open Bible, I do not have to wait until my position is doctrinally sound. God sees my heart.

The moment I prayed I opened my eyes and saw around my suitcase light beings. They were angels. It was the first and only time in my life that I had ever seen them, although I had known many, many times they were present. But this time I saw them, only for a moment, and then they were gone. But so was my fear.

I moved on through the customs line, sliding my suitcase along the stainless steel table toward the officer who was doing such a thorough inspection. At last I was before him.

"Is this your suitcase?" he asked.

"Yes, sir," I answered politely.

"It seems very heavy," he said, grasping it by the handle and picking it up.

"It is very heavy," I said.

He smiled. "Since you are the last one to come through the line I now have time to help you. If you will follow me I shall carry it for you out to your taxi."

My heart almost overflowed with hallelujahs as I followed him through the customs gate and right out to the street where he helped me get a taxi to the hotel.

So, even though we are rapidly approaching the time when the Antichrist will try to take over the world, I am not afraid. For I have an even greater promise of the constant presence of Jesus, who is greater than anything Satan can throw against me.

The apostle Peter said, "Because, my dear friends, you have a hope like this before you, I urge you to make certain that the day will find you at peace with God, flawless and blameless in his sight" (2 Peter 3:14 PHILLIPS).

Surrender to the Lord Jesus Christ must not be partial, but total. Only when we repent and turn away from our sins (using His power, of course) does He fill us with His Holy Spirit. The fruit of the Holy Spirit makes us right with God and God's love in us makes us right with men. Through that we can forgive—even love—our enemies.

Jesus Himself makes us ready for His coming.

35
Little Witness for Christ

Suffer little children, and forbid them not, to come unto me: for of such is the kingdom of heaven.

Matthew 19:14

Tante Jans lost her husband before she was forty years old. He had been a well-known minister in Rotterdam, and she had worked faithfully beside him in the church. They had no children, and after he died it was clear that her place was to be in our house in Haarlem. She was a poet, author, and organizer—especially was she an organizer! Soon after she moved into the Beje she started a club for girls where she led the meetings and began publishing a small monthly paper for them.

It was long before World War I started, but a detachment of Dutch soldiers was stationed in Haarlem. Seeing many soldiers in the streets, Tante Jans decided to open a club for them too. She approached some wealthy people and within a short time had enough money to build a military home. Twice a week Tante Jans went to the house to lead a Bible study.

Tante Jans also invited the soldiers to come to our house. Since they were lonely and did not like the street life, many of them accepted. Almost every evening we had soldiers in our home.

One sergeant was a great musician, and Tante Jans asked him to teach me and my sister Nollie to play the harmonium—an old pump organ. It wasn't long before I was joining Tante Jans at the military home to accompany the singing.

One night in my eleventh year, a large group of soldiers had gathered for the Bible study. Before I played, Tante Jans made me sing. The song I sang was about the lost sheep that was found by the shepherd. I sang it slowly and dramatically, climaxing it with the last line:

And the sheep that went astray was me.

As I finished singing, a big, blond Dutch officer reached out and pulled me to him. Picking me up and sitting me on his knee, he laughed and said, "Tell me, young lady, how did you go astray?"

All the other soldiers laughed, and I was red with embarrassment. It did seem odd that such a little girl would describe herself as a lost sheep.

I had to confess that the line just belonged to the song and that I had never, never been a lost sheep. Then I told him that as a little girl, just five years of age, I had given my heart to Jesus Christ and could never remember not having belonged to Him.

The officer grew very serious, and his eyes filled with tears. "Ah, that is the way it should be, little Sweet-Face," he said solemnly. "How much better to come to Jesus as a little child than to have to stumble as I have, always seeking the Shepherd."

Then he closed his eyes and said softly, "But tonight I think I shall stop seeking and let Him find me instead."

That night there was deep joy in the Bible meeting. The Lord had used me to lead a man to Christ. It was the first time in my life, and it had taken place not because of what I said, but because of the Holy Spirit who was in me. It was a secret I have remembered all the years of my life as I have traveled the world—a tramp for the Lord.